Legislative Deferrals

Statutory Ambiguity, Judicial Power, and American Democracy

Why do unelected federal judges have so much power to make policy in the United States? Why were federal judges able to thwart apparent legislative victories won by labor organizations in the *Lochner* era? Most scholars who have addressed such questions assume that the answer lies in the judiciary's constitutionally guaranteed independence, and thus worry that insulated judges threaten democracy when they stray from baseline positions chosen by legislators. This book argues for a fundamental shift in the way scholars think about judicial policy making. Instead of simply seeing judges as rivals to legislators, scholars need to notice that legislators also empower judges to make policy as a means of escaping accountability. The first book-length study of legislative deference to the courts, *Legislative Deferrals* offers a dramatic reinterpretation of the history of twentieth-century labor law and shows how attention to legislative deferrals can help scholars to address vexing questions about the consequences of judicial power in a democracy.

George I. Lovell is Assistant Professor of Political Science at the University of Washington, Seattle. He has published articles in *Studies in American Political Development* and *Constitutional Commentary* and reviews in *Ethics* and the *Law and Politics Book Review*. He has held teaching positions at the University of Maryland and the College of William and Mary.

Legislative Deferrals

Statutory Ambiguity, Judicial Power, and American Democracy

GEORGE I. LOVELL

University of Washington

CAMBRIDGE
UNIVERSITY PRESS

PUBLISHED BY THE PRESS SYNDICATE OF THE UNIVERSITY OF CAMBRIDGE
The Pitt Building, Trumpington Street, Cambridge, United Kingdom

CAMBRIDGE UNIVERSITY PRESS
The Edinburgh Building, Cambridge CB2 2RU, UK
40 West 20th Street, New York, NY 10011-4211, USA
477 Williamstown Road, Port Melbourne, VIC 3207, Australia
Ruiz de Alarcón 13, 28014 Madrid, Spain
Dock House, The Waterfront, Cape Town 8001, South Africa

http://www.cambridge.org

© George I. Lovell 2003

First published 2003

Printed in the United States of America .

Typeface Sabon 10/13 pt.   *System* LaTeX 2$_\varepsilon$ [TB]

A catalog record for this book is available from the British Library.

Library of Congress Cataloging in Publication Data

Lovell, George I.
Legislative deferrals : statutory ambiguity, judicial power, and American democracy /
George I. Lovell.
   p. cm.
Includes bibliographical references and index.
ISBN 0-521-82415-X (hb)
   1. Political questions and judicial power – United States.   2. Judge-made law –
United States.   3. Legislative power – United States.   4. Separation of powers –
United States.   I. Title.
KF5130 .L68   2003
342.73′052–dc21   2002074059

ISBN 0 521 82415 X hardback

For my parents,
Adrienne and Michael Lovell

Contents

Acknowledgments

I have received help from some extraordinary people as I worked on this book. The book was first a dissertation, and each member of my dissertation committee provided very valuable advice when requested and, more importantly, trusted me enough to let me work it out on my own without close supervision. Kim Lane Scheppele's enthusiasm and energy attracted me to the public law subfield and gave me a sense of direction at the beginning. Her continued support and encouragement has sustained me to the end. John Kingdon's ideas and guidance also played an important role. This project was prompted in part by a comment he made on a paper for his introductory seminar on American government, and he has continued to support the project (and helped me to remember deadlines) as I have embarked on a teaching career. Doug Dion inspired me to do work on American political history and political development. The first step toward producing this book was a paper I wrote for Doug's graduate seminar in American political development. Doug helped me with sources and with crucial ideas about measurement and strategic interaction as he oversaw that project from its initial rough formulation through publication. Terrence McDonald also made a number of very helpful and important suggestions. Other teachers at Michigan played important roles by offering encouragement, advice on research design and sources, and help with thinking about institutions and American politics. They include Martha Feldman, Mark Brandon, Hanes Walton, Jr., Kent Jennings, Ann Lin, Tom Green, and Brian Simpson. Perhaps most importantly, the graduate students in the public-law reading group at the University of Michigan provided social and intellectual companionship that made it possible to develop this project. The regular members of the group were Julie Novkov,

Jeannine Bell, Steve Dow, Joan Sitomer, Bob Stein, Ellen Andersen, Paula Denney, Michael Sherman, and Michelle Berger.

I also received advice and assistance from several Washington, D.C., area scholars. Daniel Ernst of Georgetown Law provided very useful advice and much appreciated encouragement. The late Stuart Kaufman was very generous with his encyclopedic knowledge of the Gompers-era AFL and helped me with sources at the AFL-CIO archive. Michael Singer helped with access to libraries and gave me an intellectual home by including me in seminars at his International Rule of Law Center at George Washington University. Lee Sayrs of the George Meaney Center provided help with archival sources, as did librarians at the Law Library of Congress.

A special and complicated debt is owed to Mark Graber. Mark sought me out as a shy graduate student to express interest in my work, and later provided me access to libraries and even gave me his teaching job for a year. He has offered valuable advice at several stages of the project and provided a detailed set of helpful comments on the entire manuscript. Most importantly, he took the time to help me to see that my work was original and different from his own. He is one of the kindest and most unselfish scholars I have ever known.

I also owe a special debt to Victoria Hattam. Her extraordinary book, *Labor Visions and State Power*, ignited my interest in problems of state structure and labor's development. Professor Hattam deserves special thanks for responding to an overly rabid attack that I made on her book with a very thoughtful and constructive essay from which I continue to learn.

My colleagues and students at the College of William and Mary provided much stimulation and insight as the dissertation slowly evolved into this book. New colleagues at the University of Washington have provided an ideal environment for finishing. Michael McCann deserves special thanks. At a particularly frustrating stage, Michael's interest and support reignited my desire to get the argument right. Michael provided very valuable advice on the entire manuscript and has been particularly helpful with choices about framing. Special thanks to Stuart Scheingold, Mike Lovell, Jeannine Bell, and Mark Smith for comments on chapters during the late stages.

Joel Grossman provided constructive comments on the entire manuscript. Karen Orren, Maxwell Chibundu, Jo Shaw, Sujit Choudry, Neal Devins, Larry Becker, David Jones, John Gilmour, David Dessler, Brie Gertler, Nitsan Chorev, and Brooke Livingston all provided comments on early pieces of the manuscript and valuable conversation about the ideas expressed here. Thanks also to Lew Bateman of Cambridge University Press for his interest and understanding. I must also acknowledge that I would not have finished the book if not for the outstanding baristas at Victrola in Seattle, who provided much needed stimulation and maintained a wonderful place to work.

Portions of chapters 1 and 3 have been adapted from "'As Harmless as an Infant': Deference, Denial, and *Adair v United States*," *Studies in American Political Development* 14 (Fall 2000): 212–233.

Financial support was provided by the Gerald Ford Fellowship and a Rackham One Term Dissertation Fellowship at the University of Michigan; two faculty summer research grants at the College of William and Mary; and a junior faculty development grant from the University of Washington.

The most important and complicated debts are owed to Carrie Cihak and to my parents, Adrienne and Michael Lovell. Carrie has been a constant source of emotional and intellectual support from beginning to end. Carrie has suffered through countless drafts and redrafts and has been almost always willing to talk with me about this project. More than anyone else, Carrie thought about, challenged, and helped me to develop the ideas expressed here.

It has been enormously valuable for me to have two outstanding teachers as parents. This book is dedicated with love and appreciation to two people who have been forever willing to support and nurture my interest in learning, even when that interest has taken me on some odd detours and been expressed in strange ways.

Preface

During the first round of oral arguments in the 2000 Presidential election cases, the United States Supreme Court took part in a gripping discussion regarding the Florida Supreme Court's recent rulings on the counting of disputed presidential ballots. The central question in that discussion was whether the Florida court's interpretation of state election statutes was consistent with policy choices made by Florida's legislature before the election. During an exchange with Gore attorney Laurence Tribe, Justice Antonin Scalia drew one of the few laughs in the tense proceedings when he ridiculed Tribe's suggestion that Florida's legislature had wanted state courts to play an important role creating the boundaries for resolving post-election disputes. Scalia provoked the laughter by commenting: "I mean – maybe your experience with the legislative branch is different from mine, but in my experience they are resigned to the intervention of the courts, but have certainly never invited it." In the face of the ensuing laughter, Tribe quickly backpedaled by expressing agreement with Scalia ("I have to say that my experience parallels that") and attempting to change the subject. Unwilling to let the point drop, Scalia interrupted again to dismiss the suggestion that legislatures would want to give the courts policy-making responsibilities by saying, "I just find it implausible" (*New York Times*, December 2, 2000, A12).

This book makes an empirical inquiry into the processes through which federal judges and legislators make policies in the American constitutional system of separation of powers. Among other things, I find that Scalia's claim that legislators never invite judges to intervene in policy disputes is dead wrong. The book documents several important cases where legislators deliberately empowered judges to make important policy decisions and provides some important reasons for thinking that legislators routinely invite the "intervention" of the courts by creating conditions that allow judges to make policy.

The book also tries to account for the fact that Scalia and Tribe, who disagree about almost everything else, are both willing to express agreement with the misleading claim that legislators never want judges to make policy. I argue that conservatives like Scalia, liberals like Tribe, and almost all judges and judicial scholars in between rely on the same theoretical framework to understand judicial power and judicial decision making in the American separation of powers system. This framework, which I will explain in considerably more detail in Chapter 1, is the foundation for a wide range of competing theories and models that address questions about the exercise of institutional power in the American constitutional system. The framework imagines that independent branches compete with each other for influence over policy and assumes that outcomes produced by elected legislators are more democratic than outcomes produced by unelected federal judges. The framework leads scholars and judges to address policy controversies by trying to identify the intent or meaning of choices made by elected legislators. The framework also makes it seem "implausible" that legislators would want judges to make policy because it imagines that elected legislators pursue their policy preferences by trying to minimize the powers of rival judges whose preferences are less constrained by electoral processes.

Given that thinkers as different as Scalia and Tribe publicly agree that legislators do not invite judges to make policy, my claim that legislators often invite such intervention should be quite shocking. In reality, however, it is not. At least one leading scholar has already carefully documented the importance of legislative deference to the courts as an important source of judicial power. Mark Graber's path-breaking 1993 article documents the importance of legislative deference in three important constitutional cases and makes some sophisticated theoretical claims that can help scholars to understand such deference and uncover additional cases where deference occurs. Far from being the observation of a single academic commentator, the fact that legislators deliberately leave important policy issues for judges to decide has also been the subject of commentary in mainstream media sources like the *New York Times* and *Washington Post* (Greenhouse 1998, Bardash 1998). More generally, much that is known about the way legislators make decisions suggests that Scalia's claim that legislators never invite the courts to decide substantive issues of policy is itself quite "implausible." Members of Congress very often empower actors in the executive branch and state governments to decide substantive policy issues. Legislators are obviously willing in such instances to trade control over policy outcomes for the practical and political benefits of shifting responsibility to other actors. It seems exceptionally unlikely that legislators who routinely pursue their goals by empowering independent actors in the agencies and states would *never* find it advantageous to empower judges. Legislators may have less control over judges than over state or executive branch officials, but that lack of control can sometimes make deference to the courts a politically attractive option to legislators.

Nevertheless, commentators who have drawn attention to legislative deference to the courts have faced an uphill struggle as they have tried to convince scholars and judges to take legislative deference more seriously as a source of judges' policy-making powers. Ironically, it is precisely because anomalous cases like the ones uncovered by Graber and others are *not* shocking that the importance of such cases has not yet been widely recognized. The real problem for those who want to establish the importance of such cases is not that they are "implausible," but that taking such cases seriously would require scholars to question the fundamental assumptions of a shared theoretical framework that they rely on to understand judicial policy making and separation of powers. The basic idea of that conventional framework is that outcomes created by elected legislators form a democratic baseline against which to evaluate outcomes produced by other branches, and thus that unelected judges have a responsibility in most cases to make choices that match the legislative baseline. That framework is so powerful and useful that those who rely on it have been reluctant to undermine it. The result is that scholars and judges would rather ignore legislative deference to the courts than confront the theoretical complications that would result from acknowledging deference. As I show in Chapter 1, the strategy of ignoring deference can be strained and awkward. Many scholars notice in passing that legislators sometimes make choices that empower the courts to make policy decisions, but then develop theories of judicial policy making or measures of judicial power that cannot make any sense of such cases.

The reluctance of judges and scholars to take legislative deference more seriously is understandable. For example, if Scalia and Tribe were to conclude that the Florida legislature deliberately empowered judges to make substantive policy choices as they resolved election disputes, they would be left without any familiar means of constructing legal arguments in favor of their positions. The tendency of judges and scholars to stick to the framework allows them to resolve many thorny policy issues more comfortably, but that tendency is not without costs. In the 2000 election cases, the framework led Scalia and Tribe on a quest to identify baseline policy choices that Florida's legislature had never made. That quest forced them to downplay the extent to which the Florida electoral statutes had deliberately created conditions that made it more likely that judges would make substantive policy judgments in post-election disputes. The Florida legislature had delegated important decisions to local electoral officials, but had also included provisions in the election statutes stating that a wide range of parties could file lawsuits in state courts challenging the decisions made by those local officials. Those provisions were the reason state judges were in a position to influence the vote-counting process. Moreover, the legislature also included in the statute a provision stating that the judge hearing such suits "may fashion such orders as he or she deems necessary to ensure that each allegation in the complaint is investigated, examined, or checked, to prevent or correct any alleged wrong, and to provide any relief appropriate under such circumstances" (Florida Statutes, Title IX, 102.168(8)). This provision seems like a straightforward invitation to the courts to invoke flexible equity powers in election conflicts. Such provisions make it difficult to believe that legislators wanted to minimize the role of the courts. A legislature jealously guarding policy prerogatives and wary of the influence of the courts would never have included such open-ended, judge-empowering provisions in the election law.

The conventional theoretical framework creates problems that go beyond Florida's election statutes. The more general problem is not simply that cases where legislators deliberately empower the courts are poorly understood, but also that ignoring such cases has meant that scholars fail to ask and answer a variety of important questions about institutional interaction and institutional development. The framework has meant that scholars pay a great deal of attention to questions about how judges do or should make decisions in particular cases, but very little attention to important questions about how judges end up in a position to resolve policy issues. To answer such questions, scholars would have to make more of an effort to understand how well legislators anticipate judicial decisions, how legislators who expect judicial "interference" adjust their behavior, and how legislators themselves attempt to shape the role played by judges.

This book, the first to look in detail at congressional decisions that defer to the courts and at the implications of such decisions for democratic accountability, attempts to break the pattern of denial. I make a conscious effort to undermine the conventional framework by making questions about whether and why legislators invite judges to become policy makers central to my analysis of interbranch policy making. I also uncover the often hidden assumptions of the dominant framework, show why those assumptions do not fit cases involving legislative deference, and explain why judicial decisions cannot be evaluated without paying more attention to legislative deference as a source of judicial power. The heart of the book is an exploration of four case studies that together provide several examples of legislative deference to the courts, as well as examples of more conventional interactions between Congress and the courts. My detailed examination of the case studies leads to some preliminary theory building about legislative deference. The findings show that even if legislative deference to the courts is a relatively uncommon phenomenon, scholars who rely on the dominant theoretical framework and ignore such deference will produce distorted accounts of judicial power.

The book presents a somewhat unusual combination of very detailed information about cases and very abstract theoretical claims about institutional processes and democratic accountability. Many of the theoretical claims cut across familiar divisions that scholars typically use to orient their commentary on judicial policy making, including divisions based on scholars' political orientations (e.g., liberal versus conservative), methodological perspectives (e.g., behaviorist versus rational choice versus historical institutionalist), and subject matter and focus (e.g., statutory versus constitutional interpretation, judicial decision making in individual cases versus longer term institutional and political development). Because the approach is unusual and the targets broad, it is worth sorting out three distinct levels of analysis in the presentation.

The first, least general level is my analysis of the cases. My four cases are federal labor statutes passed between 1898 and 1935, a crucial period of institutional development in American history. The cases are the Erdman, Clayton, Norris-LaGuardia, and Wagner acts. I chose these cases because many scholars of American political development and American courts have recently used these same cases to argue that the institutional and political autonomy of the judiciary allowed judges to have an important influence on the development of both public policies and political movements. Such scholars argue that judges used their independence to obstruct and distort more democratic processes in the legislative branch. In this study, I try to establish precisely the opposite conclusion. I argue that the ability of judges to influence policies was dependent on earlier choices made in the legislature and thus that the decisions that judges made cannot be fairly understood as successful reversals of a robust democratic process in the legislative branch. By deliberately selecting cases that other scholars have used to establish the importance of independent judicial power, I hope to increase the impact of my finding that judicial power is dependent on choices made by legislators.

Using previously overlooked records, I show how participants in the legislative process (legislators, labor leaders, lobbyists for employers' organizations) tried to anticipate the reactions that judges would have to legislative proposals. The evidence shows that participants were aware that choices made in Congress before legislation passed would influence subsequent decisions by judges. Nevertheless, participants deliberately made strategic choices that they expected to empower judges to exercise discretion and set policies. I conclude that the ability of judges to shape labor policies cannot be read as a sign of the independent power of judges to reverse the will of elected legislators.

My case studies show how legislators use a variety of means to empower judges to make labor policy. They sometimes empower judges by including provisions in statutes that assign to judges broad and important enforcement and oversight responsibilities. (Much like the Florida legislature did in the provision inviting judges to provide "any relief appropriate under such circumstances.") More intriguingly, legislators sometimes deliberately include ambiguous language in statutes that allows judges to make policy choices as they resolve interpretive controversies about the meaning of the ambiguous language. I call the cases where legislators empower the courts through deliberately ambiguous statutory language *legislative deferrals* to the courts. I find that the legislators who create deferrals portray them as attempts to establish clear policies, and also that the judges who interpret such statutes claim (less convincingly) that their resolution of the interpretive controversy matches the intent or purpose of Congress. Such posturing has made the judicial decisions in these cases look in retrospect like reversals of legislative choices. However, the evidence in my cases shows that participants in the legislative process understood that features of the statutes would provide opportunities for judges to influence policy, and that participants nevertheless rejected alternative legislative proposals that they expected to limit judicial discretion.

Uncovering participants' expectations about judicial reactions is difficult because the participants in the legislative process all have incentives to be deceptive as they pursue strategies that shift responsibility and blame to judges. Nevertheless, it is possible to find evidence about anticipated reactions by carefully tracing the development of competing legislative proposals. I can show, for example, that legislators deliberately made statutory language more ambiguous after clearer proposals that gave less discretion to judges failed to pass in Congress.

Taken together, the conclusions from my case studies support a dramatic reinterpretation of the labor politics of the time period. My analysis suggests that earlier scholars have overestimated labor's political success in the legislative branch, and that as a result they have overestimated the importance of judicial power. Such findings call into question the view of the "Lochner era" as a period when conservative judges repeatedly reversed the progressive outcomes of more responsive legislative processes in legislatures. My important findings about the widely studied labor cases make a very strong case for paying close attention to legislative deference as a source of judicial power.

In addition to making claims about particular cases and a particular time period, the book makes contributions at two other, more general, levels of analysis. At a second level, the book challenges conventional assessments of the relationships between electoral controls and institutional processes in the American constitutional system of separation of powers. More conventional studies are obsessed with instances where undemocratic and unaccountable courts appear to thwart victories won through political activities in the "democratic" branches. Conventional studies treat judicial decisions that appear to reverse legislative goals as though legislators (and voters) watch helplessly from the sidelines as unaccountable judges use fixed institutional powers to subvert democratically supported policies. By uncovering the important ways in which electoral pressures on Congress lead legislators to empower judges, the account here suggests that the conventional divide between "democratic" and "counter-majoritarian" branches is too simplistic to capture the complexity of the institutional mechanisms that provide accountability within a separation of powers system. Understanding legislative deference to the courts reveals that judicial policy making can be responsive to electoral controls in ways that conventional scholars ignore. At the same time, such cases show that Congress is less responsive and permeable than those same scholars assume.

At a third, most general level of analysis, the book challenges the way scholars conceptualize interaction among the different branches of government. While conventional theoretical frameworks incline scholars to see interaction between branches as conflicts between independent strategic actors seeking to pursue well-defined policy preferences, I find that the appearance of conflict between independent branches frequently masks more cooperative interaction between interdependent branches. Dropping the assumption of conflict complicates the task of understanding interaction among branches. However, it also makes it possible to uncover important forms of interaction that are invisible to scholars who look at the same processes as though they are strategic games among independent actors pursuing sharply defined policy preferences.

This book is the first to make an extended empirical inquiry into legislative deferrals to the courts, why they occur, and the effects that deferrals have on accountability and institutional development. Because it focuses on a series of cases in a single policy area and involving many of the same principal decision makers, the study is able to explore the long-term effectiveness of deference as a political strategy and to explain how deference can both help and hurt the outside organizations seeking to use electoral processes to produce changes in policies. Because the cases straddle a period of tremendous institutional change, the cases provide variation on a number of important institutional and political variables.

The book is not, however, an attempt to offer the final word on legislative deference to the courts. Because the motives that lead legislators to defer to the courts also lead legislators to use deception to disguise deferrals as clear policy choices, it is necessary to examine and interpret a tremendous amount of contextual information before concluding that a statute is or is not a legislative deferral. The detailed analysis required to code cases makes it impossible to explore legislative deference across a large population of cases. Because I can only look at a small number of cases, I am not able to draw any precise conclusions about how often deferrals occur in other policy areas and time periods. Moreover, the theoretical claims that I make about the characteristics of legislative deference are preliminary and made in a spirit that I hope invites additional empirical inquiry and refinement. Nevertheless, it is possible to draw three important general conclusions based on the case studies presented here: 1) deferrals occur in some very important and highly contested policy areas, 2) legislators are quite likely to have both motive and opportunity to defer to the courts in a much larger number of cases, and thus 3) scholars should pay much more attention to legislative deference as a source of judicial power before attempting to characterize judicial power as a threat to democratic accountability.

Several features of this study help to support these three conclusions. The factors that I identify as the reasons legislators defer to the courts in these cases are all factors that are likely to occur in a much larger number of cases. Moreover, I show that the empirical methods most scholars use to analyze interbranch interaction make it likely that they will have mis-interpreted cases involving deference to the courts. Those methods make deferrals look like cases that fit the conventional framework, and there-fore lead scholars to ignore the sources of evidence that make it possible to recognize deferrals and distinguish them from cases that better fit the conventional framework. By demonstrating the success of my alternative methods, this study suggests both that there is very good reason to think that the cases I look at here are not the only important cases where leg-islators defer to the courts, and that there is little reason to think that legislative deference to the courts is a rare or uncommon phenomenon.

While it is important for the purposes of this study to establish that deferrals do sometimes occur in important cases, it is not crucial to estab-lish exactly how often they occur. The crucial question is not whether the conventional framework accurately describes more cases of interbranch interaction than a framework that takes deference more seriously. The small number of deferral cases uncovered here demonstrates that the con-ventional framework systematically obscures important features of in-terbranch interaction. Thus, even if cases involving legislative deference to the courts are less common than cases that fit the more conventional framework, it is still important to acknowledge and account for cases where legislators defer to the courts.

The book has two introductory chapters that precede the presentation of empirical evidence. Chapter 1 explains and challenges the dominant theoretical framework by uncovering its core assumptions and showing how those assumptions are challenged by the possibility of legislative def-erence to the courts. Chapter 2 introduces the case studies, sets the his-torical context, and explains how the findings here challenge the leading interpretations of the same cases. Chapters 3 through 6 consider my four case studies in chronological order. The concluding Chapter 7 reviews some of the conclusions about deferrals that emerge across the cases and explains some of the advantages of paying more attention to deferrals.

Rethinking Judicial Policy Making in a Separation of Powers System

> There is an old adage that you can kill a person with kindness, and this is equally true when applied to proposed legislation.
>
> AFL President Samuel Gompers, *American Federationist*, May 1914, 406

In October 1914, the United States Congress passed and President Wilson signed the Clayton Antitrust Act, the first major revision of federal antitrust policy since the Sherman Act of 1890. The Clayton Act was of great interest to labor organizations because it contained provisions that seemed to prohibit federal judges from using injunctions and the antitrust laws to regulate workers and labor unions. Labor organizations had been demanding such legislation for two decades in an effort to limit the power of federal judges, who at that time had assumed much of the responsibility for regulating labor organizations and workers' collective activities.

The Clayton Act appears to be a significant political victory for labor organizations. Passage came two years after the leaders of the American Federation of Labor (AFL) made a controversial decision to endorse Woodrow Wilson's campaign for the presidency. When Wilson signed the new law, AFL president Samuel Gompers announced triumphantly that the endorsement had paid off. Gompers publicly expressed unqualified satisfaction with the labor provisions, telling rank-and-file readers of the AFL's leading publication that the new law was a "Charter of Industrial Freedom," an "Industrial Magna Carta," and that the labor provisions contained "sledge-hammer blows to the wrongs and injustice so long inflicted upon the workers."[1]

[1] *American Federationist*, November 1914, 971.

As things turned out, however, the labor provisions in the Clayton Act were less useful than a sledgehammer and the AFL got little more than the souvenir pen that President Wilson used to sign it. The act's advertised modifications in labor policies were never realized. In a pivotal 1921 case, the Supreme Court established a strained, probusiness, reading of the labor provisions that contradicted the expressed expectations of AFL leaders and the stated goals of many members of Congress.[2] As a result, the labor provisions did not produce any substantial changes in labor law. Judges continued to subject labor unions to the antitrust laws, and the rate of injunctions against workers actually increased.[3] In the end, the AFL's greatest legislative victory of the Progressive Era did little to help workers or to curtail the ability of judges to regulate workers' collective activities.

The failure of the labor provisions in the Clayton Act seems to present a classic illustration of an important and troubling structural feature of American democracy: Unelected federal judges can use their institutional powers to influence policy outcomes, often by making choices that appear to conflict with policies favored by elected officials in other branches. Scholars have long been concerned that the capacity of unelected judges to make policy in opposition to the wishes of the elected Congress is a "counter-majoritarian force" and thus a "deviant" part of American democracy (Bickel 1962, 16). Scholars worry that such judicial rulings can block policy victories won through the seemingly more democratic processes in the legislative branch. Some scholars have also been concerned that such judicial rulings have significant radiating effects that distort future democratic processes. For example, recent studies of the development of the labor movement use cases like the Clayton Act to argue that American judges who made rulings that reversed legislative policies also shaped the political consciousness of workers and thus the development of the American labor movement. By consistently thwarting labor's efforts to use conventional political processes in legislatures to achieve policy changes, the courts contributed to the uniquely apolitical labor movement in the United States and the resulting "exceptionalism" in American social and welfare policies.

---

[2] *Duplex Printing Press Company v Deering* (254 U.S. 443).
[3] Ernst 1995, 190. Forbath (1991, app. B) provides both the best estimate of the number of injunctions by decade during the late nineteenth and early twentieth centuries and the best explanation of why it is so difficult to determine the precise number of injunctions. The Clayton Act itself caused part of the increase because it gave employers a new legal basis for requesting labor injunctions by authorizing private individuals and companies to request injunctions against antitrust violations.

This book reaches very different conclusions. After reexamining the circumstances that produced the Clayton Act and three other federal labor statutes passed between 1898 and 1935, I find that scholars have misunderstood several notorious confrontations between Congress and the courts over labor policy. Other scholars have looked at judicial rulings on labor statutes as reversals of labor's legislative victories, and have linked such judicial reversals to institutional arrangements that insulate judges from democratic processes. I find, however, that the appearance of independent judges reversing clear legislative victories is an illusion that masks a more complicated set of strategic interactions. Caught between powerful constituencies with incompatible demands, legislators preferred to avoid the political costs of making clear decisions. Legislators thus decided that their political interests were best served by passing statutes that appeared to make decisive choices but that covertly empowered the courts. With such statutes, legislators could create the appearance of democratic responsiveness while allowing much of the blame for difficult policy choices to fall on less accountable judges. My finding that legislators were deferring to the courts suggests that other scholars have overestimated the independent effects of the courts on the development of the American labor movement because they have overestimated the political success of labor organizations and the responsiveness of legislatures to labor's political demands.

The bulk of the book (chapters 3 to 6) is devoted to a detailed exploration of my case studies of four pivotal federal labor statutes, the Erdman Act of 1898, the Clayton Act of 1914, the Norris-LaGuardia Act of 1932, and the Wagner Act of 1935. The case studies together support an original interpretation of labor politics and American institutional development in the first part of the twentieth century. Before presenting the detailed evidence that supports my interpretation of these cases, I use this introductory chapter to make more general theoretical claims about the importance of uncovering and understanding instances where legislators defer to the courts. Assuming for now that legislators do at least sometimes deliberately defer to the courts, I will make some preliminary observations about why such deference challenges many of the theoretical assumptions made by scholars who study judicial policy making.

THE LEGISLATIVE BASELINE FRAMEWORK AND
LEGISLATIVE DEFERRALS

> One of the duties in enacting legislation is to make legislation just as plain
> and positive as it can be made. Aside from the evils that may result from

unwise and unjust laws comes the great evil of the uncertainty of law. . . . We
pass laws about which we ourselves differ as to the use and application of
the terms, and then courts are criticized because of their interpretation of
the laws.

> Sen. Wesley Jones (R-WA) floor debates on the Clayton Act,
> 51 *Congressional Record* 14019

My findings in the labor cases reveal some important problems with the
way scholars who study judicial policy making understand judicial power
and legislative politics. Most scholars who study judges as policy makers
rely upon the same general theoretical framework to understand, measure,
and evaluate judicial power. I call that framework the *legislative baseline
framework* because its core assumption is that outcomes established by
elected legislators form a democratic baseline against which to evaluate
decisions made by less directly accountable judges. The legislative baseline
framework leads scholars to evaluate the impact and legitimacy of judicial
decisions by comparing the position established by judges to a baseline
position established earlier by legislators.

The legislative baseline framework is not a particular theory or model
of interbranch interaction, but a set of foundational assumptions from
which different scholars have constructed competing theories and models.
The studies that I group under the legislative baseline framework umbrella
sometimes differ fundamentally on important questions. The significance
of the framework is not that it always leads to the same conclusions.
Rather, the framework is important because it influences scholars' ideas
about which questions are interesting, which cases are important, and
what evidence can be ignored. Despite its ubiquity, however, the framework is difficult to define. Perhaps because it is so widely accepted, the
framework is nearly invisible. The assumptions that I associate with the
framework are not typically articulated or defended. As far as I know, I
am the first person to give the framework a name.

I will try in the next several pages to identify the theoretical and
methodological assumptions that together constitute the legislative baseline framework. I begin by focusing on some basic methodological assumptions scholars use when analyzing particular instances of judicial
policy making, I then move to more general levels of analysis by uncovering foundational assumptions about democratic processes and institutional interaction. Some of the assumptions that I list will be more familiar
than others, and the degree to which a particular scholar relies on a
particular assumption will depend in part on what question that scholar is
trying to answer. My hope, however, is that the assumptions I list will seem

innocuous and uncontroversial. They are, for many if not most cases of interbranch interaction, quite correct and quite useful. I will show, however, that the possibility of legislative deference to the courts reveals some important difficulties for each of the assumptions of the framework.

Two Basic Methodological Assumptions Used to Analyze Cases

The shared legislative baseline framework shows up most clearly in the way scholars analyze individual cases involving interaction between the courts and other branches of government. The most basic methodological assumption is:

The Policy Assumption: A congressional decision to pass legislation establishes a particular policy position for Congress. This congressional position can be identified and then compared to the positions later taken by judges and to final policy outcomes.

Scholars need to make the policy assumption in order for any legislative baseline framework analysis to get off the ground. To use the framework, scholars need to compare the policy position taken by elected legislators to the policy outcomes that occur in the aftermath of decisions made by unelected judges. If there is no baseline to be discovered, the necessary comparisons cannot be made. Once a baseline legislative policy is found, however, that baseline becomes essential to scholarly conclusions about the legitimacy and impact of judicial decisions. Scholars see judicial decisions that fail to adhere to the policy baseline as potentially substantial barriers to democratic accountability. Since judges (or, at least, federal judges) are not subject to direct electoral controls, organized groups whose interests are hurt by judicial rulings have fewer "democratic" weapons for overcoming them than they have when elected legislators make policies.

The policy assumption is part of the reason that political scientists have devoted so much attention to the power of judges to review and strike down statutes on constitutional grounds. Scholars see the power to strike down statutes as interesting and troublesome precisely because they assume that judicial decisions that strike down statutes reverse policies established by elected legislatures.[4] The policy assumption also

---

[4] Dahl's (1957) classic article on judicial influence looks only at cases involving judicial review. Bickel 1962 and Ely 1980 are two classic and very influential accounts of judicial review by law professors that are also preoccupied with judicial review as a threat to (and facilitator of) representative democracy. Such accounts pay

shows up when scholars use the legislative baseline framework to analyze instances where judges influence policy outcomes through their power to interpret statutes. Judges are often called upon to interpret statutes because the general prescriptive rules that legislators articulate in the text of statutes contain ambiguities that create interpretive controversies when the statutes are applied in concrete situations. Such controversies often lead to lawsuits, and the judges who rule on such suits have the responsibility of choosing from among competing interpretations of the relevant provisions. The policy assumption allows scholars to measure the legitimacy and impact of such judicial decisions by asking whether judges followed the intent, purpose, or meaning of the elected officials who created the statute.

The policy assumption does not imply that the policy baseline is always transparent enough to be discovered without effort or controversy. The assumption simply means that ambiguities should be treated as accidents that can be overcome through conscientious application of the correct interpretive principles.[5] The task of the deciding judges is always to use such principles to find the appropriate expression of the legislature's baseline position. Scholars who study statutory interpretation have identified a variety of factors that can lead to ambiguity in statutes. For example, legislators might have never anticipated the circumstances that give rise to the interpretive controversy, or might have simply been careless when creating the general statutory language expressing their new policy commands. (See, e.g., Carter 1998, 37–55; Sunstein 1990, 117–23; Eskridge, Frickey, Garrett 1999, 211–36.)

The importance of the policy assumption is not that it makes scholars of statutory interpretation blind to ambiguity but that it leads scholars to devote their attention to finding the best methods for finding (or inventing or imagining) a baseline legislative position that can be used to test the legitimacy of a judicial decision. Scholars disagree about whether that baseline should be identified in a congressional "purpose" discoverable

---

little or no attention to the influence judges have through their power to interpret statutes.

[5] This point about accidents is discussed in more detail later in this chapter. The desire to find a legitimating baseline is often the dominant concern for scholars of statutory interpretation, but it need not be the sole concern. Scholars are also concerned about whether competing methods of statutory interpretation are able to preserve the rule of law and respond to general pragmatic concerns associated with regulatory statutes. Eskridge, Frickey, and Garrett 2000, 211–13.

in the legislative history or simply extrapolated from the isolated legislative text.[6] Few scholars of statutory interpretation ask seriously whether legislators ever wanted to establish a baseline.

A second methodological assumption captures the effect the framework has on the way scholars understand and evaluate political processes.

The Political Power Assumption: The relative level of political power attained by different organized groups can be measured by examining the legislation Congress passes. A decision in Congress to pass legislation signals that the group sponsoring the legislation has attained a significant level of political influence through the electoral processes that influence legislative decisions.

The political power assumption is important because it allows scholars to simplify the task of analyzing the political context in which judges make policies. The assumption allows scholars who are interested in the impact of judicial decisions to focus on the effects of what judges do *after* legislation passes without worrying very much about the political processes that occurred in Congress before passage. Scholars who use the assumption will admit that legislative branch outcomes are not always perfect indicators of underlying political conditions, but are nevertheless willing to accept legislation as the best available proxy for the positions that emerge victorious from electoral processes.

The political power assumption shows up most clearly in some classic works that try to measure empirically the impact of the courts on democratic processes (Dahl 1957, but see also Casper 1976). However, the assumption also influences the work of scholars who focus on normative questions about the legitimacy of judicial decisions. The assumption is also the reason so many scholars worry that judicial policy making is a threat to the democratic accountability. However, in normative studies, the political power assumption often shows up in the form of its corollary: If the position favored by judges differs from the position favored by legislators, the difference must be a result of the fact that judges are insulated from the electoral pressures that determine legislative branch outcomes.

Legislative Deferrals and the Policy and Power Assumptions

The policy and political power assumptions provide a useful framework for understanding and analyzing a wide range of cases involving

[6] For overviews of the literature on statutory interpretation, see Eskridge and Frickey 1987, ch. 7; Eskridge 1994, p. 2; Katzmann 1997, 49–64; and Carter 1998, ch. 3.

interbranch interactions. Unfortunately, the success of the assumptions in many straightforward instances of judicial policy making has led scholars to apply the assumptions across the board to all instances where judges and legislators participate together in policy-making processes. The findings in this study suggest that there are some circumstances that present opportunities for judicial policy making that are not well suited to these conventional assumptions. In particular, there are instances where the opportunity for judges to influence policy arises because legislators deliberately avoid making choices about policies and instead allow judges to make those choices. Legislators sometimes expand the power of judges to make policy by including provisions in statutes that assign the courts broad oversight responsibilities or provisions that enable affected parties to enlist the aid of judges by making it easier to file lawsuits. In the more subtle (and perhaps more devious) instances that I call legislative deferrals to the courts, legislators empower judges by creating deliberately ambiguous statutory language.

It may initially seem unlikely that legislators would ever deliberately give away power to independent judges. However, there are a variety of reasons why legislators might sometimes create conditions that allow judges to influence policy (Graber 1993, Gillman 2002, Rogers 2001). Legislators might create a role for the judges because they think that the best way to resolve certain intractable policy questions is to give judges the discretion to apply flexible principles as they design outcomes that meet the unique circumstances of individual cases. (Some criminal sentencing may fall into this category.) Or, legislators might empower judges to reject administrative decisions because doing so provides additional oversight of executive branch agencies and an additional guarantee of due process.[7] In other instances, legislators may not particularly want judges to make policy decisions, but will nevertheless defer to the courts. For example, deliberate ambiguity might help to break a stalemate in Congress if legislators on both sides of an issue estimate that their best chance for achieving their policy goals is to support an ambiguous law and hope that their side

---

[7] Strauss 1989 and Shapiro 1988 provide overviews of judicial oversight of administration. There may be a constitutional dimension to judicial oversight. Some judges or scholars might claim that the due process clause requires legislators to provide some judicial oversight when they delegate to the executive branch. Shapiro's overview of the development of judicial oversight indicates, however, that it is not solely constitutional concerns that drive legislators to provide for judicial oversight of administration. Moreover, legislators can avoid any constitutionally required judicial oversight of administrative processes by declining to delegate.

wins in the courts. In other cases where legislators are badly divided by conflicting demands from well-organized constituencies, legislators may decide to empower judges for reasons that have little to do with their policy goals. In such cases, legislators might be willing to give up some certainty about policy goals in order to achieve important political goals. Some legislators may not care how judges resolve the controversy so long as judges take the blame for contentious and potentially unpopular decisions. A coalition supporting a deliberately ambiguous statute might include legislators responding to a broad range of motives. Legislators with strong preferences on the policy issues might agree to defer to judges because they hope to win in the courts. Other legislators may not be sure what choice judges will make, but will support the ambiguous law because they think it will force judges to absorb some of the blame from unhappy constituents.

For my purposes in this chapter, it is not yet crucial to sort out the different implications of each of these different possible motives for empowering judges. Regardless of whether legislators defer for policy or political reasons, the essential point here is that legislators who make such choices recognize that their decisions expand judicial discretion. In some of the cases I look at here, legislators decided to enact ambiguous statutes even though they knew that judges were the institutional actors who would be called upon to settle the meaning of open-ended statutory provisions. This essential point is what makes the policy assumption inappropriate in such cases. While the policy assumption can accommodate cases where ambiguities arise by accident, cases where judges rule because legislators deliberately refrain from making policy choices deserve to be treated as an entirely separate category.

A less obvious, but perhaps more troubling problem with the policy assumption is that it has led scholars to develop interpretive conventions for reading legislative records that make it very likely that scholars will misinterpret cases involving deliberate deference to the courts. These conventions for handling evidence disguise deliberate deferrals as accidental ambiguities, and thus lead scholars to mistake legislative deference to the courts as cases that fit the conventional framework. Of course, scholars disagree about precisely which conventions are appropriate. Some scholars allow judges to look at committee reports and speeches by floor leaders. Other scholars worry that such records contain distortions, and urge judges to look only at the text of statutes while ignoring all other records of congressional deliberations. Significantly, however, all scholars seem to agree that judges should ignore the overwhelming majority of legislative records. The forbidden records include most floor speeches, transcripts of committee hearings, rejected alternative proposals, and records from earlier congresses. Such sources record the expressed views of individual legislators, but are said to be unreliable as sources of information regarding the collective intent, meaning, or purpose of Congress.[8]

The demand that judges ignore such evidence works out well in cases where legislators collectively decide to establish a fixed policy baseline. However, such interpretive conventions will produce misleading results in situations where legislators refrain from making important choices and instead defer to the courts. Consider, for example, the convention that tells judges that they can look at committee reports and the speeches of floor leaders, but that they should ignore the remaining evidence of congressional deliberation. This is the convention that the Supreme Court followed in the crucial 1921 case on the Clayton Act (*Duplex Printing v Deering*, 254 U.S. 443 (1921)). The convention is supposed to prevent judges from being swayed by the distracting statements of individual legislators who do not speak for Congress as a whole. The problem, however, is that the convention leads scholars to ignore the most likely sources for evidence of deliberate ambiguity. My findings in this study suggest that committee reports and floor managers' speeches are the least likely place in the congressional records to find evidence of deliberate deference to judges. Because committee leaders and floor managers are likely to have a large stake in holding together a successful coalition built through deliberate ambiguity, they are much less likely to call attention to ambiguity than disgruntled backbenchers who want to disrupt that coalition.

The emerging rival convention telling judges to ignore *all* legislative records and look only at the text of statutes is even more misleading. Those who promote this convention claim that it limits judicial discretion by making it harder for judges to use distorted legislative records to promote their own policy preferences.[9] Ironically, however, the convention *maximizes* judicial discretion in cases where legislators deliberately write text that is ambiguous enough to support two contradictory interpretations. A judge who assumes that the legislators who wrote such text were trying to limit the influence of judges by making clear choices will

---

[8] On these conventions, see previously cited sources in note 6.
[9] The most prominent defender of this rival convention is Justice Antonin Scalia. See his opinion in *Hirschey v Federal Energy Regulatory Commission* (777 F. 2d 1, 7–8 (D.C. Cir. 1985)) or Scalia (1997).

probably have little difficulty concluding confidently that the text happens to match his or her policy preferences.

The likelihood of a deferral being misinterpreted is compounded by the fact that deferrals are likely to be accompanied by deliberate distortion. Legislators who want to avoid responsibility for a difficult decision by shifting that decision to the courts can gain the most politically by saying and doing things that disguise deferrals as clear, responsive, and responsible policy choices. Given the likelihood of deception, scholars need to be very careful about how they interpret the text of the statutes and statements of legislators as they search for a congressional position. These observations suggest that however useful it may be to ignore legislative records in cases where the policy assumption holds true, systematically ignoring such records risks distortion in cases where legislators covertly empower the courts.

The interpretive conventions that call on judges to ignore most of the record of congressional deliberations can be thought of as a very useful way to eliminate rival interpretations that found voice during congressional deliberations. Robert Cover (1983) has referred to the judicial duty to establish some single interpretation of a law by killing off rival interpretations as the "jurispathic" function of the courts. The standard interpretive conventions are very effective at performing this function. Judges who ignore evidence in a quest for a chimerical legislative intent usually succeed in finding one. For example, in the case of the Clayton Act, all the justices on the Supreme Court (including the dissenters) claimed to find baseline legislative positions that supported their preferred resolution of the interpretive controversies. They found such baselines despite the fact that the legislators who created the act deliberately left some disputed policy questions unresolved with the expectation that judges would make the choices for them. What the Supreme Court justices really found was not a baseline position of Congress but a fiction manufactured through the interpretive process.[10]

Once the policy assumption is abandoned, the arguments for ignoring most legislative records are no longer sound. Given the possibility of legislative deference to the courts, the researcher trying to understand the impact of the courts should no longer try to discover or imagine some

---

[10] To be clear: My claim is not that there are no coherent reasons for adopting the existing interpretive conventions, or that the purpose of such conventions is to disguise cases that challenge the underlying theoretical framework. Within the assumptions of the legislative baseline framework there are sound reasons for adopting these conventions.

single policy outcome that can serve as a legitimating baseline. The researcher's new goal should be to discover how well participants in legislative processes anticipated the role of the courts and whether those participants tried to shape the role judges would play. When pursuing this new goal, there is no longer any reason to ignore the statements of individual legislators simply because they are not representative of some chimerical collective entity known as "Congress." Even unrepresentative floor speeches can provide very valuable information about how well participants in legislative processes were able to anticipate the role the courts would later play.

Like the policy assumption, the political power assumption can also result in misleading conclusions when legislators deliberately defer to the courts. For example, if scholars assume that the decision in Congress to pass the Clayton Act was a victory for the labor organizations that endorsed the statute, then they will interpret passage as a signal that labor organizations had attained considerable power and influence in the legislative branch. However, once the Clayton Act is reinterpreted as a more ambiguous response that deliberately gave judges discretion, the meaning of the signal sent by passage of the statute is much less clear. My evidence shows that the bill Congress passed was not the first choice of labor leaders, that legislators made significant changes that weakened the labor provisions before passing the bill, and that both labor leaders and legislators had reservations about the likely effectiveness of the new law. Most tellingly, legislators created a law that deliberately gave discretion to judges at a time when everyone involved in the congressional process expected judges to be hostile to the interests of labor organizations. These observations make it quite difficult to believe that Congress was responding collectively to some politically powerful labor juggernaut capable of forcing congressional majorities to enact its demands into legislation. The compromises that occurred before passage of the Clayton Act suggest instead that passage of the statute might be better interpreted as a signal of the AFL's political weakness.

The political power assumption does not completely fail, however. Correctly interpreted, the Clayton Act is a reflection of the AFL's (lack of) political power in Congress. The danger of the political power assumption is not that it is wrong, but that it is typically combined with other assumptions that lead scholars to pay too little attention to the way decisions are made in Congress. Ironically, the legislative baseline framework places legislative outcomes in an exalted position as the baseline against which all other outcomes should be measured, but the policy and political power assumptions lead scholars to ignore much of what happens in Congress.

Background Assumptions about Democratic and Legislative Politics

The problems that legislative deference to the courts creates for the policy and political power assumptions point toward some deeper problems with the legislative baseline framework. In particular, deferrals call into question the framework's foundational assumptions about the relationship between electoral controls and accountability in different branches of government. To see why, it is useful to first draw out two assumptions about democratic processes that are at the heart of the legislative baseline framework. The first is:

The Electoral Constraint Assumption: The presence (or absence) of electoral constraints on the principal decision makers in a branch of government normally determines whether outcomes produced by that branch are democratic.

On the surface, this assumption seems reasonable, and the basis for its widespread acceptance appears obvious. A representative democracy seems "democratic" precisely because the officials responsible for making binding policy decisions are accountable to voters through elections. In the United States, federal legislators face regular elections. Those elections make it easy to assume that there are strong and direct connections between legislative decisions and "democracy." In contrast, judicial policy making is suspect because judges are not elected (or at least not usually subject to effective electoral constraints).[11]

---

[11] Of course, many state judges are elected officials. Since this study focuses on decisions that federal judges made regarding federal statutes, I leave this important complication for future investigation. (I discuss the politics of judicial elections in connection with judicial reversals of state statutes in Lovell 1994.) Additional complications are introduced once attention is paid to the role of the executive branch in interbranch processes. At the federal level, the president is the lone elected official among the many thousands of individuals employed in the executive branch who make decisions that have important effects on policy outcomes. In order to keep things from becoming too complicated, I focus my attention on interactions between Congress and the courts as I develop general theoretical claims in this book. However, even with that artificially narrow focus, executive branch actors do emerge as important at several crucial places in my case studies. The executive branch was crucial to shaping legislative compromises on some of the case statutes (e.g., the Clayton and Wagner Acts). Executive branch actors also made important enforcement decisions that shaped Supreme Court tests of case statutes (particularly in connection with the Wagner Act). Any complete account of accountability and separation of powers would have to pay considerably more attention to the executive branch than I do here.

It is fair to say that the electoral constraint assumption is widely shared. For example, the very first sentence of the leading manifesto of the "attitudinal model" of judicial behavior establishes that it is important to explain Supreme Court decision making by drawing attention to the fact that federal judges are unelected officials in a democratic system (Segal and Spaeth 1993, 1). More generally, the electoral constraint assumption explains why the empirical questions political scientists ask about judicial decisions are so different from the empirical questions they ask about legislative decisions. Many political scientists have devoted their careers to answering the question of whether or not judges follow their policy preferences as they vote on cases. But as far as I can tell, no one who studies Congress is interested in the question of whether or not legislators follow their personal preferences when they make decisions. Congress scholars do not think it threatens democratic accountability if legislators follow their policy preferences and many scholars interpret legislators' votes on statutes as straightforward indicators of policy preferences.[12]

The electoral constraint assumption does not mean that all judicial decisions that fail to comply with the legislative baseline are *illegitimate*. Nor does the assumption's emphasis on electoral constraints mean that scholars rely upon a purely procedural conception of democracy, that is, one where any policy outcome counts as democratic so long as it is established through an electorally constrained process. Scholars can make the assumption but still allow judges to reverse legislators when judges need to preserve rights that are essential to a democracy or to maintain some genuine constitutional limit on legislative power.[13] The importance of the electoral constraint assumption is not that it leads to any particular conception of democracy but that it leads scholars to see the task of establishing the legitimacy of judicial decisions as categorically different from the task of establishing the legitimacy of legislative decisions. The understanding of democratic accountability that results from the assumption led an entire generation of scholars to respond to Bickel's pronouncement

---

[12] There is, however, some debate about whether legislators vote strategically by taking into account the positions of potentially obstructionist actors in the other chamber or in other branches. See, for example, Martin 2001, who finds that legislators vote strategically and that their votes reflect considerations about other branches.

[13] This category of scholars includes Bickel. Other classic defenses of judicial review as part of a democratic society are Ely 1980, and the one offered by Justice Jackson in the flag salute case: "The very purpose of a Bill of Rights was to withdraw certain subjects from the vicissitudes of political controversy, to place them beyond the reach of majorities and officials and to establish them as legal principles to be applied by the courts" (*West Virginia v Barnette* 319 U.S. 624, 638 (1943)).

of a "counter-majoritarian" problem not by rejecting judicial review, but by searching for principles and methods of constitutional interpretation that could constrain judicial discretion.[14]

For scholars working within the behavioral tradition in political science, the mere fact that judges are not subject to election is enough to make most judicial policy making democratically suspect. However, some scholars working outside that tradition have made more of an effort to specify the reasons why judicial policy making is problematic. In particular, scholars associated with various "critical" movements in legal thought have specified reasons why judicial power can create barriers to democratic responsiveness. Some of their important concerns are captured in the following variation on the electoral constraint assumption:

Pure Politics Assumption: Judicial processes can create subtle but important barriers that are not present when groups are able to pursue policy change through the more pure political processes of the legislative branch. The lack of electoral constraints on judges leads judges to rely on the peculiar legitimating ideologies encoded in legal discourse to justify their decisions. As a result, groups forced to fight for policy changes in courts have to express their demands in a recognizable legal discourse, a requirement that can transform their demands and aspirations.

The pure politics assumption captures concerns about what happens when groups are forced to fight for their interests before judges rather then before elected legislators. Such groups have to translate their demands into a legal discourse judges will find recognizable. The need to absorb and parrot existing legal arguments and doctrines may lead organizations to temper their demands when they seek to protect their interests in court. Judges are unlikely to be receptive to dramatic reform proposals that challenge their foundational assumptions about justice in society. Such moderating tendencies are compounded by the need to hire lawyers to make such legal arguments, lawyers who will have undergone a socialization process that can make them reluctant to challenge the existing hierarchical system of authority. Thus, when judges assume policy-making powers, the most ambitious reform goals of insurgent organizations are likely to disappear (Pope 1997, 1012).[15]

---

[14] Bobbitt (1982); Murphy, Fleming, and Barber (1998); and Shapiro (1983) provide good overviews/introductions to the results of this effort. On the pathologies of the counter-majoritarian framework, see Friedman (2000) and Bennett (2001).

[15] Spann 1993, esp. ch. 9; Gordon 1984; and Balbus 1977 provide illuminating discussions related to these points.

The problems that critical scholars associate with judicial power intensify as groups forced to employ legal arguments begin to internalize the norms embedded in legal discourse. Judges set the boundaries for legitimate behavior and do so in a universal language that masks the underlying power relations. The power of judges to issue authoritative statements of policy in their peculiar legitimating discourse gives judges the power to influence the consciousness of mass publics and ideologies of insurgent organizations.[16]

Scholars who describe such features of legal processes often establish the importance of legal discourse by contrasting it to allegedly more pure political processes in legislatures. Such scholars expect legislative processes to allow for a more direct form of political expression and competition. Such scholars also assume that groups that have enough votes in Congress can win there whether or not their demands can be expressed as appropriate legal arguments (Spann 1993, ch. 6; Pope 1997, 1012).

Legislative Deferrals and the Electoral Constraint and Pure Politics Assumptions

The possibility that legislators strategically empower judges to make policy creates problems for both the electoral constraint and pure politics assumptions. When legislators defer to the courts, they are not responding to democratic constraints in the straightforward way that scholars imagine. As a result, neither the legislative nor the judicial decisions that occur in such cases are connected to electoral processes in the manner expected. The problem for both assumptions is that the presumed divide between democratically constrained decision making in Congress and undemocratic and unaccountable decision making in the courts can sometimes be much narrower than the two assumptions lead scholars to think.

The problem with the electoral constraint assumption is that its narrow focus on the question of whether or not decision makers are elected leads scholars to ignore some important connections between judicial decisions and electoral processes. In cases where elected legislators make decisions that empower judges, the resulting judicial decisions are no longer completely isolated from electoral processes. The officials who made the decisions that empowered judges were subject to electoral controls.

---

[16] See for example, Forbath 1991, Hattam 1993; two studies that provide empirical evidence for claims of this sort.

(Legislators who defer to the courts face election just as often as legislators who decide to establish clear policies.) Scholars who miss those connections will underestimate the extent to which democratic processes constrain judicial power. To see the connections more clearly, scholars need to shift their focus away from questions about how judges choose outcomes in particular cases and to think more carefully about why judges are sometimes in a position to resolve particular policy controversies.

Of course, any connections between electoral processes and decisions made by judges will be different from, and probably weaker than, the connections that occur when legislators make and take responsibility for policy choices. When elected legislators make the policy choice directly, the policy that results seems connected to electoral processes in a more straightforward and substantial way than when legislators shift responsibility to judges. Nevertheless, a theoretical framework that systematically ignores all connections between decisions deferred to judges and the electoral processes that constrain legislators will produce a distorted account that underestimates the links between electoral controls and judicial decisions.

This conclusion may be somewhat difficult to accept. The fact that the connections to electoral pressures are less direct in cases involving deferrals makes it tempting to condemn legislative deference to the courts as a breakdown in the democratic process. Legislators who try to shield themselves from accountability by shifting blame to others seem to be illegitimately shirking important duties. My earlier observation that legislators may try to hide such shirking with deception further suggests that the results of such legislative decisions should not be called "democratic." Moreover, my case studies show that legislators deferred to the courts to avoid responsibility for particularly important and contentious policy issues.[17] Mark Graber (1993) draws similar conclusions in his study of legislative deference to the courts. If legislators are able to shift important, polarizing issues toward less accountable decision makers, then the electoral processes that are supposed to make legislators responsive appear to be something of a sham.

---

[17] My four case studies include the statute that is undoubtedly the most important labor statute ever passed by Congress (the Wagner Act), the statute that is arguably the most radical labor statute ever passed by Congress (the Norris-LaGuardia Act), and a statute that has been at the center of several recent accounts of judicial policy making and political development (the Clayton Act). On the importance of labor to American politics and American constitutionalism, see Orren 1995. Additional deferral cases are discussed in Lovell 1994.

However, even though legislative deference to the courts may not be the most responsive or responsible way of making public policies in a democratic society, deference cannot simply be treated as though it is entirely undemocratic or unresponsive. Legislative strategies involving blame shifting may seem intuitively distasteful only because scholars' expectations about proper legislative behavior are shaped by the legislative baseline framework. To test the electoral constraint assumption and the legislative baseline framework, the relevant question is not: Does it seem democratic when legislators try to shift blame for difficult decisions to less accountable judges? The more relevant question is: Is such deference to the courts as deviant and undemocratic as the legislative baseline framework makes it seem?

The answer to that question may be "no." To answer it accurately, it is necessary to look in detail at actual cases involving deferrals, to examine how deferrals affect organizations that take part in electoral politics, and to ask whether the affected organizations would have been better off in an institutional system where it was impossible for legislators to defer to the courts. In the limited number of cases that I look at here, I make some findings that suggest surprising answers to such questions. My cases show that in addition to being barriers to direct democratic accountability, deferrals could also be important strategic weapons that labor leaders chose to employ as they pursued the long-term interests of their organizations. Labor organizations may have been better off if they had been able to win decisive legislative victories in Congress that limited the capacity of judges to issue hostile decisions. However, it also seems quite unlikely that labor organizations would have won such clear victories if it had been impossible for legislators to defer to the courts.

To be clear: My claim here is not that my case studies will prove that there is no reason to be concerned about deferrals. In fact, the labor cases show that the deferral strategies pursued by labor leaders were not very effective for achieving their most important policy goals. The claim I wish to make is simply that deferrals are quite a bit more complicated than the conventional framework makes them seem. The legislative baseline framework does call attention to some important drawbacks of blame-shifting strategies like deferrals, but the framework also misses other important problems and is completely blind to some of the important advantages that a system allowing deferrals creates.

Thinking more carefully about such advantages and disadvantages reveals a deeper, more general problem with the legislative baseline framework. The vision of democratic accountability expressed in the electoral constraint assumption cannot capture some essential elements of American constitutional democracy. In particular, the assumption underestimates the way in which the complexity and variety of institutional processes across different branches and levels of government can both facilitate and hinder responsiveness and permeability in the American state. The conventional framework's tendency to isolate decisions made in separate branches is most reasonable in instances where strategic interactions among competing groups and government officials produce a decisive victory for one side. The framework has a more difficult time with the messy, uncertain compromises that are so characteristic of American politics. Such uncertain compromises should not automatically be denigrated. The deferrals I uncover in the case studies serve as a reminder that essential features of the American constitutional system are based on the belief that institutional mechanisms that facilitate the accommodation of conflicting interests can be preferable to more divisive "winner-take-all" mechanisms. Deferrals did not help the apparent losers (labor organizations) to achieve immediately their policy goals, but they did provide the losers with important strategic resources that gave them a stake in future political processes.

Of course, one can recognize the value of compromise in general while still objecting more specifically to those compromises made by shifting responsibility and blame from elected officials to less accountable officials in other branches. For example, one could claim that blame-shifting strategies like legislative deferrals are undemocratic or illegitimate because they violate important principles of separation of powers. It is difficult, however, to isolate blame-shifting strategies as aberrational or deviant features in any separation of powers system. The problem here is that there seems to be an essential link between blame shifting and separation of powers. Institutional structures that diffuse power inevitably diffuse responsibility as well.

To see these connections, consider an alternative institutional system in which it is more difficult for elected officials to shift blame to other actors: A government with an all-powerful elected dictator. Such a system would help to solve many of the problems that now occur in the United States when unelected officials make important policy decisions. Since the dictator is all-powerful, he or she cannot blame problems on other elected officials, and voters can be assured that they are holding the right person responsible when they vote for or against the dictator's reelection.

In the United States, the Constitution rejects elected dictatorship in favor of a system where power is diffused among three branches of the federal government and between the federal government and the state

governments. It is that institutional design that makes it inevitable that unelected officials will make quite a few substantive policy decisions. The system is based on the conviction that the advantages created by the greater
transparency of the dictator system are outweighed by other problems.
It is these problems that separation of powers tries to avoid. In particular, diffusing power among the branches seems to prevent the dangerous
accumulation of power in one individual or institution (see, e.g., James
Madison, *Federalist Papers* 47). Unfortunately, one inevitable consequence
of diffusing power is that voters will have a more difficult time sorting out
which government officials are at fault for policy failures. Under such conditions, it is inevitable that strategic actors within government will exacer-
bate the problem by trying to blame other actors for difficult decisions and
policy failures. As a result, elections will not provide perfect accountability because voters will not be sure who to blame for perceived problems.

Of course, it is possible that features of institutional design could make
blame shifting more difficult. For example, a constitution could limit the
ability of elected officials to shift responsibility for difficult decisions by
carefully allocating resources and responsibilities to the different branches
of government and providing detailed instruction about how conflicts
among the branches should be resolved. Such specificity might make it
harder for elected officials to shift blame by selectively expanding the responsibilities of other branches. However, the U.S. Constitution does not
attempt such specificity. The Constitution does not fix most institutional
boundaries or even attempt to describe them in detail.[18] The Constitution
instead invites legislators to allocate the resources and responsibilities of
the other branches through, presumably, political processes. In particular, the Constitution's text invites Congress to establish executive branch
departments and the federal courts as alternative sources of power, and,
inevitably, alternative locations for blame and responsibility.[19]

---

[18] To mention just a few obvious examples, the Constitution's text does not specifically mention the power of judicial review, says very little about how the federal
commerce power is to be reconciled with the residual power of states to regulate
commerce, says very little about how conflicts between the executive and legislative
branch should be resolved, and is even ambiguous about whether the Constitution
is a compact among the states or among the people. If such ambiguities were deliberate, they raise important questions that scholars of constitutional interpretation,
particularly originalist scholars, have not yet dealt with adequately. Those questions
are, however, beyond the scope of this book.

[19] Whittington (1999) provides an account of constitutional development that emphasizes the extent to which constitutional structure has developed outside of the text
and the courts.

This does not mean that the U.S. separation of powers system is perfect. There is still room to argue that the American constitutional system is deeply flawed, in part because it allows too many moves away from majoritarian governance, allows too much power to be assigned to unelected officials, and gives elected officials too much discretion to shape, change, and distort the boundaries between the branches and levels of government. My goal here is not to defend the American Constitution, but simply to point out that any argument against blame shifting to unelected officials is question begging if it takes for granted the claim that "democracy" means that blame shifting is always bad and that it is always better when elected officials make policy decisions. A more convincing assessment of decision-making processes will result if scholars take a broader view and balance the disadvantages of allowing unelected officials to make some decisions against the important advantages that a flexible system of diffused power creates.

These observations suggest that the underlying problems with the electoral constraint assumption extend well beyond cases involving legislative deference to the courts. The real problem is that the assumption leads scholars to test outcomes in a separation of powers system by asking questions that are more appropriate to a system of majoritarian or direct democracy. It is not surprising that a separation of powers system has difficulty with such tests. Scholars could develop more appropriate tests and questions by taking separation of powers more seriously as an *alternative* to more direct, majoritarian systems of governance, rather than treating separation of powers as a clumsy attempt to *approximate* such a system. To do so, scholars need to stop conceptualizing government as being made up of "democratic" or "majoritarian" elected branches and "deviant" unelected branches. Taking separation of powers seriously as an alternative to majoritarianism reveals that democratic governance in the United States cannot be understood by counting the number of times judges seem to reverse elected legislators, or asking whether judges' decisions can be better predicted by an attitudinal model or a legal model. What is needed instead is a much better understanding of the role of compromise and ambiguity in relations among the branches, and of the actual barriers that institutional structures create for the individuals and groups that try to advance their interests through electoral politics.

It is not my intention here to offer a complete theory of democracy that can be used to evaluate competing sets of institutional arrangements. It does, however, seem likely, that any adequate institutional theory of democracy needs to recognize that the level of democratic responsiveness and permeability in an institutional system will depend on much more than the question of whether important policy decisions are made by elected officials. The level and type of accountability achieved in any political system will depend on a broad range of interrelated institutional and cultural factors. These factors include such things as basic constitutional structure (e.g., separation of powers/federal system versus parliamentary systems), system of representation (e.g., single-member districts versus proportional representation), internal decision-making rules for legislatures (e.g., agenda control, amending power, committee structure, filibusters), rules regarding elections (e.g., secret ballots or party ballots, access to the ballot, rules regarding patronage and campaign finance, procedures for drawing electoral districts), the number of viable political parties, the level of public attention to politics, voter turnout, the amount of information available to the electorate, distribution of educational opportunities, and the structure and norms of the mass media (e.g., amount of competition, partisan press versus "objective media").[20] Significant changes in any of these factors can produce significant changes in who voters elect and in the choices elected representatives make regarding policies. Structural changes can lead to changes in outcomes even when the goals and preferences of the electorate remain unchanged.

These factors also serve as a reminder that there are numerous reasons for doubting that the outcomes produced by the United States Congress deserve to be treated as presumptively majoritarian or democratic. Once attention is paid to the way congressional campaigns are financed, the way congressional seats are apportioned (including the grotesquely disproportionate system of representation in the Senate), and the low levels of participation in congressional elections, the idea that legislative outcomes should serve as a paragon of democracy or a proxy for the will of "majorities" seems almost bizarre.[21] Were it not for the additional avenues of democratic control and accountability made available because of judicial independence, the counter-majoritarian features of Congress's institutional design would be intolerable.

---

[20] One classic work on the importance of structural factors in systems of representation is Rae (1971). McGerr (1986) provides historical perspective that illustrates the importance of party structure and mass media conventions.

[21] This does not mean that there are not good things about legislators. However, the evidence presented in this book raises the possibility that the most accomplished recent defender of legislatures (Waldron 1999) may exaggerate the extent to which legislative deliberations produce agreement.

Thinking about deferrals also reveals some shortcomings of the pure politics assumption. While the electoral constraint assumption underestimates connections between electoral processes and decisions made by unelected officials, the basic problem with the pure politics assumption is that it *overestimates* the effectiveness of democratic controls on the legislative branch. Critical scholars have accurately identified some of the problems labor organizations encountered in the courts. My findings in the case studies support their claim that the aspirations of labor organizations were transformed by the expectation that they formulate those aspirations as legal arguments that judges would find acceptable (e.g., Forbath 1991, esp. ch. 5; Pope 1997, 1012). The mistake of the critical scholars, however, has been to imagine that the problems they identify are unique to the judicial branch and to suggest that things are somehow better in the legislative branch. I find that even in the cases where labor organizations were most successful, the legislative process did not provide a setting for powerful labor organizations to articulate their interests in some pure form. The labor leaders who took part in the legislative process, for example, by testifying before congressional committees, typically defended their interests using language that was saturated with legal categories, claims of legal rights, and citations to the case law. Labor organizations also had to hire lawyers as go-betweens, both as consultants who could evaluate competing legislative proposals, and as expert witnesses to defend labor interests in congressional hearings. Those lawyers sometimes expressed views before Congress that were inconsistent with, and even condescending toward, views expressed by nonlawyer labor leaders.[22]

The willingness of some labor organizations to frame their demands in an appropriately conservative legal discourse, and to engage in appropriate legal banter, is what allowed them to become active participants in legislative deliberations. Other labor organizations openly decried the legal process and openly rejected legal ideologies, and thus tended to express their sense of justice and their demands in a more pure form. The leaders of such organizations were not, however, invited to air their views before congressional committees.

Ironically, the most effective arguments made by labor leaders were not raw claims that directly asserted their preferences. Labor never had enough votes to force enactment of their unfiltered demands, and never

---

[22] This point comes across most clearly in my discussion of the Norris-LaGuardia Act in Chapter 5.

made unfiltered demands with the expectation that legislators would meet them. Rather, the most effective rhetorical strategies were those that could harness claims about legislative and judicial precedents in support of favored legislation. For example, I show in Chapter 5 that one of the most effective arguments made in favor of the Norris-LaGuardia Act of 1932 was the argument that the legislative precedent established by the Clayton Act in 1914 supported passage of the new statute. Such findings suggest that the gap between law and politics is not as wide as is sometimes hoped. However, the concern expressed here is a new one. More typically, concerns about the gap between law and politics are expressed as worries that law is too much like politics. The new problem I find here is that politics is too much like law. In a separation of powers system, there is no such thing as pure politics.[23]

Assumptions about Institutional Processes

The preceding comments about separation of powers suggest that problems with the legislative baseline framework go beyond questions of democratic accountability to broader questions regarding the relationship among institutions in the constitutional system. While the conventional framework imagines independent branches competing with one another for influence over policy, strategies involving blame shifting suggest that relations between the branches can also be more complicated and cooperative. The difficulty that such cooperation creates for the legislative baseline framework can be captured by considering two final assumptions, the conflict and competition assumptions.

The Conflict Assumption: Assessments of the relative power and impact of two branches should focus on cases where the policy preferences of one branch conflict with the preferences of the other branch. This is because the opportunity for one branch to exercise power in an interbranch conflict occurs when two branches occupy conflicting positions.

The conflict assumption helps scholars to identify the cases that provide clean tests of competing hypotheses about the relative powers of the branches. In cases where legislators and judges have conflicting

---

[23] Although this study challenges critical scholars' assumptions about legislative process, my findings ultimately support and amplify the claim that law and legal ideologies have important and potentially deleterious effects on democratic accountability. Unfortunately, the conclusion here lacks the optimism that comes from imagining that legislation offers some pure alternative to the legal process.

preferences, scholars can assess power by determining which branch's preferred position "wins," that is, which branch's position matches the ultimate outcome of the interbranch process. In contrast, cases where judges and legislators have the same goals do not provide good tests of the impact of either branch. It is much more difficult to separate the impact of judges from the impact of legislators in such cases.

The conflict assumption is one of the reasons so many scholars have looked to cases like the Clayton Act to develop claims about judicial power and the effects of legal ideology on the development of the labor movement. Such cases provide an attractive vehicle for exploring the impact of judicial power because the position favored by the courts seems to have conflicted with, and ultimately triumphed over, the position favored by a majority of elected legislators. The conflict assumption also helps to explain why the same scholars pay relatively less attention to the Norris-LaGuardia Act. Although that statute was the most important and dramatic challenge to judicial power that Congress passed during the period covered in this study, it does not attract as much attention because it did not produce any dramatic interbranch conflict after it passed.

The conflict assumption shows up not just in historical studies of labor statutes, but also in many other more general studies of judicial power. The tendency to associate power with cases involving conflicts can be traced to Robert Dahl's classic definition of political power: "A has power over B to the extent that he can get B to do something B would not otherwise do" (1961, 12).[24] Given this definition, cases where B already wants the same things as A do not seem to provide opportunities for the exercise of power. The resulting conflict assumption shows up in the work of behaviorist scholars who have studied the voting behavior of judges. Such scholars argue that judges are powerful and independent actors who can pursue their own policy goals as they vote in cases. One potential obstacle to that view, however, is the relatively large number of instances where the votes of Supreme Court justices match the preferences expressed by elected legislators. For example, the justices strike down only a very tiny percentage of the laws that they consider in their rulings. Looked at in isolation, the amount of agreement between judges and legislators might support the argument that legislators were somehow using power to force judges to conform to their will. However, as many scholars have pointed out, there are numerous reasons to expect at any given time that the

[24] McCann (1999, 65–76) discusses this view and its relevance to studies of judicial power in the United States.

persons who are federal judges will share many of the same political values as persons who are federal legislators (see, e.g., Spann 1993, ch. 2; Dahl 1957). Given the likely similarity of views, behaviorists can acknowledge a large number of cases where judicial decisions match the preferences of legislators without conceding that legislators are forcing judges to act against their preferences. Thus, accurate tests of judicial independence and power have to look at how judges behave in cases where they disagree with legislators.[25] Ironically, the conflict assumption also shows up in the leading study that presents the case *against* the independent power of judges. Gerald Rosenberg's *The Hollow Hope* (1991) is structured on the assumption that the best opportunities for the courts to demonstrate the power to produce social change occur during periods when judges take positions that are at odds with the political branches. Rosenberg tests the limits of judicial power by focusing on periods when the judiciary attempted to produce social change without the concurrence of Congress and downplays the possibility that judges were responsible for changes that occurred during periods when legislators supported the courts.

The conflict assumption reflects in part substantive ideas about interbranch processes and the exercise of institutional power. Those substantive concerns might be expressed as a separate, albeit closely related, assumption:

The Competition Assumption : Policy interaction between Congress and the courts is a competition in which actors in each branch use their institutional powers to pursue policy goals and to limit the capacity of the other branch to interfere with those goals.

The assumption that interbranch interactions are competitive is deeply embedded in much empirical work on judicial policy making. However, the assumption is usually hidden by the disagreements among scholars about what motivates different institutional actors who take part in such competitions, particularly disagreements about what motivates judges. Attitudinalists have found that judges make choices according to their individual ideologies (Segal and Spaeth 1993, Segal 1997). Rational choice scholars have suggested that judges' pursuit of their policy preferences is constrained by the institutional powers of competing legislators (Maltzman, Spriggs, and Wahlbeck 1999, 48–51). Scholars who pursue the historical variant of new institutionalism argue that judges' decisions

---

[25] These assumptions are evident in Segal and Spaeth's discussion of judicial restraint (1993 ch. 8, esp. 316–18). See also the explicit adoption of a competition assumption in the seminal rational choice paper by McNollgast (1995, 1632–3).

are shaped in part by general concerns about institutional maintenance and by the tendency of judges to internalize norms about the appropriate role of judges in a democratic system (Gillman 1999). Whether judges are motivated by individual policy preferences or broader institutional concerns, most scholars understand judges' pursuit of their goals as part of a competitive struggle with elected legislators. Thus, scholars expect legislators to pursue their goals by trying to minimize interference from the courts and expect judges to pursue their goals by altering decisions made by legislators when judges find it appropriate or desirable to do so.

Deference, Deferrals, and the Conflict and Competition Assumptions

Thinking about cases involving legislative deference to the courts reveals that the conflict and competition assumptions are not well suited to all forms of institutional interaction. In cases where actors in each branch exercise power by attempting to win conflicts with other branches, the assumptions, like the legislative baseline framework itself, work quite well. However, the two assumptions obscure other types of interaction and other important ways of exercising power in interbranch interactions. Power can be exercised not just by winning conflicts but also by avoiding conflict, manipulating the timing of conflicts, or by strategically provoking conflicts in order to secure cooperation. By conceptualizing power and influence as occurring in situations involving overt conflicts and competition, the legislative baseline framework presents an incomplete and thus distorted picture of interbranch interaction.

To see the problem with the conflict assumption, consider the following two types of interbranch interaction:

False Conflict. Legislators pass a statute that appears to respond to the legislative demands of some organized constituency. However, the decisive votes in favor of the statute come from legislators who correctly predict that judges will later prevent the law from achieving some of its most important and controversial policy goals.

Latent Conflict. Legislators decide not to pass legislation because they are convinced that the courts will interfere with the policy goals of the legislation.

The conflict assumption can lead scholars to incorrectly identify cases of false conflicts as cases where the courts reverse the collective preferences of Congress. If judges create the interference that the decisive legislators expected, the judges appear to exercise tremendous institutional power even though they may actually be producing the policy outcome favored by a majority of legislators. False conflicts can occur in cases where legislators defer to the courts by creating statutory ambiguity, or in cases where Congress enacts a statute only because some legislators expect the courts to overturn it on constitutional grounds. For example, many legislators might vote for a popular campaign finance reform law that threatens their chances of being reelected, but end up quite happy when judges predictably strike down the law on constitutional grounds.[26] Legislators who vote for a law only because they expect judicial interference are enlisting the (perhaps unwitting) cooperation of the courts. Such cases are easy to misinterpret as genuine conflicts where judges hurt the interests of legislators. Scholars who interpret such cases as instances where judges overturn the will of "Congress" will overestimate the influence of judges as adversaries of legislators and underestimate their more cooperative contribution to governance.

In contrast, latent conflicts between judges and legislators will lead scholars who make the conflict assumption to underestimate the influence of the judges. Latent conflict will fly below the radar of such scholars because no overt conflict occurs. Nevertheless, the influence of the courts can be quite real in such cases. Suppose, for example, that legislators never pass (or even consider) a law on some issue because legislators expect the Supreme Court to strike down any new law as unconstitutional. Judges will never get the chance to strike down such a law, but the influence of the courts seems quite real in such cases. A similar, but perhaps less dramatic form of influence occurs when legislators dramatically change the content of a statute in order to avoid judicial interference. While it is easiest to imagine cases where legislators enact more moderate laws to avoid judicial interference, my case study of the Norris-LaGuardia Act (Chapter 5) shows that fears of judicial interference can also lead legislators to pass much more radical laws than would otherwise be possible.

Ultimately, the false and latent conflict cases reveal the same core problem with the conflict assumption. Because actors in Congress (and the courts) have the power to manipulate the occurrence of conflict, the cases where conflicts do actually occur will not be all or only those cases where real differences in preferences exist. The strategic incentives that would

---

[26] Among the statutes that I use as case studies in this book, the Wagner Act was passed at a time when many legislators might reasonably have guessed that the Supreme Court would find it unconstitutional, and it may have attracted some votes for that reason. It is impossible, however, to say whether those votes were decisive.

lead legislators to provoke or avoid conflict will lead scholars to focus on a set of conflict cases that together provide a distorted picture of legislators' preferences.[27] Like the policy assumption, the conflict assumption works best for cases where conflicts occur by accident, for example, because legislators fail to notice an important ambiguity, or because justices raise unanticipated constitutional objections. The assumption makes less sense when applied to cases where legislators provoke conflicts in order to make some symbolic political point, where they accept the inevitability of defeat and do nothing, or where they do nothing because they are satisfied with the outcome created by judges.

Cases where legislators pursue their goals by provoking conflicts with the courts are examples of a more general phenomenon: Actors in one branch sometimes pursue their own interests by creating conditions that allow actors in another branch to exercise institutional powers. The possibility of such coordination and cooperation among the branches calls the competition assumption into question. Of course, the type of cooperation that legislators enlist in such cases is somewhat unusual. Judges may retain enough independence to make policy choices that surprise or disappoint the legislators who chose to expand the discretion of the courts. Nevertheless, even in cases where judges make unexpected or unpopular decisions, the relationship between the branches cannot be described as purely competitive or adversarial. Legislators knowingly choose to risk a surprise judicial ruling, perhaps because their preferences about policy outcomes are not as strong as their preference for avoiding blame. Even an unexpected judicial decision can be quite cooperative with respect to the sometimes-overriding goal of avoiding blame.

The most important reason for moving away from the competition assumption is not, however, that the assumption can sometimes be misleading. The bigger gain from looking more carefully at cooperation among

---

[27] These problems are further exacerbated by the fact that the Supreme Court can also strategically avoid conflicts by refusing to take certain types of cases, or provoke conflicts by making rulings that invite additional cases on certain topics. For example, the Supreme Court's ruling in *Northeastern Florida Chapter of the Associated General Contractors of America v City of Jacksonville, Florida* (508 U.S. 656, 1993) announced a new rule of standing that made it much easier to challenge the constitutionality of affirmative action programs. Such a ruling makes it more likely that conflicts over affirmative action would occur. Of course, the occurrence of conflict can also be influenced by outside actors. In 1997, interest groups concerned about how the Supreme Court was going to rule in a very unusual affirmative action case paid for a settlement to moot the case after the Court had taken *cert*. See Goodnough 1997.

the branches is that doing so can help scholars to answer some important but neglected questions about the development and maintenance of institutional power.

For example, the competition assumption makes it very difficult to explain how the bare outline of judicial power in the Constitution has evolved into the very important policy-making role played by judges today. Many scholars who follow the legislative baseline framework locate the power of judges to make policy in the provisions in Article III of the Constitution that establish the judicial branch. The problem is that the powers outlined in the Constitution do not go very far to explain the tremendous influence over policy that the federal judges have today. The Constitution gives judges some political independence by establishing that federal judges are appointed and giving judges life tenure. Behaviorists suggest that these guarantees have created the institutional context that allows judges to influence policy (Segal 1999, 238; Segal and Spaeth 1993, 69–70). However, the guarantees of appointment and life tenure do not go very far in explaining how judges manage to make binding choices that affect *any* policy issues. The provisions in Article III, Section 2 outlining the jurisdiction of the federal courts come closer to giving judges the power to influence policies, but the power granted there is conditioned on an explicit (if ambiguous) invitation to Congress to make "exceptions" and "regulations" affecting the jurisdiction of the courts. Scholars often dismiss the significance of congressional powers to control jurisdiction by claiming that Congress has not successfully pursued its power to remove jurisdiction since Reconstruction.[28] That claim, as I show in Chapter 5, is wrong. Even if it were true, however, congressional reluctance to exercise an enumerated power does not make that power unimportant. Legislators' reluctance does, however, create an important puzzle that scholars interested in separation of powers and judicial policy making should be very interested in explaining: If competitive legislators are wary of judicial power, disagree with policies created by judges, and would always rather make policy themselves, why do legislators fail to exercise their constitutional powers to strip the courts of power? This is not just a question about congressional powers to limit jurisdiction, but also about the many other important constitutional powers

---

[28] Segal and Spaeth 1993, 70–1. Many of the leading textbooks for undergraduate political science courses in American constitutional law make the mistake of teaching students that Congress has never exercised this power since Reconstruction. See, for example, Epstein and Walker 2001, 93; O'Brien 2000, 190; Ivers 2001, 71; Ducat 2000, 26–7.

that allow legislators to curtail judicial influence over policy, including the power to impeach judges, to alter the number of justices on the Supreme Court, and to change the workload of judges and the administrative capacities of courts. It is likely that the failure of legislators to exercise such powers says something important about cooperation and competition among the branches. At least part of the reason legislators tolerate judicial policy making must be that legislators have something to gain from allowing judges to maintain institutional integrity and independence.[29]

The advantages of thinking about relations between Congress and the courts as cooperative as well as competitive are further confirmed by looking beyond legislators' powers to control the courts to the powers that legislators have affirmatively given to the courts. The emphasis on competition between the branches obscures the fact that the judges who act as independent rivals of Congress are almost all the creation of Congress itself, and that the powers they exercise have been granted by Congress and remain subject to congressional revocation. The Constitution's prohibition on limiting the pay of incumbents seems utterly insignificant over the long run given that the Constitution gives Congress plenary power to eliminate judgeships on death or retirement. Looking more broadly at the choices legislators have collectively made regarding the duties of judges and the administration of the courts, the pattern that emerges seems indisputably to be a pattern of legislators making choices that give judges more rather than less power to influence policies. For example, legislators have increased the power of the Supreme Court by gradually making it easier for the justices to control the Court's agenda (Perry 1991, 294–303). Such choices are inexplicable if legislators simply resent judicial power and prefer to make policy on their own. While legislators surely disagree with some judicial decisions, they also seem to value maintenance of the courts as a separate source of institutional power (Gillman 1999, Whittington 2001, Rogers 2001).

---

[29] Two useful studies provide very valuable information about congressional attacks on the courts during two important periods when court decisions generated tremendous controversy, the *Lochner* to New Deal era (Ross 1994) and the Warren Court era of the late 1950s (Murphy 1962). Both studies document attempts by legislators to utilize Congress's constitutional powers to control the courts. The failure of those attempts was due to the fact that effective majorities in Congress supported the courts, not to some magical power of the Court to prevent Congress from using its powers. James R. Rogers (2001) provides a formal model that demonstrates a more general reason why legislators might want courts to retain power.

Once these issues are raised and taken seriously, the empirical findings of many scholars who follow the legislative baseline framework begin to look quite puzzling and incomplete. For example, consider the behaviorist finding that judges almost always follow their policy preferences, even when doing so leads them to make choices that conflict with the preferences of elected officials. Such findings may be supported by the evidence that the attitudinalists offer, but they also seem to cry out for some explanation of why legislators do not act more often to limit the power of the courts. The attitudinalists never offer a convincing explanation of why legislators tolerate the many judicial decisions that follow judges' preferences but not their own, or why a society that often takes vocal pride in calling itself a "democracy" would allow federal policy-making processes to be permanently hijacked by unaccountable judges. A convincing explanation of judicial power would not necessarily contradict the behaviorists' claim that judges' votes correlate with their policy preferences. Legislators may prefer to give up some control over policy outcomes in order to maintain the degree of judicial independence that makes it possible to blame judges for some policy outcomes. However, it seems important to explain how judicial independence serves the interests of legislators. Scholars will likely learn more by asking why legislators give judges the opportunity to make important policy choices than they can learn from making additional observations of the correlations between judges' ideologies and their votes on the merits.

This is a lesson that the actors who take part in legislative and judicial processes seem to have learned long ago. In the cases I examine in this book, all the participants in the legislative process expected judges to be hostile to the interests of labor organizations and expected judges to make rulings reflecting their ideology. My case studies show that what is interesting and important in such cases is not the observation that judges acted on their antilabor policy preferences. Rather, what is interesting is the ways in which the widespread knowledge of judges' attitudes affected the legislative and political processes that, in turn, shaped the capacity of judges to pursue their policy preferences.

My call here for paying more attention to the evolution of judicial power in changing institutional contexts resonates with the work of many new historical institutionalist scholars who have been developing alternatives to behavioral models of judicial choice (Smith 1988, Clayton and Gillman 1999, Gillman and Clayton 1999). I follow the example of such scholars by attempting in this study to pay more attention to the way institutional contexts constrain judicial power and to the often very political processes through which powers like judicial review are established and maintained (Peretti 1999; Gillman 2002; Gillman 1999; Graber 1999; Graber 1998; Whittington 1999, ch. 2). This study tries to build upon such work by demonstrating how much can be gained by focusing on legislative decisions that structure judges' opportunities to pursue both ideological and institutional goals. Progress toward understanding both judicial policy making and institutional development can be made only by carefully tracing out the political processes that link the interests of individual legislators to expanded judicial power.

DEFERRAL DENIAL: THE PERSISTENCE OF THE LEGISLATIVE BASELINE FRAMEWORK

Thus far, my discussion may suggest that in challenging a legislative baseline framework, I am attacking a straw person rather than a view that any real person holds. After all, the terminology is my own invention, and no one has articulated the precise set of assumptions that I have here. Furthermore, my observation that legislative ambiguity often shapes the role of the courts is not new. As noted previously, the leading theories for explaining judges' interpretive decisions recognize problems created by legislative ambiguity and are almost exclusively preoccupied with developing methods for resolving ambiguity. Moreover, the idea that legislatures deliberately shift controversial decisions to less accountable actors in other branches has not been missed in earlier studies of the role of the courts. While studies of blame shifting have most often focused on delegation to the executive branch (e.g., Hayes 1978, Lowi 1979, Schoenbrod 1993) recent works have also looked at the importance of legislative deference to the courts (Graber 1993) and at legislative decisions that give shape to the policy-making role of the courts (Melnick 1983, 1994). The fact that these phenomena are often noticed and discussed might suggest that my criticisms of the legislative baseline framework are not only not new, but have largely been accounted for in the best theoretical and empirical work on judicial policy making.

I nevertheless wish to take the risk of asserting that the legislative baseline framework is still relied upon by real scholars, and not just straw persons. Even though many scholars have noticed the possibility of deliberate legislative ambiguity, few scholars have been willing to bear the costs of giving up the simplifying assumptions of the legislative baseline framework. As a result, leading scholars continue to use methods and assumptions that cannot comprehend the complex forms of institutional interaction that occur in cases where legislators deliberately empower the courts. Scholars do sometimes list deliberate deference as one among many potential sources of legislative ambiguity. The problem, however, is that deliberate ambiguity has to be treated very differently from the sources of accidental ambiguity that appear on such lists. Unlike accidental ambiguity, deliberate ambiguity undermines their foundational assumptions about accountability and institutional power.[30]

One example of such scholarly ambivalence is found in Robert Katzmann's very sensible discussion in *Courts and Congress* (1997). Katzmann chides Justice Scalia's claim that judges could "compel legislators to do their jobs with greater care" by giving statutes strict textualist readings that would force legislators to avoid ambiguity (60). Katzmann responds to Scalia by noting that "exhorting the legislative branch to write unambiguous legislation will have little effect" (60) because "*ambiguity is a deliberate strategy to secure a majority coalition in support of the legislation*" (61, emphasis added).

The problem with Katzmann's account is that he appears to abandon his own insight just three pages later and in much of the rest of the book. Katzmann's own positive suggestions for improving "communication" between Congress and the courts are designed to help members of Congress to communicate their collective intentions to the courts more clearly. Katzmann suggests several strategies under the heading "Clarifying Legislative Meaning" (64–8) and then spends three chapters explaining some experiments on institutional mechanisms for improving communication between Congress and the courts. While Katzmann's suggestions are useful and may go a long way toward eliminating the (possibly very large) subset of all legislative ambiguity that is accidental, the approach assumes that legislators want to avoid uncertainty and want to make it less likely that judges will have to resolve interpretive controversies. As a result, Katzmann, like Scalia, cannot address the special problems created in those cases where legislators deliberately shift decision-making responsibility to judges.

Another example of such scholarly denial can be found in Richard Posner's method for resolving legislative ambiguity: imaginative reconstruction.[31] Posner recognizes that accidental ambiguity can give rise to

---

[30] In addition to the examples I cite in this section, see also Rosenberg (1991, 34–5), and Carter (1998, 55).

[31] Posner's most extended discussion of imaginative reconstruction is in Posner 1990, ch. 9 and 10. See also Posner 1986, 179–217.

important interpretive questions that legislators never considered. He argues that judges should resolve such controversies by trying to "imaginatively reconstruct" the decision that the legislators passing the statute would have made if it had occurred to them to do so.

Posner's method of imaginative reconstruction, like Katzmann's strategy of improving communication, makes sense for cases where ambiguity in statutory language is an accident that legislators would like to avoid. However, when the indeterminacy in the statute instead results from legislators deliberately using ambiguity to force judges to resolve controversies, Posner's method makes no sense at all. If legislators collectively decide to leave an issue for the courts to decide, there is no discoverable policy that the legislature would have produced, if only it had occurred to the legislators to vote on the issue. When legislators deliberately adopt language that empowers the courts, they do make a real decision on the precise issues later faced by the courts: Legislators decide to leave the issue for the courts to resolve.

Like Katzmann, Posner uses the conventional framework even though he is at times quite sensitive to the idea that legislators use ambiguity or uncertainty as a political tool. Posner also considers the possibility of deliberate legislative "delegation" to the courts, but then denies that such delegation poses a problem. Posner simply states, without offering any evidence, that legislative delegation to the judicial branch is too rare to be worth taking seriously (1990, 279). He also states that from the point of view of the judge faced with the interpretive question, it should not matter what the source of the ambiguity is. This last claim is rather puzzling. The discovery that ambiguity is deliberate reveals important information about legislators' preferences, information that would presumably be necessary to "reconstruct" accurately the decisions that the legislature would have made.

Cass Sunstein provides a third, somewhat different, example of an author who notices the strategic use of ambiguity but then fails to build it into his methods for interpreting statutes. After a constructive discussion of the sources and problems of legislative ambiguity, Sunstein suggests that judges solve interpretive controversies regarding statutes by following a hierarchical set of interpretive principles. Some of the interpretive principles Sunstein proposes contain substantive moral values. Sunstein argues, for example, that statutes should be interpreted in favor of political accountability and against irrationality and injustice, and that statutes protecting "traditionally disadvantaged groups" be given broad constructions while statutes embodying interest group transfers should be read quite narrowly (1990, ch. 5, 235–8).

Sunstein's argument that judges infuse moral values into interpretive principles might suggest that he has abandoned the legislative baseline framework altogether. After all, the framework is based on the assumption that judges' decisions should be made according to values and preferences of elected legislators, not according to the values of judges. However, Sunstein's commitment to the legislative baseline framework is revealed when he offers his justification for such interpretive principles. Sunstein claims that by using a clear and consistently applied set of interpretive rules, judges would make it easier for *legislators'* preferences to triumph. Clearer principles will allow legislators to predict judicial responses to legislation and thus make it easier for legislators to produce their preferred outcomes (1990, 192). The problem, however, is that such an argument is compelling only in instances where members of Congress want to resolve issues decisively and want to assume responsibility for the resulting policies. The argument makes less sense when applied to cases where legislators deliberately produce an indeterminate outcome.

A final example of the continued reliance on the legislative baseline framework comes from the theorist of statutory interpretation who pays the most attention to the ways in which judicial power is rooted in democratic processes of the legislative branch, William Eskridge. Eskridge's central claim is that judges should (and do) engage in "dynamic statutory interpretation," that is, judges should pay attention to current policy preferences in Congress at the time they make interpretive decisions rather than trying in vain to recover or reconstruct a legitimating baseline that matches legislators' preferences at the time the statute passed.[32] Eskridge's theory improves upon more static accounts of legislative intent because he is more sensitive to the fact that the capacity of judges to exercise power is dependent upon the actions and reactions of elected officials. However, the justification Eskridge offers for his approach falls short because he never fully abandons the legislative baseline framework. He instead changes the time at which the measurement of the baseline is taken.

The difference between Eskridge's account and my own comes out most clearly in Eskridge's extended discussion of the law of labor injunctions between 1877 and 1938 (1994, ch. 3), a discussion that considers many of the same statutes and court cases that I consider in this book. In his discussion of the Clayton Act, for example, Eskridge acknowledges that legislators sent "mixed signals" when they passed the Clayton Act

---

[32] Eskridge's most comprehensive statement of his position is in the book *Dynamic Statutory Interpretation* (1994).

in 1914, and that as a result the courts had a difficult time identifying a legitimating legislative intent in the statutory text and records. Eskridge uses these observations to build an original argument that the interpretation the Supreme Court offered in *Duplex* was democratically legitimate. Eskridge's argument is based on some very perceptive observations about changes in the political climate between passage of the Clayton Act in 1914 and the crucial Supreme Court ruling on the statute in 1921. In particular, Eskridge notes that conservative Republicans had swept the elections of 1920. After that election, the elected leaders in control of both the executive and legislative branches were opposed to many of the policy changes that the AFL had advocated with limited success in 1914. Thus, even though the interpretive decisions the Court made in 1921 may have been more clearly antilabor than the (non) intent that legislators expressed in 1914, the Court's decisions did match the political consensus that had emerged among elected officials. Thus, the policy selected by the Court can be called "democratic" because it was not much different from the policy that elected legislators would have chosen at the same time. Eskridge extends this argument over a sixty-year period of labor law as he reassesses several widely criticized court decisions. Eskridge shows that judges who have been criticized for failing to follow the intent of the Congress actually did a good job matching the political consensus in place at the time the court decisions were made. In a separate study, Eskridge (1991) establishes that judges have reason to be sensitive to legislators' preferences by showing that Congress overturns the Supreme Court's interpretive rulings with surprising frequency.

Despite its attractive features, however, Eskridge's account of legitimacy ultimately provides an incomplete account of the effect of judicial decisions on democratic outcomes.[33] His approach falls short because simply showing that judicial decisions at a particular time match up with preferences of elected officials is not enough to justify such decisions. The structural features that allow legislators and judges to make flexible decisions on statutes, even decisions that are responsive to election results, may also create significant barriers to electoral accountability. The problem is that intervening electoral outcomes cannot justify judicial choices

---

[33] Eskridge may not intend to provide such an account. To be fair, I think it important to note that the question of most interest to me (Were the courts barriers to efforts by labor organizations to produce change through democratic process?) is much different from the question of most interest to Eskridge (How should judges resolve interpretive questions about statutes?). I must also note in fairness that I do not offer a good answer to the question that is most important to Eskridge.

because those intervening outcomes are affected by the earlier legislative decisions that empowered the courts. To understand the problem, it is important again to recognize that congressional decisions to pass legislation do more than add new words to the U.S. Code. The act of passing legislation can also affect the way individuals organize, the relative strengths of different organized groups, and thus have significant effects on subsequent electoral outcomes. If such effects are significant, even judicial decisions that match the preferences of the elected branches can still be cause for concern.

For example, consider what might have happened if it had somehow been impossible for legislators to defer to the courts in 1914. Legislators would have been forced either to do nothing or to pass a clear law that took sides between workers and employers. Under such conditions, legislators might have responded to labor's demands by producing a clearer legislative victory for labor that curtailed injunctions and other barriers to organizing. The result would likely have been a larger and better-mobilized labor movement. If such a movement had developed, labor's interests would presumably have been in a much better political position in the 1920 elections. Even if the winners of the elections had been the same, labor's improved position may well have modified the positions taken by the major parties in that election.

Of course, forcing legislators to make a definitive decision in 1914 may not have resulted in a definitive legislative victory for labor. It seems more likely that legislators forced to choose sides would have resisted the AFL's demands and passed no legislation at all. That outcome might also have affected the way workers organized to produce changes through democratic processes. A clear "no" from Congress might have led to increased anger among workers and, as a result, to more aggressive labor mobilization for political activity. A "no" from Congress might have strengthened some of the rival labor organizations that had been relentlessly ridiculing the AFL's lobbying strategies during the period leading up to passage of the Clayton Act. Rank-and-file members of the AFL might have overthrown the moderate leaders who would have had nothing to show for their strategy of endorsing Wilson and working within the existing party system. The resulting organizational changes might have produced a more pro-labor Congress 1921. Of course, the same organizational changes might also have led to political disaster for labor and hurt labor's capacity to influence politics in the future.

Such extrapolicy organizational effects may have been quite small and are difficult to measure precisely. The comments in the preceding paragraph already suggest that evaluating counterfactual propositions about the organizational effects of legislation can quickly become an exercise in speculation. Nevertheless, it is also clear from my case studies that such organizational effects were extremely important to the participants in the legislative process who made decisions that ultimately empowered the courts to make policy decisions. Labor leaders and legislators frequently expressed interest in the effects that passage of a statute would have on the way workers organized. Many participants clearly associated such effects with the symbolic message that would be sent by the decision to pass a statute rather than with any particular policy changes that the statutes might actually create.[34]

Thus, even if it is not possible to measure all extrapolicy effects with precision, there is good reason to believe that they should not be ignored by scholars trying to understand how institutional structures affected the efforts of workers who took part in political processes. The problem with Eskridge's account is that it ignores such effects and treats intervening electoral outcomes as exogenous factors against which the legitimacy of judicial decisions can be measured. So long as it is believable that the decisions in Congress about legislation can have an effect on electoral contests, the outcomes of those contests cannot be treated as exogenous factors.

This conclusion is not just a problem for Eskridge, but for any account of judicial decision making that is based on the legislative baseline framework. When legislators and interest group leaders use statutes as tools for manipulating political and organizing processes, neither the legislative position at the time a statute passes, nor the legislative position that emerges by the time the courts decide, can serve as a pure baseline against which to evaluate the outcomes judges produce.

UNCOVERING LEGISLATIVE DEFERENCE TO THE COURTS

One reason scholars have stuck to the legislative baseline framework and paid little attention to legislative deference to the courts may be that it is quite difficult to develop clear and quantifiable evidence regarding such deference. Open legislative delegation to the courts does not seem to

---

[34] For a general argument and observations regarding symbolic politics, see Edelman 1977. Graber (1993, 44) makes a connection between legislative deference to the courts and symbolic politics. Graber suggests that legislators may enlist the aid of the court in cases where they need to make a symbolic response to some salient event but cannot reach agreement on precisely how to respond.

occur very often. While legislators more routinely assign courts important oversight responsibilities in the text of statutes, it is difficult to quantify exactly how much discretion judges are granted by particular provisions. Most difficult of all are cases where legislators empower judges by using ambiguous statutory language to create interpretive controversies that need to be resolved in the courts. I do not know of any way to develop an objective scale that can be used to identify ambiguous provisions. The meaning of statutory provisions may be quite clear in some contexts, but *any* provision could be rendered ambiguous if applied in some novel or unexpected context. Thus, instead of trying to classify legislative proposals on some objective scale of ambiguity, I use reported judicial rulings that were made in connection with each of my case statutes to identify provisions that contained ambiguities that led to judicial decisions. Once those provisions are identified, they become the focus of my analysis for each case study. The goal of that analysis is to trace the evolution of legislative language in an effort to understand whether the actual participants in the legislative process recognized the ambiguities that later had to be resolved in the courts. This is not a simple task. Evidence to support claims about what participants understood can be difficult to develop. The circumstances that make it likely that legislators will create deliberate ambiguity also make it likely that legislators will deceptively advertise such statutes as ones that make clear choices. At the same time, legislators who are opposed to legislation might claim that legislative language is too ambiguous even when it is not.

More generally, recognizing that legislators sometimes pass legislation before reaching agreement on a particular baseline position makes it extremely difficult to develop claims about the policy preferences of either individual legislators or Congress as a whole. Normally, scholars identify both collective and individual preferences by looking at roll-call votes on legislation. However, in cases where legislators leave the details of policies to be worked out later in other branches, such votes no longer contain reliable information about policy preferences. Two legislators with opposite policy preferences may cast the same "yes" vote for legislation because each predicts that judges will make rulings favorable to his or her position. Thus, absent additional contextual information, votes on legislation no longer provide the Archimedean point from which to construct accounts of congressional preferences and decision making.

Despite these difficulties, it is possible to develop evidence showing that legislators deliberately deferred to the courts. For this study, I have designed a set of procedures for analyzing individual case studies and have tried to use conservative standards to prevent exaggeration of some of the more provocative claims that I make about deliberate deferrals to the courts.[35] I do not want to claim, for example, that legislators *deliberately* made statutes ambiguous simply because the language in statutes seems inexplicably vague, or simply because opponents of a statute complained publicly that the legislative language was too ambiguous. Thus, I refrain from concluding that a particular statutory provision was a deliberate deferral to the court except in cases where all three of the following conditions are met:

1. legislators were aware of and drew attention to the precise ambiguities and interpretive questions that judges would later decide;
2. legislators specifically associated those ambiguities with a future role for the courts; and,
3. legislators specifically rejected alternative legislative proposals that were offered to clarify the language and limit the discretion of the courts.

When all three of these things are true, I feel confident concluding that the ambiguity in a statute was not accidental and that the legislators who created the statute were not doing all they could to limit the power of judges to interfere with the advertised goals of the statute. The caution introduced by using these three conditions means that I conclude that provisions were genuine deferrals to the courts in just two of my four cases. However, the effort to determine whether the conditions are met reveals in all four cases a wide variety of previously hidden strategic interactions through which legislators deliberately empowered judges and judges influenced legislative deliberations.

---

[35] The research procedures I use are described, explained, and defended in much more detail in Lovell 1997, ch. II. Because I rely heavily on official legislative records, it is worth noting that legislators can edit their comments in the *Congressional Record* before the record is published. There is sometimes little guarantee that the words in the records were actually spoken on the floor, and no guarantee that anyone there was paying attention to any words that were spoken. Such possibilities do not seriously undermine the conclusions I draw based on statements appearing in the record. The records were published before the courts had a chance to make decisions. Thus, the published comments I rely on will reveal legislators' understanding of the likely role of the courts regardless of whether the words were actually spoken as they appear in the record.

2

False Victories

Labor, Congress, and the Courts, 1898–1935

In a floor speech just before the House passed an early version of the Erdman Act in 1898, Representative Joseph Walker (R-MA) called the bill "the first step in a long line of legislation by which the twentieth century is to be ushered in." Walker claimed that the new law would be the first piece of federal legislation to "recognize and make lawful and legal the 'labor organizations' of this country" (31 *Congressional Record* 4648).

Walker was right that the Erdman Act was the first step in a larger incremental process through which labor organizations would be released from a state of "semi-outlawry" (Forbath 1991, ch. 4) and eventually receive recognition from the government as legitimate aids to economic stability. Over the next four decades, Congress passed several additional labor statutes that addressed the legal status of labor organizations and changed the way the government regulated workers' efforts to exert economic power through collective activities. The struggles that accompanied those legislative changes gradually ended the long-standing practice of allowing judges to assume primary responsibility for regulating workers' collective actions and worker organizations.

Because subsequent chapters of this book focus on small details from my four case studies, the important broader story of institutional and political change that takes place over the time period covered by all four cases can be difficult to see. To clarify the bigger picture, this chapter establishes the context for the cases and explains how the interpretation that emerges here differs from earlier accounts of the same events.

JUDGES, LEGISLATORS, AND THE SHAPING OF THE AMERICAN
LABOR MOVEMENT: A REASSESSMENT

The time period spanned by my case studies has been exceptionally important to scholars of American political development because it was a crucial
period of transformation in the American state. Most famously, the period saw enormous growth in the administrative capacities of the federal
government, a process often associated with the New Deal but that actually began much earlier (Skowronek 1982). In addition to a shift toward
centralization of power in the federal government, regulatory power also
shifted away from judges and toward legislatures and newly created administrative agencies in the executive branch. Both sets of transformations
contributed to a series of dramatic confrontations between legislators and
judges that occurred during the same period.

Scholars who have attempted to explain these transformative changes
have long recognized that the activities of labor organizations are an
important part of the story. In particular, scholars have made some of
the unique characteristics of the American labor movement an important component in explanations of some of the unique or "exceptional"
features of American politics, such as the relatively low level of social
provision in the United States. Scholars have noted that unlike the labor
movements of Britain and parts of continental Europe, American labor
failed to develop a powerful and independent political voice. During the
period covered here, the labor movement was dominated by the American
Federation of Labor (AFL), an organization that opposed efforts to build
a broad, class-based, and politically independent labor movement. The
AFL instead favored the more cautious strategy of working within the
existing two-party system to "reward friends and punish enemies."[1]

While many scholars have recognized labor's organizational and political ideologies as a cause of some unique and persistent features of the
American state, some innovative scholars have more recently pointed out
that the causal arrow also runs in the opposite direction, that is, that
unique features of the American state helped to shape the American labor movement. In particular, several recent studies of labor law and labor
movement history have focused on the capacity of judges to interfere with
labor legislation. The story that emerges from these recent studies is one
of good legislatures and bad courts. Political scientist Victoria Hattam's

---

[1] For perspectives on the AFL's voluntarism, see Hattam 1993, Horowitz 1978,
Montgomery 1987, and Rogin 1962.

Labor Visions and State Power (1993) documents judicial interference with nineteenth-century state legislation limiting criminal prosecution of labor organizations. Legal historian William Forbath's *Law and the Shaping of the American Labor Movement* (1991) documents a similar story of judicial interference during the Progressive Era, drawing particular attention to judicial interference with state and federal legislation targeting the use of injunctions. Finally, legal scholar Karl Klare argues in an influential series of law review articles (1978, 1981, 1985) that early judicial decisions interpreting the Wagner Act of 1935 were responsible for "deradicalizing" that important statute and thus for transforming an increasingly radicalized labor movement into a conservative and ineffective one.[2] These recent accounts of labor history are constructive and inventive because they focus not just on the short-term policy changes at stake in legislative and judicial decisions, but also on the radiating effects of law, legal ideology, and legal discourse on individuals and society.

Although they have covered different (but overlapping) periods and used very different assumptions and methods, the authors of these recent accounts have reached remarkably similar conclusions about the effect of law and judges on the development of the American labor movement. All three scholars find that rulings by judges who were hostile toward labor organizations helped to shape the legal ideologies that in turn shaped workers' organizing strategies and collective political aspirations. All three scholars also suggest that judicial rulings that thwarted statutory reforms discouraged labor organizations from developing a more aggressive and independent political voice in American politics.

The four statutes examined in this study cover a period that intersects with these recent and influential accounts of law's role in shaping the labor movement. Three of the four cases (the Erdman Act of 1898, the Clayton Act of 1914, and the Wagner Act of 1935) have been widely identified as instances in which conservative judges thwarted important prolabor policy reforms contained in the statutes. The fourth case (the Norris-LaGuardia Act of 1932) faced less difficulty in the courts and is included here because it provides a useful comparison case.

Like these earlier accounts, the one offered here finds that institutional (and particularly legal) processes helped to shape the American labor

---

[2] See also Stone 1981 and Atleson 1983 for arguments that judges' decisions have hurt workers' interests while shaping the values and aspirations of workers. Tomlins (1985) provides a comprehensive critique that covers a longer time period and looks at the actions of both the NLRB and the courts.

movement. However, I reject the claim that judges shaped the labor movement by thwarting important legislative victories that labor organizations
thought they had won through democratic processes in the legislative
branch. The good legislatures/bad courts story is replaced by one where
both legislators and judges fail to advance the interests of workers and labor organizations. I find that earlier accounts have overestimated labor's
accomplishments in legislatures, and thus overestimated the significance
of judicial decisions that appeared to thwart political victories. I find
instead that the hostile judicial rulings occurred in part because legislators deliberately created conditions that empowered judges to make important substantive decisions on labor policy. In two of the three cases
that scholars have associated with judicial interference (the Clayton and
Wagner acts), members of Congress built support for the legislation by
deliberately using legislative ambiguity to create uncertainty about the
meaning of the bill. In the third such case (the Erdman Act) members of
Congress deliberately expanded the discretionary policy-making powers
of the courts by giving judges vaguely defined enforcement powers that
made it easy for employers to enlist the aid of judges to defeat strikes.
Moreover, none of the four cases I look at were straightforward political victories for workers that legislators passed in response to the political might of labor organizations. The nation's largest labor organization
during the period, the AFL, vehemently opposed passage of the Erdman
Act. The AFL did eventually endorse the other two statutes that ran into
difficulties in the courts, but both of those statutes were compromise
substitutes for earlier proposals that AFL leaders expected to be more
effective.

These findings mean that the power of unelected judges to decide issues of labor policy was not simply the result of some fixed institutional
or ideological power of unelected judges, but also partly the result of
decisions made by elected legislators in Congress. As a result, the judicial rulings cannot be understood as taking place independently of, or
in opposition to, the democratic processes of legislatures. My findings
also lead to a reassessment of labor's political success in Congress during this time period. The outcomes of the legislative process were not
the clear policy choices that one would expect from responsive legislators facing a politically powerful labor movement. Moreover, I also
find that labor leaders did not experience the judicial decisions that
thwarted their goals as unexpected intrusions that betrayed a promise
held out by the transparent democratic processes in the legislature.
Labor leaders knew long before the courts ruled that troubling features

of statutes made outcomes uncertain by giving hostile judges discretion to decide policy issues. In fact, all the central participants in the legislative process (labor leaders, legislators, and representatives of employer organizations) had very sophisticated understandings of judicial doctrines and made effective efforts to anticipate and shape judicial reactions to legislation.

By recognizing that participants in the legislative process anticipated judicial reactions to statutes, this study reveals that the political strategies pursued by labor leaders were more complicated than earlier scholars have recognized. Judicial decisions were not bolts from the blue that surprised and eventually disillusioned labor leaders who thought they had won clear victories in the democratic process.[3] To understand the extent to which the courts acted as barriers to labor's efforts to pursue goals through political processes, scholars need to know more about what labor expected to gain when Congress passed statutes that labor leaders recognized as compromises rather than clear victories.

I also find that it is essential to look beyond the public pronouncements that labor leaders and legislators made at the time the statutes passed. This is because participants in the legislative process all have incentives to exaggerate as they make claims about the likely effectiveness of new statutes. To get beyond such claims and better understand what participants expected from judges, I make a much broader inquiry into legislative records that allows me to compare what participants said publicly right after legislation passed to their earlier statements regarding other legislative proposals that members of Congress rejected. In the case of the Clayton Act, for example, the statute Congress eventually passed looks very similar to earlier proposals for compromise that the AFL had vehemently criticized. For several years prior to passage of the Clayton Act, AFL leaders had rejected those similar efforts at compromise precisely because they determined that such compromises gave too much power to judges.

Taken together, my findings challenge recent accounts that have accused judges of obstructing labor's successful efforts to use legislative processes to obtain favorable policy changes. Such accounts have mischaracterized the nature of the barrier created by judges. Judges did not cause labor leaders to become disillusioned by reversing what leaders thought were clear victories in the legislature. Labor leaders were well

---

[3] This does not mean that judicial rulings are never mobilizing bolts from the blue. See Luker 1984, 137–44.

aware that they did not have the political power to produce the type of legislation that they thought would best control the courts. More generally, the findings here suggest that the approach earlier scholars have taken to understanding the effects of institutions on labor politics has been inadequate. To understand the importance of courts as barriers to democratic processes, it is not enough to compare the advertised goals of labor leaders and elected legislators to the outcomes that emerge in the aftermath of legal processes. Scholars need to reinterpret labor leaders' political strategies by examining how those leaders anticipated and tried to shape the role of the courts. Knowing what labor leaders hoped to gain from compromise statutes seems essential to understanding what, if anything, those leaders later lost in the courts. Unfortunately, however, Hattam, Forbath, and Klare have neither asked nor answered questions about how the ability of labor leaders to anticipate judicial hostility and how anticipated judicial reactions affected the strategies they pursued as legislators formulated legislative text.

Given that labor leaders expected judges to be hostile to the interests of their organizations, it is puzzling that labor leaders would accept compromises that forced them to take chances on winning from judges what they could not win directly from elected legislators. However, one of the more interesting findings in this study is that the occasional willingness of labor leaders to compromise cannot be explained by looking only at their expectations about the likelihood of achieving certain policy goals in the courts. I do not find, for example, that labor leaders were simply duped into believing that flawed statutes were certain to create dramatic policy gains for labor. The labor leaders who took part in legislative processes repeatedly demonstrated a very sophisticated understanding of likely judicial responses to competing legislative proposals. It also does not appear that the decisive factor for the decision to support compromises was that AFL leaders suddenly felt that changes in judicial attitudes had improved the prospects of winning in the courts.[4]

---

[4] For example, there is no indication in the records that the AFL supported the Clayton Act because they expected Wilson to use his appointment power to nominate prolabor judges and expected such judges to determine the meaning of the act. Wilson was not disposed by personality to use the appointment process to make the bench more prolabor, and new appointments could not make much of an immediate dent in the lower courts, where most injunction cases began and ended. AFL leaders were very attentive to changes in judicial attitudes over time. Their behavior suggests that they saw more general political pressure, rather than appointments, as the best way to nudge the courts toward more prolabor rulings.

To make sense of labor leaders' strategic decisions, scholars need to look beyond labor leaders' policy goals to other important effects that the new statutes were likely to have. The occasional decisions to endorse flawed statutes make more sense once attention is paid to organizational goals that were important to labor leaders but that had very little to do with the policy issues directly addressed in the text of the statutes. In effect, labor leaders were sacrificing some certainty about policy outcomes in order to obtain other goals that were less dependent on judicial reactions. More specifically, I find that labor leaders became more willing to compromise at crucial moments when they needed to be able to claim and celebrate a legislative victory. By declaring victory, labor leaders could justify and maintain internal support for their conventional political strategy of working within the existing two-party system. Passage of new legislation provided a concrete signal of progress, a signal that could be important and useful even if the courts later muted the long-run impact that the statute would have on actual policies. The available evidence supports the hypothesis that compromises were designed to fulfill such organizational imperatives. In addition, the hypothesis helps to explain why savvy labor leaders sometimes made Pollyannaish statements when legislation passed.

Oddly, labor leaders' organizational goals were more closely aligned with the preferences of legislators than were the labor leaders' policy goals. Members of Congress who explained their votes in favor of labor statutes often noted that the new statutes were designed to reward and thus stabilize the leadership of moderate labor organizations. For example, legislators explained that they preferred a labor movement dominated by the conservative organizing ideologies of the AFL to a more radical movement that might emerge if Congress appeared unresponsive to the AFL's relatively moderate demands. Such findings suggest that the real barrier to labor's political effectiveness was not that unelected judges did not have to face political pressures that labor organizations could create for elected legislators. However, the findings also suggest that the constraints on legislators created by congressional elections did not produce a majoritarian system that was responsive to the interests of labor organizations, as suggested in earlier accounts. Rather, the real barrier seems to have been that labor leaders were forced to covertly sacrifice policy goals for organizational goals, a finding that raises new concerns about the responsiveness of legislatures and about the transparency of democratic processes.

These findings, stated here boldly and without first presenting evidence to support them, may seem quite shocking. I seem to be portraying legislation as a medium for deception as much as a medium for policy changes. Moreover, my suggestion that labor leaders advanced their own leadership goals through deceptive compromises seems quite harsh, and perhaps so cynical that it is implausible (Hattam 1994, 110). However, the appearance of cynicism can be alleviated by thinking more carefully about what labor leaders faced and what they were able to accomplish. Given labor's precarious political position and the continuing threat that legal doctrines posed to labor's capacity to organize new workers, there is nothing cynical about noting the need for labor leaders to respond to organizational imperatives. Thus, the lesson I draw is not that labor leaders acted in bad faith or made indefensible choices. The claim that labor leaders were responding to organizational concerns seems harsh or cynical only because scholars have underestimated the many difficulties that labor faced as they attempted to put political pressure on elected legislators. If large numbers of legislators had been eager to respond favorably to the demands of powerful labor organizations, then it would be quite difficult to justify decisions by labor leaders that sacrificed attainable policy gains for organizational goals. However, by showing that legislators' apparent responses to labor were typically hollow laws that allowed judges to continue making labor policy, I shatter the illusion of a Congress that was responsive and permeable to labor organizations. In reality, the legislators in Congress were very resistant to the core demands of labor organizations, and labor lacked the political power to change the membership of Congress. Moreover, labor's difficulties were compounded because the broader institutional system of separation of powers helped to insulate legislators from political pressures for change. The eagerness of judges to regulate workers meant that an antilabor policy regime could develop without legislators having to make overt antilabor decisions on statutes. Thus, judges made it easier for legislators to avoid the political costs of making clear choices on labor policy, and more difficult for workers to hold legislators responsible.

The difficult choices made by AFL leaders can also be viewed more sympathetically once choices made at isolated points are understood as part of a longer-term strategy for securing more favorable policies. Given the obstacles that labor leaders faced, even minor accomplishments might be enough to justify some unsettling compromises. Unfortunately, however, the recent tendency to focus on the cycle of apparent legislative victories followed by judicial defeats makes it easy to think of the period as one that produced only disheartening defeats for labor organizations. Such an account misses some very dramatic changes in labor policy that occurred across the cases. My findings suggest that even though judicial rulings on compromise statutes hindered some of labor's immediate policy goals, the AFL's willingness to compromise can nevertheless be characterized as an important component in a longer-term struggle that eventually contributed to broad shifts in labor policies. For example, the Clayton Act, which failed to achieve many of its own advertised goals, later became an important weapon in the AFL's struggle to broaden public support for the right of workers to organize without judicial interference. Allegations of judicial interference with statutes like the Clayton Act helped labor organizations to clarify their grievances and ratchet-up their demands. By portraying compromise statutes as unqualified victories, labor leaders helped to create a political climate in which judicial rulings against labor organizations would be increasingly perceived as illegitimate. Those efforts seem to have made some difference. For example, one of the most powerful arguments for passing the Norris-LaGuardia Act in 1932, perhaps the most radical labor law ever enacted by the U.S. Congress, was that the Supreme Court had earlier usurped congressional power by making hostile rulings on the Clayton Act of 1914. Thus, labor leaders were able to transform even failed statutes into powerful rhetorical weapons in subsequent political battles.

These preliminary comments are meant only to establish that the compromises made by labor leaders were more complicated and defensible than they at first seem. In order to evaluate decisions to sacrifice transparency for organizational goals, it is necessary to develop a much better understanding of the goals of labor leaders and the political and institutional obstacles that they faced. In the remaining sections of this chapter, I begin to develop that bigger picture.

Before turning to that task, however, it is worth pausing for a moment to consider some of the broader implications of my findings across the labor cases. My reinterpretation of the conflicts between legislators and judges over labor policy suggests the need for a broader reevaluation of the institutional and social conflicts that took place during the crucial period spanned by my cases. Much of the growing literature on American political development takes for granted the idea that legislatures were responsive to political demands expressed by labor organizations, and that the leading barriers to the democratic aspirations of insurgent popular movements were the courts (and later the administrative agencies). The dominant story of the courts of the period has been that, for better or worse, they delayed the implementation of popular innovations favored by responsive elected officials.[5] Likewise, the dominant story of the expansion of federal administrative agencies is that, for better or worse, they took over many regulatory functions that would otherwise have been handled directly through more democratic legislative processes.[6] The findings here call into question the basis for both the positive and negative assessments of these changes. The appearance of robust and responsive democratic processes in pre–New Deal legislatures masks a more complicated system in which the willingness of judges to fill the gaps in the rules created by legislatures made it easy for elected officials to avoid responsibility for tough policy choices. Thus, the relationship between the emerging administrative state and the earlier system needs to be reassessed. The administrative state, though still problematic, may actually be an improvement over the even less transparent, judge-centered system that it replaced.[7] The lesson that emerges here is that any evaluation of the long-term effects of institutional developments has to be based on a more nuanced understanding of the complex institutional barriers to electoral accountability in the earlier "state of courts and parties" (Skowronek 1982).

THE LABOR INJUNCTION: A BRIEF HISTORY AND SOME NOTES ON CONTEXT

From the turn of the century through the Great Depression, much of the AFL's lobbying activity was focused on proposals to limit the ability of judges to use injunctions to regulate workers' collective activities. Anti-injunction legislation became the focus of the AFL's lobbying activity as injunctions replaced state criminal conspiracy prosecutions as the primary legal threat to labor's organizing activities. The quest for legislation at the federal level reflected the fact that labor policy was becoming increasingly federalized as federal judges became more willing to intervene in labor disputes.[8]

---

[5] For the "better" side of delay, see Ackerman 1991, chs. 3 and 4; on the "worse" side of delay, see Paul 1960, Forbath 1991, Hattam 1993, and Pope 1997. Recent innovative accounts of the courts of the *Lochner* era include Gillman 1993, Novkov 2001, Cushman 1998, and Horwitz 1992.

[6] Attacks on the modern administrative state as a threat to electoral accountability can be found in Lowi 1979, Schoenbrod 1993; defenses in Landis 1938, Mashaw 1997.

[7] On this point, see Orren 1991, especially the discussion (218–21) of Lowi 1979.

[8] On the expansion of federal power, see Frankfurter and Green 1930, ch. 1, esp. 5–46; Forbath, 1991, ch. 3; Dubofsky 1994, ch. 1; Paul 1960, ch. VII.

The use of injunctions as an important tool for regulating industrial strife was a uniquely American institution.[9] Labor injunctions targeted all of the most effective collective activities that workers used to exert economic pressure on employers: strikes, boycotts, and organizational drives. As a result, injunctions created tremendous difficulties for both workers and labor organizations. Injunctions made it difficult for workers to use their economic power, and threatened the efforts of labor leaders to increase the power of the labor movement by organizing new members.

Judges first issued dramatic injunctions against workers' collective activities in the Great Railroad Strike of 1877. The use of the injunction gradually spread from railroads in federal receivership to all railroads in the late nineteenth century.[10] At the end of the first decade of the twentieth century, federal judges seemed to be freely issuing injunctions in any interstate industry with labor unrest. Judges typically issued injunctions at the request of employers who were inconvenienced by labor organizations, often without first holding a hearing to give labor organizations the opportunity to contest an employer's claims. Any workers or labor leaders who violated injunctions could be charged with contempt of court, which meant that they would be tried without a jury and sentenced by the same judge who issued the original injunction (Frankfurter and Green 1930, 123–33). These features of injunction procedure reflect the broad, discretionary powers inherent in judges' authority to issue injunctions as equitable remedies. Judges technically issue injunctions in their capacity as chancellors of equity rather than judges at law. Judges acting in that capacity have broad discretion to craft remedies that balance the competing interests at stake. The power to issue equitable remedies is confined narrowly to particular types of cases, and is subject to statutory control. Nevertheless, judges exercising the powers to provide injunctive relief are

---

[9] The most thorough account of the labor injunction and efforts at legislative reform remains Frankfurter and Green's (1930) monumental study. Chapters IV and V cover efforts at legislative reform. William Forbath (1991) supplements Frankfurter and Green's account and provides a theoretically sophisticated account of the sources and effects of the injunction regime. See especially chs. 3 and 5. Ernst (1989b, 1995) gives essential background information on the interest group activity that helped to shape judicial reactions to labor activity and legislative reactions to the judicial regime. Eskridge (1994, ch. 3) gives a sharp and concise overview of the cycles of judicial decisions and political response between 1877 and 1938.

[10] The key railroad cases are *In Re Debs* (158 U.S. 564 (1905)), *Toledo, Ann Arbor and New Mexico Railway v Pennsylvania Company* (54 F. 730, (C.C.N.D. Ohio 1893)), and *In re Lennon* 150 U.S. 393 (1893).

not expected to confine their reasoning about remedies to preexisting rules from statutes or the common law.

Federal judges who issued injunctions against workers often tried to justify the use of injunctions by grounding them in claims that workers were violating federal laws. For example, judges cited statutes protecting the mail to justify the injunctions that helped to break up the dramatic Pullman Strike of 1894. Judges also invoked provisions of the Interstate Commerce Act as they targeted strikes in transportation industries. Beginning around the turn of the century, federal judges expanded the range of their injunctive powers as they became more willing to justify injunctions on the grounds that strikes and boycotts amounted to restraints of trade in violation of the Sherman Antitrust Act (Frankfurter and Green 1930, 7–9). This last development was of enormous concern to the AFL because it meant that injunctions could reach well beyond the railroads and transportation workers who were the targets of the earliest federal injunctions. AFL concerns about the antitrust laws increased after 1908, when the Supreme Court ruled definitively that the Sherman Act could be used against labor organizations (*Loewe v Lawlor* (208 U.S. 274)). During the period when labor campaigned in Congress for reform legislation, the threat of injunctions continued to expand. Labor organizations were particularly agitated by a 1917 Supreme Court decision that allowed judges to issue injunctions to prevent unions from organizing workers who had signed yellow-dog contracts, that is, agreements promising not to join unions (*Hitchman Coal and Coke v Mitchell*, 245 U.S. 229, 1917). That court decision transformed the yellow-dog contract from a mostly symbolic tool to a more effective employer weapon for resisting organizing (Bernstein 1960, 196–200; Ernst 1989a). In a later case that was perhaps even more upsetting to labor organizations, the Supreme Court endorsed the use of injunctions ordering striking workers to return to work (*Bedford Cut Stone Co. v Journeymen Stone Cutters* (274 U.S. 37, 1927)).

Perhaps the most essential thing to understand about the political context that shaped labor's complicated political response to the threat posed by the labor injunction is that workers were not well organized for politics throughout the time period covered in this study. "Labor" was never really an identifiable political actor. Workers were not able to speak with a unified voice, and were represented by organizations that were themselves experiencing divisive ideological conflicts. Different labor organizations responded differently to injunctions because of differences in the organizing ideologies that dominated different parts of the labor movement. Under the leadership of Samuel Gompers, the AFL favored organizing workers separately by craft rather than organizing skilled and unskilled workers from the same industry into a single union. The AFL's ideology of voluntarism resulted in an antistatist, *laissez faire* approach to labor relations that led the organization to oppose much proposed labor legislation. For example, until the 1930s, the AFL opposed all forms of state administration of labor relations such as government-sponsored arbitration boards. The AFL also opposed many progressive reforms that were supposed to help workers but that interfered with private bargaining, for example, most minimum wage, maximum hours, and workplace safety laws.[11]

The rise of voluntarism to a central place in the labor movement was aided by state policies that helped to destroy organizations that pursued more radical strategies. The broad republican and associative vision of the Knights of Labor declined in importance after the first wave of injunctions defeated the massive strikes of 1877. Eugene Debs' attempt to build an industrial union movement with the Pullman Strike of 1894 was no match for the federal troops sent in to imprison labor leaders and end the strike by threat of violence. The AFL eventually had to abandon elements of its voluntarism when the Great Depression forced its leaders (and everyone else) to rethink core ideas. However, voluntarism had a profound effect on the AFL's early political responses to injunctions, and the painful ideological battles that were prompted by voluntarism's decline continued to influence AFL strategies long after the Depression.[12]

Scholars sometimes equate the AFL with "the labor movement" during the time period covered in this study. That mistake would never be corrected if scholars looked only at the witness lists for congressional hearings for evidence showing the existence of labor organizations. Along with the conservative railroad brotherhoods, the AFL was the only national labor organization whose demands were entertained at the conventions of major political parties, in congressional hearings, and in meetings with executive branch leaders. Leaders of unaffiliated locals and more radical national organizations did participate in some state legislative campaigns during the same period, but they did not respond to

---

[11] There were exceptions to this stance, particularly when statutes restricted women's access to employment. On this point, there are odd parallels between the attitude of the AFL and the attitude of judges. See Novkov 2001.

[12] The same issues of organizing ideologies contributed to the AFL/CIO split and to the AFL's destructive efforts to sabotage the NLRB (Gross 1981, chs 4–10).

the labor injunction with an active lobbying campaign for new federal legislation.[13]

However, the apparent dominance of the AFL masks the importance of other labor organizations to the political context in which the AFL operated. Debs's American Railway Union, the syndicalist Industrial Workers of the World (IWW, or the Wobblies), and later Sidney Hillman's Amalgamated Clothing Workers successively challenged the ideological pillars of the AFL's national leadership.[14] Other labor organizations could not match the AFL for number of members, organizational strength, or political contacts. However, the alternative political visions and campaigns to organize unskilled workers along industrial lines were very much a part of the consciousness of workers, employers, and political leaders during the campaign for antiinjunction legislation. AFL president Samuel Gompers often responded quite defensively to challenges from such organizations in the pages of the *American Federationist*.[15] The occasional massive strikes and campaigns of civil disobedience engaged in by more radical groups like the IWW were also important because they helped to shape public consciousness of the labor movement. Voluntarist labor organizations like the AFL and the Railroad Brotherhoods sometimes seemed to be as repulsed as judges by the disruptive tactics of some radicals, and AFL leaders would often remind legislators that the AFL could be displaced by a more radical labor movement if legislators did not respond appropriately to the AFL's moderate demands. The radicals' open contempt for the legal process often led federal judges to enlist the aid of private security guards and federal troops to defeat them. Debs and other "radical" leaders encountered much harsher repressive measures from the government than were ever dealt to the more powerful AFL.

However, one measure of the reach of injunctions is that even Samuel Gompers barely escaped jail time after he staged a symbolic refusal to obey an injunction.[16] Usually, however, the AFL's size, resources, and

---

[13] A catalog of state-level legislative activity can be found in Forbath 1991, apps. A and C.

[14] On Debs and the ARU, see Salvatore 1982. On the IWW, see Dubofsky 1969. On Hillman, see Fraser 1991.

[15] For example, March 1914, 126–7; discussed in more detail in ch. 4.

[16] Gompers was spared prison by two Supreme Court rulings resting on technicalities. See *Gompers v Bucks Stove and Range Co.* (221 U.S. 418 (1911)) and *Gompers v United States* (233 U.S. 604 (1914)). The cases and conflicts surrounding them are discussed in detail in Ernst 1995, ch. 7.

moderate political ideology protected its leaders from repressive measures and made it possible for the federation to pursue an insider strategy of direct lobbying for legislative change. The federation built political contacts and had friends in Congress who would introduce bills written by AFL leaders. Members of Congress often invited AFL leaders to air their grievances at committee hearings. This insider strategy exemplified, but also ran up against, another broad change in the political context: The growth of lobbying organizations and interest groups. AFL organizing and lobbying was matched by increased organizing and lobbying among employers. Some of the judicial rulings that the AFL complained about most bitterly were the result of the prototypical litigation strategy pursued by the American Anti-Boycott Association (AABA), an innovative organization of antiunion employers. For example, the notorious case where the Supreme Court subjected the Danbury hatters to the penalties of the Sherman Act was a lawsuit sponsored by the AABA (Ernst 1995, ch. 3). Representatives of a large number of local and national employers' associations appeared regularly at congressional hearings on injunctions to challenge the AFL's arguments.

The rise of interest groups and lobbying was itself a reflection of important changes in party politics. The AFL's interest-group style lobbying became more viable with the overthrow of the strict party leadership in Congress, as exemplified by House Speaker "Uncle Joe" Cannon, in 1910.[17] Republicans dominated national politics during the campaign for antiinjunction legislation until a split in the party contributed to Democratic gains in 1910 and victory in 1912. The electoral shift reflected changes in party coalitions as Democrats worked to attract additional urban and immigrant voters, the first steps in a larger process that eventually produced the FDR coalition of the 1930s (Mink 1986).

While this study focuses mostly on the campaign to end injunctions through legislation, it is important to realize that proposing legislation was not the only response that labor organizations made to injunctions. Both the AFL and the Wobblies developed campaigns to draw public attention to First Amendment rights that were violated when injunctions prohibited communicating information about strikes and boycotts. Some workers responded to the perceived injustice of labor injunctions with high-profile campaigns of civil disobedience. Sometimes moderate labor leaders like Samuel Gompers risked imprisonment by staging a symbolic violation of an injunction. In other instances, more radical

[17] On Cannon's style of leadership, see Jones 1968.

organizations led mass refusals to abide by court orders.[18] These more radical tactics led some federal judges to enlist private security guards and federal troops to break strikes, a response that contributed to the unusually high levels of violence associated with labor unrest in the United States.[19]

THE LEGAL CONTEXT

At the same time that the labor movement was experiencing internal ideological divides in a changing political climate, the judiciary was going through its own ideological struggles. The AFL's fight against injunctions began during the final stages of what Grant Gilmore (1977) has called the "Age of Faith" in American legal thought. That period began after the Civil War as Harvard Law School Dean Christopher Columbus Langdell promoted the idea of developing "legal science." Those sharing Langdell's faith believed that careful development of the case law method would distill a core set of objective legal principles. By developing an authoritative canon of leading cases, Langdell thought it possible to develop a legal system where objective principles could eliminate the influence of judges' preferences and whims (Gilmore 1977, ch. 3). At the turn of the century, hopes for a pure legal science were beginning to founder on the rocks of legal realism and the emerging sociological jurisprudence.

Such changes in legal thought are relevant here because they sometimes meant that the justifications judges offered for their decisions in labor cases were evolving more rapidly than the AFL's statutory proposals for curtailing injunctions.[20] In particular, changes in legal thought affected the legal categories and tests that judges used when determining the legality of workers' collective activities in injunction cases. Perhaps the most important example is the way changes in legal thought affected the legal concept of malice. Malice is important to the labor injunction story because injunction cases often hinged on whether the judge interpreted workers' collective activities to constitute a "malicious combination," a legal category covering collective activities that interfere with the rights of third parties. In the early years of labor's fight against injunctions,

---

[18] Rabban 1994; Forbath 1991, 142.
[19] On violence in American labor relations, see Forbath 1991, 106, note 30.
[20] My discussion in this section owes much to Ernst 1995, ch. 4. Gillman (1993) provides a sophisticated account of the complexity of judges' constitutional jurisprudence during the *Lochner* era. Horwitz (1992) provides an account that ranges more broadly into tort and property law.

many conservative judges saw almost any collective activity by workers as actionable malice toward the inconvenienced employer. Judges often claimed that such actions violated the employer's absolute right to carry on business without interference. However, the emerging challenge to orthodox legal thought developed by the legal realists of the early twentieth century made it increasingly difficult for judges to ignore the fact that such absolutist rights formulations were not objective "legal science" but merely masks for enforcing class privileges.

Thus, judges gradually began to abandon absolutist rights talk in favor of more pragmatic balancing approaches like those advocated by Oliver Wendell Holmes. In a series of influential articles and opinions, Holmes developed a formula for evaluating otherwise lawful conduct that interfered with rights of third parties.[21] According to Holmes's formula, such actions could be justified if they were motivated by a legitimate self-interest. By making the determination of malice hinge on the motives for actions that interfered with rights rather than on the absolute nature of the rights, Holmes's formula asked judges to look more carefully at the context in which interference with rights occurred. When applied to cases involving workers' collective activities that interfered with the rights of employers, the formula asked judges to be more sensitive to the need for workers to defend their interests, and thus sensitive to the broader causes and consequences of various forms of collective activity. For example, a strike undertaken to improve working conditions could be justified on grounds of self-interest even when the strike interfered with an employer's business operations. In contrast, a strike undertaken to bankrupt an unpopular employer could still be ruled a malicious combination.

Judges gradually began to abandon absolutist claims about employers' rights in favor of Holmes's balancing formula during the period covered in this study. However, even though Holmes's formula encouraged judges to address the motives of workers in labor cases, the open-ended formula did not always lead judges to reach outcomes that favored workers. In Holmes's hands, the formula helped labor organizations because

[21] See Holmes (1894). See also Holmes's opinions in *Vegelahn v Guntner* (167 Mass. 92, 106 (1896)) (Holmes, J., dissenting), *Plant v Woods* (176 Mass. 492 (1900)). The roots of the Holmes formula are in a British case, *Mogul Steamship Co. v. McGregor and Gow & Co.* ((1892) App. Cas. 25 (1891)). The prescriptive principles Holmes was attacking have been identified as having roots in both the "Victorian gentility" of the judges and attorneys (Ernst 1995) and in English feudal law going back to the fourteenth century (Orren 1991).

Holmes recognized connections among the economic interests of large groups of workers. However, the same formula allowed more conservative judges to rule against workers. Such judges would recognize a legitimating self-interest only when they could see very clear and direct connections between workers' collective activities and workers' interests. Thus, Holmes's formula made some judges more tolerant of activities aimed at securing higher wages, shorter hours, or better working conditions. However, when the connection between the activities and self-interest was more remote, conservative judges were unable to recognize any legitimating self-interest and attributed workers' activities to unlawful malice.[22] For example, in the leading Supreme Court case on the Clayton Act, *Duplex Printing v Deering*, the conservative judges in the majority could not find the requisite connection to self-interest when unionized machinists organized a strike and boycott against a company that refused to recognize the union. The justices in the majority applied a Holmesian balancing formula rather than making absolutist rights claims. However, the judges ruled against the workers after finding that the boycott was illegitimately motivated by a "sentimental or sympathetic" rather than a "proximate and substantial" interest in the dispute (254 U.S. 443, 472). The justices in the majority simply could not recognize any connection between working conditions at the targeted company and the self-interest of the boycotting workers who were employed by competing firms in the same industry. Dissenting justices Holmes and Brandeis disagreed, but were outvoted.[23] Thus, even as judges adopted balancing formulas that bore some resemblance to Holmes's, they continued to argue well into the 1930s that many activities designed to strengthen workers' bargaining position (e.g., closed-shop drives, boycotts, and sympathy strikes) were "malicious combinations" and thus enjoinable (Frankfurter and Green 1930, 26–7).

Different labor leaders responded in different ways as changes in legal thought changed the way judges justified their efforts to regulate workers' collective activities. Radical organizations like the IWW, sounding like the critical legal scholars of the late twentieth century, delighted in pointing out the contradictions and class biases lurking behind judges' claims, whether those claims took the form of a "legal science" or the

---

[22] See, for example, the discussion of *Arthur v Oakes* (63 Fed. 310 (C.C.A. 7th, 1894)), in Frankfurter and Green 1930, 27.

[23] See also *Hitchman Coal and Coke Co. v Mitchell* (245 U.S. 229 (1917)), where Holmes joins the dissent of Justice McKenna.

newer sociological jurisprudence. Such leaders were sophisticated enough to blame judges for contributing to false consciousness among workers.[24] AFL leaders likewise harbored few illusions about the objectivity of judges. However, the AFL was much more restrained in its attacks on judicial reasoning. Instead of shunning conventional legal reasoning, AFL leaders trained themselves in the law and tried to argue on the judges' own terms.

The path taken by the AFL's legislative representative, Andrew Furuseth, provides a striking illustration of the AFL's response. The founder of the Seamen's union, Furuseth became a self-taught expert in the history of the equity powers of federal courts. He designed legislative proposals for the AFL that reflected his learning, and defended his proposals with lengthy lectures before startled congressional committees, lectures that included copious citations to British and American case law. Furuseth's position was straightforward: Federal judges did not have jurisdiction to use equitable remedies like injunctions in labor disputes. Thus, almost all labor injunctions were illegitimate. The argument in support of his claims went as follows. Article III of the Constitution extends the jurisdiction of federal courts to cases in "equity." According to Furuseth, the only powers granted by that provision are the equity powers that the framers of the Constitution recognized, that is, the powers of English and colonial courts. At the time the Constitution was written, those courts understood the equitable remedy of injunction to be applicable only in cases where injunctions were needed to protect physical property. Based on this understanding of legal and constitutional history, Furuseth claimed that the problem in the labor cases was that federal judges were issuing

---

[24] See the following articles from the *Industrial Worker:* "LAW, LAW, How Capitalists Uphold the Law" (December 22, 1910, 1); "The Sanctity of the Law" (August 22, 1912, 2), ("Belief in the sanctity of the law spells slavery for the working class . . . It is the veneration in which the mandates of the masters are held that holds us in thrall. We are vassals to precedent."); "The Injunction" (January 2, 1913, 2), ("And what is more laughable than a set of supposedly sensible men dressed in black Mother Hubbard wrappers, trying to prevent organized workers from wielding their might.") The last article claims one ironic result of the IWW radical attitude: the Wobblies felt immune to injunctions. "The injunction is feared only by those who are afraid of it," the article declares, claiming that Lawrence mill owners failed to ask for injunctions in a recent strike because they would have been ignored; "Past precedents would have been scattered to the four winds and the sham of legality bared to the workers' gaze." The article also chided the AFL: "The injunction still strikes terror to the hearts of the aristocrats of labor, but for those rebellious and propertyless workers, to whom jail is no reproach, the 'holy writ' of capitalism is a huge joke."

injunctions even when the physical property of the employer was not threatened. Some judges had claimed in early labor injunction cases that the "right to conduct business" was "property" for the purposes of establishing equity jurisdiction. However, according to Furuseth, that claim was incorrect and had never been properly tested in court. The right to conduct business was not considered "property" for the purpose of determining equity jurisdiction at the time the Constitution was adopted. Thus, in the absence of any statutory change expanding the injunctive powers of the courts to cover such "property," any injunction that went beyond protecting traditional property was an illegitimate usurpation of legislative powers.[25]

Although Furuseth's argument reaches the somewhat dramatic conclusion that a very large number of labor injunctions were completely illegitimate, it is based on very conventional arguments about precedent and Framers' intent. The willingness to rely upon such arguments signals that unlike the Wobblies, the AFL was not interested in challenging foundational assumptions about the legal order. The AFL's traditionalism also made its leaders quite wary of efforts by realists and progressives to improve upon the old rights-based formalism with the new sociological jurisprudence. The AFL remained ambivalent about the Holmes formula and continued to articulate its demands using absolutist rights claims, for example, claims about an absolute right to strike or to organize (Forbath 1991). Ironically, the rights-based approach adopted by the AFL placed them closer ideologically to lobbying opponents, like the AABA than to progressive judicial reformers like Holmes and Brandeis (Ernst 1995).

LABOR'S GRIEVANCES AND PROPOSALS FOR REFORM

Between 1898 and 1935, Congress considered a wide variety of proposals designed to alter the way labor organizations were regulated in the American state. The content of those proposals changed over time in response to changes in the political and legal context.

One type of legislative proposal attempted to establish some formalized system of state-sponsored or state-protected collective bargaining between employers and employees. Such proposals typically involved trade-offs for

[25] Furuseth's original history lecture is in the 1906 *House Hearings*, 18–25. He was still making the argument in the 1928 hearings on the Shipstead bill. See 1928 *Senate Hearings*, 18–35.

unions. The proposals would give legal recognition to labor unions and limit the capacity of government or private actors to interfere with labor's collective activities. In return, labor organizations agreed to abide by certain administrative procedures for settling disputes, and agreed to the creation of legal mechanisms for enforcing the agreements reached through those administrative processes. An early example of this type of legislation is the first case considered in this study, the Erdman Act of 1898.[26] The Erdman Act established a system of state-administered arbitration for railroad labor disputes. It contained not only provisions that limited the ability of employers to interfere with workers' collective activities, but also provisions allowing judges to force workers to abide by the terms of arbitrators' rulings. The AFL opposed the act, both because of their general opposition to all state-sponsored arbitration, and because the act contained a provision that limited the right of workers to quit while arbitration was pending. Some railroad labor organizations did endorse the bill, largely because the strategies the government used to end the Pullman Strike had made it difficult for railroad workers to use strikes to exert economic pressure on employers. However, in 1898 the railroads were very much a special case. Labor organizations in other industries still expected to be able to use the strike weapon to exert economic power independently of state assistance. The AFL remained unwilling to endorse any state-administered bargaining or arbitration until the federation reluctantly endorsed the Wagner Act of 1935.

Thus, as federal regulation of railroad labor began a shift toward an administrative model at the turn of the century, AFL leaders continued to oppose legislative proposals that conflicted with their *laissez faire* ideology. The AFL did, however, push for legislation that made it easier for workers to exercise collective economic power without judicial interference (Hattam 1993, 165). Proposals for antiinjunction legislation were the most important components of this strategy.

During the time period covered here, legislators considered numerous proposals drafted by labor leaders as well as alternatives drafted by legislators or academic experts. Distinct legislative proposals were, at

---

[26] The Erdman Act is something of an anomaly among my cases because it is not an antiinjunction statute and did not have much direct effect on AFL-affiliated unions. It is included because it set off a confrontation in the courts over yellow-dog contracts that contributed to the expansion of the injunctive powers of federal courts, and because the system of arbitration established in the act is an imperfect precursor for the system of administrative regulation established in my fourth case, the Wagner Act.

various points, combined into single bills, and antiinjunction provisions were sometimes attached to bills that were primarily concerned with other topics. For example, several provisions from earlier AFL-sponsored antiinjunction bills were, in modified form, adapted as part of the Clayton Antitrust Act in 1914.

One type of antiinjunction proposal tried to limit injunctions by amending the statutes that judges used to justify labor injunctions. The most important of these proposals tried to exempt labor organizations from the antitrust laws. The AFL sought such an exemption both to prevent judges from using the antitrust laws to justify injunctions that were supposedly needed to prevent restraints on trade and also to exempt labor organizations from liability for damages in private antitrust suits. Congress passed such a provision as Section 6 of the Clayton Act, but subsequent judicial rulings limited the reach of the exemption.

A second type of proposal targeted the jurisdiction of the federal courts to issue injunctions in labor disputes. Proposals of this type were the centerpiece of the AFL's legislative strategy against injunctions for much of the period covered in this study. The proposals reflected Andrew Furuseth's reading of legal history and his resulting conviction that the courts had illegitimately expanded their jurisdiction. Proposals that pursued the jurisdiction-curbing strategy were often quite short, consisting mainly of the assertion that the right to conduct a business was not a property right and thus not subject to protection through equitable remedies like injunctions. Furuseth expected such a straightforward statutory pronouncement to restore the jurisdiction of the federal courts to what he saw as its proper place. Such a provision was included in the several bills that the AFL backed adamantly between 1906 and 1912 as the only acceptable legislative response to the threat of labor injunctions (H.R. 18171, 18446, 18752, 59th Congress; H.R. 94, 60th Congress; H.R. 11032, 62nd Congress). Congress never enacted the AFL's favorite proposal, which was initially known as the Pearre bill. But legislators did copy some of the language about property rights from the Pearre bill into the compromised and ultimately ineffective Section 20 of the Clayton Act. After that truncated version of the Pearre bill provision failed to have any impact on judges and labor injunctions, Furuseth revived the jurisdiction-curbing strategy in 1928 when he returned to Congress to defend another bill attacking injunctions with a new definition of property (the Shipstead bill; S. 1482, 70th Congress; S. 2497, 71st Congress). However, legislators instead passed less direct limits on equity jurisdiction in the more complicated Norris-LaGuardia Act of 1932. That statute turned out to be much more effective at curbing injunctions than the earlier Clayton Act, but not because of its watered-down property provision, which did not seem to have much of an impact on judges.[27]

A final category of legislative reform tried to limit injunctions by changing the procedures that governed the use of injunctions. A wide variety of proposed provisions fall into this category, including proposals to limit temporary injunctions, proposals to require judges to hold adversarial hearings or to make certain findings of fact before issuing injunctions, proposals to prevent judges from issuing injunctions with vague or sweeping descriptions of the forbidden activities, proposals requiring judges to specify carefully who was covered by the injunction, and proposals requiring that violations of injunctions be charged as criminal offenses (with jury trials) rather than as contempts of court.[28] Provisions falling into this category were enacted as part of both the Clayton and Norris-LaGuardia acts. However, this type of proposal was never the first choice of labor leaders. Leaders like Furuseth worried that such provisions would have a difficult time controlling judges because judges would themselves be responsible for interpreting the meaning of the immunizing language in the provisions. Moreover, Furuseth complained that judges might read any specified limitations on injunctions in some types of labor disputes as an implicit congressional endorsement of labor injunctions in other labor disputes that did not fit the specified exemptions. Thus, Furuseth thought that legislation directly attacking the jurisdiction of federal courts was preferable because such proposals were less dependent upon favorable judicial interpretations.

Few of the legislative proposals considered by Congress were ever enacted. The ones that did pass were usually not the first choice of labor organizations but modified compromises that, with the exception of Norris-LaGuardia, *extended* the powers of the courts. Most of the judges who resolved interpretive controversies about the meaning of ambiguous statutory provisions chose interpretations that hurt the interests of labor. These observations suggest that the political strategies pursued by the AFL were a complete failure. However, it is also undeniable that both the legal status of labor organizations and the possibilities for future labor legislation improved considerably during the time period covered by these cases. One way of seeing the broader improvements that are masked by

---

[27] I discuss the Pearre bill in more detail in ch. 4; and the Shipstead bill in ch. 5.

[28] Frankfurter and Green (1930, ch. III, and 182–98) document numerous cases where judges issued questionable injunctions that inspired these reform proposals.

TABLE 1 *Legislation and Legislative Proposals Related to the AFL's Antiinjunction Campaign, 1898–1935*

Type of Provision	Location
Administrative regulation of collective bargaining	Erdman Act (1898) Wagner Act (1935)
Limits on application of antitrust laws to labor organizations	Littlefield Bill (1900) Clayton Act (1914) Section 6
Limits on equity jurisdiction to cases involving threats to "property"	Pearre Bill (1906–1912) Clayton Act (1914) Section 20 Norris-LaGuardia Act (1932) Section 7(b)
Changes in injunction procedures	Clayton Act (1914) sections 17–19 Norris-LaGuardia Act (1932) sections 7 and 8
Limitations on yellow-dog contracts	Erdman Act (1898) Section 10 Norris-LaGuardia Act (1932) Section 3, 4(i) Wagner Act (1935) Section 7(3)
List of collective activities that cannot be enjoined	Clayton Act (1914) Section 20 Norris-LaGuardia Act (1932) Section 4

the more striking failures is to compare the position the Supreme Court took in a 1908 ruling on the Erdman Act to the position the Court later took on the Wagner Act of 1935.

In the 1908 case *Adair v United States* (208 U.S. 161), the Supreme Court rejected the idea that legislators could act to protect members of labor organizations from discrimination. Writing for the Court, Justice Harlan considered the suggestion that Congress had included a provision protecting the interests of unionized workers because legislators had decided that favoring worker organizations would help to preserve industrial peace and induce workers to submit to state-administered bargaining. Harlan rejected that suggestion, and hinted darkly that the Court would not let any compromises that protected the interests of unionized workers stand:

Will it be said that the provision in question had its origin in the apprehension, on the part of Congress, that, if it did not show more consideration for members of labor organizations than for wage-earners who were not members of such organizations, or if it did not insert in the statute some such provision as the one here in question, members of labor organization would, by illegal or violent measures, interrupt or impair the freedom of commerce among the states (179)?

After asking this (apparently rhetorical) question, Harlan claimed that it would be unfair for the Court to read any statute as establishing such an arrangement:

We will not indulge in any such conjectures, nor make them, in whole or in part, the basis of our decision. We could not do so consistently with the respect due to a coordinate department of the government. We could not do so without imputing to Congress the purpose to accord to one class of wage-earners privileges withheld from another class of wage-earners, engaged, it may be, in the same kind of labor and serving the same employer. Nor will we assume, in our consideration of this case, that members of labor organizations will, in any considerable numbers, resort to illegal methods for accomplishing any particular object they have in view (179).

Taken seriously, Harlan's odd outburst regarding legislative efforts to induce the support of the railway unions threatens the very possibility of labor law reform. Even if labor organizations did manage to convince enough legislators that statutes favorable to labor organizations were in the public interest, the justices seemed poised to pounce on any statute that they perceived as an effort by Congress to favor labor organizations.[29]

The four statutes that are case studies in this book can be thought of as part of the difficult process through which labor organizations were able to get out from underneath the incredulity and potential obstructionism that Harlan articulated in *Adair*. Between *Adair* and passage of the Wagner Act, the continuous agitation of labor organizations contributed to a process through which the old system of regulation by judges was replaced by a system of administrative control that was potentially much more responsive to the interests labor organizations expressed through political processes. One sign of the progress that was made is that the same tradeoff that Harlan rejected in *Adair* was embraced by the Supreme Court three decades later. The Supreme Court defended the constitutionality of the Wagner Act of 1935 by repeatedly interpreting the law as an effort by Congress to preserve industrial peace and promote economic growth by protecting labor organizations and collective bargaining (Klare 1978, 281–93, 325–39).

Ironically, the judicial rulings claiming that the goal of the Wagner Act was to use collective bargaining to insure industrial peace have themselves been attacked for "de-radicalizing" the Act (Klare 1978). Such claims are

---

[29] On the Supreme Court's constitutional objection to such "class legislation," see Gillman 1993, esp. chs. 2 and 3.

ironic because the position classified as "de-radicalizing" in the late 1930s was too radical for the Court even to consider in 1908. The processes that made such shifts possible must be understood in terms of the AFL's tireless efforts to use lobbying and legislation, even "failed" legislation, to change public and judicial attitudes toward workers' organizations and collective activities.

Had legislative and judicial processes been more transparent, it may not have taken more than three decades for the AFL's campaign against injunctions to result in legal recognition and state protection. More transparent processes may also have meant that labor organizations would not have had to give up so much autonomy to administrators in order to receive such legal recognition and protection. Nevertheless, it is still a mistake to characterize failed statutes like the Clayton Act as proof of the independence of the courts, or the responsiveness of legislators. The institutional system that produced compromise statutes created barriers to democratic accountability because it forced bad choices on the leaders of labor organizations as they tried to develop and exercise political power. Judges, however, were not all-powerful or completely isolated from political processes that influenced decision making in other branches of government.

3

"As Harmless as an Infant"

The Erdman Act in Congress and the Courts

> This bill may benefit organized labor, or it may be like many other laws now on the statute books – a dead letter. It will depend to a great extent on the courts. We can not tell now just how the courts will construe some of the provisions of this bill, and until that is done no one can tell whether this bill will be in the interest of the workers or not.
>
> > Rep. William Sulzer (D-NY), on the Erdman Act (31 *Congressional Record* 4647)

> I do not think it really amounts to anything, either for or against labor. . . . The bill, in other words, is . . . a species of buncombe. It is a step taken, ostensibly, in the interest of labor, which can neither be benefited nor injured by it. It is easy to get such legislation through, but hard to get any that will really benefit our laboring people.
>
> > Rep. William L. Greene (Populist-PA), on the Erdman Act (31 *Congressional Record* 5052)

> [T]oo many measures come into this House masked with favor or benefit to the poor, but carrying beneath the surface the iron hand of oppression exerted in behalf of power.
>
> > Rep. James H. Lewis (D-WA), on the Erdman Act (31 *Congressional Record* 5051)

In 1908, the Supreme Court struck down Section 10 of the Erdman Act of 1898 in the notorious case of *Adair v United States* (208 U.S. 161). Section 10 made it a misdemeanor for employers in the railroad industry to blacklist members of railroad unions or to require employees to sign yellow-dog contracts, that is, contracts promising that the employee would not join a labor union. The Court ruled that Section 10 was unconstitutional because it interfered with a "liberty of contract" allegedly protected by the United States Constitution.

The Supreme Court's ruling in *Adair* seems to present a classic case of unelected judges interfering with the democratic process. The ruling in *Adair* came after elected officials in Congress appeared to signal their strong disapproval of yellow-dog contracts and discrimination against union members. (The act passed overwhelmingly, by 226 to 56 in the House and 47 to 3 in the Senate.) Scholars of American government have long worried about the power of unelected judges to reverse the outcomes selected in Congress. Presumably, if democratic government means anything, it means that successful legislative campaigns by insurgent groups like labor organizations should produce important policy changes. Yet the Supreme Court's decision in *Adair* meant that the policy changes encoded in Section 10 of the Erdman Act were never realized.

The Court's ruling in *Adair* turned out to be quite damaging to the interests of organized labor. *Adair* not only neutralized any legislative gain made with passage of the ban on yellow-dog contracts in Section 10, it also discouraged subsequent legislative action against yellow-dog contracts and other forms of discrimination against organized workers. More devastatingly, *Adair* later served as a precedent for judicial enforcement of yellow-dog contracts through injunctions, the era's most egregious form of judicial interference with workers' efforts to organize.[1] The fact that the Supreme Court relied on the now-suspect constitutional doctrine of "liberty of contract" makes the seemingly counter-majoritarian ruling in *Adair* even more troubling.

The successful judicial reversal of the apparent consensus in Congress is especially striking in this case because the Erdman Act seems on the surface to be a congressional attempt to limit the power of judges. The act was the first piece of railroad labor legislation passed in the aftermath of the dramatic Pullman Strike of 1894. The intervention of federal judges in that strike signaled an increase in both federal and judicial involvement in

---

[1] In 1915, the Court used *Adair* as a precedent to rule that a state statute banning yellow-dog contracts was unconstitutional (*Coppage v Kansas*, 236 U.S. 1). Two years later, in *Hitchman Coal and Coke v Mitchell* (245 U.S. 229 (1917)), the Court ruled that federal courts could issue injunctions to prevent unions from organizing workers who had signed yellow-dog contracts. The ruling in *Hitchman* transformed the yellow-dog contract from a mostly symbolic tool used to intimidate workers to a powerful weapon against unionization. Bernstein 1960, 196–200.

labor disputes.[2] Upset with the recent expansion of federal power and with a longer history of judicial hostility toward workers, labor organizations repeatedly asked Congress to pass legislation limiting judicial power in the years before and after the Erdman Act passed. The ostensible purpose of the Erdman Act was to establish a new system of arbitration for railroad labor disputes as an alternative to the judicial intervention used to defeat the Pullman Strike.

Recent scholars who have analyzed the consequences of judicial rulings on labor legislation from the same "*Lochner* era" have identified *Adair* as one of a series of judicial rulings that reversed important legislative victories won by labor organizations, and have claimed that those judicial rulings were barriers to labors' efforts to use the democratic process to produce changes in government policies. The conclusions these scholars reach about *Adair* are based in part on the assumption that the Erdman Act was a political victory that legislators passed in response to the political demands of labor organizations. William Forbath lists the Erdman Act as one of many examples of legislative victories won by labor organizations that were struck down or vitiated by hostile judges during the time period (1991, 199). Melvyn Dubofsky identifies the act as part of a "rush to mollify labor" in the aftermath of the Pullman Strike, and says that the act allowed labor leaders to "glory in congressional recognition of their legitimacy" (1994, 32). Karen Orren has claimed that Section 10 was an "integral part of the Erdman Act" (1991, 205) and the "major reason for labor's support of the legislation" (187).

Looking only at the vote tally in Congress and the Supreme Court's decision in *Adair*, it is easy to see why scholars have assumed that the Erdman Act was a congressional concession to powerful labor organizations angry about the expansion of judicial power in the Pullman Strike. Section 10 makes it easy to imagine that Congress was making important policy changes because labor organizations beat on the doors of the Capitol and insisted that the most democratic branch either provide some measure of protection from judges or face severe consequences at the polls. Such a picture of the reasons for the Erdman Act's passage makes it easy to assume further that judges were willing to reverse the legislators' decision only because judges were not susceptible to the same electoral pressures that labor organizations had used effectively on legislators.

---

[2] For accounts of the role of railroad strikes in the evolution of federal and court power in labor disputes, see Frankfurter and Green 1930, 18–24; Dubofsky 1994, ch. 1.

However, the real story of labor's role in the passage of the Erdman Act, revealed here after a more detailed look at the political context in which legislators made decisions, is considerably different. The message sent by Congress's collective decision to pass the Erdman Act is more complicated and ambiguous than it first appears. By exploring the meaning of that decision more carefully, I show that *Adair* was not an exercise of raw judicial power that reversed labor's successful utilization of democratic processes in the legislative branch.

Scholars employing more conventional methods to analyze the impact of *Adair* have reached different conclusions because they look at Section 10 in isolation from the rest of the statute. Such a focus on Section 10 elevates the significance of that provision in a way that is tremendously misleading. Section 10 was less than peripheral to the political conflicts that animated legislators and labor organizations in 1898. By focusing on the broader conflicts at the heart of the political processes that shaped the Erdman Act, I am able to place the ruling in *Adair* into a context that makes the conflicts between Congress and the courts seem much less apocalyptic. The courts no longer seem to have been barriers to a robust democratic process or to efforts by Congress to control the courts.

I do not, however, conclude that Section 10 of the Erdman Act was itself a deliberate deferral to the courts. The evidence does not show, for example, that Congress passed Section 10 only to provoke an adverse court ruling that would lead workers to blame judges for ongoing discrimination against unions. In sharp contrast to my other three case studies, I do not find here that the participants in the legislative process anticipated the difficulties that the courts created during implementation of Section 10. There is no evidence that any members of Congress expected the Supreme Court to strike down Section 10 as a violation of liberty of contract. In fact, the provision banning yellow-dog contracts was barely mentioned during public congressional deliberations on the Erdman Act.

Nevertheless, the case study does show how conventional assumptions about the relationship between Congress and the Courts can be misleading. Other scholars have looked at Section 10 in isolation, and guessed that legislators' willingness to pass such a provision reflected an underlying political terrain on which labor was in an influential position. Closer scrutiny of the Erdman Act as a whole reveals a more complicated political situation. Section 10 was part of an almost completely ineffective statute that purported to establish a framework for arbitrating railroad labor disputes. That statute was, at best, a mixed bag for labor organizations. The seeming victory in Section 10 was offset by several other provisions that leading labor organizations vigorously opposed. Far from being an attempt to remove the courts from labor disputes, the act included provisions that gave courts new powers to intervene. Furthermore, legislators did not pass the Erdman Act in response to pressure from politically powerful labor organizations. The bill that later became the Erdman Act was not drafted by labor organizations, friends of labor in Congress, or labor sympathizers in the executive branch. The bill was drafted by Richard Olney, the Attorney General who had just engineered the violent put-down of the Pullman strike and subsequent prosecution of Eugene Debs.[3]

In addition, it is inaccurate to claim that "labor" supported the bill. The nation's largest and most politically powerful labor organization (the American Federation of Labor (AFL)) strongly opposed the bill. The illusion of labor's political power is fed by the fact that one group of railroad labor organizations (the railroad brotherhoods) did endorse the bill, and by the fact that supporters of the bill in Congress often cited that endorsement as a reason to vote in favor of the bill. However, the broader record shows that the apparent responsiveness of Congress to the brotherhoods does not indicate that those organizations had a decisive role in the bill's passage. The brotherhoods did not play a very active role as three congresses deliberated on the act. After endorsing Olney's original bill in 1895, the brotherhoods did not make any visible effort to influence any of the subsequent amending activity that dramatically altered the content of the bill. It may be true that Olney and some members of Congress wanted to reward the brotherhoods and strengthen their position. However, that solicitude was less a reflection of the brotherhoods' existing political power than the result of a desire to strengthen the brotherhoods as a bulwark against the radicalism exemplified by Debs.

Furthermore, the Erdman Act cannot be characterized as an attempt by Congress to reward or "mollify" labor organizations upset with the use of injunctions to end the Pullman Strike. Given that members of Congress overwhelmingly supported violent federal intervention in the Pullman Strike, it seems unlikely that Congress was trying to rebuke the executive

---

[3] Olney's role is described in Eggert 1967, 217–22. Olney devised the bill at the request of Rep. Lawrence E. McGann (D-IL) who was chair of the House Labor Committee in 1895, and who had been working on a bill with Carroll D. Wright and John D. Kernan of the United States Strike Commission. Representative Lawrence E. McGann (D-IL) introduced the original bill. Representative Constantine Erdman (D-PA) was the author of the first House committee's report on the bill, but played little visible role in its development.

and judicial branches for their violent intervention in that strike.[4] A better indication of labor's political power was that legislators had collectively refused to pass any of the legislative proposals backed by the AFL, including anticonspiracy and antiinjunction bills that were much higher priorities for labor organizations than bills limiting yellow-dog contracts.

The actual content of the Erdman act provides additional support for the view that labor's political position was not strong. Perhaps the most striking feature of the Erdman Act was that it was, in its final form, a complete mess. As the bill moved toward passage, its meaning gradually became obscured by a series of amendments that weakened the language in the arbitration provisions. Those changes also made it unlikely that participants in railroad labor disputes would invoke the provisions of the bill. As they deliberated on these changes, legislators openly disagreed about what the bill meant and how it would operate in practice. Many legislators expressed doubts about whether the bill would have any affect at all. Despite an inability to reach agreement on a coherent bill, many members of Congress did feel compelled to pass something. Legislators wanted to make some response to the Pullman Strike and to the potential for further labor unrest on the railroads. However, because members could not agree on how to respond (and apparently did not know how to respond effectively), they passed a law that failed to make clear policy choices or establish workable procedures.

Recovering the broader story of the Erdman Act's passage through Congress leads to an improved account of the impact of the Supreme Court's ruling in *Adair*. The broader lesson that emerges is that scholars cannot understand the relationship between a ruling like *Adair* and the broader democratic process without developing a better understanding of the political context in which Congress enacts the statutes that give rise to judicial rulings. Attention to the act's other provisions may not be necessary for a conventional assessment of the legitimacy of the Supreme Court's doctrinal and constitutional arguments regarding Section 10. However, this chapter shows that such attention is crucial for understanding how severely the Court's decision interfered with democratic processes in the legislative branch. To reach accurate answers to questions about judicial policy-making powers, scholars need to broaden their conceptions of what information is relevant for assessing the impact

---

[4] One indication of Congress's support for the violence used to end the Pullman strike is that the Senate overwhelmingly passed a resolution praising the actions of the president and courts (26 *Congressional Record* 7284).

of court decisions on democratic processes. When scholars look at legislative provisions in isolation, and take those legislative provisions at face value, they are likely to develop misleading assessments of the impact of the courts. The congressional decision to pass the act had little to do with either labor's political power or the specific policy goals that appear on the surface to be the act's primary preoccupation. Despite all the contested details in the statutory language about such things as how boards of arbitrators would be chosen and compensated, many members of Congress did not expect the statute to create a workable system of arbitration, or, for that matter, to produce any significant changes in policy. Passage of the bill did help to signal legislators' concern about the Pullman Strike and legislators' willingness to respond to labor organizations that engaged in nonthreatening tactics. However, these subsidiary goals are invisible until scholars look beyond the text of isolated statutory provisions to the broader political context in which a statute is passed.

SYMBOLISM OVER SUBSTANCE: THE ERDMAN ACT
IN CONGRESS AND THE COURTS

The Erdman Act is chiefly remembered because of the Supreme Court's landmark constitutional ruling in *Adair v United States*. In that case, the Supreme Court heard a challenge to a federal indictment against William Adair, a master mechanic who supervised employees at the Louisville & Nashville Railroad Company. Adair was charged with violating the clause of Section 10 of the Erdman Act that made it a misdemeanor for a railroad employer to "threaten any employee with a loss of employment" or to "unjustly discriminate against any employee because of his membership in ... a labor corporation, association, or organization." According to the indictment, Adair had threatened and then fired a locomotive fireman named O.B. Coppage, because Coppage was a member of a labor organization called the Order of Locomotive Firemen. The Court ruled, however, that the case could not be tried because Section 10 violated the Constitution.

Although Adair was charged only with violating the antidiscrimination clause of the Erdman Act, the Court's ruling invalidated all of Section 10, including clauses making it an offense for railroad companies to use yellow-dog contracts or to blacklist union members.[5] The Court used a

---

[5] The statute defined a yellow-dog contract as: "an agreement, either written or verbal, not to become or remain a member of any labor corporation, association or

two-part argument to strike down Section 10. First, the court ruled that the provision interfered with the "liberty of contract" guaranteed by the Fifth Amendment to the Constitution. Second, the interference with that liberty was not justified as a legitimate exercise of legislative power (in Article 1 Section 8 of the Constitution) to regulate interstate commerce.

The Court went beyond the existing case law and forged a new doctrinal path with each of the two grounds in its opinion. The Court's ruling under the still-emerging doctrine of liberty of contract was a departure from earlier rulings because the statute under consideration had been passed by the U.S. Congress rather than a state legislature. Earlier liberty-of-contract rulings had involved state legislation challenged as a violation of the Fourteenth Amendment. Because the Fourteenth Amendment did not apply to federal legislation, the Court had to expand the liberty-of-contract doctrine before it could be applied to the Erdman Act. The court accomplished this by grafting the liberty of contract found in the *due process* clause of the Fourteenth Amendment onto the *due process* clause of the Fifth Amendment, which did apply to the federal government.

The Court's ruling on the commerce clause issue was also something of a departure. Although the Court had sometimes restricted Congress's power to regulate manufacturing industries, the Court usually allowed the federal government wide latitude to regulate the railroad industry as part of interstate commerce.[6] The reasoning that the court used in defense of its reading of the commerce clause in *Adair* reveals a great deal about how the justices conceptualized industrial relations at the time that the ruling was made.[7] Harlan stated that Congress could only regulate activity that had a "substantial connection" to interstate commerce. To demonstrate that there was no "substantial connection" in the activity regulated by Section 10, Harlan asked: "what possible legal or logical connection is

organization." The antiblacklisting provision made it an offense to "conspire to prevent" an employee from "obtaining employment" after the employee quit or was fired. Although the Erdman Act applied only to the railroad industry and railroad unions, I examine it in this study of more general labor legislation because the Supreme Court later used *Adair* as a precedent in rulings that covered all industries. The later rulings appeared to block further legislative action and expanded the role of the courts on the yellow-dog issue.

[6] Compare, for example, *United States v E.C. Knight* (156 U.S. 1 (1895)) with the *Shreveport Rate Cases* (234 U.S. 342 (1914)).

[7] The evolving doctrines the court relied upon were not universally recognized or accepted. Very shortly after the ruling was made, Harvard Law School Dean Roscoe Pound (1909) wrote a law review article attacking the decision as emblematic of a misguided formalism that led the Court to reach conclusions at variance with common sense and common conceptions of justice.

there between an employee's membership in a labor organization and the carrying on of interstate commerce?" Harlan then answered: "Such relation to a labor organization cannot have, *in itself,* and in the eyes of the law, any bearing upon the commerce with which the employee is connected by his labor and services" (178). Despite Justice McKenna's vigorous dissent, Harlan's position carried the day on the court by a vote of six to two.

The Erdman Act in Congress: 1895–1898

My analysis of the Erdman Act's passage through Congress is based on the large official record of deliberations in three congresses. The first version of the bill that became the Erdman Act was introduced in Congress in January 1895, two and a half years before final enactment. Versions of that bill passed three houses, in 1895 (H.R. 8556, 53rd Congress), 1897 (H.R. 268, 54th Congress), and 1898 (H.R. 4332, 55th Congress), before the Senate finally agreed to pass an amended bill in 1898.[8] The House then hastily agreed to the Senate version to avoid a conference and the Erdman Act became law under President McKinley's signature.

The record left from these three rounds of congressional consideration reveals that neither the Erdman Act nor the Supreme Court's ruling in *Adair* was what it appears to have been. Passage of the Erdman Act was not a political victory for "labor." "Labor" had very little to do with its

---

[8] Congress made a number of substantive changes to Olney's original 1895 bill before it was finally enacted. The original bill by Olney provided for each side to choose one arbitrator while the ICC chair would choose a third. The House committee successfully changed the bill so that the first two arbitrators selected would be responsible for choosing the third. Several representatives suggested changes in the size of the board, but Congress kept the size at three. All versions also specified procedures for maintaining the status quo during the pendency of the arbitration. In the original bill, failure to follow the award was made a misdemeanor subject to a $1,000 fine and a year in jail. In 1895, the House changed the provision to decriminalize violations and instead hold the party liable for damages. The Senate added a provision in 1898 (discussed later in this chapter) stating that the act did not allow courts to issue injunctions to compel service. Both bills also contained provisions modifying U.S. statutes on the incorporation of railroad unions. (Section 8 of the bill, modifying an act for incorporating railroad unions from 1886.) The provision required incorporated railroad unions to have bylaws stating that members would be kicked out for violence, or intimidation during disputes. The provision was symbolic. Railroad labor organizations did not want to incorporate because doing so made it easy to sue them for damages. For a discussion of the debate over incorporation of railroad unions in connection with the Erdman Act, see Tomlins 1985, 85–6. For background on the broader ideological controversies implicated in the debate over incorporation, see O'Brien 1998, ch. 2.

design or enactment. Furthermore, even though the Act was ostensibly a legislative alternative to the system of judicial control of railroad strikes that had expanded in the aftermath of the Pullman Strike, the law was not, as Karen Orren suggests, an attempt by Congress to "assault" judicial power or to place the courts "under siege" (1991, 188). Rather, legislators included provisions that expanded the powers of the courts by giving judges important but vaguely defined oversight and enforcement responsibilities.

Before turning to these legislative records, a few observations about the content of the Erdman Act and the results of its passage are in order. Attorney General Richard Olney drafted the original bill. In proposing the legislation, Olney was following the recommendation of the United States Strike Commission, which had conducted extended hearings on the Pullman Strike in 1894. The commission had recommended a government-supported system of mediation and arbitration in order to prevent future strikes. The amended version of Olney's bill that passed as the Erdman Act turned out to be an almost complete failure. That failure was not, however, the result of the Supreme Court's decision in *Adair*, which struck down only the peripheral Section 10. The act failed because parties in labor disputes were reluctant to invoke its weak and risky procedures. The Act was invoked only once between passage in 1898 and 1906 before being temporarily revived and invoked in sixty-one railway labor disputes between 1906 and 1913. During that period of revival, the act's provisions proved incapable not only of settling disputes, but also of channeling disputes through the institutional procedures established in the act: Only four of the sixty-one cases even made it to the point where arbitration boards made rulings. Eventually, universal recognition that the Erdman Act was inadequate led legislators to replace it with a new railroad labor arbitration law, the Newlands Act of 1913 (Lecht 1955, 17–20).

The degree to which participants in the legislative process anticipated the ineffectiveness of the arbitration provisions is difficult to determine with precision. Despite the fact that it was considered by three different congresses before it was passed, the records of congressional deliberations on Olney's bill are not always illuminating. Opponents of the bill were disorganized and critics were given little time to explain their concerns during floor debates. Despite the shortcomings in the official record, however, the evolution of the language in the Erdman Act and the expected reactions of participants before passage provide valuable information about how those participants understood the role the court would play and how expectations regarding judicial reactions affected congressional deliberations.

The Sound of Silence: Section 10 in Congress

The first questions to consider are how well legislators anticipated judicial interference with Section 10 of the Erdman Act and what steps they took to prevent or minimize such interference. The evolution of the statutory text enacted as Section 10 is uncomplicated. The first bill drafted by Olney in 1895 (H.R. 8556, 53rd Congress) already contained a provision that was nearly identical to the one eventually enacted as Section 10 of the Erdman Act. The provision remained unchanged in each of the bills passed by the House in the years leading up to enactment. The apparent explanation for the yellow-dog and blacklisting provisions is that the United States Strike Commission's report on the Pullman Strike recommended that such a policy be enacted.[9] Olney incorporated many of the commission's other recommendations into the bill.[10] Nothing in the official record suggests that Olney, members of Congress, or any of the other participants attached much significance to Section 10. Although Section 10 was reported and passed four times by the House and once in the Senate, there was almost no discussion of the constitutionality of this rather remarkable provision.[11]

---

[9] United States Strike Commission 1894, LIV. For a later statement of Olney's own views on yellow-dog contracts and *Adair*, see Olney 1908, 161–7.

[10] Eggert 1967, 213–17; Lecht 1957, 15–16. The strike commission was established in 1888 as part of the previous time Congress responded to a railroad strike by passing a symbolic bill with ineffective arbitration provisions.

[11] A few legislators did mention a concern that the Erdman Act went beyond Congress's power to regulate interstate commerce. However, only one member (Representative Maguire (D-CA)) suggested the bill was likely to be held unconstitutional on those grounds. The 1895 House debates: Rep. G.W. Fithian (D-IL), 27 *Congressional Record* 2799–2803; Rep. Franklin Bartlett (D-NY), 27 *Congressional Record* 2799. The 1897 House debates: Representative Maguire, 29 *Congressional Record* 2389. Other members expressed confidence that the bill was a legitimate exercise of the commerce power (Representative Hepburn (R-OH) (26 *Congressional Record* 2799), Rep. C.H. Grosvenor (R-OH) (31 *Congressional Record* 4640)). None of these comments about the commerce clause was made in connection with Section 10 of the Erdman Act.

Liberty of contract was only mentioned two times during all the debates concerning the various versions of Olney's bills. (Representative Bartlett 26 (*Congressional Record* 2799), Representative Van Voorhis (R-NY) (27 *Congressional Record* 2791)). The concerns were not expressed in connection with Section 10, and no one suggested that judges were likely to strike down Section 10 as an unconstitutional interference with liberty of contract. The fact that members of Congress did not call attention to potential problems created by the liberty-of-contract doctrine should

In fact, there was almost no discussion of Section 10 at all. No member of Congress took the trouble to explain publicly why Congress should criminalize yellow-dog contracts and blacklisting.[12] Section 10 was not even mentioned in the Senate report or any of the three House reports on Olney's bill. In three rounds of House floor debates and one in the Senate, the provisions in Section 10 that were later struck down by the Supreme Court in *Adair v United States* were mentioned only twice.

The first mention of Section 10 came from Rep. J.H. Lewis (R-WA), just before the House passed the bill for the third time. Although Lewis had serious doubts about the bill and suggested that it was something of a trap, Lewis mentioned Section 10 as a reason for swallowing his doubts and supporting the bill:

I have very little hope and less confidence that the arbitration feature of this bill will prove an advantage to anybody. But I have some hope of and much reliance on the features of the bill which prevent corporations and employers from discharging or blacklisting their employees because they may be members of labor organizations. This provision may be effective. Therefore my support of this bill is rather in the line of the Merchant of Venice: "I do a little wrong that I may do a great good" (31 *Congressional Record* 5051).

The only other reference to Section 10 during all the floor debates on the Erdman Act came in an even more doubtful speech by Senator Allen (P-NE) in the Senate (31 *Congressional Record* 4795). Allen claimed that the provision would likely be meaningless because it would remain nearly impossible to prove the existence of a blacklist in court. Other than these two comments, Section 10 went unnoticed during floor debates. The lack of interest in Congress seemed mirrored among labor leaders as well. Shortly before passage, AFL president Samuel Gompers exchanged letters with both the head of the railroad brotherhoods and the AFL's legislative representative. The letters contain nuanced and prescient discussions of

not be surprising. Most of the cases establishing the doctrine were decided after passage of the Erdman Act. The Supreme Court had never decided to strike down a *state* law on liberty-of-contract grounds until 1897, only a year before Congress enacted the Erdman Act (*Allgeyer v Louisiana* (165 U.S. 578)). That case did not cause alarm among progressive critics of the Court because the Court's use of the doctrine was benign in the years immediately following the decision (Ross 1994, 39). The doctrine was not recognized as a threat until later decisions like *Lochner v New York* (198 U.S. 45 (1905)) and *Adair*.

[12] Daniel Ernst (1989) provides a fascinating discussion of the ideological fight over the yellow-dog contract in the first third of this century. Ernst finds that Congress did eventually respond to an elite consensus in opposition to the yellow-dog contract, but that consensus did not form until the early 1930s. See also Cushman 1992.

the plusses and minuses of various provisions in the bill, but express almost no interest in Section 10.[13] Gompers was responding to a legal opinion he received from two labor lawyers who reviewed the bill at Gompers's request in January 1887. The two lawyers wrote Gompers a detailed, section-by-section critique. They dismissed the ban on blacklisting and yellow-dog contracts, saying that it was not of "any considerable importance." They noted that similar state statutes had been ineffective because "the offenses are of such a covert nature."[14]

The silence of legislators and other participants regarding Section 10, like the sound of no dog barking in the Sherlock Holmes story, is remarkable. However, such evidence is too weak to conclude that "Congress" expected the Court to strike down Section 10 or that members voted for Section 10 only because they expected the courts to strike it down. Nevertheless, the fact that legislators gave so little attention to this "integral" part of the bill suggests, if nothing else, that it is worth taking a closer look at the events that prompted passage the peculiar railroad arbitration bill that was the subject of the Court's ruling in *Adair*.

Creating a Role for the Courts

To develop the full picture of the Supreme Court's interference with labor's efforts to produce change through democratic processes, it is important to look not only at the legislative provision that the court struck down, but also at other provisions in the Erdman Act that gave the courts important responsibilities in the new system of arbitration. Each version of Olney's bill, including the final Erdman Act, contained provisions that specifically mentioned the courts and assigned them an important role in carrying out and shaping the meaning of the legislation. Each version included open-ended provisions authorizing the courts to hear suits for liability if workers quit while arbitration is pending (Section 7), to enforce arbitrators' awards after they were issued (Section 3), to compel testimony and production of documents needed for arbitration (Section 5), and to hear appeals of arbitrators' awards (Section 4). The

---

[13] Gompers to Frank Sargent, Grand Chief of Brotherhood of Locomotive Firemen, January 28, 1897, in Kaufman, Albert, and Palladino 1991, 292–4, Gompers letter to Andrew Furuseth, March 20, 1896, *ibid*; 141–2.

[14] Jackson H. Ralston and Frederick L. Siddons letter to Samuel Gompers, January 23, 1897, Files of the Office of the President, General Correspondence, reel 59, frames 290–9, *American Federation of Labor Records: The Gompers Era* (Microfilming Corporation of America). The quotes are on frame 299.

provisions did not, however, attempt to define these new judicial powers with specificity, or to place coherent limits on the exercise of those powers.

The fact that the Erdman Act gave courts new powers to interfere in labor disputes is tremendously important. One of the most important legislative demands expressed by labor organizations during (and for decades after) deliberations on the Erdman Act was a demand for relief from judicial supervision of labor organizations. By 1898, judges had established a clear pattern of hostility toward organized labor. Thus, the fact that legislators invited judges to take part in the Erdman Act's arbitration procedures suggests that other scholars are wrong to see the Erdman Act as an indication of labor's political strength. The statute may more fairly be characterized as a sign of labor's political ineffectiveness.

Unlike Section 10, the court empowering provisions of the Erdman Act did not go unnoticed as three congresses considered the various Olney bills. Each of the provisions extending powers to the courts was subjected to discussion and amending activity in Congress, and legislators rejected several alternative provisions establishing clearer limits on the power of judges before adopting the provisions from Olney's bill. The attempts to change these court-empowering provisions, and the debates those attempts inspired, provide the best available window on the participants' attitudes toward judicial supervision of labor unrest.

The provision that I will focus on here is the one that attracted the most attention and debate: The third clause of Section 3 of the Erdman Act. This clause gave the courts the power to use injunctions to enforce arbitration awards. The controversial provision stated that awards were to be filed with the circuit court and then "enforced in equity so far as the power of courts of equity permit." Because injunctions were the only remedy "in equity" that was likely to be used to enforce an award of arbitration, the provision amounts to the first-ever direct congressional authorization for the courts to use injunctions in labor disputes.[15] The decision to

---

[15] Each version of Olney's bill that Congress considered contained additional provisions that supported this grant of judicial power by adding provisions limiting workers' right to quit and employers' right to fire employees without notice. Olney's original bill also contained a clause that gave the attorney general the power to request injunctions to stop railroad strikes, a power that Olney had seized in the Pullman Strike through some rather creative readings of federal antitrust statutes and postal statutes. That clause was too much for the House committee, and the House adopted the committee's recommendation that the provision be removed. The issue is discussed in a speech by Representative Bartlett (27 *Congressional Record* 2799).

include this "equity" provision in Section 3 suggests that most members of Congress were not yet ready to accept the most important legislative demand of mainstream labor organizations like the AFL: The demand that Congress pass legislation prohibiting the use of injunctions in labor disputes.

The extent to which Olney's bill failed to limit the power of the courts in labor disputes can be seen by comparing it to other railroad labor bills introduced in 1895. While some of the alternative proposals gave the courts even greater powers,[16] some bills tried much harder to restrict the power of the courts. A bill introduced by Sen. James C. George (D-MS) attempted to prevent the courts from becoming involved in disputes by specifically denying judges the power to use injunctions to end strikes.[17] The George bill stated that it was not "lawful" for a U.S. Court to grant an injunction against employees of a railroad company if the company had earlier refused a request to submit the dispute to arbitration.[18] The George bill seems based on the observation that judicial intervention in labor disputes through injunctions usually benefited employers, and that as a result employers had little incentive to submit disputes to arbitration. Why, after all, would employers submit disputes to arbitration if they could count on judges to break up strikes with injunctions? Thus, George's bill tried to encourage employers to submit

---

[16] For example, bills introduced by Representative Tawney (H.R. 7382, later reintroduced in a modified version as H.R. 8214, 53rd Congress) and Representative Hudson (H.R. 7697).

[17] S. 2177, 53rd Congress.

[18] The George bill was no doubt inspired by the ARU's complaint that the Pullman Company had refused the union's request to submit the dispute to arbitration before the Pullman Strike. Exactly who was at fault in the Pullman Strike was a matter of some dispute in Congress. As the Senate debated a resolution praising the use of force to end the Pullman Strike, Senator Daniel (D-VA) proposed an amendment noting the refusal of the Pullman Company to go to arbitration. Senator Dolph (R-OR) replied "Why stop to throw a bone to Cerberus, to conciliate the elements which are seeking to overthrow the government" (26 *Congressional Record* 7282). Daniel quickly withdrew his suggestion, and the resolution that passed expressed only support for President Cleveland's actions (26 *Congressional Record* 7284). Other bills tried to limit injunctions like the one used in the Pullman Strike by amending the federal laws that judges had relied on to justify the injunctions against Debs's union, for example, a bill introduced by Senator Allen (P-NE) (S1563) limiting the application of statutes protecting the mails. A bill introduced in the House by Representative Boatner (D-LA) (H.R. 7362) limited the use of injunctions more generally. These early efforts to control injunctions were the beginnings of a long legislative campaign that later produced the labor provisions of the Clayton Act. I discuss the evolution of legislative strategies for curtailing injunctions in ch. 4.

to arbitration by denying the protection of the courts to employers who refused.

Had it passed, the George bill might rank as a sincere effort by Congress to limit the power of the courts in labor disputes. But George's bill went absolutely nowhere. The House committee instead reported Olney's bill as the one bill worthy of serious consideration. Significantly, each time Olney's bill came to the floor in either the House or Senate, the provisions expanding the equity powers of the federal courts in Section 3 came under attack. Those attacks resulted in a series of changes in the legislative language. The first change came in 1895 after Rep. (later Speaker) Joseph Cannon (R-IL) attacked the expansion of equity power (26 *Congressional Record* 2791). In response, Rep. James A. Tawney (R-MN) offered a floor amendment adding the following proviso: "Except that no employee shall be punished for his failure to comply with the award as for contempt of court." Cannon immediately announced that he would support the bill with the amendment, and the House added the provision without a recorded vote (26 *Congressional Record* 2804). That amendment remained part of each bill passed by the House until the Senate modified it in 1898.

The Tawney amendment was enough to quiet Cannon, but it led other members of the House to worry that it rendered Section 3 self-contradictory and thus dangerously ambiguous. Without the amendment, the provision seemed to invite the courts to issue injunctions to prevent workers from quitting to avoid arbitrators' rulings. The amendment did not revoke that invitation, but did seem to limit the power of the courts to punish persons who violated injunctions. Critics worried that the contradictory language would simply empower judges to choose an interpretation that would allow them to enforce awards. For example, judges might claim that the unlawful "contempt" was the workers' refusal to obey the injunction rather than their refusal to "comply with the award."

The confusing provision came under repeated attack in subsequent floor debates. When the Tawney amendment was first added to Olney's bill, an opponent of the bill, Rep. John Van Voorhis (R-NY) sarcastically raised a "parliamentary inquiry": "Does not the adoption of that amendment kill the whole bill?" (27 *Congressional Record* 2791). Other members of Congress who were more sympathetic to labor's interests openly doubted whether the amendment would protect workers. When the amended bill reached the Senate floor for the first time in 1898, Senator Allen (P-NE) referred to the equity provision as a "death trap" for labor organizations, and called the bill "one of the most vicious bills in the manner in which it is drawn that ever came before Congress" (31 *Congressional*

Record 4790). After drawing attention to the contradiction created by the
Tawney amendment, Sen. John Spooner (R-WI) called it one of the most
"artful" provisions in the bill (31 *Congressional Record* 4794). Similar criticisms were repeated by Senator Turner (Fusionist-WA), who also pointed
out that the real danger in the bill was that it marked the first time that
Congress specifically authorized judges to use equity powers in labor disputes (31 *Congressional Record* 4799).

Responding to criticisms of the language in the Tawney amendment,
Sen. George F. Hoar (D-MA) offered a substitute stating that "no injunction or other legal process shall be issued which shall compel the perfor-
mance by any laborer against his will of a contract for personal labor or
service." Hoar claimed that the substitute reconciled the apparent conflict
between the general grant of equity power and the limit on proceedings
for contempt. But the amendment also appeared to narrow workers' immunity from injunctions because it seemed to limit the immunity to just
one type of injunction. Thus, the new amendment failed to satisfy critics
of the Tawney version. Senators continued to express uncertainty about
how judges would read the confusing legislative language. Some critics
were also concerned that the limit on judicial enforcement powers in the
amendment would make the bill ineffective by making it impossible to
enforce arbitrator's awards.

Senators Turner (Fusionist-WA) and Spooner (R-WI), for example,
both stated that they were dissatisfied with Hoar's substitute. These senators suggested, correctly as it turned out, that the ambiguous expansion
of judicial powers would make labor organizations reluctant to submit
disputes to arbitration under the Act. Spooner stated that he had advised
representatives of railroad workers that both versions of the proviso were
"utterly useless" but that the leaders still endorsed the bill because they
"thought there might be some moral effect from it which would be beneficial to them" (31 *Congressional Record* 4801). Senators did not, however,
respond by attempting to alleviate such doubts with a clearer amendment. Even though no member could answer the concerns of Spooner
and Turner, the Senate adopted Hoar's amendment the next day without
making any improvements aimed at resolving the uncertainty (31 *Congressional Record* 4843).

Senator Allen (P-NE) later made one additional attempt to add a provision establishing a clear limit on the powers of the federal courts to use
injunctions to enforce arbitrators' rulings. Allen proposed an amendment
adding a new Section 12, stating that nothing in the Act "shall be so construed as to enlarge the remedies at law and in equity in courts of the

United States now enjoyed by private persons, firms, or corporations."
Allen's amendment also tried to prevent further judicial interference
through the use of injunctions on behalf of private employers by adding
a provision stating: "no statute of the United States shall be construed
as permitting the equitable jurisdiction of the courts of the United
States to be invoked except by the Attorney General of the United
States."[19]

Allen's colleagues rose to object to his proposal. Significantly, they
objected precisely because it took away the discretion of the courts to
decide important issues with substantive policy consequences. Senator
William J. Sewell (R-NJ), for example, stated: "I will say that you ought
not to pass a bill which will deprive the courts of the right to do what
they consider proper in the case of any citizen or in the case of any
corporation in anything which involves great business interests or the
rights of the individual concerned" (31 *Congressional Record* 4845). Sewell
claimed that taking away the discretionary power of the courts would
deprive one class of "citizens" of rights that were enjoyed by others. The
Senate apparently agreed with Sewell's rather expansive conception of
the proper range of judicial discretion. Allen's amendment was quickly
rejected (31 *Congressional Record* 4846). The bill that passed the Senate
retained only the ambiguous Hoar amendment as a limit upon the court's
newly granted powers to use injunctions to end labor disputes.

The House later rushed to pass versions of the bill approved by the
Senate in order to avoid a conference. During the very short time allotted
for debate, Rep. John S. Rhea, a Democrat and Populist from Kentucky,
complained repeatedly about the Senate change to the proviso on the
equity provision. He claimed the Senate version allowed contempt proceedings, or at least left the bill "open to doubtful construction" (31 *Congressional Record* 5050). Rhea stated that "every lawyer of this House"
knew that the clause would "not rob a court of equity of its power to rule
for contempt any person who disobeys the decree entered" (31 *Congressional Record* 5052) because judges would claim that a contempt proceeding was not a "legal process." However, Rhea's objections were drowned
out by partisan wrangling between Democrats and Republicans.[20]

---

[19] According to Senator Allen, the proposed section would limit the expansion of
injunctive powers and end "the indiscriminate issuing of injunctions on behalf of
private individuals" (31 *Congressional Record* 4845).

[20] Representative Grosvenor (R-OH) asked Rhea to defend the Democrats' position
(31 *Congressional Record* 5052) despite Rhea's plea that he was speaking as a member
of the Labor Committee and lawyer rather than on behalf of Democrats.

The Senate version of the bill was quickly rushed to passage as the Erdman Act.[21]

"Their Blood Will Be on Their Own Heads": Labor Organizations and Congressional Support for Olney's Bill, 1895–1898

It usually seems quite safe to assume that passage of a bill in Congress by a very wide margin indicates that there is strong support in Congress for a particular policy outcome (*policy assumption*) and that the outside organizations that supported the bill are politically powerful (*political power assumption*). In the case of the Erdman Act, those assumptions suggest that Congress passed the law to establish a workable system of arbitration that would benefit or "mollify" politically powerful railroad labor organizations.

There are, however, numerous indications that the lopsided vote in favor of the Erdman Act obscures the true nature of the decision made in Congress and the influence of outside groups on that decision.[22] Taken together, the evidence suggests that passage of the Erdman Act did not reflect the arrival of a broad consensus on a particular policy. Rather, passage reflects the fact that participants in the legislative process came to understand the Erdman Act as a symbolic measure that was unlikely to be invoked, unlikely to be effective, and unlikely to create any significant changes in public policies.

But why did legislators pass any act at all? Any adequate answer to that question has to begin with the Pullman Strike of 1894. Although it was not until four years after the Pullman Strike that the Erdman Act was finally enacted, the strike was very much on the minds of many members

---

[21] While the vague provisions in Section 2 allowing the courts to enforce arbitrators' awards through injunctions attracted the most attention in Congress, the other provisions of the Erdman Act assigning a role to the courts also confirm that the act was not an effort to keep the courts out of labor disputes. For example, Section 4 of the act established procedures allowing parties to arbitration to file appeals in circuit court. The provision gave those courts broad powers to adjust arbitrators' rulings.

[22] The lopsided House votes in favor of Olney's bill in 1895 and 1897 came as members acknowledged that it was too late in the term for the Senate to consider the bill. (See comments by Representative Lacey, 27 *Congressional Record* 2803; Representative Hulick, 2804; and Representative Henderson, 2804.) It was relatively easy for legislators to cast votes in favor of a symbolic bill that had no chance of enactment and attracted no organized opposition. That the bill had no chance of enactment may also be one of the reasons why the bill did not generate sharp debate or discussion on the House floor. Criticisms of the bill in the House were much sharper in 1898, when the bill was finally acted on early enough to allow Senate consideration.

of Congress from the time the bill was first introduced in January 1895 to the moment of passage in 1898. In the first set of House floor debates on Olney's original bill in 1895, Representative Dunn (D-NJ) reminded his colleagues that "we are today as every member of this House knows, on the very brink of what may be an industrial revolution" (27 *Congressional Record* 2795). As the bill finally approached passage in 1898, the Senate Committee on Education and Labor's report explained: "The necessity for the bill arises from the calamitous results in the way of ill-considered strikes arising from the tyranny of capital or the unjust demands of labor organizations, whereby the business of the country is brought to a standstill and thousands of employees, with their helpless wives and children, are confronted with starvation." The same committee stated that the bill was an effort to "reduce to a minimum labor strikes which affect interstate commerce," in order to protect the interests of both the workers and the railroads. The committee suggested that the "only alternative is industrial wars."[23]

In order to understand such concerns, it is important to recall how the dramatic 1894 strike and boycott against the Pullman Company changed the political and legal context. The strike, led by Eugene V. Debs and the American Railway Union (ARU), captured the public imagination by dramatically illustrating the potential power of industrial unions. It also led to a dramatic expansion of federal power over labor relations after federal judges helped to create the pretense for using federal troops to bring a violent end to the strike and destroy the union. However, even though the Pullman Strike caused many legislators to fear the potential power of radical labor organizations, it is wrong to conclude that legislators were responding to the existing strength of any particular labor group. Some railroad brotherhoods did endorse the Erdman Act, but the political power of the groups making those endorsements does not appear to have been the main reason legislators passed the act. The brotherhoods were politically weak. They did not even offer a more favorable alternative to Olney's bill, and were not strong enough to sponsor any successful amendments to Olney's bill or to block any of the amendments that weakened it.[24] Moreover, the brotherhoods clearly could not endorse

---

[23] Senate Report 591, 55th Congress, 2nd Session, on S. 3662, 1–2.
[24] Supporters of the bill did try to silence criticism of the bill by calling attention to the brotherhoods' endorsements. However, the endorsement of the brotherhoods was not given as a reason to vote for or against any amendments. The brotherhoods did not visibly attempt to make their endorsement conditional on any changes.

the bill on behalf of "labor" or even on behalf of "railroad labor." The
fact that the leaders and some members of the brotherhoods took sides
against the ARU during the strike made it difficult for those same leaders
to speak later on behalf of all railroad labor (Eggert 1967, 174).[25]

Attorney General Richard Olney's decision to draft the Erdman Act
is best understood not as a concession to the established political power
of railroad unions, but as part of his effort to consolidate his victory
over the radicalism of Eugene Debs by strengthening the conservative
railroad trade unions as a bulwark against future labor radicalism. After
the Pullman Strike ended, Olney took actions to reward the leadership of
the railroad brotherhoods for their cooperation in putting down the strike,
including unsuccessful intervention on behalf of a brotherhood in a federal
receivership case.[26] Such efforts on behalf of the railroad brotherhoods
may feed the illusion of labor's independent political power. However, the
power was coming from the top-down, not from the bottom-up. There
is nothing in the congressional records to suggest that the brotherhoods
had much influence on either Olney's or legislators' decisions about the
actual content of the bill.

Additional evidence that the Erdman Act was not simply a bill passed
on behalf of "labor" can be found by looking at the reaction the AFL
had to the Erdman Act. Speaking to the membership of the nation's
largest labor organization in an editorial in the *American Federationist*
in February 1897, AFL President Samuel Gompers warned:

The Erdman Arbitration bill, so called, is a piece of legislation destructive of the
best interests of labor, ruinous to the liberties of our people, a step in the direction
for the creation of an autocracy or an empire on the one side and a class of slaves
or serfs on the other. Against such conditions of affairs the whole sentiment – the
entire interest – of the wage workers should be directed.

[25] The forced dissolution of Eugene Debs's American Railway Union left the brotherhoods as the leading remaining organizations of railroad workers. Eugene Debs
had been affiliated with the Brotherhood of Locomotive Firemen before forming the
ARU, but the leadership of the brotherhoods opposed Debs's vision of a single union
organized across trades, and opposed his strike against the Pullman Company. In
testimony before the government commission investigating the Pullman Strike, two
representatives from railroad brotherhoods explain their reasons for not cooperat-
ing with the ARU, and their preference for trade unionism over organizations (like
the ARU) that organize workers across trades. See testimony of P. H. Morrisey,
Brotherhood of Railroad Trainmen (United States Strike Commission 1895, 180–5)
and Edgar E. Clark, Order of Railway Conductors (185–7).

[26] Eggert 1967, 206–12. Olney emerges as a more complicated figure than his virulently
antilabor reputation would suggest in Eggert 1974.

We therefore urge not only the defeat of this iniquitous bill by every means at the command of our people, but the thorough organization of labor to defend, protect, and advance the rights and interests of all. There is danger ahead; meet it and conquer it, and labor will yet be emancipated and man really free (259).

The Erdman Act was objectionable to the AFL because it sanctioned forms of state intervention that violated some of the most important pillars of the AFL's voluntarist conception of industrial relations. The AFL's opposition has to be taken seriously. No other labor organization came close to the AFL in terms of political influence in Congress. Moreover, the AFL's objections were not unthinking reflections of ideology. AFL leaders very carefully analyzed the provisions of the bill, and tried to communicate their concerns to the leaders of the brotherhoods. AFL leaders were particularly animated by the provisions in Section 3 of the Erdman Act that invited judges to use injunctions. They also singled out a provision in Section 7 requiring workers to give thirty days notice before quitting after arbitration because it invited judges to interfere with the sacred right of workers to quit.[27]

Ironically, the railroad brotherhoods that endorsed the bill were the railroad labor organizations closest in ideology to Gompers and the AFL. The brotherhoods' decision to endorse the Erdman Act came as circumstances forced railroad labor organizations to undergo transitions in ideology and strategy. The successful deployment of federal troops in the Pullman Strike rested on a consensus among all three branches of government that it was appropriate to imprison labor leaders and use armed force to defeat railroad strikes. That consensus and the violence used to back it up made it impossible for railroad workers to follow Debs's strike-based strategy for building a centralized industrial union. Debs's defeat also meant that the remaining railroad labor organizations could no longer afford the luxury of the AFL's ideological consistency. The leaders of the brotherhoods were forced to accommodate the reality of being denied the right to strike by adjusting their voluntarism and supporting state-sponsored arbitration. Thus, despite a shared commitment to a conservative form of voluntarism and trade unionism that made them natural allies, the brotherhoods supported the Erdman Act while the AFL remained adamantly opposed.

[27] The AFL's objections are outlined in the most detail in a legal opinion given to Gompers by two attorneys. See Siddons and Ralston letter to Gompers, January 23, 1897, *American Federation of Labor Records: The Gompers Era*, reel 59, frames 290–9.

In an apparent concession to the AFL, legislators did add amendments exempting seamen and street railway workers from the act. Those changes helped to quiet the AFL because they meant that no members of AFL-affiliated unions would be covered by the Erdman Act.[28] After a difficult internal fight, the AFL decided not to fight publicly against Olney's bill during the final stages of congressional deliberation. Although the AFL remained opposed, nothing like Gompers's harsh editorials of early 1897 appeared in 1898.

Two of Gompers's letters from the period reveal some of the internal discussion that preceded the AFL's decision to become silent. Andrew Furuseth, President of the Seamen's Union, future legislative representative for the AFL, and a remarkable self-trained expert on judicial reactions to labor legislation, wrote to Gompers in 1896 expressing his strong objections to Olney's bill. Furuseth urged the AFL to take a strong stand and to try to prevent passage of the bill. In his response, Gompers expressed agreement with Furuseth's complaints about the bill, but explained that the AFL would not interfere with the internal decisions of the railroad trade unions about what was best for railroad workers.[29] Later, after receiving a very critical report on the bill from two attorneys in January 1897, Gompers sent a respectful and conciliatory letter to Frank Sargent of the Brotherhood of Locomotive Firemen, explaining the AFL's opposition and politely warning the brotherhoods against defects in the bill.[30]

While the AFL's silence in 1898 may have helped the bill to pass, the AFL's opposition and restraint also makes it difficult to believe that the brotherhoods had the power to exert much influence in Congress. Given that the AFL's vehement opposition did not prevent the House from passing the bill in 1895 or 1897, it seems quite unlikely that the endorsement of the much smaller brotherhoods was sufficient to force legislators to enact the Erdman Act in 1898. Members of Congress were serving other constituencies.

---

[28] The House added the provision exempting seamen in 1895. The Senate added the provision exempting street railways in 1898. Gompers later explained that the AFL leaders decided not to become involved in the final congressional deliberations on the Erdman Act because the exemptions meant that the final version of the bill did not apply to any workers in AFL-affiliated unions (Gompers 1925, 136).

[29] See Gompers letter to Furuseth, March 20, 1896, cited in note 13.

[30] Gompers to Frank Sargent, Grand Chief of Brotherhood of Locomotive Firemen, January 28, 1897, cited in note 13; Siddons and Ralston to Gompers, January 23, 1987, cited in note 14.

Nevertheless, it would be an exaggeration to say that the endorsement of the brotherhoods was irrelevant to congressional deliberations. Supporters of the Erdman Act in Congress did feel that it was important to maintain both the endorsement of the railroad brotherhoods and the silence of the AFL. Each of the four House and Senate committee reports was careful to establish that the railroad brotherhoods supported the bill.[31] And during floor debates, the floor managers were careful to avoid open discussion of the AFL's strong opposition and careful to change the subject whenever that issue arose. The broader record makes it clear, however, that the endorsement of the brotherhoods was not important because the brotherhoods were politically powerful organizations capable of forcing large numbers of legislators to do their bidding. The endorsement did, however, provide cover for legislators who supported a bill that was opposed by most labor organizations and widely understood as unlikely to create an effective arbitration framework.

Some of the most revealing exchanges during floor debates on the Erdman Act came when critics of the bill attempted to draw attention to the AFL's opposition. Usually, the bill's sponsors were able to quiet such criticisms by claiming that legislators should listen to only those labor organizations whose members would be directly affected by the law, the brotherhoods. Nevertheless, some members of Congress continued to question whether the bill was really in the interest of railway workers, and whether the leaders of the brotherhoods were capable of representing the interests of rank-and-file railroad workers. During floor debates in 1895, Rep. William P. Hepburn (R-OH) expressed concern that harsh economic conditions were forcing the brotherhoods to consent to the bill. Hepburn worried that the same economic conditions would prevent the system of arbitration from being fully voluntary (27 *Congressional Record* 2791).

Challenges to the railroad brotherhoods' endorsement became more intense as the bill moved closer to enactment. During the second set of House debates on the bill in 1897, Rep. James G. Maguire (D-CA) called the bill a "dangerous surrender of the individual liberty of all American laborers" (29 *Congressional Record* 2387). A year later, Representative Lewis (D-WA) suggested that the railroad brotherhoods were being duped

---

[31] Letters in support of the bill from the leaders of the Railroad brotherhoods, rather than detailed explanations of the provisions, were the centerpiece of the committee reports for the House in 1895, 1897, and 1898 (House Report 1754, 53rd Congress, on H.R. 8556; House Report 1058, 54th Congress, on H.R. 268; House Report 4334, 55th Congress, on H.R. 4332). The Senate report on the bill in 1898 included similar letters from the brotherhoods (Senate Report 591, 55th Congress, on S. 3662).

into supporting a bad bill. Lewis worried that the leaders of the labor organizations were "unaccustomed to the criminal sinuosities of the law and
the sneaking methods and corrupt purposes of legislative 'workers.'"[32]

When the Senate took up the bill for the first time in 1898, members
made much stronger challenges to the claim that the brotherhoods' endorsement was sufficient reason to vote for the bill. Senator Allen (P-NE)
scoffed at the claim that Congress was passing the bill to help the labor
organizations. Allen claimed the bill was "Janus faced" (31 *Congressional
Record* 4790) and "not drawn . . . as an honest lawyer would draft an honest bill" (31 *Congressional Record* 4793). Senator Turner (Fusionist-WA)
later went even further. Turner questioned whether the railroad labor organizations were competent to evaluate the bill. He stated that it would
be "cruel and wicked to take advantage of the inexperience of this class
of our citizens for the purpose of fastening upon them legislation which
would be injurious to their true interests" (31 *Congressional Record* 4799).

The next day, the debate over how much weight should be given to the
brotherhoods' endorsement continued. After three Senators responded
to an attack on the bill by noting that the railroad unions were happy
with it, Senator Turner urged that the support of the brotherhoods
was "not conclusive upon the judgment and conscience of the Senate"
(31 *Congressional Record* 4849).[33]

While critics like Turner in the Senate and Lewis in the House seem to
have felt that labor leaders were making an honest mistake by endorsing
the Erdman Act, other critics of the bill attributed sinister motives to
the brotherhoods. Senator Rawlins (D-UT) argued that the leaders of the
brotherhoods supported the bill because it served their own interests, not
the interests of workers:

I can well understand how certain labor leaders would desire to put this through.
They, like every other person, will arrogate to themselves as much power as
they can. . . . These labor leaders come here not in the interest of the men – the

---

[32] 31 *Congressional Record* 4641. The bill's floor leaders never allowed such criticisms
to become the focus of discussion. No one responded to Lewis's speech. After Lewis
used up the short time allotted, he was quickly cut off and his remarks in the *Record*
are followed by a long speech by Representative Cochran (R-MO) on the irrelevant
topic of war bonds (31 *Congressional Record* 4642–5).

[33] Senator Mallory (D-FL) made the attack (31 *Congressional Record* 4848). Senators Cullum (R-IL), Lindsay (D-KY), and Kyle (Independent-SD) responded (4848).
Turner did concede that, "The views of the labor organizations, of course, are entitled to a very great respect in considering the provisions of the bill because their
interests are affected by it" (4848).

individuals whose rights are to be affected – but they come here asking Congress to vest in them the power to submit the rights of person and the right of property of the membership of their organization to arbitration without their direction or authorization or consent. No wonder they come here and say this bill is satisfactory to them (31 *Congressional Record* 4852).

For the most part, however, criticisms like these were drowned out as the floor managers devoted much of the allotted time to seemingly irrelevant matters.[34] Despite these attacks, most of the members of Congress who spoke appeared willing to swallow doubts about the value of the bill so long as the brotherhoods remained unflinching in their official endorsement.[35] Just before the House adopted the final version of the Erdman Act and sent it to the president, Rep. Thomas McEwan (R-NJ) captured the sentiment of many when he declared that responsibility for problems with the bill would fall not on the legislators who voted for the bill, but on the leaders of the brotherhoods who urged the House members to do so. Demonstrating a unique capacity to mix metaphors, McEwan noted, "their blood will be on their own heads" (31 *Congressional Record* 5053).

"As Harmless as an Infant": The Erdman Act as Symbolism over Substance

Passage of the Erdman Act also appears to have been aided as more and more participants in the congressional debates began to realize that the bill was unlikely to have much effect at all on railroad labor disputes. By 1898, even the most vocal supporters of the bill conceded that the bill's impact would be largely symbolic. As the bill moved closer to passage, efforts to tinker with technical aspects of the bill were interrupted with jokes and laughter as members became increasingly vocal in expressing the view that such changes, like the bill itself, were irrelevant.

The best example of a supporter of the bill conceding its likely ineffectiveness can be found in a sympathetic speech made by Representative Sulzer (D-NY) just before initial House passage of the bill in 1898.

---

[34] Rawlins's speech is followed (in the record, at least) by a long discussion of the merits of the gold standard, and the attack went unanswered until much later, when Senator Caffrey mentioned it briefly in a speech supporting the bill (31 *Congressional Record* 4854–5).

[35] Even Senator Allen, who gave the harshest attack on the leadership of the brotherhoods, ended up voting for the bill. This was perhaps in pursuit of his promise (31 *Congressional Record* 4794) that he would vote for the bill if the brotherhoods still supported it after hearing his criticisms.

Sulzer announced that he was in favor of the bill, but expressed limited expectations about its likely effect:

The bill is necessarily in the nature of an experiment. It is a step, however, in the right direction. It is but the beginning of what we hope will be accomplished in the near future, when labor shall receive its just reward and its just recognition. . . . The bill does not go far enough to suit me. It gives no additional benefit to, and confers no more advantage on, the men who work for the railroads . . . but I want to see the bill pass . . . on the theory that half a loaf is better than no bread (31 *Congressional Record* 4647).

After explaining that the meaning of the bill would have to be determined in the courts, Sulzer made an overt effort to shape the interpretation the courts would later give to the statute:

In case the question of legislative intent should subsequently arise in some legal proceeding growing out of a contention regarding the construction and meaning of this bill. . . . I now deliberately place this statement on record, for the guidance and information of the court, that this bill is a labor bill intended to aid organized labor, and should be construed, where any doubt exists, liberally and favorably in the interest of the employee. If this is done, it will prove a good law, if it is not done, but on the contrary the provisions of this bill are construed by the courts in the interests of the employers, the railroads, then I am afraid this measure will be a delusion and a snare so far as organized labor is concerned. Let us pass this bill this afternoon and hope for the best (31 *Congressional Record* 4647).

Unfortunately, as Sulzer was no doubt aware, conventions for interpreting statutes made it unlikely that judges would encounter his advice in the record, and even more unlikely that they would take it seriously.

Sentiments similar to Sulzer's were later expressed in the Senate as well. Senator Teller, an Independent Silver Republican from Colorado, declared "it is a trial bill, an experiment, which a great many people believe will not succeed. I confess I have very little hope of its success myself, but if we make the effort we at least can then determine whether we can proceed hereafter in this way or whether it will be necessary to adopt some other method" (31 *Congressional Record* 4844). Senator Spooner acknowledged that mere passage of the bill would not guarantee its success, and suggested that the meaning of the bill would be determined by the efforts of affected parties to construct its symbolic impact (31 *Congressional Record* 4848).

In the final stages of congressional consideration of the bill, the House avoided a conference by voting to adopt the version of the bill passed in the Senate. Some members of the House claimed that the bill's supporters were avoiding the conference because they feared that many Senators had already changed their minds and would use the opportunity to vote on a conference report to scuttle the bill.[36] Under these unusual conditions, the people's representatives were positively giggly about the weakness of the bill and its likely irrelevance. In a speech that was several times interrupted by laughter, Rep. William L. Greene (P-NE) claimed that neither the supporters nor opponents of the bill had "elucidate[d] its vague and mysterious sections" and called the bill "a species of buncombe" (31 *Congressional Record* 5052).[37] But after asking rhetorically, "Why not bring forward a bill that will really relieve labor, and not a mere sop like this?" Greene also announced that he would still vote "yes" on the bill. A raucous House, led by Rep. Charles Henry (R-IN), asked Greene why he still wanted to support the bill. Greene explained that he would because "it is as harmless as an infant. While it does no good, it is also powerless for harm, but may tend to agitate the question until something effectual will be done" (31 *Congressional Record* 5052).[38]

These comments serve as a powerful final reminder that the meaning of the decision in Congress to pass the Erdman Act and the later Supreme Court decision overturning Section 10 must be considered in the context of the broader congressional decision-making processes that produced a symbolic but ultimately ineffective law. The Erdman Act inspired more laughter than passion when it finally emerged from Congress.

CONCLUSION

My inquiry into the Erdman Act reveals that the impact of the judicial decision in *Adair* was different than it appears in more conventional accounts. While the Court's ruling did strike down one provision of the statute, the ruling cannot be understood as some counter-majoritarian negation of any labor organization's successful efforts to use its political power to win favorable changes in policies through the democratic

---

[36] As the House leaders announced they would take up the Senate amendments rather than request a conference, Representative McEwan claimed that the reason for doing so was that many senators had changed their minds and now opposed the bill (31 *Congressional Record* 5048). McEwan claimed the Senate amendments to the House bill were made at the request of the railroad companies, but also noted that he had received written communication from the brotherhoods saying that they still supported the bill.

[37] Greene identified the following specific weaknesses: There was no provision for compelling parties to submit to a judgment, and no enforcement procedures, other than the equity provision in Section 3, which made it unlikely that many disputants would bind themselves to arbitration.

[38] There is another exchange of jokes and laughter later between Rhea and Greene (31 *Congressional Record* 5053).

process. The Erdman Act was neither a clear-cut victory for labor organizations nor the result of labor organizations flexing political muscle.
At the request of the Attorney General who had engineered the violent
defeat of the most significant and potentially transformative democratic
uprising of the era, legislators produced a bill of uncertain meaning that
consciously assigned the courts a large role in making substantive policy
decisions. Although the Erdman Act ostensibly provided an alternative
to the judge-centered policy of labor injunctions that had defeated the
Pullman Strike, it was not an attempt to reverse a judicial policy, to rein
in the courts, or to prevent the courts from continuing to play an important role in the regulation of labor's collective activities. If labor had been
politically powerful, it seems likely that the legislators in Congress would
have passed a very different law, and likely that legislators would have
responded more favorably to other legislative demands that were higher
priorities for larger labor organizations.

More generally, the Erdman Act case reveals some of the pitfalls of
the dominant *legislative baseline framework*. Because other scholars have
overestimated the responsiveness of legislators, they have overestimated
the success labor organizations had in the legislative branch. This in turn
has led scholars to overestimate the importance of the courts as barriers
to democratic processes.

A number of other general lessons about interbranch interaction
emerge from this inquiry into congressional consideration of the Erdman
Act. The first is that when some dramatic event like the Pullman Strike
provides legislators with an imperative to make some response, legislators
may base their response on expectations about effects that have little to
do with the policy issues ostensibly addressed by the statute. Legislators
will sometimes also be willing to build support for a bill by making compromises that create uncertainties about the meaning and effectiveness of
the bill. When the Erdman Act passed, even its supporters conceded that
its meaning was uncertain and that the law's value was mostly symbolic.
The perception that many compromises in the bill's language made it less
likely that it would be invoked appear to have made it much easier for
many members of Congress to swallow doubts and vote for the bill.

Second, members of Congress sometimes invite the courts to play an
important policy-making role in the text of a new law. In the case of the
Erdman Act, legislators rejected proposals that would have placed clearer
limits on the power of the courts to interfere in future labor disputes.
Members instead consciously enlisted the aid of the courts by assigning
judges a broadly defined enforcement role that would allow judges to

determine the outcome of particular conflicts and to decide substantive policy issues.

Third, the Erdman Act demonstrates that the willingness of members of Congress to pass legislation on behalf of the representatives of one group of labor organizations need not be taken as an indication that "labor" had attained a high level of political power. If "labor" or the railroad brotherhoods had been powerful enough to force a majority in Congress to support their positions, Congress would undoubtedly have passed a very different bill. Legislators would also have responded to demands that were much higher priorities for labor organizations in 1898 than a criminal ban on blacklisting and yellow-dog contracts.

Labor organizations were not primarily responsible for shaping the language in the Erdman Act or shaping congressional attempts to modify Olney's original proposal. The preferences of legislators and the preferences of labor leaders did not converge around any particular policy outcome. The common ground was instead the belief that the organizing ideology of the railroad brotherhoods was preferable to the radicalism exemplified by Eugene Debs. However, the desire of Olney and many members of Congress to reward and strengthen the brotherhoods does not establish that the existing level of political power possessed by the railroad brotherhoods was greater than the power of other organizations. Passage of the bill in part reflects legislators' desire to manipulate the relative power of different types of labor organizations in order to establish conservative railroad labor organizations as an alternative to labor radicalism.

Thus, the legislative outcome does not provide a very straightforward baseline against which to measure which groups had political power and influence. In fact, passage of the bill was less a reflection of the relative strengths of different labor organizations than a result of a conscious decision by legislators to strengthen one group in order to weaken potentially more powerful rivals. Such efforts to use legislation to manipulate the underlying political terrain should be of enormous interest to scholars interested in assessing democratic responsiveness in our constitutional system. Many scholars dismiss concerns about elite influence in the democratic process by citing instances where Congress appears responsive to insurgent organizations. Troublingly, however, a case like the Erdman Act reveals that elite manipulation can easily be mistaken for democratic responsiveness by scholars who use the conventional theoretical framework. Developing a better appreciation of how legislators use symbolic legislation to manipulate the way people organize themselves should lead to a reassessment of the responsiveness of the "democratic" branches.

The fourth and final lesson is that researchers should not try to understand the impact of the courts by looking only at how the courts shape the policy outcomes with which isolated statutory provisions are ostensibly occupied; in this case, the policy banning yellow-dog contracts. Such an approach can be very misleading. Legislators' reasons for passing laws, and labor leaders' reasons for endorsing laws, sometimes have little to do with their expectations about the precise technical policy changes that such statutes purport to make. Participants in the legislative process might be more concerned about the extra-policy side effects of new legislation, for example, the effect passage of legislation will have on the relative strengths of different organized interests. The comments of Representative Sulzer and Senator Teller reveal that legislators make decisions about statutes after making calculations about how the symbolic impact of passage might shape subsequent political battles. In such cases, scholars who assess the effectiveness of democratic processes by looking only at whether a statute attains its advertised policy goals are likely to draw misleading conclusions.

It is clear that the significance of the Supreme Court ruling in *Adair* was not simply that judges reversed clear majoritarian outcomes of democratic processes. Section 10 and *Adair v United States* are merely the sideshow to a more complicated longer term struggle that shaped not only labor policies but also labor organizations. The judicial branch's more significant impact came long before the ruling in *Adair,* when legislators took advantage of the presence of judges as interpreters of statutes and thus distorted the democratic process in Congress that produced the Erdman Act.

Note, finally, that the most significant distortion of the democratic process came not from unelected judges courts, but from the allegedly democratic and responsive Congress. By assigning the courts the responsibility for deciding the particular contours of policy, legislators shirked their responsibility to make a clear response to an important policy problem. Furthermore, it was legislators who tried to use a symbolic enactment to manipulate the way workers organized for future economic and political actions. It is a mistake to ignore those effects, and a mistake to identify such a statute as a baseline against which to measure the legitimacy of outcomes in a democratic system.

4

Killing with Kindness

Legislative Ambiguity, Judicial Policy Making, and the Clayton Act

> This pen with which the President signed the Clayton bill has been added to the collection of famous pens at the A.F. of L. headquarters – trophies of humanitarian legislation secured for the workers of America. This last pen will be given the place of greatest honor – it is symbolic of the most comprehensive and most fundamental legislation on behalf of human liberty that has been enacted anywhere in the world. The Clayton law gives bones and sinews to an academic ideal of freedom – it secures industrial freedom and makes the workers free in thought and in act.
>
> AFL President Samuel Gompers, *American Federationist*, November 1914, 974

> It is but declaratory of the law as it stood before.
>
> Justice Mahlon Pitney, Opinion of the Supreme Court on the Clayton Act, in *Duplex v Deering*, 254 U.S. 443, 470

Upon passage, the labor provisions of the Clayton Act were celebrated by the leaders of the American Federation of Labor (AFL) as a landmark reform, the most important legislative victory ever achieved by the American labor movement. Its subsequent failure to achieve its apparent policy goals has been the subject of continual scholarly interest and concern (Frankfurter and Green 1930, 165–73; Jones 1957; Kutler 1962; Bernstein 1960, ch. 4, esp. 209–10; Forbath 1991, 147–58). Because the failure of the labor provisions is directly traceable to the interpretation that the Supreme Court imposed on each of the celebrated labor provisions, the Clayton Act has become one of the central building blocks of the claim that unelected judges reversed gains made by labor through democratic processes in legislatures.

The most important Supreme Court ruling on the celebrated labor provisions grew out of a dispute between the Duplex Printing Press Company
and the International Association of Machinists (*Duplex Printing v Deering*
(254 U.S. 443)). Duplex was one of four press manufacturers in the United
States, and the only one that refused to recognize the machinists union as
the bargaining representative of its workers. The dispute that reached the
Supreme Court began when the machinists organized a boycott of Duplex
products in order to prod Duplex to recognize the union. The boycott
came after the other press manufacturers threatened to abandon existing
agreements with the union because Duplex held a competitive advantage
as the sole nonunion shop. During the boycott, members of the union
refused to handle, transport, or install Duplex presses. The boycotting
activity took place mostly in New York, where the other printing press
companies were located and where demand for printing presses was
highest.

The boycott hurt Duplex's business and the company sought an
injunction in the federal court to forbid the union and its members from
continuing the boycott. The company sought the injunction under provisions in the Clayton Act authorizing private parties to request injunctive
relief from unlawful restraints of trade. Before passage of the Clayton Act,
judges had often issued injunctions against similar labor boycotts after
finding such activity to be unlawful. However, two lower federal courts
refused Duplex's request for the injunction in this case. Both the district
and circuit courts ruled that sections 6 and 20 of the Clayton Act exempted
the boycott from injunctive relief.[1] If other federal courts had followed
the interpretation offered by those courts, the Clayton Act may well have
become the dramatic prolabor reform that Samuel Gompers seemed to
expect when the Clayton Act passed in 1914. Things did not work out
that way, however. The Supreme Court rejected the labor-friendly interpretation of the lower courts and instructed the district court to issue the
injunction requested by the Duplex Company.

The Court's ruling was devastating to the policy goals of labor organizations. Before the Court ruled, the attorneys for the workers and
the company had offered competing interpretations of language in the
labor provisions. The ruling eventually made by the Court established the
authoritative reading of provisions in Section 6 immunizing labor from
the antitrust laws, and of several provisions in Section 20 that placed
limits on the use of injunctions in certain types of labor cases.

---

[1] 253 Fed 722, 2d Cir. 1918, affirming 247 F. 192; 1917 U.S. Dist, S.D. New York.

The language in sections 6 and 20 grew out of a vigorous and complicated political campaign for injunction reform that the AFL had been engaged in since before the turn of the century. Yet at every interpretive crossroads, the Supreme Court majority chose an interpretation that favored the interests of employers over workers. In effect, the Court read the labor provisions not as an attempt by Congress to change the law of industrial relations, but as a mere legislative codification of the much-criticized judge-made law that was in place before passage of the Clayton Act. The Court thus preserved the status quo, and the Clayton Act's labor provisions made no dramatic reforms to existing labor laws.

As noted in Chapter 1, many scholars have blamed the hostility of judges toward labor organization for the failure of the Clayton Act to achieve its advertised goal of curbing injunctions (Kutler 1962; Jones 1957; Forbath 1991, 154–8, 200–1; Hattam 1993, 163–4). Such scholars have found the Court's reading of the statute as a codification of existing law to be inconsistent with the spirit of provisions that members of Congress passed on behalf of labor organizations; provisions that were celebrated as major reforms upon passage. On the other hand, Justice Pitney's opinion of the Court claimed repeatedly to be following the intent of Congress. Pitney quoted floor speeches in Congress to support some of his conclusions. More importantly, Pitney's opinion relies heavily on a detailed parsing of the actual text of the statute. While the Court's critics may be right that Pitney could have chosen other, more pro-labor readings that would also have been consistent with the confusing statutory text, nothing in Pitney's reading appears to contradict the text of the statute.

The ambiguities in the statutory text seem to have affected the outcome produced by the Court. It may be that the justices would have voted to allow the injunction no matter what language Congress had enacted. Judges can always invent ambiguities where none really exist, give odd readings to seemingly clear statutory language, or simply declare that a disliked law is unconstitutional. However, the ambiguous language in the Clayton Act made it easy for the Supreme Court to give a hostile reading to the statute while maintaining at least a veneer of legitimacy. Because of the ambiguity in the statute, the Court majority was able to impose a probusiness outcome without striking down any of the Clayton Act's labor provisions and without ignoring or openly contradicting any text in the statute. As a result, criticisms of the Courts' ruling, both at the time and more recently, have been based less on claims about the text than

on claims about the broader reform ambitions expressed by the legislators and labor leaders who sponsored the labor provisions. Scholars have
used the exuberant statements of labor leaders like Samuel Gompers to
provide support for their critiques of the court and assessments of the
courts as barriers (e.g., Forbath 1991, 157). The claims made by labor
leaders deserve more careful scrutiny than they have previously received,
however. Statements of participants cannot be taken at face value without scrutinizing the broader record. Moreover, the record of participant
reactions is also ambiguous. The Supreme Court was also able to find
some support for its position in speeches by congressional leaders and in
committee reports.

The question that I address in this chapter is why the version of the
Clayton Act enacted by Congress contained ambiguous language that
is consistent with both the prolabor interpretations offered by unions
and the contradictory probusiness interpretation that the Supreme Court
imposed on the statute. As noted in Chapter 1, scholars and judges typically treat ambiguity in statutory text and history as though that ambiguity
is the result of some unavoidable accident or oversight. Such scholars
might point out correctly that it was very difficult to create legislative
language that could address complicated issues of labor relations law
with complete clarity and finality. Such difficulties made it inevitable that
questions about the meaning of the statute would arise during implementation, and thus inevitable that judges would have to make decisions
that established the authoritative meaning of the statute. Such an explanation was suggested even before Congress passed the Clayton Act by
Rep. Robert Thomas (D-KY). Thomas, an active participant in the deliberations on the act, suggested during House floor debates that creating
clear statutory language is "sometimes one of the most difficult things to
accomplish." Thomas claimed that the difficulty "arises from the meaning of which words in the English language in combination with other
words is susceptible" and suggested that judges were difficult to control
because they sometimes invent "constructions which never occurred to the
legislator in framing the statute" (51 *Congressional Record* 14020). Legislators and scholars who feel that ambiguity and interpretive controversies
simply cannot be avoided usually want judges to resolve ambiguities by
making a conscientious effort to discover and match a baseline position
established by elected legislators.

However, even though the difficulties that Representative Thomas mentions are real, scholars should not assume that the constructions offered
by judges "never occurred to" members of Congress without first making

empirical inquiry into the circumstances that produced ambiguous statutory text and history. This chapter makes such an inquiry by looking in detail at the legislative processes that created the ambiguities in the Clayton Act. I find that the ambiguities and uncertainties in the Clayton Act that empowered hostile judges to determine the act's meaning were not accidents. The ambiguities were the result of deliberate compromises made by legislators. Those legislators understood that they were creating uncertainty that would have to be resolved by judges. Given these circumstances, efforts to identify the legitimate outcome by finding the appropriate legislative baseline are misguided. There is no policy baseline to be discovered because legislators consciously decided not to create one.

My inquiry into legislative records is not an attempt to identify some true legislative intent, and my conclusion is *not* that the judges who ruled on the Clayton Act were correctly following some baseline position established in Congress. Rather, my claim is that legislators deliberately refrained from establishing any specific policy position and instead deliberately created ambiguity that gave judges discretion to make substantive policy choices. To reach this conclusion, I shift my focus away from the conventional quest for some imagined legislative intent. I focus instead on questions about how well legislators were able to anticipate the role later played by the courts, and about whether legislators took available steps to limit judicial discretion. It seems essential to ask and try to answer such questions before deciding whether independent judges thwarted the will of the legislature. Thus, for this chapter I try to understand the relevant strategic choices by tracing the evolution of the Clayton Act's labor provisions from their origins in a series of more radical reform proposals that the AFL began to advocate as early as 1900.

Unlike other accounts of the court rulings on the Clayton Act, the goal of this inquiry is not to determine whether judges were hostile to labor (they were) or whether judicial hostility toward labor affected the choices that judges made as they gave meaning to the labor provisions (it did). Observations about judicial hostility, while interesting, do not explain why judges were able to be so influential with respect to the policy issues addressed in the Clayton Act. To understand the importance of courts as barriers to democratic accountability, it is more essential to know how participants in the legislative process made strategic decisions that created or limited the opportunities for judges to influence labor policies. Without first understanding the strategic choices that participants made before statutes passed, it is not possible to understand or explain the inability of labor organizations to use legislation to advance their goal of ending injunctions.

THE ANTITRUST EXEMPTION : SECTION 6 IN CONGRESS AND THE COURTS

The first interpretive question confronted by the Supreme Court in *Duplex* concerned language in Section 6 of the Clayton Act that appeared to exempt labor from the antitrust laws. Section 6 resolves:

That the labor of a human being is not a commodity or article of commerce. Nothing contained in the antitrust laws shall be construed to forbid the existence and operation of labor, agricultural, or horticultural organizations, instituted for the purposes of mutual help, and not having capital stock or conducted for profit, or to forbid or restrain individual members of such organizations from lawfully carrying out the legitimate objects thereof; nor shall such organizations, or the members thereof, be held or construed to be illegal combinations or conspiracies in restraint of trade under the antitrust laws.

The labor organizations that supported the Clayton Act claimed that Section 6 responded to one of labor's long-standing grievances by fully exempting labor from the antitrust laws. Attorneys for employers, however, claimed that Section 6 provided only a very limited form of protection for the activities of labor organizations.

Justice Pitney's opinion of the Court in *Duplex* chose the interpretation favored by employers. Pitney's opinion scrutinized the text of the provision in detail, and focused almost exclusively on the lengthy second sentence. Pitney's most important claim was that the language in that sentence established two levels of protection for labor organizations. The first part of the sentence articulates a very broad protection for labor organizations by telling judges not to use the antitrust laws to "forbid the existence and operation" of labor and other organizations. However, Pitney argued that the second part of the provision established a more limited type of protection for the "individual members of such organizations." Pitney found evidence for the claim that the statute provided less protection for the *activities* of labor than for labor *organizations* in the text of the provision. In particular, Pitney noted that the protections afforded activities were qualified by the words "legitimate" and "lawfully." These qualifying phrases, Pitney argued, meant that the broad language stating that labor organizations could not be declared unlawful did not extend to the immunities given to labor's activities. Pitney noted:

there is nothing in the section to exempt such an organization or its members from accountability where it or they depart from its normal and legitimate objects, and engage in an actual combination or conspiracy in restraint of trade. And by no fair or permissible construction can it be taken as authorizing any activity otherwise unlawful (469).

In effect, Pitney reads the qualifying phrases as a signal that instead of giving a blanket antitrust exemption to labor, legislators wanted judges to continue to apply the antitrust laws when members of labor organizations engaged in unlawful conduct. This reading was potentially fatal to the claims made by the workers engaged in the boycott against the Duplex Company. If judges decided that the workers' conduct was "unlawful," the decision by Congress to exempt the "lawful" conduct of labor organizations was simply not relevant to their case.

Given Pitney's focus on the qualifying words, the crucial issue for the justices became the question of whether the machinists taking part in the boycott were "lawfully" carrying out the "legitimate" objects of a labor organization. Unfortunately, however, the legislators who passed the act had not defined the terms "lawfully" and "legitimate" anywhere in the statute. The absence of a new definition for those key terms is what gave the Supreme Court discretion as the justices assigned meaning to the Clayton Act. Absent clear instructions from the legislature, determining what counts as "lawful" behavior is typically very much the prerogative of judges. Thus, the Court majority was able to treat the congressional decision to include general words like "lawfully" and "legitimate" in the provision as an invitation to judges to continue to apply the widely known (and widely resented) judge-made standards that judges had developed prior to passage of the Clayton Act. Pitney's claim, in effect, is that legislators would have said something specific in the text of the statute if they had wanted the courts to alter their conduct and follow some new definition of "lawful."

The Court's stance meant that Section 6 did not prevent judges from issuing an injunction against the machinists who targeted the Duplex Company. Before the Clayton Act passed, judges had established that boycotts like the one against Duplex were "unlawful." Absent a redefinition of "unlawful" in the new statute, Pitney assumed that the decision by Congress to include the word "lawfully" in Section 6 meant that legislators wanted judges to leave such practices undisturbed. Because the Supreme Court's ruling established the authoritative interpretation of Section 6, it meant that all such boycotts would remain subject to injunctions.

Many observers since 1921 have criticized Pitney's reading of the statute. Such criticisms seem easy to make. While Pitney's reading does not obviously contradict the confusing text of the provision, his interpretation creates a puzzle that Pitney never addresses: Why would legislators go to the trouble of enacting a provision that did not make any changes in existing law? It seems difficult to explain the decision to pass Section 6 as anything other than an attempt to respond to the AFL's long-standing demand for relief from judicial applications of the antitrust laws to labor organizations. Justice Louis Brandeis suggested such an explanation in his dissenting opinion when he reminded his colleagues that the statute "was the fruit of unceasing agitation, which extended over more than twenty years" (484). Many scholars have followed Brandeis's suggestion and assumed that legislators passed Section 6 to satisfy the AFL's demand for a full exemption from the antitrust laws. Perhaps legislators never imagined the judges would think that the statue made a distinction between prohibiting the existence of organizations and prohibiting the activities of members of organizations.

However, critics of the court have their own puzzle to explain: Why was Pitney able to find at least some support for his position in the text of Section 6? Why, for example, did legislators include qualifying words like "lawfully" in the clause exempting worker activities if legislators had intended to provide a full exemption? Perhaps the support Pitney found for his reading in the text of the statute was simply the result of some accident or carelessness in drafting. If it had "never occurred" to members of Congress that the courts would read the word "lawfully" as an invitation to exercise discretion, then perhaps scholars are right to conclude the Court's probusiness reading of Section 6 amounted to a judicial reversal of legislators' reform intentions. A second possibility, however, is that legislators did anticipate that judges would interpret phrases like "lawfully" and "legitimate" as qualifications that empowered them to exercise discretion; and also that legislators anticipated that judges would thus find different levels of protection for labor organizations and the activities of such organizations. If this second explanation is correct, then any assessment of the courts as barriers to Congress has to await a more thorough explanation of the reasons why legislators would deliberately include language that empowered the courts.

The Antitrust Exemption in Congress 1890–1914

Two key questions about legislators' decisions on Section 6 are: 1) How did legislators expect judges to respond to words like "lawfully" and "legitimate"? and 2) Did legislators expect judges to find different levels of protection for labor organizations and for the activities of their members? I find that participants clearly anticipated that judges would interpret words like "lawfully" as substantial qualifications on the antitrust exemption that expanded judicial discretion. Moreover, questions about whether language like that in Section 6 of the Clayton Act would cover the *activities* of organized workers as well as workers' organizations had not only been anticipated by members of Congress before the Clayton Act passed, but had been discussed and debated extensively and repeatedly by legislators for fourteen years.

The task of uncovering the evolution of Section 6 is complicated by the fact that language in the provision has roots in two related but distinct AFL legislative campaigns. The two campaigns proceeded in different legislative tracks and produced separate bills through different congressional committees from 1890 until the campaigns merged in 1912. The first AFL campaign was an effort to add a provision containing a labor exemption to any new statute amending the nation's antitrust laws. This campaign heated up each time legislators seriously considered bills to revise laws related to restraints on trade, that is, with the Sherman Act of 1890, the Littlefield bill of 1900, the Hepburn bill of 1908, and the Clayton bills of 1912 and 1914.[2] The AFL's second campaign was an effort to include an antitrust exemption in the freestanding antiinjunction bills that the AFL was backing during the same period. The AFL backed at least one antiinjunction bill in every Congress between 1900 and 1914. Each of those bills included provisions that were designed to provide some protection from the antitrust laws to labor's collective activities.

The campaign for a labor exemption in antitrust bills. The roots of the AFL's campaign for an antitrust exemption go back to before Congress passed the Sherman Act in 1890.[3] As legislators debated that statute, AFL leaders

---

[2] The Clayton bill was the only one of these bills to become law.
[3] The history of the AFL's antitrust campaign is summarized by Rep. Robert Henry (D-TX) in a floor speech as 51 *Congressional Record* 9540–1, and by Gompers 1925, vol. II, ch. XXXVI. Gompers also describes his role in the 1890 negotiations in the 1908 House Hearings, 54–5. For secondary accounts, see Ernst 1989b and Ernst 1995, ch. 9. Forbath (1991, 147–58) provides an account of related state legislation.

lobbied for a provision exempting labor organizations from its operations. At one point, the Senate voted to add a provision that seemed responsive to such concerns. The provision stated:

> this act shall not be construed to apply to any arrangements, agreements, or combinations between laborers made with a view of lessening the number of hours of labor or the increasing of their wages

This labor exemption never made it into the Sherman Act. After Senate leaders promised AFL President Samuel Gompers that the law could never be used against labor organizations, the amendment was removed by a Senate committee, and the Sherman Act passed without any provision regarding the application of the antitrust laws to labor unions.[4]

Although the Supreme Court did not officially confirm that the Sherman Act could be applied to unions until 1908 (*Loewe v Lawlor* (208 U.S. 274)), the AFL's lingering concerns led its leaders to push for a labor exemption when legislators attempted to modify the Sherman Act with the Littlefield bill of 1900 (H.R. 10539, 59th Congress).[5] During floor debates on the Littlefield bill, the House passed an amendment that added the following exemption for labor organizations to the bill:

> Nothing in this act shall be so construed as to apply to trade unions or other labor organizations organized for the purpose of regulating wages, hours of labor, or other conditions under which labor is to be performed.

The Littlefield bill passed the House with this amendment intact, but the bill later died in a Senate committee and thus never became law.

The next serious attempt to amend the antitrust laws came when both the House and Senate conducted lengthy hearings on antitrust reform in 1908. The AFL sent representatives to the hearings and again requested an explicit exemption from the antitrust laws. Congress did not ultimately pass any new antitrust legislation that year, but the hearings did provide another forum for a lively debate between the AFL and various

---

[4] Frankfurter and Green (1930, 139–43) discuss what happened as a result of the Sherman Act's silence on the labor question: The Sherman Act ended up being applied quite frequently to labor unions. Ambiguity in the Sherman Act was not limited to the labor question. Graber (1993) uses the open-endedness of other provisions in the Sherman Act as an example in his analysis of legislative deference to the judiciary and judicial review.

[5] In the minority report on the Littlefield bill, the supporters of this amendment noted with dismay that the *only* successful criminal convictions under the Sherman Act to that time had been against labor organizations rather than corporations (*House Report* 1506, pt. 2, p. 4, 56th Congress).

employers' associations about the wisdom and constitutionality of such an exemption.[6]

Six years later Congress began considering the proposal that eventually became the Clayton Act. The original bill contained a provision that was in many respects similar to the labor exemptions added to antitrust bills in 1890, 1900, 1902, and 1908. There was, however, one crucial difference: The earlier proposals had all stated that the antitrust laws shall not "be construed to apply" to labor organizations, while the Clayton Act version stated that the laws shall not "be construed to forbid the existence of" labor organizations. That important difference, which turned out to be very important in *Duplex*, did not go unnoticed. The difference was noted repeatedly by legislators during House floor debates on the Clayton bill, and also in a letter that Gompers and the leaders of the Railroad Brotherhoods sent to the House in 1914 demanding restoration of the original "shall not apply" language.[7] Yet even though members of Congress were clearly concerned about the adequacy of the language, legislators never restored the "shall not apply" language to Section 6.

Antitrust Provisions in the AFL's Antiinjunction Bills. To understand what members expected to result from the "forbid the existence" language in Section 6, it is important to place the decision to adopt that language in the context of the AFL's long campaign for antiinjunction legislation. There are some strong and revealing links between the language adopted as Section 6 of the Clayton Act and provisions in the AFL's early antiinjunction bills that restricted judicial remedies for labor activities that restrained trade. Looking at the record of congressional consideration of these earlier legislative proposals reveals that questions about whether

---

[6] Before 1914, Congress enacted only one piece of legislation connected to the controversy over the application of the Sherman Act to labor unions: the "Hughes Amendment" to a sundry civil appropriations bill. The amendment stated that the Justice Department could not use funds from the appropriation to pursue labor organizations for violations of the Sherman Act. The amendment passed the House in 1910 but was rejected by the Senate. Both houses passed the same rider in 1912, but President Taft vetoed it. After the rider passed again the next year, it finally became law under Woodrow Wilson's reluctant signature. Despite being elected on a platform pledging relief from the antitrust laws for labor, however, Wilson sent Congress an ominous message saying that Justice would sidestep the restraint by finding funds in other appropriations bills to conduct prosecutions (Jones 1957, 205).

[7] The difference was discussed in detail in an exchange between MacDonald (P-MI) and Murdock (R-KA), 51 *Congressional Record* 9545. Letter from Gompers, et al. to U.S. House of Representatives, May 5, 1914, *American Federation of Labor Records: The Samuel Gompers Era*, reel 26, index number 2369.

Section 6 fully exempted only labor organizations or exempted both the organizations and their activities did not arise unexpectedly for the first time when the Court decided *Duplex* in 1921. The record reveals that confusion and controversy about the scope of the antitrust exemption can be traced back two decades to the AFL's earliest antiinjunction proposals.

The debate about exempting organizations or activities first arose during debates over the Hoar bill of 1900 (H.R. 8917). That bill, like all the other bills in this second legislative campaign, attempted to curb injunctions by changing the laws judges used to justify injunctions against labor organizations. The Hoar bill aimed to narrow the definition of criminal conspiracy, an early legislative strategy that the AFL soon abandoned as judges stopped regulating labor organizations as criminal conspiracies (Gregory and Katz, 1979, chs. III and IV). Even though the strategy was abandoned, the striking parallels between the Hoar bill and Section 6 of the Clayton Act are worth exploring.

The provision in the earlier bill describing the exemption from conspiracy prosecutions stated:

no agreement, combination, or contract by or between two or more persons to do, or to procure to be done, or not to do, or procure not to be done any act in contemplation or furtherance of a trade dispute … shall be deemed criminal. …

The relevance of this general provision to the antitrust laws is established in a later clause declaring:

nor shall such agreement, combination, or contract be considered as in restraint of trade or commerce.

What is striking about this provision is that it appears to have the same limitation that the Supreme Court discovered in Section 6 of the Clayton Act two decades later: It protects the "agreement" or "combination" from being declared criminal, but does not protect the activities undertaken in pursuit of the agreement. In the context of the Hoar bill, however, this apparent limitation was not as devastating as the similar limitation in Section 6 of the Clayton Act. Unlike the Clayton Act, the Hoar bill supplemented the provision providing protection for *organizations* with additional provisions that specified additional protection for *activities* of workers who were parties to labor agreements.[8]

---

[8] For example, the Hoar bill's redefinition of conspiracy declared that activities undertaken by combinations of individuals were illegal only if the same activities would be illegal if engaged in by a single individual: "nor shall those engaged therein be indictable or otherwise punishable for the crime of conspiracy if such act committed

It may seem like a stretch to claim that the content of the obscure and ultimately unsuccessful Hoar bill has any relevance to debates that took place more than a decade later on the Clayton Act. However, instead of being quickly forgotten, the questions first raised in 1900 arose again and again as each intervening Congress considered similar proposals in the years leading up to passage of the Clayton Act in 1914. Congressional debates on the Hoar bill and subsequent bills raised interpretive questions almost identical to the interpretive questions that later arose about the Clayton Act in *Duplex v Deering*. At a minimum, this finding makes it difficult to maintain that the distinction that the Supreme Court made between the organizations and activities was a strained and unforeseeable reading that had never occurred to legislators. Given that a debate about precisely the same issues had already been taking place in Congress for fourteen years, it seems reasonable to assume that members of Congress in 1914 could have anticipated that the Supreme Court might choose the narrower reading of the ambiguous language in Section 6.

Furthermore, the records regarding congressional debates on the earlier proposal suggest that members of Congress (and outside organizations) consciously used ambiguity about the scope of the antitrust exemption to build support for the bill. The relevant debate occurred for the first time when the House Judiciary Committee recommended that the entire provision referring to "restraint of trade" be removed from the Hoar bill in 1900. The conservative committee majority that voted to remove the provision was obviously quite aware of the distinction between exempting organizations and exempting the activities of their members. The committee report explained that the "restraint of trade" provision was removed precisely because it exempted the activities of labor organizations from the antitrust laws and not just the organizations themselves.[9]

A committee minority's report opposed removing the provision. Significantly, however, the minority members did not argue that the provision should be kept because it was a good idea to exempt the activities of labor organizations from the antitrust laws. They instead argued that the

---

by one person would not be punishable as a crime." The authors of the Hoar bill were obviously conscious of the distinction between protecting the "existence" and protecting the "activities" of labor organizations, and thus used a separate provision to make it clear that the bill protected both. The distinction is lost, however, if language like that in the Hoar bill is removed from its original context.

[9] House Report 2007, 56th Congress, 2nd Session. The relevant part of the report is missing in the CIS series, but is reprinted in the *Congressional Record* for February 18, 1901, 2589.

provision should be maintained precisely because the courts were unlikely to interpret it as providing the broad exemption for activities that the conservative majority feared. The minority argued that the provision applied only to the "agreement, combination, or contract" itself and not to any of the actions carried out in pursuit of such an agreement.[10] Legislators were also clearly aware that the reading offered by the minority severely limited the reach of the provision. For example, members of the majority later pointed out that the interpretation favored by the minority transformed the bill from a "victory" for labor to an "insult."[11]

What is especially fascinating about this debate is that the committee minority, which was ostensibly acting in the interests of labor organizations, was offering an interpretation of the provision that was very different from the interpretation being offered at the same time by the AFL. The AFL representatives who testified in support of the Hoar bill in 1900 clearly hoped that the courts would adopt the broad interpretation feared by the committee majority rather than the narrow interpretation promised by the committee minority.[12] Ironically, the AFL's favored interpretation was closer to that of the conservative committee majority that wanted to remove the provision altogether than it was to the committee minority that claimed to be acting on the AFL's behalf.

The Hoar bill was defeated when it came to the House floor under a rule that did not allow a separate vote on the committee amendment to remove the restraint on trade provision.[13] Before the vote on the amended bill early in 1901, there was considerable confusion about whether or

---

[10] House Report 2007, pt. 2, 56th Congress, 2nd Session, 2.

[11] The claim is made by former members of the majority in a House minority report issued when the same bill was reported in the next Congress (57th Congress, House Report 1522, pt. 2). In 1914, the House committee reporting the bill that became the Clayton Act was also divided over whether the language in what became Section 6 could help labor. One committee member, Rep. Dick Morgan, wrote separately, and echoed the earlier claim that a compromised provision would not help labor (House Report 1168, pt. 4, 63rd Congress, 2nd Session).

[12] The AFL's support was not offered blindly. When pressed by members of the committee about the exemption during the hearings, AFL representatives admitted that their favored interpretation might not win out in the courts and that the language in the bill could be made clearer. Appearing on behalf of the AFL, attorney Clarence Darrow even complained that the bill was ambiguous and did not go far enough (1900 House Hearings, 18–19).

[13] The committee also attached another amendment that limited the application of the new definition of conspiracy. The committee minority objected to this amendment because its vague provisions left too much discretion to the courts. The chair of the committee (Rep. George Ray (R-NY)) denied that the wording was unclear (34 *Congressional Record* 2594).

not labor organizations still wanted legislators to adopt the bill after the "restraint on trade" provision had been removed. Eventually, AFL leaders announced publicly that they opposed the amended bill and it was overwhelmingly defeated.[14]

The issues raised in this first fight about exempting organizations or activities were not forgotten by the AFL and members of Congress between 1901 and passage of the Clayton Act in 1914. The same issues kept arising. Legislators first returned to the controversy when a bill that was nearly identical to the Hoar bill was introduced in 1902 as the Grosvenor bill (H.R. 11060, 57th Congress). The 1902 bill restored the original restraint-of-trade provision that had been removed by the preceding Congress. The second time around, the makeup of the closely divided House committee shifted and the committee reported the bill in 1902 without removing the restraint-of-trade provision. However, members of the committee still could not agree on the meaning of the provision. As a result, another similar debate about the scope of the restraint-of-trade provision took place before the bill passed the House. The courts never had the opportunity to resolve that controversy because the bill died in the Senate after that chamber's Judiciary Committee reported it with a killer amendment.[15] The same bill was introduced in the next two Congresses,

[14] Shortly before the vote, the committee chair (Representative Ray) claimed to have fifty "communications" from labor organizations expressing support for the amended bill (34 *Congressional Record* 2595). However, opponents of the amendment were able to respond by introducing hastily prepared statements from leaders of the AFL and the Railroad Brotherhoods expressing opposition to the amended bill (34 *Congressional Record* 2597). Just before the House voted, a representative noted that the reported bill contained an error in transcription that made the labor provisions meaningless. The committee leaders blamed the labor representatives who drafted the bill for the mistake, but an agreement to fix the error could not be secured and the bill was defeated.

[15] The Senate amendment led the labor organizations that supported the House version to drop their support for the bill (see the leadoff testimony of H. R. Fuller at the 1906 House Hearings). The Senate Judiciary Committee initially reported a different bill (S. 4553) that authorized the courts to issue injunctions in some labor disputes. In proposing these changes, the committee quickly discovered that there were limits on the willingness of labor organizations to support compromises on reform legislation. Two hundred sixty-seven labor organizations, most of them affiliated with the Railroad Brotherhoods, communicated their unqualified rejection of S. 4553 in letters later documented by the Senate (*Petitions and Remonstrances for and Against the Passage of the Bills "To limit the Meaning of the word 'conspiracy' and the Use of 'Restraining orders and injunctions' in Labor Disputes,"* unnumbered Senate Document, 1903, Library of Congress, partially reprinted in Senate Document 190, 57th Congress). The lobbying labor organizations insisted that any version of the provision had to be worded so that it did not explicitly or implicitly authorize the

in 1904 and 1906.[16] Additional hearings were held each time, but the later bills never escaped the House Committee.

In 1906, the AFL gave up on the moderate but perennially unsuccessful Hoar/Grosvenor bills and instead introduced a more dramatic and comprehensive reform proposal. Representative George A. Pearre (R-MD) introduced the bill that became the most important AFL-supported anti-injunction bill from the period between 1900 and passage of the Clayton Act. The most important and innovative sections of the Pearre bill are relevant to my discussion of Section 20 of the Clayton Act later in this chapter. However, the Pearre bill also contained provisions that are indirectly connected to the antitrust exemption.

While the Pearre bill did not contain any explicit reference to the antitrust laws, it did contain a more general clause that the AFL expected to prevent judges from issuing injunctions based on the antitrust laws. The strategy behind that Pearre bill provision was similar to the one used in the Hoar bill's definition of conspiracy. The provision stated that agreements "between two or more persons concerning the terms or conditions of employment of labor" and "any act or thing to be done or not to be done with reference to or involving or growing out of a labor dispute" could not constitute "a conspiracy *or other criminal offense* or be punished or prosecuted as such unless the act or thing agreed to be done or not to be done would be unlawful if done by a single individual" (emphasis added). AFL attorney T. C. Spelling, one of the authors of the bill, made it clear to the House Committee that this provision was aimed at the antitrust laws. He claimed that one of the beneficial effects of the bill was that it "would...repeal the antitrust law, at least in so far as it applies to boycotts affecting interstate commerce" (1908 House Hearings, 29).

The language exempting labor organizations in the Pearre bill, unlike the earlier Hoar and Grosvenor bills, explicitly stated that it covered both the activities ("any act or thing to be done") and the formation of labor organizations ("entering into or the carrying out of" labor agreements). The new language in the Pearre bill silenced the concerns about ambiguity that

use of injunctions in labor disputes. The AFL continued to insist on this point until 1912 when it agreed to endorse the compromise that eventually became the Clayton Act.

[16] H.R. 89, 58th Congress, known as the Grosvenor bill in 1904; H.R. 9328, 59th Congress, known as the Little bill in 1906. The concerns about ambiguity continued. James Beck of the American Anti-Boycott Association and the Contractors League of Chicago expressed concern that "the bill is ambiguous and will give rise to a flood of evils" (1904 House Hearings, 67).

had been expressed so often in connection with the earlier bills, concerns that would return when members of Congress considered the Clayton bill. None of the witnesses in three sets of congressional hearings on the Pearre bill ever suggested that the Pearre bill would exempt only labor *organizations* from the antitrust laws while leaving the *activities* of the organizations subject to penalties. The problem with the Pearre bill was not that it was ambiguous, but that its clarity made it unacceptable to legislators. None of the variations on the Pearre bill that the AFL supported between 1906 and 1912 reached the floor of either the Senate or House.[17]

Changes to Section 6 in 1914: From Clayton bill to Clayton Act. As the bill that later became the Clayton Act became a focus of congressional attention in 1912 and 1914, legislators abandoned the clarity of the Pearre bill for language that was much closer to the troublesome language in the earlier Hoar and Grosvenor bills. The consequence of this reversion did not go unnoticed by legislators. Many participants remembered the earlier debates.

More generally, members of Congress complained repeatedly during later debates on the Clayton bill that Section 6 was too ambiguous to be of much help to labor organizations. In part of the House report on the bill, Rep. Dick Morgan (R-OK) declared:

It would hardly seem necessary in this day and age of the world to enact a law which merely permits the existence of labor organizations. If labor and farmer organizations are not to be given some substantial recognition by statutory enactment, it would seem unwise to place a new provision in the law, which can be of no material benefit to labor organizations, but which is bound to bring doubt and uncertainty as to what, if any, additional rights labor and farmers' organizations and members thereof have under the new statute. If the provisions of our antitrust laws should not apply to labor organizations Congress should in plain and clear

---

[17] There were several versions of the Pearre bill. In 1906, friends of the AFL in Congress introduced three versions of the bill before they were satisfied that the Pearre bill they introduced was free from various minor errors in transcription and style (H.R. 18171, H.R. 18446, and H.R. 18752, 59th Congress). H.R. 94, 60th Congress, 1908 was identical to H.R. 18752 of the 59th Congress. The Wilson bill of 1912 (H.R. 11032, 62nd Congress) was essentially the same. A more complicated bill that incorporated much of the Pearre bill, the Bartlett-Bacon bill (H.R. 23189, 62nd Congress), did escape the House Labor Committee in 1912 (House Report 588, 62nd Congress, 2nd Session), but that bill was never voted on by the full House because of a jurisdictional dispute between the Judiciary and Labor Committees (48 *Congressional Record* 4683). Much of this history was recounted in a sarcastic speech by Representative Volstead (R-MN) during the Clayton Act debate (51 *Congressional Record* 9083).

language so declare. We should not speak in the doubtful uncertain, indefinite terms which characterize the provisions of [Section 6] (House Report 1168, 63rd Congress, pt. 4).

These concerns were echoed in floor debates. Representative Robert Thomas (D-KY) declared the provision to be as "ambiguous as the prophecy of a Roman oracle.... As a matter of fact it means nothing."[18] Representative Andrew Volstead (R-MN) attributed the ambiguity in the bill to sinister motives, noting that, "It looks as though it has been drawn to deceive somebody" (9564).[19]

In response to such criticisms, AFL leaders and members of both the Senate and the House suggested amendments to clarify the meaning of the section. Negotiations over changes to Section 6 were difficult, however, because President Wilson opposed adding any blanket exemption for the activities of labor organizations. Despite Democratic Party campaign promises to provide relief from labor injunctions, Wilson objected to an unqualified labor exemption on the grounds that it was "class legislation" at odds with his New Freedom ideology and commitment to market-based solutions. Wilson also wanted to maintain the support of business interests during the prolonged recession that began in the fall of 1913 (Jones 1957).[20]

Perhaps because of Wilson's reservations, the first version of the Clayton bill developed by the House Judiciary Committee did not contain *any* provisions regarding the application of the antitrust laws to labor unions. Only after the AFL insisted that the Democrats fulfill their campaign pledge did the House committee add the following provision:

nothing contained in the antitrust laws shall be construed to forbid the existence and operation of fraternal, labor, consumer, agricultural, or horticultural organizations, orders, or associations instituted for the purposes of mutual help, and not having capital stock or conducted for profit, or to forbid or restrain individual members of such organizations, orders, or associations from carrying out the legitimate objects thereof.

Representatives from the AFL at first expressed satisfaction when the committee added the new language (Jones 1957, 209). Later, however, Gompers and the AFL later had an attack of buyer's remorse. The AFL

---

[18] 51 *Congressional Record* 9544. Remaining page references in this section are to volume 51 of the *Congressional Record*.

[19] Senator Wesley Jones (R-WA), 14011, expressed similar sentiments during Senate debates.

[20] Jones (1957) provides an extended account of Wilson's role in the negotiations.

requested that the language be changed to say that the antitrust laws "shall not apply" to labor unions rather than that the laws "shall not be construed to forbid the existence of" unions. Anticipating the Supreme Court's exact reasoning, Gompers requested the change in part because he wanted to make sure the provision applied to labor's *activities* as well as labor *organizations*.[21] However, President Wilson rejected the request. Wilson insisted that the AFL's retracted endorsement proved that the committee's version of the bill fulfilled the Democrat's campaign promise and thus was unwilling to make further concessions.

The AFL continued to object, however, and the result was a stalemate that held up the bill for weeks. To break the deadlock, the committee had to find compromise language that both the AFL and President Wilson would be willing to endorse. Given that the two sides were on opposite sides of a crucial issue, however, it was not possible to find a clear solution that could satisfy both sides. Not surprisingly, then, the agreement brokered by Committee Chair Edwin Webb (D-NC) added language that rendered the provision ambiguous. Webb agreed to introduce an amendment adding the following provision:

Nor shall such organizations, orders, or associations, or members thereof, be held or construed to be illegal combinations or conspiracies in restraint of trade under the antitrust laws.

Webb's compromise amendment solved the immediate political problem: The Clayton bill went to the House floor with the endorsement of both the administration and the AFL.

Webb's amendment did not, however, produce much agreement about what the amended version of Section 6 actually meant and what policies would result. During floor debates, members of the House offered two contradictory interpretations of the Webb version of Section 6. The first interpretation, offered by supporters of the AFL, was that Section 6 fully exempted both labor unions and the activities of their members from the antitrust laws.[22] The second interpretation, offered by administration

---

[21] The change of heart came after AFL leaders consulted with Alton B. Parker, a federal judge, former Democratic presidential candidate, and political nemesis of Woodrow Wilson. See Gompers 1925, vol. II, 295; Jones 1957, 209, note 58. See also the circular letter sent by Gompers and the heads of the railroad trade unions to the House (cited in note 7).

[22] During floor debates, the first interpretation was suggested by Rep. Walter Hensley (D-MO) and Rep. Alben Berkeley (D-KY). Hensley said the Webb amendment exempted labor organizations from the "operations" of the antitrust laws and associated Section 6 with labor's earlier fight for full exemption (9551). Berkeley

loyalists like Webb, was closer to the position Wilson favored and the position eventually adopted by the courts. According to this interpretation, Section 6 prevented suits for the dissolution of labor organizations under the antitrust laws but did little else.[23] The administration loyalists who offered this second interpretation revealed some clues about their motivations by repeatedly reassuring their House colleagues that Section 6 fulfilled the Democratic platform pledge.[24] They also emphasized that the Webb version of Section 6 had the full support of "labor" (meaning, of course, the support of the AFL).[25] However, they failed to mention that the AFL's support was offered only in connection with the AFL's claims that the provision meant something very different.

The existence of these two conflicting interpretations among the key supporters of the antitrust exemption did not go unnoticed by Republican opponents of the proposal during floor debates. Representative Volstead noted the "peculiar" circumstance that the AFL was claiming one interpretation for the amendment while the administration was claiming another. He pointed out that the Webb amendment would "of necessity go into the courts after it becomes a law before anybody will know definitely just what it means" (9564). Volstead urged adoption of clearer language that would resolve the ambiguity, suggesting that "we ought to know what we are voting for" (9564).

Representative Victor Murdock (R-KA) also suggested that Congress was leaving it up to the courts to determine the scope of the protection:

> Some of the friends of labor say that the amendment does exempt organized labor from the provisions of the Sherman antitrust law, but its enemies say that it does not exempt organized labor. Who knows? No man on the floor of this House. Who will determine? The Courts (9542).

Noting the AFL's heightened lobbying activity in the aftermath of the 1908 Supreme Court ruling that the antitrust laws applied to labor

---

claimed, among other things, that judges could never apply the antitrust laws to workers under the new law (9552–5).

[23] This interpretation was most actively defended by Webb and House Rules Committee Chair Henry (D-TX), but also by Rep. Isaac Sherwood (D-OH) (9171) and Rep. David Lewis (D-MD) (9565).

[24] Webb: "It is the Baltimore [Democratic Party] platform in exact words. It is the spirit, the substance, the verbiage, and the promise of the Democratic platform" (9541).

[25] See, for example, Representative Henry (9540) who claimed (erroneously) that the language in the bill matched the original 1890 Senate Amendment to the Sherman Antitrust Act.

organizations,[26] Murdock noted that "the tragedy of this transaction... is...[t]hat after labor went to the courts and after the courts had sent it back to Congress, Congress sends labor back to the courts again" (9542).

It seems likely that the complaints made by Republicans were not motivated by a sincere desire to help labor unions. Volstead and the other Republicans who noted the ambiguity in the section probably hoped calling attention to the multiple interpretations would shatter the fragile compromise between the administration and the AFL that was allowing the bill to move toward passage.[27] The lesson suggested by the failure of the Pearre bill was that a clear statute that clearly expressed labor's policy preferences would have less chance of becoming law. Volstead and his friends were probably hoping to continue that pattern.

However, not all the members of Congress who called attention to the ambiguities in the bill were opponents of the exemption seeking to embarrass the opposing political party. Legislators who sympathized with labor also tried to resolve the ambiguity by proposing amendments to clarify the legislative language. In the House, several representatives introduced amendments to clarify Section 6. The most important of these was introduced by Representative Thomas (D-NY).[28] The Thomas amendment replaced Section 6 and the Webb amendment with a proposal that would have restored the "shall not apply" language from the earlier antitrust exemption bills backed by the AFL. The straightforward Thomas amendment stated:

The provisions of the antitrust laws shall not apply to agricultural, labor, consumers, fraternal, or horticultural organizations, orders, or associations (9538).

Although it did not pass, the Thomas amendment focused attention on the ambiguity of Section 6 and forced supporters of the Webb amendment to back off on some of their extravagant claims about its likely effects.[29] The debate over the Thomas amendment also produced a very revealing

---

[26] *Loewe v Lawlor,* (208 U.S. 274)
[27] The other Republican complainer was Representative Madden (9081). Volstead (9081, 9564) and Madden (9081) both delighted in claiming that the ambiguity meant that the bill would not fulfill the Democratic Party platform pledge.
[28] MacDonald also introduced an amendment as an alternative to Thomas's that MacDonald hoped would have a similar effect. It combined the Thomas amendment with the Webb amendment favored by many Democrats and President Wilson.
[29] Compare, for example, Representative Henry's initial broad defense of the Webb amendment (9450) with the more modest claim he made after Thomas and other representatives attacked its ambiguity (9544).

exchange between Webb and Rep. William MacDonald (P-MI). When MacDonald pointedly asked Webb whether his version would exempt labor "in every respect from the law" Webb's first reply was that "It certainly does exempt their existence and operation." When pressed further about whether the activities of labor organizations would remain subject to the antitrust laws, Webb could only reply vaguely, "Of course it is an organization subject to the law." When MacDonald suggested that the Webb Amendment left labor organizations "confined under the antitrust laws to a mere inactive existence," Webb was forced to abandon Section 6 altogether and point to additional protections afforded to labor's collective activities in other parts of the Clayton Act (9567).

What is perhaps most interesting about the debate over the Thomas amendment is that the AFL refused to come out in support of it. Earlier in the legislative battle, Gompers sent a letter to the House stating that the only way to create an effective exemption for the activities of labor organizations was to restore the "shall not apply" language from the earlier bills.[30] However, the AFL had to back down from that position when it agreed to the fragile compromise on the Webb amendment. The AFL stuck to the script by refusing to endorse the Thomas amendment. The AFL's unwillingness to endorse the Thomas amendment is important because it provided cover for representatives who voted to stick with the Webb version instead of adding Thomas's stronger protections. Several representatives claimed that they were voting for the Webb Amendment over Thomas's only because Webb's had the support of "labor." These legislators said this even as they expressed doubts about whether the Webb version would be effective.[31] A frustrated Representative Thomas claimed that labor leaders really wanted his amendment, and explained that they would not publicly endorse it out of fear that clearer language would defeat the bill. In response, administration loyalist Rep. Edward Keating (D-CO) offered the ambiguous claim that AFL leaders had told him that the Webb amendment was "better, from the viewpoint of organized labor than the Thomas amendment" (9569). Without further explanation, the Thomas amendment went down to defeat and the Webb compromise survived in the bill passed by the House.

[30] Gompers, et al. to U.S. House of Representatives, May 5, 1914, *AFL Records*, reel 26, index number 2369.
[31] Representatives Towner (R-IA, 9547), Lenroot (R-WI, 9550), Raker (D-CA, 9551), Morgan (R-OK, 9564), and Brumbaugh (D-OH, 9564).

Subsequent events suggest that Thomas was right that the AFL endorsed the Webb version only to preserve the fragile compromise in the House. As soon as the bill moved over to the Senate, the supposedly satisfied AFL started lobbying senators to change the language in the House version of the exemption.[32] Perhaps in response to the AFL demands, the Senate adopted several changes that had been recommended by the Senate Judiciary Committee during an early round of floor debates. However, the amendments went both for and against the interests of the AFL. The most significant committee amendment was the one that added an additional "lawfully" to Section 6.[33] The senators seem to have been as divided as their House counterparts about the political meaning and likely effect of Section 6.

Meanwhile, Samuel Gompers was meeting behind the scenes with Senate Judiciary Committee Chair Charles Culberson (D-TX) and Sen. Albert Cummins (R-IA) to change the House language in the antitrust exemption. Cummins agreed to introduce an amendment on the floor that would replace the House version of Section 6 with an entirely new provision. Gompers later remembered that he was particularly thrilled with the first sentence of Cummins's amendment, a declaration that "the labor of a human being is not a commodity or article of commerce."[34] The Senate eventually rejected the Cummins amendment, but Senator Culberson later introduced a successful amendment that made the first sentence from the Cummins amendment the first section of Section 6 of the Clayton Act.[35]

---

[32] The additional AFL lobbying in the Senate came despite the following plea in the July 1914 *American Federationist*: "The insidious antagonists as well as the pretending friends of labor are studiously endeavoring to kill labor provisions of the Clayton bill, HR15656, by 'kindness'; that is by 'improving' upon or 'clarifying' its language. Real friends will insist upon the enactment of the bill as it passes the House of Representatives" (573).

[33] The other Senate amendments removed consumer (adopted, 13925) and fraternal organizations (13963–4) and three occurrences of the phrase "orders and associations" after "organizations" (14028). The Senate also eliminated an entire second paragraph from the House version of Section 6 concerning associations of common carriers. Senate Report 698, 63rd Congress, 2nd Session.

[34] Gompers 1925, vol. II, 296.

[35] The rejected Cummins amendment differed from the House version of Section 6 because it specified what organizations counted as labor organizations by making reference to the objectives of an organization. The amendment also exempted an enumerated list of *individual* actions from the antitrust laws. The list was similar to the one in Section 20. Anticipating the Supreme Court's ruling in *Duplex* exactly, Cummins thought it was important to repeat those exemptions to prevent judges from saying that Section 20's exemptions applied to "employees" of labor

With the declaration that labor is not a commodity, Senator Cummins hoped to establish a justification for a full labor exemption from the antitrust laws. Cummins explained that the commodity declaration was meant to respond to the potential judicial argument that exempting labor from the antitrust laws was a form of unconstitutional "class legislation" (14586).[36] The amendment established a distinction between labor and other commodities in order to make it clear why the antitrust laws should not regulate commodities and workers in precisely the same way. The goal, apparently, was to show that the exemption was not "class legislation" that gave workers special protection not afforded to other groups. As Cummins carefully explained, the antitrust exemption was not an unfair attempt to place the activities of organized workers beyond government regulation.[37] The declaration was an attempt to articulate legislators' belief that a different type of regulation was appropriate for labor than for the production of commodities. As one supporter of the amendment explained: "Legislation for the regulation and control of one may be no more suitable for the regulation and control of the other than would legislation for the control of a flying machine" (Senator Jones, 14013).

The declaration that "labor is not a commodity" has been seized on as a key accomplishment of the Clayton Act. In 1914, Gompers called the words in the commodity declaration "sledge-hammer blows to the wrongs and injustice so long inflicted upon the workers" (971) and "the Industrial Magna Carta upon which the working people will rear their structure of industrial freedom" (971–2). Gompers's belief that the declaration was the key accomplishment in the Clayton Act never dimmed even though the Supreme Court ignored it in *Duplex* and subsequent cases.[38]

---

organizations. I discuss the "employees" issue in more detail later in this chapter in connection with Section 20 of the Clayton Act.

[36] Gillman (1993) describes the Supreme Court's class legislation jurisprudence from this period in considerable detail.

[37] Senators Chilton (14020) and Borah (14591) were not convinced on this point, and raised concerns about whether the provision would take away Congress's power to regulate labor under the commerce clause.

[38] In his 1925 memoirs, Gompers proudly described his trembling excitement as the Senate voted to add the commodity declaration to the Clayton Act (Gompers 1925, vol. II, 297). For years, the declaration graced the frontispiece of AFL reference publications and the *American Federationist*. More recently, Ernst (1989) has argued that the recognition that the distinctive nature of labor organizations required different regulatory schemes is significant because it signaled the rejection of the individualistic analogy between the right to work and the right to manage. Ernst notes that the declaration established that "a rival way of understanding the employer-employee

Although the "not a commodity" declaration did become part of the Clayton Act, there was no widespread agreement in the Senate about what the declaration meant and what its effect would be. In explaining why they could not support the full Cummins amendment, several senators expressed doubts about whether the courts would recognize the "not a commodity" declaration as the bold legislative initiative supporters claimed it was. For example, Senator Williams declared, "the committee amendment is broader and more unmistakable, covering the ground more completely, than the substitute proposed by [Cummins]" (14588).

With or without the first sentence of the Cummins amendment, the meaning of Section 6 of the Clayton Act was no clearer in the Senate than it had been in the House. Opponents of a strong labor exemption, like Republican Senators William Borah (ID) (13918) and Atlee Pomerene (OH) (13912) suggested that Section 6 accomplished very little besides confirming what courts had already established regarding the legality of labor organizations.[39] A second group of senators who seemed to favor a strong labor exemption did not challenge such claims. They instead expressed regret that the law did not go further, but seemed to agree that the courts would adopt a narrow interpretation. For this group, the AFL's decision to support the compromise again provided cover. Senator William Hughes (D-NJ) admired the "humble and suppliant" workers and their willingness to compromise and "take what they could get" (13972). Although he stated that he "would like to go farther" (13972) and that he wished the Senate committee had more "courage" (13971), Hughes recognized that labor organizations were "afraid to jeopardize their chances of getting any legislation by insisting upon getting more than there is in this bill as it came from the House" (13974). Despite his concerns, Hughes was willing to accept the AFL's request for the House version of the bill: "They are satisfied, and nobody is authorized to go any further in their name. So much for that" (13974).

---

relationship had reached maturity" (1173). Without denying that broader significance of Congress's symbolic decision to pass the provision, I think it is equally important to note that in practice the provision had almost no legal effect. The federal courts universally ignored it, even in opinions that found in labor's favor. The provision also appears to have had little influence on the way judges handled "class legislation" arguments in subsequent cases involving state labor legislation. See, for example, *Bogni v Perotti* (244 Mass. 152, 112 N.E. 853 (1916)).

[39] With respect to dissolution of labor organizations, Senator Pomerene pointed out that courts did not usually entertain suits for dissolution anyway (13909). Borah said that any fears of the courts issuing orders for the dissolution of labor organizations were unfounded (13918).

Some senators suggested that the Senate had responsibilities that went beyond simply adopting whatever legislation happened to be publicly endorsed by labor organizations. Senator Hoke Smith (D-GA) claimed:

We can not legislate because a class of people are satisfied. A class of people might be satisfied with a piece of legislation, thinking it would accomplish a certain thing, when it would not. Finally, the responsibility comes to us, even though they thought it would do a certain thing for them, if we found that it would do a very different thing to them we could properly be responsible if we passed the legislation, though they misapprehend its effect, were satisfied with it (14366).

Senator Wesley Jones (R-WA)[40] added:

one of the duties in enacting legislation is to make legislation just as plain and positive as it can be made. Aside from the evils that may result from unwise and unjust laws comes the great evil of the uncertainty of law. . . . We pass laws about which we ourselves differ as to the use and application of the terms, and then courts are criticized because of their interpretation of the laws (14019).

Senator Jones also connected the ambiguity in the Clayton bill with a more general problem, claiming that, "We pass laws almost every day of doubtful meaning and uncertain intention" (14011).[41]

Concerns about ambiguity in Section 6 turned out to be well founded when the Supreme Court later found the commodity declaration did not prevent the injunction in *Duplex*. The ruling in *Duplex* did not come out of the blue, however, and did not give an interpretation that "never occurred to" members of Congress. The ruling came more than twenty years after legislators first began discussing questions about whether an antitrust exemption phrased like the one in the Clayton Act would exempt from the antitrust laws only organizations or both organizations and their activities.

The legislative records that reveal the evolution of Section 6 of the Clayton Act have also revealed that all three of the conditions I set out for declaring a provision a legislative deferral have been met. Legislators were aware of and drew attention to the ambiguities and interpretive questions that later arose in court; associated those ambiguities with a

[40] I am not making this up. There really was a Smith and a Jones.
[41] Other senators expressed worries about outside groups expecting too much from the law. Senator Thomas stated, "we can not afford to enact legislation that is going to prove a disappointment in its practical operation" and said that the bill would not "wholly exempt any class of citizens" (14020). Senator Borah was more direct, calling the bill a "farce" (13978).

future role for the courts; and, rejected alternative legislative proposals that attempted to limit the discretion of judges.

JURISDICTION AND PROPERTY RIGHTS: THE FIRST
PARAGRAPH OF SECTION 20

The difficulties with Section 6 were not the only problems with the labor provisions of the Clayton Act. Before ruling that the lower court could issue the injunction to end the boycott against the Duplex Printing Press Company, the Supreme Court had to consider several provisions in Section 20 of the Clayton Act that articulated limits on the powers of federal courts to issue injunctions in labor disputes. Those provisions generated another series of interpretive controversies that the Supreme Court had to resolve in *Duplex Printing v Deering*.

The court looked first at the opening paragraph of Section 20, which prohibits judges from issuing injunctions in labor disputes:

unless necessary to prevent irreparable injury to property, or to a property right, of the party making the application, for which injury there is no adequate remedy at law.

The attorneys for the boycotting workers claimed that this provision prevented the courts from issuing an injunction. Although the attorneys conceded that the boycott interfered with Duplex's business operations, they claimed that such interference did not amount to an injury to "property" or any "property right." The right of the Duplex Company to conduct its business was a *personal* right rather than a *property* right, and thus not subject to relief by injunction under the language in Section 20.

Pitney and the Court majority apparently did not think much of this argument. The majority simply asserted that the Duplex Company's "business of manufacturing printing presses and disposing of them in commerce is a property right entitled to protection against unlawful injury or interference" (254 U.S. 443, 465). Of course, in declaring that the right to conduct business free of boycotts was a property right, the Court was declaring that the first paragraph of Section 20 made no changes at all in existing law. Pitney readily admitted as much in his opinion: "The first paragraph merely puts into statutory form familiar restrictions upon the granting of injunctions already established and of general application in the equity practice of the courts of the United States. It is but declaratory of the law as it stood before" (254 U.S. 443, 470). The Court could not identify any congressional intention to change the existing judge-made law in the paragraph.

The ease with which the Supreme Court rejected the claim that the "property" provision limited labor injunctions makes it easy to overlook an important fact that is abundantly clear in the broader legislative record: Questions about what counted as a property right were at the very heart of the AFL's long legislative campaign against the labor injunction. The language about property rights in Section 20 of the Clayton Act was copied verbatim from a provision in the earlier Pearre bill, the AFL's bold antiinjunction proposal that was introduced in every congress from 1906 to 1912. The main point of that Pearre bill was to redefine what counted as a property right so that the courts could no longer issue injunctions against worker activities that interfered with the right to conduct business. However, while one part of the Pearre bill was copied into Section 20 of the Clayton Act, another crucial provision from the Pearre bill was missing. In order to understand the significance of what was included and what was left out, it is necessary to uncover and understand the original jurisdiction-curbing strategy of the Pearre bill. Looking at the AFL's strategic choices, first to endorse and then to abandon the full Pearre bill, provides the essential clues for understanding the failure of the Clayton Act in the hands of hostile judges.

In 1906, the Pearre bill strategy of limiting the equity jurisdiction of the federal courts abruptly replaced the earlier Hoar bill strategy of changing the substantive law of conspiracy and restraint of trade. From 1906 until 1912, the AFL adamantly refused to endorse any bill that did not contain the full Pearre bill provision defining "property" and limiting the jurisdiction of the courts. In 1912, the AFL finally backed down and agreed to support the compromise antiinjunction bill that was later incorporated into the Clayton Act. That compromise bill, like the Clayton Act, included part of the Pearre bill provision verbatim but also omitted a crucial sentence defining what counted as "property." However, the first sentence of the Pearre bill was included in the Clayton Act virtually unchanged while the crucial second sentence disappeared without a trace. That decision was significant because the omitted second sentence stated that the right to do business was not a property right for purpose of equity jurisdiction. It was the decision to remove that sentence that left the Supreme Court free to say that the right to conduct business was a "property right" under Section 20 of the Clayton Act.

The AFL's campaign for the Pearre bill's limitation on the jurisdiction of the federal courts began during a House committee meeting on a Hoar bill clone in 1906. The AFL, frustrated with legislators' repeated failure to pass the highly compromised Hoar and Grosvenor bills, abruptly switched positions and announced to a startled committee a newly aggressive strategy. The change in strategy was presaged earlier in the hearings when the AFL's legislative representative Andrew Furuseth refused to endorse a procedural reform bill (H.R. 9328) that had just been lauded by a trade union ally of the AFL, H. R. Fuller of the Railroad Brotherhoods. It was at that hearing that Furuseth presented the first long lecture on the history of equity procedure in English and American courts and the constitutional limits on the equity powers of the federal judges that I discussed in Chapter 2. Furuseth's position, as explained in Chapter 2, was that injunctions were remedies of equity courts, and thus only justified in cases involving threats to physical property. Since most labor injuction cases did not involve threats to such property, most of the injunctions issued in labor disputes amounted to illegitimate judicial usurpations of legislative powers.[42] The Pearre bill was supposed to reestablish traditional limits on equity jurisdiction by restating the traditional limitation of that jurisdiction to cases involving threats to property.

From the day of that 1906 hearing until 1912, the leaders of the AFL insisted that the only effective way to limit injunctions was to pass a statute like the Pearre bill that directly attacked the jurisdiction of the courts with an explicit, narrowing definition of what counted as a property right. Because the AFL leaders felt other procedural reforms would be less effective, the AFL refused to endorse any other antiinjunction bills until deciding in 1912 to endorse a bill that was later incorporated into the Clayton Act of 1914.

The Pearre bill was relatively short and straightforward. In language nearly identical to that eventually enacted as the first paragraph of Section 20 of the Clayton Act, the first sentence of Section 1 of the Pearre bill states that no injunctions should issue in labor disputes unless necessary to protect a "particularly described" property right of the applicant. The crucial second sentence of the Pearre bill, which was not made part of the Clayton Act, was a statement restricting what could count as a "property right":

for the purposes of this act, no right to continue the relation of employer and employee, or to assume or create such relation with any particular person or persons, or at all, or to carry on business of any particular kind or at any particular

---

[42] *1906 House Hearings*, 18–25.

place, or at all, shall be construed, held, considered, or treated as property or as constituting a property right (H.R. 18752, 59th Congress).

The importance of the second sentence can be seen by considering Furuseth's arguments about the legitimacy of equity powers. According to Furuseth, judges had not expanded their equity powers in labor disputes by ignoring the traditional requirement that injunctions be limited to cases involving threats to property (the issue addressed in the first sentence of the Pearre bill). Rather, judges had extended their jurisdiction and issued injunctions in labor disputes by expanding the concept of property rights to include an employer's right to conduct business (the issue addressed in the second sentence of the Pearre bill). The unreflective declaration by the Supreme Court in *Duplex Printing v Deering* that the right to conduct business is a property right provides an example of the problem that Furuseth was seeking to solve in that essential second sentence.

It is abundantly clear from the earlier debates on the Pearre bill that members of Congress and the leaders of the AFL recognized that the second sentence was essential to limiting the ability of judges to issue injunctions. The AFL's most effective witness in support of the juris-diction curbing bills, attorney T. C. Spelling, repeatedly emphasized the central importance of the property rights issue to the injunction contro-versy. Four years before passage of the Clayton Act, Spelling told a House committee:

... there is one germ of usurpation in all those [labor injunction] cases. The central idea of ... [the Pearre] bill, the basic principle, is to lop off and get rid of that seed or germ of usurpation. This is the assumption ... in these cases that business or the right to do business, as expressed in this bill, or the right to continue business, is property or a property right. Now if the opponents of this legislation dared concede that our contention on this point is correct ... then I could show error and usurpation in 95 percent of the cases of which we complain (1908 House Hearings, 5).

During hearings on jurisdiction curbing bills in 1906, 1908, and 1912, the AFL's representatives insisted repeatedly that the only way to get the courts to return to the narrower definition of property rights was to have Congress pass a provision that explicitly established a restrictive defini-tion. In the 1908 hearings, Spelling argued that the "real point at issue here ... is the distinction between personal and property rights" (1908 House Hearings, 145). This was true because "courts have never yet had the hardihood to openly and avowedly use the remedy for the protection of personal rights" (145).[43] A statute explicitly limiting the definition of property was necessary because, as Spelling explained, the courts had already established so many bad precedents in labor injunction cases. Those precedents made it exceedingly unlikely that judges would decide on their own that the right to conduct business was somehow no longer a property right. It was thus essential that legislators include language restricting the definition of property in order to prevent judges from continuing to follow such precedents.

The importance of the second sentence is further confirmed by the fact that so many opponents of the Pearre bill conceded the main premise underlying the bill. Employers' representatives did not deny the AFL's claim that the courts had no jurisdiction to issue injunctions in cases that did not involve any threats to property. They instead responded to the AFL's claims by applauding the case law that had already established that the right to conduct business was a property right subject to relief by injunction.[44]

These earlier controversies were not forgotten during the debates on the Clayton bills in 1912 and 1914. Evidence that members of Congress understood that the meaning of the word "property" in Section 20 was crucial to the effectiveness of the provision can be found in the Senate hearings held in 1912 and in the 1914 floor debates on the Clayton Act in both the House and Senate. Legislators clearly understood the significance of the decision to remove the restrictive definition of "property" in the Pearre bill, and also understood that by endorsing this decision, the AFL had abandoned the legislative strategy that the same AFL leaders had earlier declared to be the most effective way to establish limits on judicial power. Nevertheless, legislators repeatedly rejected attempts to restore the original Pearre bill language or to take other steps to clarify the meaning of the "property right" language in Section 20. In the end, legislators decided not to resolve the controversy about property rights that had been at the

[43] Spelling also argued that the earlier cases should not go unchallenged as precedents that permanently settled the property-rights issue. He noted that the defendants in the earlier cases had never raised any challenge to the court's jurisdiction, and blamed the failure to raise the crucial jurisdictional question on the inadequate legal representation the unions received in the early cases (1908 House Hearings, 14).

[44] Both the employers and the AFL spent most of their energy in the 1906 and 1908 hearings arguing about what the various court precedents on property rights established. The most interesting exchanges were between Spelling and Daniel Davenport of the American Anti-Boycott Association. Despite a growing unwillingness to accept the authority of what he considered bad precedents, Spelling spent time addressing the employers' claims in detail. Spelling either questioned the employers' reading of the cases or challenged the authority of the courts that decided them.

center of the antiinjunction fight since 1906. Congress instead passed a law that stated a proposition about property rights that was so bland that everyone who took part in the legislative debates already agreed with it. It is thus not at all surprising that the Supreme Court was able to strip the remaining provision of meaning without even taking the trouble of producing an argument in favor of its position.

The first bill to contain the truncated version of the property rights requirement that ended up in the Clayton Act was reported in 1912 by the House Judiciary Committee as a replacement for a Pearre bill clone that had been backed mightily by the AFL (the "Wilson bill" H.R. 11032, 62nd Congress). The replacement bill (H.R. 23635) did not pass in 1912, but later reappeared as part of the 1914 Clayton bill and eventually became Section 20 of the Clayton Act. The AFL agreed to support the House Committee's replacement bill in 1912. That agreement marked a dramatic change in strategy for the AFL.

The significance of that change did not go unnoticed in Congress. When the replacement bill came before the Senate Judiciary Committee in 1912, the crucial question of whether the right to conduct business was a property right continued to dominate the discussion even though the new bill said nothing about what counted as "property" or about the right to conduct business. That the members of the Senate Committee understood the significance of the decision to remove the property rights definition is clear from some of the pointed questions asked at the hearings. Under questioning, many witnesses for employers' organizations switched from complaining that the bill was ambiguous to admitting that they were satisfied that the new bill left the key issue of jurisdiction and the right to conduct business to the discretion of judges.[45]

The AFL's decision to endorse the compromise bill was undoubtedly the result of a strategic calculation that it was better to compromise and get a new law passed than to hold out for a more perfect bill.[46] In the 1912

---

[45] See, for example, Walter D. Hines, appearing on behalf of several large railroad companies, who insisted that any new statute should leave the issue for the courts to resolve (1912 Senate Hearings, 31). George Monaghan of the National Founder's Association expressed some satisfaction that the "extremely radical wording" of the original Pearre bill had been changed but still complained that the new bill left the issue uncertain (1912 Senate Hearings, 49).

[46] In the 1912 hearings on the replacement bill, the AFL's representatives never stopped arguing that the bill made it *possible* for the courts to change their position. Spelling devoted more than fifteen pages of patient testimony to questions of equity jurisdiction and property-rights. He cited various legal treatises, dictionaries, and selected cases to argue that the property-right requirement was not met in cases involving only the right to do business. But Spelling never claimed that the courts were *likely*

hearings, there is a palpable change in the tone of the AFL's presentations to congressional committees as the organization backed off its more aggressive court-curbing strategies. While AFL representatives had made aggressive attacks on judges when defending the Pearre bill in hearings in 1906 and 1908, the AFL representatives of 1912 promised repeatedly that the Clayton bill left judges free to decide the property-rights issue. Several senators were apparently surprised by the change in the AFL's stance. After being pressed by Sen. (and later Horseman) George Sutherland (R-UT) about the adequacies of the protection for labor in the new bill, AFL attorney T. C. Spelling acknowledged that the omitted definition of property was "the very heart of the Pearre bill" (1912 Senate Hearing, Spelling Testimony, 41). Spelling had a difficult time explaining why the AFL was supporting a bill that left it to the judges to resolve such an important policy issue as the definition of property rights. Spelling's only expressed reason for optimism was that the employers' continued obsession with the property-rights issue indicated that the issue was "irrepressible" and might eventually be decided in labor's favor. Yet, however "irrepressible" the issue may have been, the AFL had obviously given up the long fight to have the issue resolved in Congress rather than in the courts.[47]

The 1912 bill died in the Senate, but was reintroduced two years later as part of the bill enacted as the Clayton Act. In 1914, floor debate on the Clayton Act's property-rights requirement was short but quite revealing. On the very first day of debate over the Clayton Act in the House, Rep. Martin Madden (R-IL), a conservative opponent of labor provisions, read the Pearre bill into the record and noted the differences between the earlier bill and what later became Section 20 of the Clayton Act. He stated that the restrictive definition of property in the Pearre bill would have prevented injunctions in antitrust cases (51 *Congressional Record* 9082). In contrast, he said that any claim that the truncated version in Section 20 "exempts anybody from any legal danger or interference" was "the rankest nonsense." Madden added that the property requirement remaining in the Clayton bill "embodies a legal proposition never disputed

to reach the same conclusions if they were given the opportunity to interpret the replacement bill.

47 Spelling later broke with the AFL after becoming more outspoken in his criticism of the way the Pearre bill was altered and made into Section 20. His criticism of the bill before the Commission on Industrial Relations angered Gompers and apparently contributed to Gompers's efforts to disown Spelling as a labor spokesperson. See Ernst 1995, 187 and Gompers's letter to Frank Walsh, September 15, 1915, *Gompers Letterbooks,* Library of Congress.

by any court nor by any respectable authority" (9082). Madden also marveled at the "subserviency" of the AFL and the willingness of the AFL's leaders to so "stultify themselves and disappoint their followers as to accept so miserable a makeshift, so utterly ruinous a measure" (9083) as the Clayton bill.

Representative MacDonald (P-MI), who unlike Madden was a supporter of injunction reform, also called attention to the problems in the provision. MacDonald offered an amendment to add a restrictive definition of property similar to the one in the original Pearre bill.[48] However, the House rejected MacDonald's amendment without much debate regarding its significance (9611).

Things played out a bit differently when the Senate debated the bill. The issue of property rights and Section 20 first arose when an apparently confused Senator Pomerene (R-OH) questioned why the Clayton bill contained *any* language restricting equity jurisdiction to property rights. Senator Pomerene asked why "property has become more sacred than life or limb" and offered an amendment to get rid of the word "property" so that the bill required only that the complainant demonstrate a threat to "a right."

In response to Senator Pomerene's confusion, Sen. Knute Nelson (R-MN) offered a revealing explanation for the presence of the "property rights" language in Section 20. Nelson explained:

Mr. Gompers maintains, and he argued very strenuously before the Judiciary Committee, that the right to do business and the right to labor are not property and therefore are not entitled to protection by injunction . . . this was put into the bill to meet that argument.

Nelson added, however, that the concession to the AFL was not very important.

It is my opinion that the courts will hold that the right to carry on business, the right to run a factory, is property. . . . [The provision in the first paragraph of 20] was put in here as a sop to encourage and make labor organizations believe they are getting something in this section that is not provided for in the other section (14533).

---

[48] The language in MacDonald's amendment was taken from the 1912 Bartlett-Bacon bill, a failed AFL-supported measure that incorporated language from the Pearre bill on jurisdiction (H.R. 23189, 62nd Congress). The amendment would have added the definition of property rights to Section 17 of the Clayton Act rather than Section 20. Section 17 contained new procedures for issuing temporary injunctions but it did not state that a threat to property rights need be established before an injunction could be issued. MacDonald worried that Section 17 permitted "by implication" the issuance of injunctions to protect personal rights (9610).

After Nelson gave vent to his skepticism, another supporter of the bill in the Senate tried to defend the property-right requirement with a less sinister explanation. Sen. James O'Gorman (D-NY) noted that the limitation on equity jurisdiction to property rights was supported by 300 years of case law and established in Rule 73 of the Supreme Court (14534). However, O'Gorman's explanation made it difficult to explain why a restatement of established law on equity jurisdiction should be included in an antitrust bill, and difficult to explain why Samuel Gompers would have gone to so much trouble to add such an innocuous provision to an antitrust bill. After further prodding O'Gorman, Nelson again suggested that supporters of the property-rights provision in Section 20 were "holding out a false promise" (14534). The Senate rejected the Pomerene amendment and thus decided to retain the uncertain language regarding property rights in Section 20.

Nelson's suspicion that the "promise" afforded by that open-ended provision was "false" turned out to be well grounded. In *Duplex* and subsequent cases, the Supreme Court essentially ignored the remnants of the Pearre bill jurisdictional language that were made part of Section 20 and the Court instead added to the growing list of precedents that recognized the right to conduct business as a property right subject to injunctive relief. Of course, it remains an open question whether the courts would have acted differently had the AFL successfully forced legislators to pass the Clayton Act with the second sentence of the Pearre bill intact.[49] However, by removing that second sentence, legislators decided to avoid a confrontation altogether. In making that decision, legislators knowingly left it to judges to decide whether to reconsider the precedents they relied on to justify the injunctions that limited workers' rights to engage in collective activities. The resulting interpretive controversies in cases like *Duplex* could not have been surprising to those members of Congress who participated in the formation of the Clayton Act.

EMPLOYERS, EMPLOYEES, AND LABOR DISPUTES: THE SECOND PARAGRAPH OF SECTION 20

On the surface, the second paragraph of Section 20 is a more promising source of protection for labor organizations than the provisions in either

---

[49] Some states did enact Pearre bill style definitions of property in antiinjunction reform bills, and those bills were struck down, but for reasons that would not necessarily have applied to Federal statutes (Frankfurter and Green 1930, 150–4; Forbath 1991, chs. 3 and 4 and app. C).

Section 6 or the first paragraph. The Supreme Court majority thus devoted more space in its *Duplex* opinion to the complicated and confusing language in that paragraph than it did to any other part of the Clayton Act.

The second paragraph of Section 20 seems to exempt a list of collective activities from some forms of injunctive relief. The paragraph states that "no such restraining order or injunction" shall "prohibit any person or persons, whether singly or in concert" from engaging in six categories of behavior:

1. *quitting or striking:* "terminating any relation of employment, or ... ceasing to perform any work or labor, or ... persuading others by peaceful means so to do"
2. *picketing:* "attending at any place where any such person or persons may lawfully be, for the purpose of peacefully obtaining or communicating information, or ... peacefully persuading any person to work or to abstain from working"
3. *boycotting:* "ceasing to patronize or to employ any party to such dispute, or ... recommending, advising, or persuading others by peaceful and lawful means so to do"
4. *paying benefits to strikers:* "paying or giving to, or withholding from, any person engaged in such dispute, any strike benefits or other moneys or things of value"
5. *assembling:* "peaceably assembling in a lawful manner or for lawful purposes"
6. *general:* "from doing any act or thing which might lawfully be done in the absence of such dispute by any party thereto"

A final clause of the paragraph extends the protections beyond a mere prohibition on injunctions, stating: "nor shall any of the acts specified in this paragraph be considered or held to be violations of any law of the United States."

In *Duplex*, the Supreme Court argued that the exemptions and immunities described in this paragraph, including the provision that seemed on its face to apply to boycotts, did not prevent the courts from issuing an injunction against the machinists. The Supreme Court reached this conclusion by shifting attention away from the question of *what* activities were immunized by the paragraph to the question of *whose* activities were immunized. The Court concluded that *none* of the exemptions in Section 20 could ever apply to any activities of the machinists who engaged in the boycott against the Duplex Company. The Supreme

Court reached this conclusion after deciding that Section 20 immunized the six listed activities only when those activities were part of a particular type of dispute over "employment." Since the dispute between the machinists and the Duplex Company was not the appropriate type of dispute, the Court concluded that nothing in Section 20 protected the machinists.

At first, this seems like a very odd reading of the broad immunities expressed in the statute. Once again, however, Pitney's opinion of the Court purported to stick very closely to the text and intent of the statute. According to Pitney, the question of whether the machinists were engaged in a dispute with Duplex over employment was made important by language in the opening phrase of the second paragraph of Section 20. The relevant phrase stated: "And no *such* restraining order or injunction shall prohibit *any* person or persons" (emphasis added) from engaging in the activities described in the paragraph. The key to understanding Pitney's reading of the provision is to recognize that Pitney chose to focus on the word "such" rather than the word "any" when construing that phrase. Pitney determined that the word "such" referred back to the first paragraph of Section 20, which established that courts could not issue injunctions in certain types of labor disputes unless there was a threat to property. The relevant provision from the first paragraph stated the paragraph applied to disputes:

between an employer and employees, or between employers and employees, or between employees, or between persons employed and persons seeking employment, involving, or growing out of a dispute concerning terms or conditions of employment.

By deciding that the word "such" in the second paragraph referred back to this provision from the first paragraph, Pitney created a limitation on the scope of the immunities in the second paragraph. The crucial issue in the *Duplex* case was the question of whether the dispute between Duplex and the machinists fit the definition of immunized disputes in the first paragraph.

While Pitney's opinion eventually made choices that established the meaning of the two provisions in Section 20, those choices were not easy to make. The precise nature of the first paragraph as a qualification on the second was quite difficult to determine. Competing parties were able to offer a variety of conflicting interpretations, each of which seemed to be at least consistent with the confusing text of the statute. Because of various ambiguities and seeming contradictions in the text of the provisions, it was difficult for the parties to defend any interpretation as the best reading of the text.

Justice Pitney's opinion considered several possible interpretations. Pitney first considered and quickly rejected the broad interpretation favored by some supporters of the boycotting machinists. On that reading, the machinists qualified as participants in the labor dispute simply because they belonged to the same union as some of Duplex's employees. Ironically, Pitney's justification for rejecting that reading was that Section 6 of the Clayton Act actually did create such a broad immunity, that is, one based on membership in labor organizations. Pitney noted that Congress had gone to the trouble of using different language to define the scope of the immunities in Section 20, and thus insisted that the Court find a reading of Section 20 that treated those differences as significant. Pitney thus concluded that the immunities in the second paragraph could not "be regarded as bringing in all members of a labor organization as parties" to a dispute "which proximately affects only a few of them" (472).

The Court also considered and rejected the interpretation favored by many employers: The provisions in Section 20 applied only to workers who were actual employees of the firms targeted by collective activities. This reading is in some respects tied quite closely to the text of the first paragraph, given that the paragraph repeatedly uses variants on the words "employee" and "employer." Such a reading would also have sharply curtailed the scope of Section 20. For example, the boycotting machinists could not be covered since they were not employees of the Duplex Company.

The Court was not, however, willing to accept this second reading of the text. The problem was that if the Court had read the first paragraph as covering only persons who were actual employees of the targeted company, then the Court would have rendered nonsensical some of the clauses in the second paragraph. For example, the provision protecting strikes would be silly if legislators intended it to only apply to "employees." Striking workers were often no longer "employees" of the company targeted by the strike. Moreover, if the "employee" reading of the statute was correct, employers would have always been able to escape the limitation imposed by Congress and suddenly qualify for an injunction if they simply fired their striking workers. Thus, while many of the justices on the Supreme Court may otherwise have been happy to adopt this probusiness reading of the statute, the Court did not adopt the second interpretation of Section 20.

Yet another possible reading of the text was the one offered by the circuit court judges who first heard *Duplex*. After noticing the same contradiction between the "employee" language in the first paragraph and the strike clause in the second, the circuit court decided that Congress must have intended the terms "employer" and "employee" to invoke membership in broad social classes rather than to the technical employment relationship that exists between particular workers and companies (252 Fed. 722, 2d Cir., 1918, 748). This third reading would have greatly expanded the protection given to workers by Section 20 because it meant that the second paragraph covered all workers. However, that reading did not survive. The Supreme Court simply declared that the lower court's reading was unacceptable.

The reading that the Supreme Court ultimately adopted seems rooted in a desire to find middle ground between the broad reading of the lower court and the much narrower but ultimately nonsensical reading favored by employers. To find such middle ground, Pitney had to go beyond the text of the statute and invent a new test for determining what types of disputes and disputants were covered by the immunities in Section 20. Pitney's test borrowed from the emerging Holmesian formula for determining the lawfulness of actions that interfered with the rights of third parties. As noted in Chapter 2, that formula distinguished acts that were unlawful because they were motivated by malice from acts that could be justified because they were undertaken as part of the pursuit of a legitimate self-interest. The test Pitney announced in *Duplex* was that the immunities in Section 20 covered "parties affected in a proximate and substantial, not merely a sentimental or sympathetic, sense by the cause of the dispute" (472). Since Pitney could not cite anything in the text directly inviting the application of the Holmesian formula, he simply noted that any other reading "would do violence to the guarded language employed" (472) by Congress in the statute. Pitney's own reading may have gone beyond the text, but it also provided a way of reconciling the difficulties in the text without openly contradicting the text.

The way in which the majority of the Court applied the test to the boycotting machinists was more important than their decision to adopt it. The Court majority was either unable or unwilling to understand that the Duplex Company's refusal to recognize the union affected the material well being of employees of the other three press manufacturers in the United States. The Court concluded that the machinists were not involved in a dispute with the Duplex Company because they were affected only in a "sentimental or sympathetic sense" by the dispute.[50]

In making this ruling, the Court chose a reading of a labor provision that left judges with considerable room to exercise judgment when resolving legal disputes that arose in connection with strikes and boycotts. The Court also chose a reading that meant, once again, that a celebrated Clayton Act provision made no substantial changes in existing law. Invoking "self-interest" formula as a means of testing the connection between workers' collective actions and their grievances against targeted employers meant that the reach of the Clayton Act's immunities would not depend on a new substantive legal rule laid down by elected legislators. Rather, labor relations law would remain dependent on judges' mostly unarticulated background assumptions about industrial relations.

Controversies in Congress about Who was Covered by Section 20

Although Justice Pitney claimed that the Court was attempting to uncover and follow the will of Congress, the choices Pitney made regarding the scope of the immunities in Section 20 seem to fit the criticism that the judges who interpreted the Clayton Act violated the spirit of a statute that was hailed upon passage as a dramatic reform. Once again, however, it is impossible to assess the impact of the courts without a more complete understanding of the political processes that shaped the details of the statutory text. It turns out that the difficulties in the courts can be directly traced to compromises made in Congress that rendered the text of the statute ambiguous. With respect to the question of who was covered by the second paragraph of Section 20, the story of the changes made in Congress is shorter, and the nature of the changes more subtle. The whole controversy over the scope of Section 20's exemptions hinges, in fact, on the decision in Congress to remove a single two-letter word from the statute.

The Clayton Act was not the first injunction reform proposal that defined the scope of its immunities using terms like "employer" and

[50] Although the dissenters disagreed with this characterization of the interests that were at stake in the boycott, they did not challenge the test Pitney used to determine who was covered by Section 20. Brandeis's dissent argues that the machinists had a self-interest in the dispute that was sufficient to qualify them under Pitney's test.

"employee." The Hoar and Grosvenor bills of 1900–6, for example, stated that they protected any:

agreement, combination, or contract by or between two or more persons to do, or procure to be done, or not to do, or procure not to be done, any act in contemplation or furtherance of any trade dispute between employers and employees.

However, even though the phrase "employers and employees" appears in this earlier proposal, the provision as a whole seems to provide broader protections for workers than the ones the Supreme Court later found in Section 20 of the Clayton Act. The quoted provision seems to make a person's participation in a collective agreement or combination, not a person's employment status, the salient fact for determining when the exemption applies.

The original source for the language in the first paragraph of Section 20 of the Clayton Act can be found in an almost identical provision in the Pearre bill of 1906 (H.R. 18446, 59th Congress). The similarities between the provision from the Pearre bill and the Clayton Act provision can be seen in the following modified quote:

in any case between an employer and an employee [employees], or between employers and employees, or between employees, or between persons employed to labor and person[s] seeking employment as laborers, or between persons seeking employment as laborers, or involving [,] or growing out of [,] a dispute concerning terms or conditions of employment.

In the preceding quote, underlining indicates the words or phrases that were omitted in Section 20 of the Clayton Act. The brackets around the word "employees" and the two commas indicate what was added to the Clayton Act but not in the Pearre bill.

Most of the differences between the Pearre bill provisions and the final version in the Clayton Act were not of any consequence in the judicial rulings. However, one seemingly minor difference between the two proposals narrowed the scope of the provision considerably and directly influenced the outcome in *Duplex:* The removal of one instance of the word "or." The missing "or" is the last underlined word in the preceding passage.[51]

In the Pearre bill version with the "or" intact, the clause following the "or" appears to establish an additional category of protected dispute:

[51] The "or" was missing in the compromise bill that the AFL endorsed in 1912 (62nd Congress, H.R. 23635). The commas appeared for the first time when that bill was incorporated into the Clayton Bill in the next Congress (H.R. 15657).

"*or* involving or growing out of a dispute concerning terms or conditions of employment" (emphasis added). In the Clayton Act version with the "or" omitted, the final clause takes on a different meaning. The provision in the Clayton Act read:

in any case between an employer and employees, or between employers and employees, or between employees, or between persons employed and persons seeking employment, involving, or growing out of, a dispute concerning terms or conditions of employment.

Instead of adding an additional category preventing judges from issuing an injunction in "any case ... involving or growing out of a dispute concerning the terms of condition of employment" the clause instead appears to add a qualification restricting the application of the preceding four categories. That difference matters. Rather than covering any case between an employer and employees *or* growing out of a dispute concerning terms or conditions of employment, the modified provision covered only cases that were *both* between employers and employees *and* growing out of such a dispute.

The decision to remove the "or" did not go unnoticed. The "or" was at the center of a more general debate about the meaning of Section 20 during House floor debates on the Clayton Act in 1914. The controversy first arose after Judiciary Committee Chair Webb twice made the broad claim that the House need not worry about shortcomings in Section 6 because Section 20 provided protection that filled in any gaps (9541, 9567).[52] The second time Webb made this claim, he was challenged by Representative William MacDonald (P-MI). The questions that MacDonald raised almost perfectly anticipated the reasoning of the Supreme Court in *Duplex*. He noted that the language in Section 20 referred to "employers" and "employees" and not to members of labor organizations. MacDonald worried that the language in Section 20 would lead the courts to continue to issue injunctions against members of labor organizations who were not themselves employees of a targeted company (9567).

---

[52] Floor debate page references are again to vol. 51 of the *Congressional Record*. Interestingly, Samuel Gompers later made the same argument about Section 20 that Webb tried to make on the floor. Gompers often cited the protections in Section 20 when defending the Clayton Act from attacks it received soon after passage. See letters from Gompers to David Kreyling, January 19, 1915, to Margaret Dreier Robbins, August 31, 1915, and to Frank Walsh, September 15, 1915, *Gompers Letterbooks*, Library of Congress. These letters are also discussed in Foner 1980, 140.

The following day, the same controversy arose again when Representative Murdock (R-KA) directly raised the issue of the missing "or." Murdock argued that with the original "or" still in place, the earlier Pearre bills provided much broader protection than the Clayton bill (9654). Murdock was especially concerned that the missing "or" would mean that striking workers who were no longer employees of a firm would not be covered. Webb responded first by claiming that Murdock was "mistaken" about the missing word. Webb later said: "I am sorry that this argument appears to me to be extremely technical. I cannot understand the difference" (9654). But when Murdock proposed an amendment to restore the "or," Webb protested: "I think the use of that word might make it uncertain" (9655). Without offering any explanation for the decision to remove the "or," Webb protested that the committee had maintained the language in the Clayton bill for two years, and had "gone over this very carefully and drawn the section, having in view the decisions on the matter" (9655).

Supporters of the committee's language defended the wording as adequate. Rep. George Graham (R-PA) said rather cryptically that restoring the "or" would "destroy the symmetrical construction of the real meaning of the sentence" (9655). Rep. John C. Floyd (D-AK) claimed that restoring the "or" would "complicate" the passage but would not strengthen it (9656). Rep. Frank Buchanan (D-IL) asked more general questions about the ability of legislators to do anything to control future judicial interpretations. Buchanan said: "I do not think that as long as judges are going to construe laws in the narrowest possible way against labor that we will ever get anything right" (9655).

Despite the reassurances that the existing language was adequate and the suggestions that legislators were powerless to make the outcome in the courts more definite, six more representatives rose to offer suggestions for alternative language that could clarify the meaning of the passage and thus ensure that the courts would read the provision as covering all the affected members of labor organizations.[53] Webb continued to insist that such changes were unnecessary. He claimed that the passage covered "every case involving or covering every phase of employment" (9660). Webb also claimed (erroneously) that the passage came directly from the AFL-supported Bartlett-Bacon bill of 1912 (H.R. 23189, 62nd Congress),

---

[53] Suggestions were made by Representatives Graham (R-PA), Floyd (D-AK), Gardner (R-MA), Gorman (D-IL), Dickinson (D-MO), Phelan (D-MA), and Hulings (P-PA) (9655–6).

and that it had been endorsed "probably by every labor union in the United States" (9660).

The floor discussion of the ambiguity in the opening paragraph of Section 20 and the missing "or" resulted in votes on three amendments in the House.[54] The House rejected all three amendments, and decided to stick with the original language from the Judiciary Committee. They did this despite the fact that so many representatives found the language confusing and feared that it would allow the courts to make substantive policy choices about who Section 20 covered.

The missing "or" and the question of who was covered by the immunities in Section 20 did not attract nearly as much attention when the bill reached the Senate. However, senators did express concern about which workers would be covered by the language in Section 20. Some senators questioned whether the language in Section 20 was clear enough to remove the discretion of judges in labor injunction cases. Senator Cummins anticipated perfectly the Court's reasoning in *Duplex* and expressed concern that membership in labor organizations would not be the Court's basis for deciding who was covered by Section 20. Cummins's substitute amendment for Section 6 (discussed previously) included a provision adding exemptions for all members of labor organizations for many of the same activities described in Section 20. Other senators agreed that the House version of the bill left judges tremendous discretion to decide which workers were immunized by Section 20. Senator Borah (R-ID), for example, noted that lingering questions about who was covered by Section 20 would mean that outcomes would continue to depend on individual judges' attitudes toward workers' collective actions and workers' interests in the outcomes of labor disputes (13925).

---

[54] The first was one offered by Representative MacDonald to restore the "or." The amendment also added a provision that extended protection "in the case where a strike or lockout exists or is threatened." A second amendment, also offered by MacDonald, removed the word "such" from the first sentence of the *second* paragraph of Section 20 so that the phrase read "And no restraining order or injunction shall prohibit..." rather than "And no such restraining order or injunction shall prohibit...." This amendment also anticipates perfectly the reasoning used by the Supreme Court in *Duplex*. The amendment would have made questions about who was covered by the first paragraph of Section 20 irrelevant to the interpretation of the second paragraph. The third amendment, offered by Representative Hulings, struck all the "employer" and "employee" categories from the first paragraph of Section 20, leaving only the broad category "any case involving, or growing out of, a dispute concerning terms or conditions of employment." All the amendments are in 51 *Congressional Record* 9660.

Thus, the record of congressional deliberation shows once again that the participants in the legislative process noticed that legislators had replaced strong provisions in earlier bills with less decisive language in the Clayton Act. The complaints about the ambiguity of the legislative language and the proposals to improve that language perfectly anticipate the interpretive controversy settled by the courts in *Duplex*. Despite these concerns about how the Courts would interpret the labor provisions, members of Congress decided not to limit judicial discretion by clarifying the language.[55]

"NOTHING BUT A HUMBUG AND A SHAM": WHAT ACTIVITIES ARE COVERED UNDER SECTION 20?

Because the *Duplex* Court concluded that the boycotting machinists did not qualify as "employees" covered by the immunities in Section 20, the Court did not have to say much about exactly what activities were covered by those immunities. The Court's answer to the question of *who* was covered made it unnecessary to fully consider *what* activities would be covered in cases where workers involved in collective activities were employees of a targeted company. Nevertheless, the justices in the majority hinted at things to come when they briefly considered the machinists' claim that their boycott was covered by one of the clauses of that second paragraph.

The clause in question stated that the courts could not issue an injunction to prevent "any person or persons" from "recommending, advising, or persuading others by peaceful and lawful means" that other persons cease to patronize a party to a labor dispute. In his opinion, Justice Pitney claimed that this provision would not have covered the boycott even if the machinists in New York had been involved in a legitimate labor

---

[55] Note, however, that in the case of Section 20, the doubters in Congress did not always predict accurately how the courts would react to the ambiguous language. Many House members worried that the courts would respond to the contradiction by reading all protections for striking workers out of the statute. In *Duplex*, these worries did not prove justified: Both the majority and the dissenters of the Supreme Court took the strike provision seriously as they strained to provide interpretations of Section 20 that could at least occasionally cover striking workers. However, the issue of coverage for strikers did contribute to the Court's difficulty in reaching a consensus on what Section 20 meant. In his dissent, Brandeis made it quite clear that he felt the Court needed to find an interpretation that would cover striking workers. The decision by the majority to go beyond the terms "employee" and "employer" appears to be rooted in similar concerns.

dispute with the Duplex Company. Pitney called attention to the qualifying adjectives "peaceful" and "lawful" in the provision and declared
that the machinists' boycott did not fit the description. Pitney stated that
a "sympathetic strike in aid of a secondary boycott cannot be deemed
'peaceful and lawful' persuasion" (474).[56]

Pitney's dictum provided yet another way for judges to continue to issue
injunctions, even in cases where the workers targeted by injunctions were
covered "employees" involved in an appropriate "labor dispute." The
alternative strategy in such cases was for judges to issue injunctions after
calling attention to the qualifying phrases in the descriptions of immunized
activities in Section 20. Section 20 contained five instances of the words
"lawful" or "lawfully," and five instances of "peaceful," "peacefully," or
"peaceably." Because legislators had added so many qualifying phrases
in the language describing the law's immunities, it was hard to argue
that the congressional intent in Section 20 was to establish a broad
barrier to injunctive relief in all cases involving activities like boycotts,
pickets, or strikes. Judges were free to interpret the qualifying phrases as
an indication that legislators wanted judges to continue to exercise discretion when sorting lawful from unlawful, enjoinable from immunized
conduct.

For many judges, the qualifying phrases meant that Section 20 did not
make any change in the way they would respond to labor disputes. There
was a large body of case law directly relevant to the question of what
kinds of worker activities were "lawful." As with Section 6, legislators
did not attempt to indicate what was meant by the word "lawful" in
Section 20. Thus, it is not surprising that judges read the statute as an
indication that they should continue to draw the line between lawful
and unlawful behavior by citing the same doctrines and precedents that
had been cited in labor injunction cases *before* passage of the Clayton
Act. Those doctrines and precedents allowed judges to exercise a great
deal of discretion and to take into account a broad range of surrounding
circumstances when determining whether workers' collective activities
were unlawful (Frankfurter and Green 1930, ch. II and III).

Brandeis's dissenting opinion argues against such conclusions by
claiming that the Clayton Act "was designed to equalize before the law

---

[56] Pitney cited the committee reports and floor statements of the chair of the committee with jurisdiction to support his contention that the statute was not meant to
legalize "secondary boycotts." Pitney's interpretation of the record was based on a
distinction between a primary and secondary boycott that was not the same as the
distinction used by the members of Congress he was quoting.

the position of workingmen and employer as industrial combatants" (484); and that legislators had passed the act in order to clear up the "great confusion" (485) caused by disagreements among judges regarding which purposes of labor organizations were "socially and economically harmful." Brandeis further claimed that the Clayton Act was an effort to establish "the opinion of Congress" on the propriety of workers' collective actions, so that the congressional opinion could substitute for the conflicting opinions of different judges (486). However, Brandeis's position is rooted less in the text of the statute than in the general *ethos* surrounding the decision in Congress to pass the statute. While Brandeis's reading is perfectly consistent with the text, the presence of so many qualifying phrases also provides some support for Pitney's more restrictive reading. Thus, before choosing to side with either Brandeis or Pitney, scholars need to answer the question of why legislators included qualifying phrases in the provisions establishing worker immunities.

Section 20 in Congress: What Actions are Immunized by Section 20?

The record of congressional deliberations on the second paragraph of Section 20 is much shorter than the record on some of the other controversial provisions in the Act. Provisions containing lists of immunized activities did not appear in any of the AFL-supported bills until 1912, two years before the Clayton Act passed. The reason the AFL never pursued such legislation earlier was that AFL leaders like Andrew Furuseth were convinced that statutes that attacked the jurisdiction of the courts by narrowing the definition of property rights would be more effective. Furuseth feared provisions like those eventually enacted in Section 20 because he was convinced that judges would read any attempt to specify immunities for some listed array of activities as an invitation to issue injunctions whenever judges found that activities somehow fell outside the listed immunities.

A first useful window into what the participants in the legislative process expected Section 20 to accomplish is found in the AFL's explanation for its decision to support the new provision. The explanation was given by T. C. Spelling, an attorney who was the AFL's most effective advocate for the provision before the Senate Judicial Committee in 1912.[57] Spelling adopted an interpretation of the bill that was quite similar to the one

---

[57] Spelling's testimony, on H.R. 23635, 62nd Congress, is in 1912 *Senate Judiciary Hearings*, 380–451. See esp. 382–404.

Justice Brandeis would give in his dissent almost a decade later. Spelling claimed that the list of immunized activities was needed because much of the existing law on such matters had been made by judges with little statutory guidance from legislators. Spelling claimed that in the absence of clear statutory guidelines, outcomes would remain dependent upon the attitudes of individual judges, or as he put it, the "obnoxious paternalism" (1912 Senate Hearings, 394) of judges and the "whim of the courts" (382). According to Spelling, even the most conscientious judges were having a difficult time deciding cases. Lack of guidance from Congress had led to a proliferation of contradictory rulings that made the case law an unreliable guide for judges in injunction cases. In most cases, judges could find precedents that would justify either a decision to issue an injunction or a decision not to issue one. Thus, clear statutory guidance was needed to remove judicial discretion in the broad class of cases fitting the descriptions of immunized activity that ended up in Section 20.

Unfortunately for labor organizations, legislators passed the Clayton Act without ever agreeing to adopt the clear legislative language that was needed in order to limit judicial discretion. Although the decision to pass the Clayton Act seems at first to be an attempt to respond to Spelling's concerns, closer scrutiny reveals that members of Congress never agreed to pass a statute that pursued the goals articulated by Spelling. Instead, legislators weakened the provisions as the bill moved toward passage by adding numerous qualifying adjectives like "lawfully" and "peaceably" to the language describing immunized activities. The decisions legislators made to modify the bill did not send any clear message about what those legislators wanted the bill to mean. As if to compensate for the effect of the qualifying phrases that narrowed the protections, members of Congress also voted to make one change that seemed to broaden the scope of the bill. The result of such contradictory changes was not a statute reflecting broad agreement on a particular set of policies, but a confusing hodgepodge of provisions that passed despite widespread disagreement among legislators about what the provisions meant.

One initial indication of the effect of the amendments is provided by changing reactions of the AFL's longtime lobbying nemesis, Daniel Davenport of the American Anti-Boycott Association. During the 1912 hearings, after Spelling first introduced the provisions immunizing a list of specified activities, Davenport called the provisions "half-baked, ill-considered, preposterous" and vigorously opposed them.[58] Two years

---

[58] 1912 *Senate Judiciary Hearings*, 257.

later, after those provisions had been watered down by numerous qualifying phrases like "lawful" and "peaceably," Davenport confidently told
a member of Congress that those changes made Section 20 meaningless;
"nothing but a humbug and sham."[59]

Davenport's early objections seem to have helped him to get what he
wanted. Legislators decided to weaken the protections afforded labor by
adding the qualifying language. The picketing provision provides a good
example of the types of changes that were made. The 1912 version of
the provision stated that the courts could not prohibit workers "from
attending at or near a house or place where any person resides or works
or carries on business, or happens to be, for the purpose of peacefully
obtaining or communicating information." Before the bill was introduced
in 1914, an additional clause was added: "or peacefully persuading any
person to work or abstain from working." When the bill reached the
Senate, a committee amendment removed the original clause from the
1912 bill and kept only the provision that the House added in 1914.
Later, the Senate adopted a floor amendment by Senator Cummins that
substituted new language for the entire provision: "from attending at any
place where any such person or persons may lawfully be for the purpose
of peacefully obtaining or communicating information." The Cummins
substitute seemed to cover a broader range of activities than the provision
kept by the Senate committee. However, including the word "lawfully"
belies any claim that the amendment was an effort to eliminate judicial
discretion or to prevent the courts from relying on existing precedents
when deciding which activities were lawful. None of these changes satisfied members that uncertainties about the meaning of the bill had been
eliminated. Nevertheless, the Senate adopted the Cummins version and it
remained in the final version of the Clayton Act.

The Senate also fiddled with the boycotting provisions by adopting
two committee amendments. The first changed the phrase "ceasing to
patronize" to "withholding patronage from." No one articulated why
this change was important. The second appeared once again to weaken
the protection by adding the qualifying word "lawful." The House/Senate
conference committee later restored the House "ceasing to patronize"
language, but retained the "lawful" that had been added to the Senate
version.

The legislators who took part in deliberations on the Clayton Act
did not miss the importance of the qualifying phrases that legislators

[59] From a letter from Davenport to Senator Borah, quoted in Ernst 1995, 188.

added to the statute. When the House Judiciary Committee first reported the bill in 1912, the committee did not claim that the bill provided the broad immunities that Spelling had asked for and defended. Like Spelling, the committee claimed that the bill was needed because the courts had developed "divergent views" regarding the legality of the acts enumerated in the bill.[60] However, the committee's explanations for each item on the modified list of immunized activities implied that the immunities conferred in Section 20 were much narrower than Spelling had originally claimed. For example, the committee emphasized that the language regarding picketing applied only when the picketing communicated information and did not involve coercion or threats. A similar limitation was found in the language applying to boycotts. The committee stated that the immunity for boycotts applied only if the "primary object" of the boycott was the self-interest of those conducting the boycott rather than a simple desire to "inflict harm" on the targeted firm.[61] The committee suggested that the same self-interest standard applied to the immunity for assemblies of workers.[62]

Many of the new limitations articulated by the committee appeared to invite, not eliminate, judicial discretion. For example, the meaning of the "self-interest" standard the committee found in the boycotting and picketing provisions was likely to vary depending on the personal views of the judge who heard the case. Thus, even before legislators finished adding qualifying words to the statute, the committees appear to have been moving away from Spelling's goal of establishing a uniform standard through clear instructions to judges.[63]

A minority report issued by the same committee challenged the majority's reading and warned that there was no guarantee the courts would recognize the limitations suggested by the committee. The minority called the paragraph containing the list of immunities "the most vicious proposal of the whole bill"[64] and complained that the implied limitations on the immunities were not expressed with sufficient clarity in the text. Curiously, the pattern noted in connection with Section 6 of the Clayton Act reappears in connection with Section 20: The opponents of the AFL

---

[60] House Report 612, 62nd Congress (on H.R. 23635), 8.

[61] House Report 612, 62nd Congress (on H.R. 23635), 8.

[62] House Report 612, 62nd Congress (on H.R. 23635), 10–11.

[63] The committee had not changed its mind in 1914. Instead of issuing a new report on the bill, the committee simply incorporated the 1912 report into its report on the Clayton bill.

[64] House Report 612, 62nd Congress (on H.R. 23635), pt. 2. Quote is from p. 7.

in Congress offered an interpretation of the bill that was closer to the AFL's interpretation than the one given by the alleged friends of the AFL who were voting for the bill.

Two years later, the same controversies about the likely meaning of the provisions in Section 20 arose a second time. As introduced in the 1914 Clayton bill, the provision describing immunized activities was identical to the corresponding provision of the 1912 House judiciary bill except for an additional provision in the description of picketing.[65] As the bill moved toward passage, legislators continually expressed disagreements about the meaning of the provisions. Nevertheless, the legislators once again failed to develop legislative language that eliminated the smoldering controversies over what the bill meant.

What happened instead was that Section 20 was subjected to a flurry of amending activity. Many of the changes seemed to make the meaning of the provision even more obscure and thus to make outcomes even more dependent upon the attitudes of judges. Amendments substituted language that many members felt was more ambiguous to describe the conduct that was immunized. In the end, the version of Section 20 that emerged from the drawn-out legislative process failed to choose decisively among the unqualified interpretation originally favored by the AFL and a number of more limited interpretations that were offered during debates.

While the addition of qualifying language like "lawful" seems to have been an effort to limit the application of the provision, the many changes in the various descriptions of the immunized conduct do not fit any simple, uniformly antilabor pattern. One of the important changes appears to have narrowed the protections by inviting judicial discretion, others appear to have broadened the protections.[66] For example, during floor debates on the Clayton Act, legislators voted to add a final phrase to Section 20: "nor shall any of the acts specified in this paragraph be considered or held to be violations of any law of the United States." This change appeared to expand the coverage of the entire provision. While

---

[65] The new bill added the phrase "or peacefully persuading any person to work or abstain from working" to the picketing section.

[66] The Senate committee and conference committee made some other changes to the descriptions of the acts that appear to have been of even less consequence. The opening phrase of the House version covered "person or persons"; the Senate changed the language to "any individual or individuals, whether singly or in concert." In the final version of the bill, the passage read "any person or persons, whether singly or in concert." "Or of" in a provision regarding peaceful persuasion was changed to "or from." None of these changes figured in any reported cases arising under the Clayton Act.

the original 1912 version of the bill provided only that the enumerated acts be immunized from a particular judicial remedy (the injunction), the final version of the bill added a clause that transformed Section 20 into a change in substantive law.[67]

The new clause originated in an amendment of even broader scope that Representative Webb had introduced at the AFL's request during House consideration of Section 20.[68] The House debate on the Webb amendment to Section 20 did not specifically address the wisdom of what appeared on the surface to be a major change in the scope of the provision. However, the introduction of the amendment did intensify the debate about Section 20 and led to a revealing discussion of the overall meaning of the labor provisions in the bill.

The Webb amendment to Section 20 animated an odd coalition of legislators who claimed that the new provision was holding out a false promise to labor: Legislators associated with the Progressive Party who wanted to make the bill stronger and conservative Republicans who wanted to narrow the protections. The Progressives predicted that the Webb amendment would not provide the sweeping coverage the committee claimed and that the AFL wanted. Meanwhile, conservative Republicans used the debate over the Webb amendment to complain about the possibility that Section 20 might take away some of the discretion of the courts.[69] Both conservative and progressive House members introduced clarifying amendments that were supposed to clarify the meaning of the Webb amendment, but the House voted against all the attempted clarifications.

When the bill reached the Senate, the Judiciary Committee decided that the new language added by the House in the Webb Amendment was too sweeping. They changed the provision to state that the immunized activities could not be held to be "violations of the antitrust laws" rather than to say that they could not be held "unlawful." The committee amendment was supported by senators who questioned the constitutionality of the Webb amendment. Some senators claimed that "unlawful" might be

---

[67] Ernst 1989b, 1163, explains the symbolic significance of this change.

[68] The Webb version read: "nor shall any of the acts specified in this paragraph be considered or held unlawful." Representative Henry noted in an exchange with Representative Mann (9654) that the change was being made at the request of the AFL.

[69] During debate over the Webb amendment, Volstead challenged Webb on whether the bill would legalize the secondary boycott (51 *Congressional Record* 9652–3). Justice Pitney later quoted the exchange in his opinion for the Supreme Court in *Duplex*.

interpreted as an attempt by legislators to supersede state laws.[70] Other senators said that anything less than the House version would make the bill too weak.[71]

A compromise was eventually reached when Senator Culberson (D-TX) proposed changing the House language so that the described actions would not be "violations of any law of the United States." This compromise language provided broader protection than the Senate Committee version while at the same time alleviating the federalism concerns raised by the House version. It was Culberson's language that survived the conference committee and appears in Section 20.

As the final version of Section 20 was being worked out in the Senate, several senators continued to warn that the bill held out a false promise to labor and that it might backfire and hurt labor's interests.[72] While some senators (e.g., James Reed [D-MO], 51 *Congressional Record* 14322) defended the bill by noting that it was the AFL that requested that the House add the final phrase to Section 20, senators again expressed concerns about relying on the AFL to decide how the Senate could best assist labor. For example, Senator Smith argued that the Senate should not rely on the endorsements of the AFL when deciding how to help workers:

it does not matter that labor approves of the bill as worded. The Senator from New Jersey [Hughes] says that the laboring people are satisfied with it. We can not legislate because a class of people are satisfied. A class of people might be satisfied with a piece of legislation, thinking it would accomplish a certain thing, when it would not. Finally the responsibility comes to us, and even though they thought it would do a certain thing for them, if we found that it would do a very different thing to them we could properly be responsible if we passed the legislation, though they, misapprehend its effect, were satisfied with it (51 *Congressional Record* 14366).

In the end, however, the senators chose not to listen to Smith or to adopt clarifying language. The heavily qualified language in Section 20 was enacted before legislators reached any collective agreement about what

---

[70] Senator Shields (14333); Senator Culberson (14364).

[71] For example, Senator Reed (D-MO) pointed out that many of the injunctions that the AFL had complained about were not issued under the antitrust laws (14332). Senator Thomas complained that if the amendment specified that the described acts did not violate the antitrust laws, Section 20 could be taken as implying that the acts were illegal under other, unspecified laws (14333).

[72] Smith, for example, argued that the bill created immunities for employers that would make it harder for employees to recover against employers who broke agreements with workers. On the important problem of legislation backfiring, see Forbath 1991, 135.

the qualifications meant or what activities were covered by the six categories in Section 20.

It is clear in retrospect that Section 20 was not strong enough to prevent judges from continuing to issue injunctions when labor disputes led workers to boycott, picket, or quit work. In later cases involving Section 20, judges took the proliferation of words such as "peaceful" and "lawful" as an indication of a legislative intention that they continue to weigh surrounding circumstances and apply existing common-law precedents when deciding cases.[73] The evidence presented here, however, shows that at least some of the blame lies with the legislators who created the statute. The decision to add such qualifying phrases despite frequent warnings that the phrases invited judicial discretion demonstrates at least some congressional complicity in continued judicial regulation of labor by injunction. Many of the decisions legislators made while converting earlier antiinjunction bills into Section 20 made it easier for judges to justify injunctions. As the different opinions in *Duplex* demonstrate, outcomes were still dependent upon differences in the way *judges* understood industrial relations and the connections among workers' interests. The provisions in Section 20 were, as Brandeis pointed out, the "the fruit of unceasing agitation" (484). However, one result of the compromises made to get the Clayton Act passed was that the unceasing agitation would bear bitter fruit for the workers affiliated with the AFL.

Nevertheless, even though legislators deserve some of the blame, the overall record of Congress on Section 20 is somewhat ambiguous. As already noted, legislators did make some changes that seem like attempts to strengthen the protection afforded by the bill. In addition, some of the debates over the language in Section 20 suggest that at least some members of Congress worried about whether it was possible to find descriptive language that would curtail the interpretive power of the courts. The problem may have been that ordinary language was not powerful enough to describe immunized activities in a way that would make it impossible for judges to exercise discretion, especially judges whose hostility to labor might lead them to find loopholes in statutory immunities.

Nevertheless, difficulties with ordinary language do not mean that there was nothing legislators could have done to make it more difficult for judges to issue injunctions in cases like *Duplex*. The eventual failure of the descriptions of immunized conduct underscores some of the reasons

---

[73] Frankfurter and Green (1930, 165–77) discuss the problems with the statutory text in considerable detail.

why the AFL had earlier pursued the Pearre bill strategy of limiting the jurisdiction of the courts to cases involving threats to property. It is no accident that none of the early AFL-supported bills tried to curtail injunctions by describing actions to be immunized from judicial interference. AFL leaders like Furuseth understood that any such descriptions would have to be interpreted by judges and would thus allow judges to scrutinize workers' collective activities in each case that arose.

The strength of the earlier Pearre bill was that the judges' interpretive task would not have involved any choices about whether or not particular activities engaged in by labor organizations were "peaceable" or "lawful." If the original Pearre bill language had remained in the first paragraph of Section 20, it would not have mattered how the judge felt about the behavior if the judge could not establish that the behavior threatened the physical property of the employer. Thus, Duplex's request for an injunction might have been thrown out *before* the justices ever reached the web of "peacefuls" and "lawfuls" that legislators added to the second paragraph. The difficulties with the language in Section 20 were relevant only because of a very conscious congressional decision to reject the Pearre bill's more comprehensive strategy for limiting the discretion of judges by limiting the jurisdiction of the courts.

In conclusion, it may well be true that the legislators who passed the Clayton Act reached a consensus that the courts had abused their equity powers in labor disputes. There are quite plausible grounds for arguing that some judges read the language in the Clayton Act more narrowly than many members of Congress would have liked or anticipated. Nevertheless, it does not seem accurate to characterize the labor injunctions issued after passage of the Clayton Act as bold judicial reversals of a clearly established desire by elected officials to end the labor injunction. Whatever agreement Congress reached that allowed passage of the Clayton Act, it was not an agreement to prevent judges from issuing injunctions in all labor disputes.

The discussion of the immunities in the second paragraph concludes this discussion of Section 20. That complicated provision gave rise to a number of significant interpretive controversies that had to be settled by the courts. Looked at in the context of the legislative decisions that produced the language in Section 20, it seems that all three of the conditions for identifying legislative deferrals, as explained in Chapter 1, have been met for Section 20. The participants in the legislative process noticed and called attention to ambiguities in the legislative language before the Clayton Act passed, specifically associated the ambiguities with the ability of judges to influence policy outcomes, and rejected alternative proposals that participants felt would better prevent the courts from interfering with the stated goals of the new law. The fact that legislators passed the Clayton Act without resolving such uncertainties makes it impossible to conclude that the judicial rulings reversed some clearly expressed intent of Congress. In this case, there is no baseline indicating a legitimating intent because Section 20 of the Clayton Act was a deliberate deferral to the courts.

CONCLUSIONS

The power possessed by the justices on the Supreme Court who interpreted the Clayton Act has been identified as a threat to democratic responsiveness in the American political system. Decisions like the one in *Duplex v Deering* are thought to threaten democratic legitimacy because they appear to reverse the achievements that organized social groups like labor make through seemingly more democratic legislative processes. The evidence presented here suggests that in the case of the Clayton Act, the interaction between interest groups, Congress, and the courts was much more complicated than such criticisms recognize.

After the Clayton Act passed, judges were called upon to resolve interpretive controversies about what the new law meant. The interpretation established by the Supreme Court in *Duplex* ensured that the Clayton Act would not achieve the two central goals of the AFL's long legislative campaign: Curtailing labor injunctions and exempting labor organizations from the antitrust laws. Such court rulings are often treated as cases where judges reverse policy choices established by legislators. The evidence here suggests, however, that the judges were making choices that legislators had declined to make at the time the Clayton Act passed. Instead of using the new law to establish a clear congressional position on the injunction and antitrust issues, legislators deliberately created conditions that allowed judges to continue to make crucial policy decisions. Because the confusing language in the labor provisions could support multiple interpretations, the justices who settled interpretive questions faced a choice between plausible alternatives rather than a choice between following or rejecting the clearly expressed will of Congress.

Because the ability of the Supreme Court to shape policies grew out of deliberate legislative deferrals, the basic assumptions about interbranch policy making that grow out of the legislative baseline framework do not fare very well in the case of the Clayton Act. Legislators did not establish a particular policy position when it passed the labor provisions of the Clayton Act. Furthermore, passage of the Clayton Act does not provide a straightforward reflection of the political power of the sponsoring labor organizations. There was, of course, strong support for the goals of some labor organizations among some key members of Congress. Legislators did at times mention the AFL's position as a reason to vote for or against a particular amendment or the statute itself. However, the broader record reveals that there were no labor organizations in a position to force legislators to pass anything but a very compromised bill in 1914. The AFL could not prevent opponents from adding the various qualifying amendments that weakened the immunities given to workers. The AFL also could not extract meaningful concessions from some of their most important political allies, particularly President Wilson and his supporters in Congress. The AFL had backed Wilson for President in part because of a campaign promise to support antiinjunction legislation. While AFL leaders may have believed that Wilson would support the AFL's proposals, Wilson and the Democrats did not feel so indebted. The AFL was unable to convince Wilson and the Democrats to switch to the AFL's preferred version of the antitrust exemption in Section 6 by withholding support for the bill developed by Wilson's allies in Congress. Such evidence shows that passage of the Clayton Act should not be taken as a signal that the AFL had achieved a high level of political power.

This is not, of course, the same as saying that labor had no power or even that labor was politically weak. Many members of Congress appear to have taken AFL endorsements into account when they decided how to vote on proposals or amendments. The fact that many members of Congress had an interest in voting for the Clayton Act as a symbolic response to the AFL's legislative demands also shows that those members were not willing to ignore the AFL completely. Nevertheless, the inability of the AFL to prod legislators to pass stronger legislative proposals shows that the AFL's broadest goals were not supported by majorities in Congress.

The failure of the policy and political power assumptions means that it is impossible to characterize the relationship between democratic accountability and electoral controls on decision makers in the way envisioned by the legislative baseline framework. Nor is it possible to characterize the relationship between Congress and the courts as a competition among independent branches. The collective decision made in Congress was that the meaning of the legislation should emerge only in the broader context of judicial rulings on ambiguous legislative language. Members of Congress and other participants were able to anticipate each of the interpretive questions that later arose in the courts. Such participants nevertheless produced an outcome that failed to resolve those questions, even though they knew that leaving them open would ultimately empower judges to make policy.

Given that labor's problems with the courts grew out of labor's inability to win a more decisive victory in Congress, any adequate explanation of the impact of the courts has to look beyond the fact that federal judges are not elected. The reason judges were able to produce an outcome that differed from the AFL's stated expectations was not that the judges did not have to stand for election against an AFL juggernaut that had produced a prolabor Congress. The problem was that the AFL could not find a majority in the divided Congress that would enact stronger legislation that better secured the AFL's policy goals.

Building an Alternative Account of the Impact of the Courts

To understand fully the impact of the judicial decisions that grew out of the legislative deferrals, it is necessary to look at the reasons why the AFL was unable to force members of Congress to act more decisively and, equally importantly, the reasons why the AFL agreed to endorse the Clayton Act after earlier holding out for stronger legislation. The evidence on these points suggests that the decisions that allowed judges to resolve important policy questions did have an important effect on the development of the labor movement and labor policies. However, that effect can only be seen by looking beyond the immediate policy consequences of passage of the Clayton Act and the Court's decision in *Duplex v Deering*. Attention must also be paid to the way legislative compromises served organizational goals that were only distantly related to the policy goals expressed by AFL leaders like Gompers. Passage of the Clayton Act had little immediate impact on labor injunctions and the antitrust laws, but that does not mean that AFL leaders got nothing as a result of its passage. Passage also affected the AFL's leadership strategies and the AFL's capacity to continue to exert political pressure on legislators.

The importance of the extrapolicy side effects of the Clayton Act emerges after considering what the AFL's leaders hoped to gain by agreeing to endorse the Clayton Act's final version despite the many damaging compromises that had to be made on the way to passage. The evidence presented in this chapter makes it clear that the AFL's leaders made conscious decisions to accept compromises even when they realized that such compromises would empower hostile judges to make policy decisions.

Labor leaders were not duped. The AFL's representatives showed a very sophisticated understanding of the likely role the courts would play under competing legislative proposals. AFL leaders had earlier rejected the same compromises precisely because they concluded that such language gave too much discretion to hostile judges. Thus, whatever the reasons for the AFL's decision to abandon the Pearre bill's jurisdiction-curbing strategy in favor of the modified Clayton Act, it was not that labor leaders naively believed that the compromise legislation would automatically achieve their stated policy goals.

The AFL's eventual decision to compromise in 1912 and 1914 remains puzzling in part because the decision to compromise came at a time when the AFL seemed to be in a stronger political position than it had been when the AFL had been holding out for the Pearre bill. The Democrats who controlled Congress and the White House had promised to produce antiinjunction legislation in the 1912 campaign, and were quite obviously eager to avoid breaking with AFL over that promise. In some circumstances, such political conditions would put the AFL leaders in a very good position to bargain for a very favorable legislative outcome. However, the seeming strength of the AFL's bargaining position was hurt because AFL leaders were facing important organizational imperatives that made it very difficult to hold out for their ideal bill.

One indication that the AFL's position may have been hurt by internal organizational pressures can be found in the recollections of Samuel Gompers. In his 1925 autobiography, Gompers recalls his efforts to win legislative victories during the Progressive Era, and emphasizes that those efforts took place in the context of frequent challenges to his leadership. Gompers came under attack from within the AFL because of his moderate strategy of working within the existing party system to "reward friends" and "punish enemies," rather than building permanent ties to one of the existing parties or forming an independent labor party. Looking back on the long period when the AFL struggled to produce injunction reform, Gompers remembered, "My leadership was on trial" (1925, v. II, 269).

Historian Philip Foner's (1980) account of the AFL during the period provides more background on the nature of the challenges to the AFL's leaders. Foner confirms that there was increasing opposition within the AFL to the modest political strategies of leaders like Gompers in the years leading up to passage of the Clayton Act. Leaders of Gompers's own cigar-makers local in New York and several state federations voted several times to form an independent labor party at AFL conventions (Foner 1980, 95–6). Gompers's decision to support Woodrow Wilson in

1912 was controversial within the AFL because the Progressive Party's platform contained more prolabor planks than the Democrat's.[74] Once Wilson and the Democrats won the election, Gompers and the other AFL leaders who orchestrated the endorsement were under tremendous pressure to demonstrate the effectiveness of their political strategy. It was that pressure that made it difficult for the AFL to win the standoff with Wilson.

Gompers and the rest of the leadership knew that the best way to demonstrate their effectiveness was to produce legislative victories. In his editorials in the *American Federationist,* Gompers often claimed that the AFL's ability to produce legislation was the test of the credibility of his leadership. For example, as Congress was moving toward passage of the Clayton Act in early 1914, Gompers wrote an editorial responding to criticisms made by the New York Socialist Party. The socialists had ridiculed an earlier article in the *American Federationist* that had outlined the strategy the AFL would use to secure antiinjunction legislation. The socialists suggested that the AFL was agreeing to compromises that would render the legislation ineffective. More generally, the socialists criticized the AFL for failing to adopt a more aggressive political stance, and claimed that the AFL was too willing to accommodate the interests of its enemies. Gompers was troubled enough to respond to such attacks in the *Federationist.* Gompers explicitly connected the continued survival of effective labor organizations with the ability of those organizations to win concessions through political action. Gompers defended his willingness to compromise as an effective form of pragmatism. In contrast, Gompers claimed, "the socialist party is no real menace to the present order of things." Socialist concerns for some "dim distant future" did not, according to Gompers, amount to an aggressive political strategy (*American Federationist,* March 1914, 126). In the same article, Gompers noted:

Is not all life a struggle for existence? ... Experience proves to all that defensive as well as offensive tactics and policies are necessary for progress. ... The policies of organized labor are the result of years of actual experience in promoting the interests of the working people and in defending the rights that have been secured. They are not perfect, but they are the best that the toilers have as yet been able to

---

[74] Wilson received the AFL endorsement in part because the Democratic platform was closer to the AFL leaders' voluntarism. Both the Democrats and Progressives had an antiinjunction plank, but the Progressives also had a plank in favor of safety, wage, and hours laws that was opposed by voluntarists like Gompers (Foner 1980, 110–11).

think out. The organized labor movement does not exist for propaganda purposes or for theoretical gymnastics, but is a practical movement for toilers living in a world of men and women. It gets results (127).

Here Gompers tellingly associates the continued existence of the AFL with the ability of its leaders to "get results" from the political process. After the election of 1912, getting results meant securing enactment of legislation that could be characterized as a concrete gain and associated with the decision to endorse Woodrow Wilson.[75]

As the first year of the new Democratic Congress's term passed without any antiinjunction legislation being passed, the internal pressure on Gompers increased. Rumblings for an independent labor party began anew at the AFL's convention in November 1913. Gompers had already sent a message to the Democrats in Congress saying that if they did not fulfill the AFL's demands for legislation, he would no longer be able to withstand the growing demand that the AFL abandon the Democrats and form an independent labor party (Foner 1980, 96). Thus, the danger for Gompers was that holding out for the strongest possible law would leave him with nothing to show for his endorsement of Wilson, and thus little basis for resisting calls to form an independent labor party in time for the 1916 presidential election.

Given that the Democrats were likely aware of Gompers's position, it was possible to find common ground. While the preferences of the AFL leaders and the Democrats seemed to diverge on some of the specifics of injunction and antitrust policies, their preferences seemed to converge around the desire to prevent an independent labor party from forming. That converging interest could best be served if the two sides could agree on some moderate antiinjunction bill.

By pointing out Gompers's need to "get results," I do not mean to suggest that his decision to support the Clayton Act was simply a selfish effort to serve his own personal needs by tricking the rank and file with a doomed compromise. AFL leaders no doubt hoped that the interests of workers would be better served by taking a chance on the courts than by risking the potential damage that failure to reach a compromise might do to the ideological direction of the labor movement. Furthermore, AFL leaders may have hoped that even if the provisions failed in the courts, they would still mark an important symbolic victory that would make

[75] The need for interest groups to produce symbolic victories to solve internal organizational goals has been explored by Dennis Chong (1991) in the context of the civil-rights movement.

it easier to win more decisive legislation from Congress the next time around.[76]

In conclusion, it is worth noting an important similarity between the Erdman Act and the Clayton Act. In both cases, the new statute was passed before any majority in Congress emerged in favor of a decisive resolution to the crucial policy controversies addressed in the statute. In both cases, the participants' strong desire to pass new legislation was connected to expectations about the organizational side effects that the participants associated with passage of the statute. In both cases, participants were concerned about the symbolic value of new legislation as well as the policy consequences. In both cases, participants supported the bill in part because they expected passage to affect labor's political strategies and to affect the relative strengths of different labor organizations. Finally, in both cases, participants understood before passage that language in the enacted statute would leave judges with broad discretion to decide substantive issues of labor policy.

[76] Gompers's letters defending the Clayton Act shortly after passage make it clear that he was 1) hopeful that the new law would be successful, 2) aware that success was by no means certain, and 3) very much concerned that labor organizations help to pressure the courts by making it clear that they expected the law to provide relief. Gompers's letters also show that he was upset about criticisms of the bill from other labor leaders. He hints that it was important to maintain the impression that the bill was a big victory for labor because such an impression would pressure the courts and also shape any political reaction if judges continued to issue decisions that hurt the interests of workers. See letters from Gompers cited in note 52.

5

The Norris-LaGuardia Act, for Once

Learning What to Learn from the Past

> We speak about the abuse of equity powers, we denounce the courts. Oh, let us put the fault where it lies – our legislators, subject to election, realizing the public mind, evade their responsibility by delegating it to the court in order that they may accomplish their end, and yet stand with a clear slate before the popular vote to which they must be responsible.
>
> AFL Vice President Matthew Woll, explaining the failure of the Clayton Act to the 1930 AFL Convention

Any bitterness felt by labor organizations as a result of the Supreme Court ruling on the Clayton Act in *Duplex v Deering* did not quickly translate into effective political campaigns for new legislation limiting the power of the courts. The ruling came at the beginning of a very difficult decade for labor organizations in national politics (Bernstein 1960). That lean political period seems to have ended, however, with passage of a new antiinjunction statute in 1932, the Norris-LaGuardia Act.

Measured against the longstanding legislative goals of curtailing yellow-dog contracts and injunctions, the Norris-LaGuardia Act was a success in precisely the areas where federal labor legislation of the preceding decades had failed. The act contained provisions that closely parallel failed provisions in the Erdman and Clayton acts. Yet judges read the Norris-LaGuardia provisions with much more sympathy for labor's expressed goals than the judges who interpreted earlier laws. Early rulings on Norris-LaGuardia helped things to come full circle for labor organizations: The reforms promised labor in the Clayton and Erdman acts but later thwarted by the courts seemed finally (if temporarily) to have been realized.[1]

The success of Norris-LaGuardia is especially remarkable because the act is by no means modest or innocuous. Labor lawyer Thomas Geoghegan may exaggerate when he claims that the Act allowed labor to "run naked in the streets," (1991, 44) and the act never allowed labor organizations to "kill a thousand people" with impunity, as Rep. Thomas Blanton (D-TX) claimed during floor debates (75 *Congressional Record* 5483). Nevertheless, Norris-LaGuardia has a legitimate claim to being "the most revolutionary piece of labor legislation ever adopted by Congress" (Gregory and Katz 1979, 191). The statute directly attacks the power of the federal judges. It seeks to reverse the effects of several Supreme Court decisions by stripping federal courts of jurisdiction to hear many types of cases related to labor disputes. By successfully narrowing the jurisdiction of the federal courts in an effort to reverse a line of Supreme Court decisions, Norris-LaGuardia demonstrates the importance of the congressional power to limit judicial policy making by controlling the jurisdiction of federal courts. (As noted in Chapter 1, court and constitutional law scholars often dismiss that power as irrelevant after claiming incorrectly that Congress has not exercised it since the Civil War.) Moreover, by sharply curtailing the use of injunctions in labor disputes, the act dismantled the primary institutional means through which labor organizations were regulated. Perhaps most significantly, and unlike any other American labor law, Norris-LaGuardia dismantled an existing system of labor regulation without simultaneously establishing a new regulatory apparatus to replace it.

Despite its uniqueness and radical content, Norris-LaGuardia has not attracted nearly as much scholarly attention as other labor statutes passed before and after it. The Wagner Act of 1935, in particular, attracts much

---

[1] In one Norris-LaGuardia case, the Supreme Court revived the moribund Section 6 of the Clayton by reading Norris-LaGuardia as providing protection against the antitrust laws, despite the fact that no provision in Norris-LaGuardia mentions antitrust or restraint of trade. *United States v Hutcheson* 312 U.S. 119 (1941). The Court's solicitude did not last forever. After Congress passed the Taft-Hartley Act in 1947, the courts established some important limitations to Norris-LaGuardia's exemptions. See *Bakery Sales Drivers Local Union No. 33 v Wagshal* (333 U.S. 437 (1948)) (injunction against a secondary boycott) and, more notoriously, *Boys Markets, Inc. v Retail Clerk's Union Local 770* (398 U.S. 235 (1970)), allowing an injunction to enforce a "no-strike" clause in a union contract (Klare 1990). I am concerned in this chapter with court rulings on Norris-LaGuardia that took place *before* legislators made post-Wagner Act changes in the labor statutes.

more notice, no doubt because that statute created the administrative system for regulating collective bargaining that remains in place to this day. Among scholars who acknowledge the existence of Norris-LaGuardia, many emphasize its links to subsequent legislation like the National Recovery Act (NRA) and the Wagner Act.[2] By emphasizing those links, such scholars paint Norris-LaGuardia as the pregnant precursor to the system of administrative regulation that soon emerged under subsequent statutes associated with Roosevelt and the New Deal. However, even though links between Norris-LaGuardia and subsequent laws are real and important, it is also very important to remember that Norris-LaGuardia became law in a very different political climate than the Wagner Act. Although hindsight makes it clear that the new regulatory apparatus of the Wagner Act would follow, there was no guarantee when Congress passed Norris-LaGuardia that legislators would be able to establish some new system of administrative regulation of labor relations. Furthermore, Norris-LaGuardia was by no means a Roosevelt or New Deal reform: It was signed into law by President *Hoover*, at a time when FDR's campaign vision was that balancing the federal budget was the key to recovery!

Some scholars have already recognized the uniqueness and radical nature of Norris-LaGuardia as originally enacted. A few scholars have offered accounts that see Norris-LaGuardia as a potentially very interesting, but ultimately short-lived, triumph for a vision of labor regulation very different from the one later created by the Wagner Act. Scholars in this group have seen Norris-LaGuardia as a triumph for *laissez faire* individualism (e.g., Gould 1993, 25; Tomlins 1985, 104; Gregory and Katz 1979, 197), as the triumph of a progressive vision of labor regulation emerging from one wing of the Republican party (O'Brien, 1998), or as the belated triumph of a liberal state centered around legislatures rather than judges (Orren 1991, 209–21).

However, even the scholars who recognize Norris-LaGuardia as an important and potentially transformative statute have not tried to provide a detailed account of why it passed in the form that it did. They have been content to point out the broad political and social factors that led politicians to enact antiinjunction and anti-yellow-dog legislation in 1932. These include 1) the 1930 midterm elections, which made it possible for progressive Republicans and liberal democrats to form the coalition that passed the bill, 2) the external shock of the stock market crash

---

[2] Among those emphasizing links are Zinn 1959, 228; Ernst 1989a; Forbath 1991, 163–6.

and Depression, which created conditions that made legislators unusually receptive to reform legislation, and 3) the fact that injunctions and yellow-dog contracts had already fallen out of favor with many employers organizations.[3] Scholars have not attempted to establish why legislators prone in 1932 to adopting reform legislation passed the particular statute that it did, or whether participants in the legislative process expected the new law to avoid the difficulties that earlier statutes had encountered in the courts.

The relative lack of attention to Norris-LaGuardia is especially striking in studies that have drawn attention to judicial decisions on other labor statutes passed before and after Norris-LaGuardia. Since the Norris-LaGuardia Act stands as a lone exception to the apparent pattern of judicial hostility toward labor legislation, understanding Norris-LaGuardia's success seems essential to understanding the importance of the courts as barriers to democratic processes in other cases. As a case that fails to fit the broader pattern, Norris-LaGuardia is a potentially very valuable vehicle for testing competing hypotheses about labor's other encounters with political and legal institutions during the first part of the twentieth century.

The most frequently proffered hypothesis for the success of Norris-LaGuardia is that the legislative language in the act was much clearer than language in earlier statutes.[4] The ease with which scholars accept this *legislative language hypothesis* is somewhat surprising, given the standard explanation for the failure of the Clayton Act. It would seem that the corollary of the claim that improvements in legislative language explain the success of Norris-LaGuardia is that weak legislative language, and not

---

[3] Ernst (1989a) argues for the third point. O'Brien (1998) analyzes the evolving position of the Republican Party. During debates over Norris-LaGuardia in Congress, supporters of the bill often pointed out that both major parties had planks in their campaign platforms calling for injunction reform. See, for example, 1930 Senate Report, 9.

[4] Scholars who note Norris-LaGuardia's improvements in legislative language include: Gould 1993, 23; Bernstein 1960, 397–403, 414; Forbath 1991, 161–2; Gregory and Katz 1979, 184–99; Dubofsky 1994, 104, 255–6, note 68. Although this group includes some sharp critics of court rulings on earlier statutes like the Clayton Act, none of these authors fully considers the implications that their account of Norris-LaGuardia's success has for the standard view that the Clayton Act failed because of judicial usurpation. Numerous commentaries made *before* enactment of Norris-LaGuardia also emphasized that legislative language would be the key to the success of any new legislation. See, for example, Cochrane 1927, Hunt 1928, Witte 1929, Frankfurter and Green 1930, 207–28. Some contemporaneous observers were more skeptical, however, for example, Joseph 1928, Christ 1932.

judicial usurpation, is the reason earlier statutes failed in the courts. Thus, the legislative language hypothesis, if confirmed, would *support* my claim in the preceding chapter that changes made to legislative language during legislative deliberations contributed to the failure of the Clayton Act.

The legislative records on Norris-LaGuardia provide some support for the legislative language hypothesis. The leading architects of the bill in Congress were very attentive to the problems earlier labor laws faced in the courts, and worked hard to craft legislative language that avoided some identified shortcomings of the Clayton Act. Moreover, floor leaders in both the House and Senate often invoked memories of *Duplex Printing v Deering* as they successfully argued against proposed amendments that would have weakened the statutory language describing labor's immunities.

These findings suggest an assessment of American democracy that is more optimistic than the one offered by critics who focus on the courts. If clear legislative language can tame the mighty judiciary, then hostile judicial rulings like the ones on the Clayton Act no longer prove that undemocratic powers of the courts rendered workers helpless in their efforts to change state policies. Rather, the success of Norris-LaGuardia seems to prove that labor was able to get what it wanted just as soon as labor organizations had the political strength to force elected officials to take decisive action.

Unfortunately, however, as the length of this chapter indicates, things turn out to be too complicated to fit such a straightforward (and optimistic) reading of events. While there are substantial differences in legislative language between Norris-LaGuardia and the Clayton Act, such differences cannot be isolated as the cause of Norris-LaGuardia's success. For one thing, the language in Norris-LaGuardia did not prove so crystal clear that every judge found it impossible to give interpretations that thwarted labor's reform ambitions. More importantly, events that occurred between passage of Norris-LaGuardia and the first Supreme Court test cases create some plausible alternatives to the legislative language hypothesis, alternatives that are hard to rule out on the available evidence. The most significant of these events was the New Deal constitutional crisis and subsequent changes in judicial personnel.[5] Put simply, the

---

[5] Ross (1994) shows that the New Deal crisis has roots in conflicts between Congress and the courts that go back to the end of the nineteenth century. Cushman (1994, 1998) argues against the commonly held view that justices were bullied into switching to a pro–New Deal position. Gillman (1993) also helps to explain the development

problem is that the Supreme Court justices who issued definitive rulings on Norris-LaGuardia were very different, in attitude and ideology, from the judges who issued definitive rulings on the Clayton and Erdman Acts. One instructive indication of these changes is that the Supreme Court opinion that gave the single most prolabor reading to Norris-LaGuardia was written by Felix Frankfurter, one of the statute's principle drafters and a leading academic critic of the labor injunction before ascending to the Supreme Court bench.[6]

Thus, the legislative language hypothesis has to be tested against a second plausible explanation for Norris-LaGuardia's success: The *judicial attitudes hypothesis*. This second hypothesis is that Norris-LaGuardia achieved its advertised reform objectives because the judges who ruled on it, unlike the judges who ruled on the Clayton Acts, had prolabor policy preferences. The changes in legislative language appear important on the surface, but the more decisive factor was that new judges had different policy preferences. Significantly, this second hypothesis suggests a less rosy assessment of American democracy than the legislative language hypothesis. It suggests that it is much more difficult for Congress to control judges who determine the effectiveness of democratic reforms. After all, elected officials can change legislative language more easily and quickly than they can change judicial attitudes.

While it would be nice to be able to confirm one of these two hypotheses and rule out the other, historical events conspire to make it impossible to do so. For example, it is not possible to know for certain whether the judges who ruled on the Clayton Act in 1921 would have responded differently if legislators had passed a statute in 1914 containing the same strong language later included in the Norris-LaGuardia Act. Luckily, however, it is not essential for my purposes here to draw a firm distinction between the contribution made by changes in legislative language and changes in judicial attitudes. My goal is not the impossible one of isolating some single factor as the *cause* of Norris-LaGuardia's success, but the more

---

and decline of Lochner era jurisprudence by providing crucial background information on the views of the justices. My point here is simply that new judges were on the Court by the time of the crucial Norris-LaGuardia rulings, judges who were more deferential to legislatures and, in some cases, more sympathetic to labor organizations. It is also very important to note that Congress had already passed the Wagner Act by the time the Supreme Court ruled definitively on the injunction restrictions in Norris-LaGuardia. Judges may have been less willing to read Norris-LaGuardia's limits on their powers so broadly if the Wagner Act had not created an alternative administrative apparatus for regulating industrial conflict.

[6] *United States v Hutcheson* 312 U.S. 119 (1941).

limited goal of understanding how the participants in the legislative processes that produced both statutes encountered the courts as barriers to their efforts to exercise political power. It is possible to gain at least some insight into these issues by carefully considering the expressed views of the participants in the legislative processes that produced Norris-LaGuardia. I find that from the point of view of those participants, changes in legislative language and judicial attitudes both figured as deeply interconnected elements of a strategy for preventing judicial interference. Taking participants' perspectives into account results in a more complete account of the impact of the courts than accounts that focus narrowly on judicial attitudes or legislative language and the rule of law. Knowing that judicial attitudes had changed, and even that those attitudes affected the way judges voted, ultimately tells us very little about how judges impacted the political strategies of labor organizations or about the profound effect that anticipated judicial reactions had on congressional decision making.

The records of congressional deliberations on Norris-LaGuardia provide information that is very helpful for understanding the courts as barriers to labor's democratic aspirations during this period. The debates that preceded passage of Norris-LaGuardia became a forum for legislators, labor leaders, and employers to discuss competing explanations for the failure of earlier labor statutes, particularly the Clayton Act. The participants in those discussions engaged in spirited debates about whether judges or legislators were to blame for the failure of earlier labor legislation. The participants also expressed a variety of more general views about the nature of judicial power in the American constitutional system.

Significantly, participants from all sides of the debates eventually reached the conclusion that the failure of the Clayton Act was not due to judges usurping legislative powers, as claimed publicly by labor leaders of the time and by many legal and labor historians today. Almost all the participants eventually took the position that the Clayton Act failed not because judges refused to follow the expressed will of Congress, but because legislators and labor leaders made bad compromises on legislative language that empowered judges to issue the damaging rulings.

By uncovering the expectations of the participants in the legislative process, this chapter challenges earlier accounts that have blamed judges for usurping legislative powers and stunting labor's political development. However, the chapter ultimately presents an assessment of the responsiveness of legislative institutions that is no more optimistic about American democracy than the vision offered by the recent scholars who

TABLE 2 *Corresponding Provisions from the Erdman, Clayton, and Norris-LaGuardia Acts*

Norris-LaGuardia Provision	Corresponding Provision in Earlier Statute	Content of Provision
Sections 3 and 4(i)	Erdman Section 10	Limits on yellow-dog contracts
Sections 7 and 8	Clayton Section 20, 1st paragraph	Limits equity jurisdiction of federal courts to cases involving "property"
Section 4	Clayton Section 20, 2nd paragraph	List of several collective activities that are immunized from judicial intervention
Sections 4 and 13	Clayton Section 20	Indicates which workers are covered by the immunities in the statute

have blamed the courts. Looking closely at the legislative records reveals that whatever Norris-LaGuardia may be, it is not an example of labor organizations effectively exercising political power to extract concessions from a permeable democratic state. Furthermore, I find that judges and judicial decisions did play a very important role in shaping the content of the act. However, that influence was subtler than the influence that appears when scholars focus more narrowly on the overt conflicts between Congress and the Courts that occur after legislation passes.

NORRIS-LAGUARDIA IN CONGRESS AND THE COURTS

My discussion in the remainder of this chapter focuses on four sets of provisions from the Norris-LaGuardia Act that closely parallel provisions in the Clayton and Erdman acts. The relationships between the provisions in Norris-LaGuardia and the earlier statutes are indicated in Table 2.

Before turning directly to the evolution of these provisions, a more general overview of Norris-LaGuardia's path through the Congress is in order. Legislators eventually approved the Norris-LaGuardia Act by overwhelming margins in 1932, but the margin of victory masks a four-and-a-half year struggle that was not smooth and easy.[7]

The story of Norris-LaGuardia begins in 1928, when congressional deliberation on antiinjunction legislation began in earnest for the first

[7] Norris-LaGuardia passed the Senate by a vote of 75 to 5 and the House by 362 to 14.

time since passage of the Clayton Act in 1914. Senator George Norris (R-NE) chaired a series of hearings before a special subcommittee of the Senate Judiciary Committee. The hearings were convened to consider an antiinjunction bill introduced by Sen. Henrik Shipstead (Farmer-Labor-MN). Shipstead's original bill was much shorter and considerably less complicated than the bill Congress enacted as the Norris-LaGuardia Act four-and-a-half years later. Shipstead introduced the bill on behalf of its author, Andrew Furuseth, the American Federation of Labor (AFL) legislative representative who had authored the Pearre bill that the AFL had first endorsed in 1906. Like the earlier Pearre bill, the Shipstead bill attempted to use a restrictive definition of what counted as "property" to limit the equity jurisdiction of the federal courts.

The 1928 hearings on the Shipstead bill reveal that criticism of the courts had become sharper in the years since the hearings on the Clayton Act. Even many *employers* acknowledged that judges had issued unjust injunctions, and expressed support for the general legislative goal of preventing abuse of injunctions. Nevertheless, many participants, including some who were sympathetic to labor organizations, harbored doubts about Furuseth's new bill. One was Senator Norris. At the close of hearings, Norris convened a group of academic experts on labor relations and labor laws and asked them to evaluate the Shipstead bill and suggest improvements.[8] The experts rejected the Shipstead bill in its entirety and drafted the entirely new bill that later became known in different versions as the "Norris bill." This 1928 Norris bill already had the essential framework and much of the same legislative language as what eventually passed in 1932 as the Norris-LaGuardia Act.[9]

Norris's subcommittee voted to recommend Norris's bill as a substitute for Shipstead's in 1928, a decision that was immediately attacked by Andrew Furuseth. Furuseth objected after concluding that the new bill had many of the same defects that led to the failure of the Clayton Act. Furuseth protested before the subcommittee and later convinced the 1928

---

[8] The group was Felix Frankfurter of Harvard Law School, Herman Oliphant of Johns Hopkins, Edwin Witte of the University of Wisconsin, Francis B. Sayre of Harvard, and attorney Donald Richberg. See Norris 1945, 312–14.

[9] The original Shipstead bill was S. 1482, 70th Congress. The Norris substitute retained that number. The Shipstead bill was again introduced in the 71st Congress as S. 2497. The Norris substitute again retained the number of the Shipstead bill. Norris's version was introduced as its own bill in the 72nd Congress as S. 935, and as H.R. 5315 (the bill that went to conference and became the Norris-LaGuardia Act).

convention of the AFL to withhold its endorsement of the substitute bill and insist on Shipstead's original.

After the withdrawal of AFL support, the Norris bill died quickly in the 70th Congress without being reported by the Senate Judiciary Committee. In the next Congress, a slightly modified version of Shipstead's original bill was reintroduced in the Senate, but the Senate subcommittee decided instead to recommend a substitute bill almost identical to the 1928 Norris substitute.[10] The second time around, the AFL relented and agreed to endorse Norris's bill, despite howls of public protest from Andrew Furuseth. Even with the AFL's endorsement, however, the bill died in the 71st Congress after the full Senate Judiciary Committee voted narrowly to report adversely on the bill.[11]

After the 1930 elections made both the committee and Congress as a whole more receptive to reform legislation, Senator Norris and Rep. Fiorello LaGuardia (Progressive Republican-NY) each reintroduced bills nearly identical to the substitute Norris bill that had failed in the two previous congresses. It was an amended version of that bill that passed both chambers and became law over President Hoover's signature in March 1932.

The New Legislative Attack on Yellow-Dog Contracts: A Constitutional Confrontation that Barely Arose

Section 3 and Section 4(i) of Norris-LaGuardia aim directly at two earlier Supreme Court rulings that protected yellow-dog contracts: *Adair v United States* (208 U.S. 161, 1908) and *Hitchman Coal and Coke v Mitchell* (245 U.S. 229, 1917). Section 3 declares that yellow-dog contracts are "contrary to the public policy of the United States," that they "[s]hall not be enforceable in any court of the United States," and that they "shall not afford any basis for the granting of legal or equitable relief by any such court." The provision specifies that this is true whether the contracts were "written or oral, express or implied." The prohibition on enforcement applied to "promises not to join, become, or remain a member of any labor organization" and "promises that [the worker] will withdraw from an employment relation in the event that he joins, becomes, or remains a member of any labor organization."

---

[10] S. 2497. The new version added a provision repealing Section 4 of the Sherman Act.
[11] Senate Report 1060, 71st Congress, "Define and Limit the Jurisdiction of Courts Sitting in Equity."

Parts of Section 4 of the act provide additional support for the yellow-dog language in Section 3. Section 4 declares that "No court of the United States shall have jurisdiction" to issue an injunction in a labor dispute to prevent persons from engaging in nine categories of collective activities, including "[b]ecoming or remaining a member of any labor organization or of any employer organization, regardless of any such undertaking or promise as is described in Section 3 of this Act" and "[a]dvising, urging, or otherwise causing or inducing without fraud or violence the acts heretofore specified, regardless of any such undertaking or promise as is described in section 3 of this Act."[12]

These provisions are clearly aimed at reversing the effects of earlier court decisions on yellow-dog contracts. The declaration in Section 3 that yellow-dog contracts were not "enforceable" was an alternative to the criminal ban on yellow-dog contracts in the Erdman Act that the Supreme Court struck down in *Adair*. In 1917, the court reaffirmed that ruling as it struck down a similar state law provision in *Coppage v Kansas* (236 U.S. 1). The provisions in Section 4 denying the court jurisdiction to issue injunctions against organizing campaigns was aimed at the Supreme Court's decision in *Hitchman*, which authorized an injunction that prevented the United Mine Workers (UMW) from organizing Hitchman employees who had signed a yellow-dog contract (*Hitchman Coal and Coke v Mitchell*, 245 U.S. 229 (1917), Bernstein 1960, 196–200).

Given that the yellow-dog provisions in Norris-LaGuardia aim to reverse a line of Supreme Court decisions enforcing such contracts and striking down laws that attempted to regulate them, it seems reasonable to expect that the provisions would have led to a dramatic constitutional showdown in the Supreme Court.[13] The provisions in Section 4 seemed especially likely to attract Supreme Court attention since they marked a rare successful attempt by legislators to reverse a judicial ruling by removing the jurisdiction of the courts. Such a legislative attempt to reduce the power of the court strikes at the separation of powers between the branches of government.

---

[12] Sections 4(b) and 4(i). I discuss the remaining categories Section 4 in more detail later in this chapter.

[13] Before the Norris bill passed, members of Congress and outside observers certainly anticipated that a constitutional showdown over these provisions would occur. For example, Chicago Business School professor Jay Finley Christ's long and scholarly analysis of judicial rulings on labor law predicted immediately after passage that the yellow-dog provisions of Norris-LaGuardia "will undoubtedly be attacked with vigor and determination" (1932, 293).

Oddly enough, however, constitutional challenges barely materialized and never reached the Supreme Court. In fact, there is only one reported case where the provisions of Section 3 were even cited in a dispute involving an employment "contract" limiting workers' collective activities. That case never went beyond a federal trial court, was not settled on constitutional grounds, and did not involve a traditional yellow-dog contract.[14]

One reason that the expected constitutional test of the yellow-dog provisions never occurred is probably timing. Employers did mount several early constitutional challenges aimed at other provisions in Norris-LaGuardia that were much closer to the heart of Norris-LaGuardia. Those early challenges failed. Even judges who were openly hostile to labor quickly dismissed constitutional challenges to Congress's power to place limits on court jurisdiction.[15] Such rulings signaled to employers that the courts had become considerably less willing to gut labor laws on their behalf, and may have discouraged challenges to the yellow-dog provisions.[16]

---

[14] *Colorado-Wyoming Express, et al. v Denver-Local Union No. 13 of the International Brotherhood of Teamsters, Chauffeurs, Stable Men and Helpers of America* (35 F. Supp. 155 (1940)). The case involved a challenge to a union's promise not to engage in sympathy strikes. This is the only one of the five reported cases citing Section 3 of Norris-LaGuardia (U.S.C. 29 §103) where a court considers an agreement to refrain from union membership activity. The other cases cite Section 3 only incidentally. There are other cases citing the broadly applicable Section 4(i) of the act, but the contracts in those cases were not traditional yellow-dog agreements.

[15] Early Norris-LaGuardia cases upholding the limits on jurisdiction include *Knapp-Monarch Co. v Anderson, et al.* (7 F. Supp. 332, E.D. Ill. (1934)), *Cinderella Theater Co., Inc. v Sign Writers' Local Union No. 591* (D.C. Mich. 1934, 6 F. Supp. 164), and *Levering & Garrigues Co. v Morrin* (C.C.A. N.Y. 1934, 71 F. 2d 284). The Supreme Court upheld the constitutionality of the jurisdictional limitation in both *Senn v Tile Layers Protective Unions* (301 U.S. 465 (1937)) and *Lauf et al. v E.G. Shinner & Co., Inc.* (301 U.S. 315 (1938)). The courts often cited the Supreme Court's 1922 decision in *Kline v Burke Construction Company* (260 U.S. 226), and ruled that there was no constitutional barrier to Congress circumventing an unpopular court ruling by removing jurisdiction from the court.

[16] Among the other plausible reasons for the lack of a Supreme Court test of the Norris-LaGuardia provisions is that Norris-LaGuardia was followed by more broadly framed provisions in the Wagner Act (1935) that declared agreements interfering with organizing activities to be unfair labor practices. These provisions reinforced Norris-LaGuardia and likely made judges more willing to uphold the act by giving the NLRB and the circuit courts the power to decide which practices were unfair. The Wagner Act provisions also failed to generate a Supreme Court case touching directly on the issue of yellow-dog contracts.

Congressional Discussion of the Constitutionality of the Yellow-Dog Provisions

The records of congressional debates on Norris-LaGuardia's yellow-dog provisions suggest that many members of Congress expected a bigger court test of the constitutionality of the yellow-dog provisions than what actually occurred. Congressional debates on the yellow-dog provisions focused almost entirely on the question of whether the courts would strike down the provisions limiting such contracts. The chief supporters of Norris-LaGuardia in Congress openly expressed concern about potential judicial interference, and spent a great deal of energy explaining and defending distinctions between their new bill and the failed Erdman act.

On the Senate floor in 1932, supporters of the Norris bill pointed out that the new statutory language tried to fit through some loopholes in the Supreme Court's rulings in *Adair* and *Coppage*. The most important difference, according to supporters of the bill, was that the Norris bill made yellow-dog contracts *unenforceable* rather than criminal. Senator Thomas Walsh (D-MT) explained the relevance of this distinction. Walsh pointed out that "there is a vast class, a great variety of contracts which the law will not permit to be made" (75 *Congressional Record* 4691) and cited laws against prostitution, gambling, usury, and insurance fraud to show that the tactic of using statutes to render some types of contracts unenforceable had been used before. Senator Robert Wagner (D-NY) also tried to distinguish the provisions in the new bill from the ones that the Supreme Court had struck down in *Adair* and *Coppage*. In *Adair,* Wagner argued, the Supreme Court objected to the Erdman Act's interference with an employer's right to discharge employees, while "the bill which is before us . . . do[es] none of the acts condemned by the court" (75 *Congressional Record* 4917).[17] In addition, Senator Norris noted that the declaration of "public policy" in Section 2 of the bill would help judges to recognize problems caused by yellow-dog contracts that earlier judges had difficulty understanding (75 *Congressional Record* 4683). As noted in Chapter 3, legislators had never articulated a reason for banning yellow-dog contracts when the Erdman Act passed. Norris apparently hoped that the courts would respond more favorably to legislation clearly expressing Congress's collective judgment that such contractual arrangements caused public harms.

---

[17] Two years later Wagner would introduce the bill that eventually became the Wagner Act. The Wagner Act did go directly against *Adair* by interfering with the power of employers to discharge and discriminate against unionized workers.

Supporters of the Norris bill successfully protected the integrity of the new bill's legislative language by blocking all attempts, both hostile and friendly, to alter the bill. The result was that the language in the yellow-dog provision of Norris's bill went virtually unchanged between the bill's initial appearance in 1928 and its eventual passage in 1932. Legislators did not reject any alternative proposals for a yellow-dog ban that members claimed would have a better chance of surviving court scrutiny.[18]

Taken together, the detailed explanations of the improvements in the bill and the successful efforts to preserve the integrity of the legislative language suggest that Norris-LaGuardia was a more sincere effort to limit the role of the courts than earlier statutes. Things are not quite so simple, however. Many participants in the legislative process were never completely confident that improvements in the new bill guaranteed success in the courts. Even strong supporters of the bill indirectly acknowledged that hostile judges could still make decisions that would limit the effectiveness of the legislation. However, such supporters also repeatedly provided their colleagues with substantial reasons for believing that the likelihood of such judicial usurpation was small.

Senator Norris, for example, made detailed doctrinal arguments documenting that recent Supreme Court decisions had demonstrated the justices' new willingness to give broad readings to statutory protections of workers' rights to organize.[19] Norris explained how the new bill took advantage of these trends. Norris also pointed out that the Supreme Court was divided in its earlier yellow-dog opinions, and suggested that the Court was ready to rethink its position because "those cases were decided at a time when the 'yellow-dog' contract had not reached the culmination of it wickedness" (75 *Congressional Record* 4683).

Senator Walsh also made a speech citing a long list of conservative legal and political voices opposed to yellow-dog contracts. He noted that even William Howard Taft had become an opponent of the yellow-dog

---

[18] Representative LaGuardia did include a differently worded yellow-dog provision in the antiinjunction bills he introduced in the House in 1928 and 1929 (H.R. 10082, 70th Congress; H.R. 122, 71st Congress), but switched his support to Norris's bill without reservation once the Senate settled on that version. Neither LaGuardia nor any other member of the House ever expressed the view that the language in the discarded LaGuardia bills was more likely to be effective than the language in the Norris bill.

[19] The most promising case was one where the Supreme Court allowed a railroad union to obtain an injunction against an employer for interfering with organizing efforts under the Railroad Labor Act of 1926, *Texas-New Orleans Railroad v Brotherhood of Clerks* (281 U.S. 548 (1930)). See Senate Report 163, 72nd Congress, 1st Session, 15.

contract during his service on the War Labor Board (4691). In a later speech, Walsh went even further, citing cases decided after *Coppage* to suggest that the courts had given up on the abstract formalism of the "freedom of contract." Since the court had relied on such arguments in the earlier yellow-dog cases, Walsh suggested that the provisions in the new statute limiting the *enforcement* of yellow-dog contracts would provide judges with the opportunity to rethink their position. Walsh stated: "A wide change has come over the judicial minds of the country as to the question of liberty of contract, the earlier decisions having been induced, as everybody must now realize, by reason of the judges entertaining antiquated and obsolescent views concerning economic questions" (5018).

Senator Wagner also made an effort during floor debates to establish that recent changes in judicial attitudes made it more likely that the yellow-dog provisions in Section 3 would withstand the scrutiny of the courts. Wagner noted that the "major evils of the anti-union promise were born after the Hitchman case" (75 *Congressional Record* 4917) and suggested: "A judiciary accustomed to current conditions would never have permitted the . . . routine repetition of sterile precedents to grow wild like a tropical jungle" (4915). Like Norris and Walsh, Wagner demonstrated an impressive command of legal precedents that extended well beyond the subject of labor relations. Wagner cited cases involving retail pricing agreements where the Supreme Court had established a distinction between courts punishing a person for forming a particular contract (unconstitutional) and courts refusing to enforce a lawful promise after the promise is made (no constitutional objections) (4917).[20]

When the bill reached the floor of the House, opponents raised fewer questions about the constitutionality of the yellow-dog provisions. Nevertheless, Rep. Emmanuel Celler (D-NY) assumed the task of explaining why the new statute might better survive the scrutiny of the courts. Celler cited the dissents in *Coppage* and *Hitchman*, a conciliatory speech by Taft, and doctrinal arguments made by Frankfurter and Green in *The Labor Injunction* to support his argument that the courts would recognize that they had been wrong in the earlier cases (75 *Congressional Record* 5489).

The comments made by Norris-LaGuardia supporters about the constitutional issues reveal an interesting feature of Supreme Court precedents

---

[20] *U.S. v Colgate* (250 U.S. 300 (1919)), *Dr. Miles Medical Co. v Park and Sons* (220 U.S. 373 (1911)), both involving agreements among retailers not to cut prices.

as seen through the eyes of legislators. Members of Congress looked at recent Supreme Court cases on related topics as indirect signals that the attitudes of judges had changed since the rulings in *Adair, Coppage,* and *Hitchman.* Because of the way the members of Congress were reading those signals, the meaning of those earlier cases as barriers to legislative action had changed even though the courts had not directly revisited the issues in those cases. Interestingly, the comments about changed judicial attitudes suggest that Norris-LaGuardia supporters did not believe that the success of the new statute hinged entirely on the substantive improvements in legislative language. The distinctive features of the new bill were important not because they would make it impossible for hostile judges to rule against labor, but because they provided moderately sympathetic judges with an opportunity to save face while backing off earlier rulings.

Not every member of Congress was as confident as the Norris-LaGuardia supporters. During Senate floor debates in 1932, the Senate's leading opponent of the bill, Republican Felix Hebert of Rhode Island, warned that the yellow-dog provisions "will not only not be effective but will not stand the test of constitutionality, and therefore will result in a mere gesture" (75 *Congressional Record* 4677). Hebert argued that the drafters of the Norris bill had not successfully circumvented the Supreme Court doctrines developed in *Hitchman, Adair,* and *Coppage.*[21] Hebert pointed out, for example, that even liberal dissenter Brandeis had conceded the *legality* of the yellow-dog contract in *Hitchman.* Hebert also drew the attention of his colleagues to an advisory opinion issued by the Massachusetts Supreme Court in 1931 declaring that a proposed state law that was much like Norris-LaGuardia would be unconstitutional under the *Adair, Coppage,* and *Hitchman* rulings.[22]

Even some supporters of the bill were willing to express doubts about whether the bill would survive. Senator Wagner conceded that Congress had never before tried to overcome a Supreme Court ruling through a statement of public policy (75 *Congressional Record* 4917). Senate Judiciary Committee Chair Borah noted that although some recent precedents provided grounds for optimism, legitimate doubts also remained because "questions involving the 'yellow-dog' contract have never gone

---

[21] Hebert discusses *Hitchman* at 75 *Congressional Record* 4684–5, *Coppage* and *Adair* at 4683.

[22] 75 *Congressional Record* 4685.

to the Supreme Court under the circumstances in which they will now go there under this measure" (5019).[23]

To help allay these lingering doubts, supporters of the bill in Congress worked hard to signal to the courts that congressional sentiment against the yellow-dog contract was quite strong. Senator Neely expressed an apparently widely shared sentiment when he noted:

regardless of the place where the "yellow-dog" contract was brought to life, it is high time that this iniquitous instrumentality of intolerable tyranny be put to death. And after death it should be buried in a grave so wide and deep and secure that no black robed Gabriel from his high seat of authority on a Federal bench can ever resurrect it with trumpet or tongue or pen (75 *Congressional Record* 5014).

Although not all members of Congress were so prone to waxing poetic, not a single member of Congress went on record defending the yellow-dog contract. Even Senator Hebert, who attacked the yellow-dog provisions and predicted that they would not survive judicial scrutiny, never defended the use of yellow-dog contracts. Hebert repeatedly claimed that his goal was only for Congress to pass a ban that would survive judicial scrutiny, not to preserve the yellow-dog contract as a weapon for employers.

The ability of legislators to make such strong attacks on the yellow-dog contracts reflects what Daniel Ernst calls the "moribund condition of a once vital consensus" in favor of a particular vision of industrial relations and individual rights (Ernst 1989a, 274). Earlier judicial support of the yellow-dog contract was a manifestation of a vision of industrial relations that focused on individual rights to contract rather than collective interests. Ernst points out that as the twenties progressed, the individualist vision went into decline, yellow-dog contracts became less common, and most firms developed more sophisticated methods like company unions for controlling and channeling their workers' desire to organize. By the time members of Congress considered the Norris bills, yellow-dog contracts persisted mainly in proprietary firms on the fringes of the economy (Ernst 1989a). As a result, the threat that yellow-dog contracts posed to labor organizations declined so much that in 1934,

---

[23] Outside comments made shortly after passage of the act also indicate that not everyone was convinced legislators had succeeded in neutralizing the courts. See, for example, Christ (1932) whose lengthy, scholarly article on Norris-LaGuardia and relevant court precedents states that "the Norris Act is not likely to be very effective in curbing the use of the yellow-dog contract" (1932, 300).

even before the meaning of Norris-LaGuardia was settled in the courts, AFL representatives told legislators that they had lost interest in statutes attacking yellow-dog contracts and had turned their attention to the new enemy, company unions.[24] All of these events suggest that passage of the yellow-dog provisions in the Norris-LaGuardia Act may be less the sudden *cause* of any judicial change of heart or of the decline of the yellow-dog contract, but rather a *reflection* of the yellow-dog contract's gradual demise as an important employer weapon for preventing union organizing.

The Jurisdictional Strategy Revisited: Sections 7 and 8 of Norris-LaGuardia

Sections 7 and 8 articulate limits on the conditions under which courts can issue injunctions in labor disputes and are thus analogous to similar limits in the first paragraph of Section 20 of the Clayton Act. There are a number of striking parallels between the development of these provisions and the development of the corresponding provisions of the Clayton Act. First, in both cases the bill Congress eventually enacted was a substitute for an earlier bill written by representatives of labor organizations. The decision to adopt the Norris bill as a substitute for Shipstead's resembles the decision to adopt Clayton's bill as a substitute for Pearre's. Second, in both cases the original proposals that legislators replaced were shorter than the bills that were enacted, and pursued the simpler strategy of limiting the jurisdiction of the courts by articulating a narrowing definition of what counted as property. Third, in both cases the enacted bill omitted the narrowing definition of property in favor of a list of procedural requirements that courts had to meet before assuming jurisdiction in labor injunction cases. Finally, in both cases, at least some participants in Congress expressed doubts about the ability of the proposed legislative language to withstand judicial scrutiny. Against the background of

---

[24] In the 1934 Senate hearings on the original bill introduced by Wagner that later became the Wagner Act, AFL President William Green praised Congress for banning the yellow-dog contract in the Norris-LaGuardia and National Industrial Recovery Acts, but stated: "Now it must be remembered that only a small number of employers ever used a yellow-dog contract. The majority of company union shops depended on other tactics for the promotion of their homemade unions. And now company unions are spreading to many more companies. The bona fide labor movement is attacked on a much wider front." See the NLRB's *Legislative History of the National Labor Relations Act* (1949), 101.

these similarities, however, there are some substantial differences in final product that distinguish Sections 7 and 8 of the Norris-LaGuardia from the corresponding provisions of the Clayton Act.

In particular, Norris-LaGuardia uses different language and adds a number of important new features to the Clayton Act provisions. Section 7 states that "No court of the United States shall have jurisdiction to issue a temporary or permanent injunction in any case involving or growing out of a labor dispute" until a set of procedural and substantive restrictions are satisfied. The Norris-LaGuardia provisions state that before an injunction could be issued, the judge has to hold an open, adversarial hearing and make the required findings of fact.[25] These procedural requirements improve upon the corresponding provision in the Clayton Act, which required only that the party requesting the injunction attest that a shorter set of requirements had been met.

Section 7 of Norris-LaGuardia also required judges to make five findings of fact before issuing an injunction, only two of which correspond to provisions in the Clayton Act. The holdovers from the Clayton Act were requirements that there be a "substantial and irreparable injury to property" (clause b) and that the "complainant has no adequate remedy at law" (clause d). To these familiar restrictions Section 7 added three new requirements: 1) "That unlawful acts have been threatened and will be committed unless restrained or have been committed and will be continued unless restrained" (clause a);[26] 2) "That as to each item of relief granted greater injury will be inflicted upon complainant by the denial of relief than will be inflicted upon defendants by the granting of relief" (clause c); 3) "That the public officers charged with the duty to protect complainant's property are unable or unwilling to furnish adequate protection" (clause e).

Section 8 of the act added another novel jurisdictional restriction to the list: "No restraining order or injunctive relief will be granted to any complainant who has failed to comply with any obligation or who has failed to make every reasonable effort to settle such dispute either by

[25] The only exception to this rule is established in a provision specifying narrow conditions where the courts could issue temporary injunctions. However, the party requesting a temporary injunction had to file an undertaking with adequate security to compensate the defendants if a court later ruled that the improperly requested injunction caused damages.

[26] The same clause contains the further limitation that the court's order could only be directed at those who committed the act or those "actually authorizing or ratifying the same after actual knowledge thereof."

negotiation or with the aid of any available governmental machinery of mediation or voluntary arbitration."

Taken together, the requirement that the judge hold a hearing and make the specified findings of fact appear to extend Norris-LaGuardia's protections well beyond the requirements that were in the Clayton Act. That appearance is confirmed by the reluctance of many judges to issue injunctions in early Norris-LaGuardia cases. In the years following passage of Norris-LaGuardia, judges again and again cited provisions in sections 7 and 8 as they refused to issue injunctions in labor disputes. Even judges who appeared to be quite hostile to organized labor had a difficult time ruling that employers met the entire gauntlet of procedural and jurisdictional limitations specified in the statute. An example can be found in the opinion written by a Judge Wham of an Illinois district court in one of the first Norris-LaGuardia cases.[27] Wham offered interpretations of some of the restrictions and exemptions in Norris-LaGuardia that rendered them useless to labor organizations. Wham ruled that the provision in Section 4(e) stating that judges could not issue injunctions against "giving publicity" to a labor dispute did not apply to cases involving picketing. Wham conceded that the provision mentioned "advertising, speaking, patrolling," but placed enormous weight on the absence of the word "picketing." Wham read the absence of "picketing" as a sign that Congress wanted judges to continue to issue injunctions in order to prevent "coercive" or "intimidating" picketing. This interpretation came even though the words "coercive" or "intimidating" do not appear anywhere in the provision. Yet Wham's obvious talent for giving restrictive readings to labor laws did not, however, lead him to issue an injunction in the case. Wham eventually claimed that he could not issue the injunction because he could not make *one* of the five required findings of fact, the clause 7(e) requirement that local authorities could not protect the complainant's property.[28]

---

[27] *Knapp-Monarch Co. v Anderson et al.* (7 F. Supp. 332, E.D. Ill. (1934), 339).

[28] Another indicator of the effectiveness of the procedural restrictions on jurisdiction in sections 7 and 8 of Norris-LaGuardia is that judges sometimes refused to issue injunctions even in cases involving provocative worker conduct. In another 1934 case, a judge refused to enjoin a union's campaign against a theater even though the campaign allegedly involved mass picketing, mutilation of theater property, and stench bombs. The judge ruled that theater owners could not meet the Section 8 requirement. *Cinderella Theater Co., Inc. v Sign Writers' Local Union No. 591* (D.C. Mich. 6 F. Supp. 164 (1934)). In another case, a judge refused to enjoin the seizure of a hosiery plant because the requirement that there be no available legal remedy as an alternative to an injunction (clause (d)). The judge ruled

Norris-LaGuardia's jurisdictional limits did not, however, make it *impossible* for judges to issue injunctions in labor disputes. Judges did issue some injunctions, usually in cases where judges found there had been "violence."[29] However, even in these cases the judges at least followed the procedural requirement by holding hearings and making the required findings of fact. The tendency of lower court judges to interpret Norris-LaGuardia as restricting their power to issue injunctions was eventually reinforced by the Supreme Court. In one of its first Norris-LaGuardia cases, the Supreme Court scolded a lower court for failing to make required findings in a case involving a violent strike growing out of a jurisdictional dispute.[30]

Ironically, the one Norris-LaGuardia provision that proved ineffective in limiting the ability of judges to issue injunctions was the provision limiting injunctions to cases involving threats to "property" (clause (b) of Section 7). The courts were as successful at gutting this provision as they had been in gutting a similarly flawed provision of the Clayton Act in *Duplex Printing v Deering* (254 U.S. 443, 1921). Legislators had made two changes that could be called improvements over the Clayton Act's "property" provision with Norris-LaGuardia. First, the Norris-LaGuardia provision referred only to an injury to "property" rather than the Clayton Act's reference to "property, or a property right." Second, the Norris-LaGuardia provision specified that the injury to property had to be "substantial and irreparable" rather than just "irreparable." Despite these changes, the "property" provision of the Norris-LaGuardia Act shared the most important weakness of the Clayton Act provision: Like the Clayton Act, it did not define what counted as "property." That weakness explains why no judge ever declined to issue a labor injunction solely because of the Norris-LaGuardia requirement that there be an injury to "property."[31]

---

that a state law for recovering damages resulting from unlawful detainer provided an "adequate remedy at law." *Richard H. Oswald Co. v. Leader* (D.C. Pa. 1937, 20 F. Supp. 876).

[29] *Tri-Pac Shoe Co. v Cantor* (D.C. Pa. 1939, 25 F. Supp. 996), *Lake Charles Stevedores v May* (D.C. La. 1937, 20 F. Supp 698). However, in *Heintz Mfg. Co. v Local No. 515 of United Automobile Workers* (D.C. Pa. 1937, 20 F. Supp. 116) a court refused to issue an injunction even after a finding of violence.

[30] *Lauf v Shinner* (303 U.S. 315 (1938)).

[31] The ineffectiveness of the two changes in legislative language can be seen in the opinion by Judge Wham in *Knapp-Monarch* (7 F. Supp. 332, E.D. Ill. (1934), 339). Judge Wham simply noted that the judges who interpreted the Clayton Act had "used interchangeably the terms 'property' and 'property right' ... without distinguishing the terms." Based on this assessment, Wham argued that "no marked significance can be given to the fact that only the term 'property' was retained in

Even though all the Norris-LaGuardia provisions were not equally successful in limiting injunctions, judges in the early Norris-LaGuardia cases eventually settled on interpretations of the jurisdictional restrictions in sections 7 and 8 that produced substantial changes in the practices of the federal courts, changes that many judges cited when they refused to issue injunctions in labor disputes. Even when confronted with provocative and violent behavior that judges would have routinely enjoined as "coercive" or "unlawful" a decade earlier, judges adhered to the statutory procedures and refused to issue injunctions when they could not make the required findings of fact.

Sections 7 and 8 in Congress

Looking at the legislative records on the development of sections 7 and 8 in Congress reveals some important differences between Norris-LaGuardia and the Clayton Act. The debate over congressional attempts to limit the jurisdiction of the federal courts began during consideration of the Shipstead bill in Senator Norris's subcommittee. Those hearings were the first congressional hearings on labor injunctions since passage of the Clayton Act. They provided an important opportunity for some of the participants in the earlier debates to renew old battles and express their feelings about the Clayton Act's failure in the courts. With the fate of the Clayton Act very much in mind, some supporters of injunction reform initially attacked the jurisdictional limits in Senator Norris's bill as likely to be just as ineffective in controlling the courts.

Early on in the debates, supporters of the Shipstead bill suggested that the failure of the Clayton Act was the result of judicial hostility toward labor organizations. Because they blamed hostile judges for earlier failures and anticipated additional hostility in the future, Shipstead bill supporters felt that the Norris bill strategy of using procedural requirements and removing court jurisdiction in specified types of disputes would be no more effective than the Clayton Act was at controlling judges. Hostile judges would find some way to twist any such legislative language to render it ineffective.

In contrast, supporters of Norris's substitute bill began to believe that weaknesses in the statutory language of the Clayton Act had contributed to judicial interference with that law. As a result, they became

---

the Norris Act" (7 Fed. Supp. 332, 336). Thus, he concluded that the property-right language in Norris-LaGuardia did not prohibit the injunction.

more confident that carefully crafted legislative language limiting the jurisdiction of the courts in labor disputes could prevent judicial interference. For Senator Norris, and other advocates of reform, the process of selling his bill to colleagues in Congress was a process of learning to understand the failure of the Clayton Act and explaining that failure to other participants.

Some of the same people who participated in earlier debates over the Clayton Act returned to Congress in 1928. Andrew Furuseth was still pursuing antiinjunction legislation with the intensity of Captain Ahab, impressing and sometimes startling the Senate committee with his command of the case law and legal history, and his reflections on the failure of the Clayton Act.[32] Furuseth's views on the history of equity and the jurisdiction of the courts in labor disputes had not changed in the twenty-two years since he had first defended the Pearre bill in Congress. The Shipstead bill did contain some innovations. While the Pearre bill had contained a provision specifying that the right to conduct or carry on a business did not count as a property right, the Shipstead bill contained a more general legislative corrective based on the same underlying principle. After identifying the 1911 Judiciary Act that it was amending, the entire Shipstead bill consisted of the following declaration:

Equity courts shall have jurisdiction to protect property when there is no remedy at law; for the purpose of determining such jurisdiction, nothing shall be held to be property unless it is tangible and transferable, and all laws and parts of laws inconsistent herewith are hereby repealed.[33]

Like the earlier Pearre bill, the Shipstead bill reflected Furuseth's belief that the injustice of the typical labor injunction was its illegitimate expansion of the federal courts' equity jurisdiction to cases that did not involve threats to physical property.

Furuseth's bill reflected his distrust of judges, a distrust that had only been deepened by the failure of the Clayton Act. Since Furuseth believed that judges had repeatedly demonstrated their hostility toward labor organizations in cases occurring both before and after passage of the Clayton Act, he also believed that the only way to prevent another legislative failure was to prevent judges from hearing labor cases altogether. And the only way to do that was to establish (or, perhaps, restore) general restrictions on equity jurisdiction rather than restrictions limited to various enumerated

[32] Weintraub 1959, 188, notes the odd respect in which Furuseth was held in Congress and among experts in labor relations.
[33] S. 1482, 70th Congress.

activities or disputes.[34] According to Furuseth, the fatal flaw in the longer and more complicated Norris bill was that its effort to place *limits* on injunctions in some defined cases would be read by judges as implicitly authorizing injunctions in other cases where those limits were met. Thus, Furuseth's preferred strategy was for legislators to strip the courts of all jurisdiction in labor cases, and then to avoid saying anything else.[35]

Other supporters of injunction reform at the 1928 hearings appeared at first to share Furuseth's belief that poor drafting and judicial hostility had led to the failure of the Clayton Act. AFL President William Green and Secretary Frank Morrison both claimed that the courts had illegitimately ignored the expressed will of Congress as they interpreted the Clayton Act. Morrison recollected that in 1914 AFL leaders fully expected the Clayton Act to succeed because "the plainly written words gave recognition of practically all the rights that we urged in our bill of grievances" (1928 Senate Hearings, 150).

However, not all the witnesses shared the view that the failure of the Clayton Act grew out of bad judicial interpretations. Opponents of the Shipstead bill defended the judiciary by offering an alternative explanation for the Clayton Act's failure, one that placed responsibility on Congress rather than the courts.[36] The senators on the committee initially greeted

[34] Furuseth articulates these objections to the Norris bill in testimony and other materials included in the published 1928 Senate Hearings, 890–8. Although Furuseth reserved the bulk of his scorn for judges, he also hinted that legislators could have avoided problems in the Court by adopting the original Pearre bill and making a more direct attack on the Court's jurisdiction in the Clayton Act. (See, e.g., his discussions of the *Bedford* case (23) and the effectiveness of the Clayton Act (146–7).) For Furuseth, ongoing judicial hostility and the Court's record of ignoring less dramatic legislation justified using an as yet untried strategy.

[35] Furuseth never explained why he was certain that hostile judges would not ignore, strike down, or distort the Shipstead bill. He appeared convinced that judges would be able to interfere with Shipstead only at great cost to their own legitimacy. During one of his appearances, Furuseth said that if the Shipstead bill failed: "the only thing left to do is to burn the law books, discharge the law courts. Elect poobahs and call them 'equity judges,' and if anybody thinks that somebody is about to do evil, hale them before an equity judges and let him prohibit it" (146).

[36] Those defending judicial conduct during the 1928 Senate Hearing included Alfred Thom, General Counsel for Association of Railway Executives (171–87), W. H. Latta of the Indianapolis Street Railway Company, (243–70), and Reeves Strickland of the ABA (375–7). Some opponents cited the same court cases of "judicial excess" that had been cited by the supporters of the Shipstead bill. But for the opponents, those harsh decisions were used to argue that the legislative interference with equity powers in labor disputes was likely to be ruled unconstitutional, for example, Latta (269), Thom (175). Other attacks on the Shipstead bill came from more conciliatory witnesses who objected less to the goal of banning labor injunctions than they did to

this alternative narrative with disbelief. Eventually, however, the alternative account caught on and began to shape the committee's decisions about how to proceed.

As participants considered competing explanations for the failure of the Clayton Act, they revealed a great deal about their expectations regarding judicial responses to any new legislation. The alternative narrative was presented most notably by Walter Gordon Merritt of the League for Industrial Rights and James Emery of the National Association of Manufacturers. Citing materials from the legislative record as well as personal remembrances, Merritt argued that at the time the Clayton Act passed many observers did not think it would immunize activities like the ones the courts had continued to enjoin under the new law (1928 Senate Hearings, 300–2). Merritt also suggested that even the AFL leaders who had supported the Clayton Act understood it as being something of a fake. He claimed that the "immediate purpose" of the labor leaders who supported the bill was simply to get a statute passed, and that the labor leaders were thus willing to accept a compromise that made it uncertain whether the bill would produce any real changes in the law (315). Later in the hearings, Emery made an extended defense of judicial interpretations of the Clayton Act, and added additional evidence from the *Congressional Record* to demonstrate legislators' ambivalence at the time the Act passed (485–91).

Merritt and Emery's arguments turned the claims of the Shipstead bill's supporters on their heads. Both challenged the broader claim that the courts had demonstrated a pattern of hostility toward labor organizations or labor legislation. Merritt argued that most of the advances labor had achieved in the United States had come from the judges and not legislators (285). (Demonstrating that he possessed not the normal human reluctance toward disingenuousness, Merritt quoted Brandeis's dissent in *Duplex* to support this claim.) Emery later echoed this argument, noting that American judges had been out ahead of both the American Congress and the British courts in recognizing the rights of unions (514). Both Merritt and Emery reached the same conclusion: The courts were being unjustly criticized by labor leaders disappointed by the continued use of injunctions after passage of the Clayton Act. If judges had done

the broad sweep of the Shipstead bill. Two witnesses from the American Patent Law Association, for example, expressed concern that the "tangible and transferable" requirement would wreak havoc on patent law. Karl Fenning (209–22), J. Austin Stone (222–5).

nothing wrong, new and drastic restrictions on their jurisdiction were not warranted.

Senator Norris at first had a difficult time accepting Merritt and Emery's defense of the judges who interpreted the Clayton Act. Norris immediately challenged the sincerity of Merritt and Emery's claims by asking why employers' groups had so vigorously opposed the injunction provisions in the Clayton Act in 1912 and 1914. If, as Merritt and Emery suggested, employers believed at the time that the labor provisions made no substantive changes in the law, there would have been no reason for employer representatives to lobby vigorously against the law. Merritt explained that employers opposed the labor provisions in the Clayton Act because confusing and ambiguous language created uncertainty about how it would be treated in the courts. Merritt explained, "I think we should oppose a bill which may present such perplexing questions, and not rely upon what one side believed to be the correct interpretation" (317). Thus, Merritt and Emery's main point held: "The courts should not be embarrassed and subsequently criticized for its interpretation of a bill which no one can understand" (317).

As the hearings went on, other witnesses who supported injunction reform offered additional, if inadvertent, support to the view that legislative insincerity rather than judicial usurpation was responsible for the failure of the Clayton Act. One of the more startling examples came when Winter S. Martin, an attorney appearing on behalf of the AFL, made a startling attack on the Clayton Act. Martin declared at one point that the "Clayton Act is worthless" (702). To illustrate his point, Martin attacked the provision in Section 6 of the Clayton Act declaring that the "labor of a human being is not a commodity or article of commerce." Martin scoffed:

The straightforward and direct way was to insert language which changed the antitrust act. What they did was to cater to the unfounded apprehensions of certain misinformed erratic persons, who had no clear conception of what the courts had held on the subject, and to inject into the hodge-podge section such language as almost any pupil at a night school should be ashamed to use (709).

In making this attack, Martin was at least a few steps ahead of the labor federation he was allegedly representing. The provision he ridiculed was so cherished by AFL leaders that it continued to be quoted at the top of the masthead in the *American Federationist* and in other AFL publications.

Martin's conduct also illustrates some problems with the way scholars conceptualize the differences between judicial and legislative processes. Recent critics of court rulings in labor cases have suggested that some unique barriers to democratic action occur in court battles that are not present when political battles are instead fought out in legislatures. The Norris-LaGuardia debates reveal, however, that the politics of the legislative branch may be more like the judicial process than such scholars realize. For example, James Gray Pope (1997, 1012) claims that the "jurisgenerative" capacities of outside groups like labor are limited when they make arguments before judges. He notes that the efforts of such groups are hindered in the courts because of the need to articulate demands in a legal discourse recognizable to judges, and the need to use lawyers as go betweens who articulate those claims. While Pope's claims about presenting arguments in courts may be true, Andrew Furuseth seems to have encountered precisely the same difficulties as he tried to advance his alternative interpretive world in the "pure politics" forum of Congress. Before lobbying Congress, Furuseth had to spend a tremendous amount of time studying the history of English equity courts. In his testimony before Congress he supported his position by citing legal treatises and case law. Note also that the organization he represented later sent an attorney to testify before Congress, an attorney who openly contradicted Furuseth's vision and the claims made earlier by other AFL leaders. Ultimately, the legislators chose the vision offered by the attorneys over the vision offered by self-trained legal expert Andrew Furuseth.

During the 1928 hearings, Senator Norris struggled to evaluate the competing explanations of the Clayton Act's failure. At first, Senator Norris appeared no more convinced by Winter Martin's argument than he had been by Merritt's or Emery's. He told Martin that the "Clayton Act came after a long series of debates, and after long consideration" and that "there is no doubt in my mind, and I do not think there is any doubt in anybody's mind" that the Clayton Act was passed "to prevent injunctions such as have been issued over and over again since its passage" (711). However, while Norris still doubted congressional culpability in these March 1928 hearings, his decision a few months later to introduce a substitute bill suggests that he later changed his mind. Although Norris himself never fully articulated his objections to the Shipstead bill, his growing acceptance of the claim that weaknesses in legislative language contributed to the failure of the Clayton Act came through repeatedly as he spent the next four years defending his substitute bill.[37] Norris often

---

[37] Norris's most extended discussion of the failure of the Clayton Act is in comments he made during the brief public hearings on the second Shipstead bill of 1930 (1930 Senate Hearings, 22–4). Norris never fully explained his objections to the Shipstead

defended the new bill by reminding his colleagues that the best available legal experts had carefully drafted the language so that the bill would avoid earlier problems in the courts.[38]

After Norris's "experts" had weighed in, only one participant in public congressional deliberations continued to claim that the Shipstead bill was preferable to Norris's substitute: Andrew Furuseth. In 1928 and 1930, Furuseth angrily denounced the Norris bill in both testimony before the subcommittee and in a more detailed set of letters and articles that were incorporated into the record.[39] Defenders of the Norris bill were touched by Furuseth's commitment, but remained convinced that his bill went too far. For example, Frankfurter and Green wrote that Furuseth defended the Shipstead bill with "indomitable tenacity," and noted that there "is much that is gallant in the picture of this self-taught seaman challenging with power and skill an entire learned profession." The problem, however, was that "almost without exception, the informed opinion of lawyers, even of those most sympathetic with Mr. Furuseth's aims, regards his proposal as an attempt to throw out the baby with the bath" (207). Frankfurter and Green cited testimony that the Shipstead bill threatened court jurisdiction in thirty-two categories of litigation other than labor disputes and claimed that the better strategy was to adopt a bill that focused on equity jurisdiction only in labor disputes.[40]

Furuseth dismissed such attempts to defend the Norris bill. When supporters mentioned Frankfurter's role, Furuseth scoffed that asking a "professor of equity" for an opinion on the bill was like asking a priest for an opinion on a dispute between Catholics and Protestants.[41]

---

bill in the public records of congressional hearings. He simply stated that the legal experts he had consulted found the Shipstead bill to be defective. See, for example, his response to Shipstead (75 *Congressional Record* 5008) or the explanation in his autobiography (1945, 313). Norris mentioned constitutional concerns, but did not fully explain them. It was clear early on in the hearings that Norris was interested in considering alternatives to the Shipstead bill. See, for example, an exchange early in the hearings with Morris L. Ernst of the ACLU (1928 Senate Hearings, 166).

[38] Norris relates the story of the bill's drafting in Norris 1945, 312–13.

[39] 1928 Senate Hearings, 883–97; 1930 Senate Hearings, 4–19. In his autobiography, Norris recounts Andrew Furuseth's anger upon hearing of the decision to offer the substitute bill, and suggests that Furuseth was personally hurt by the experts' suggestion that the Shipstead bill was inadequate (Norris 1945, 312). Furuseth's subsequent behavior suggests, however, that his objections went beyond personal feelings to deep conviction.

[40] Frankfurter and Green (1930, 207, note 15) cite a memo by Alfred P. Thom, General Counsel for Association of Railway Executives (1928 Senate Hearings, 924).

[41] *AFL Proceedings*, 1930, 360.

The debates in Congress were mirrored by debates within the AFL. When the substitute Norris bill was first introduced in 1928, Furuseth was able to persuade the AFL to come out in opposition and to insist on the original Shipstead bill. A special committee reported to the AFL convention that the Norris bill did not meet the demand of the previous year's convention for a bill "clearly defining the jurisdiction of equity courts" (1928 *AFL Proceedings*, 250). Furuseth came out on the losing end of the same argument at the following year's AFL convention, however. After a spirited debate (Furuseth at one point accused AFL Vice President Matthew Woll of being a "pettifogging lawyer" (1929 *AFL Proceedings*, 342)), the AFL convention of 1929 voted to endorse Norris's substitute bill.

Furuseth remained bitterly opposed to the substitute and continued to attack the Norris bill in subsequent AFL conventions. Echoing the argument he had been making for nearly thirty years, the bitter Furuseth warned when the AFL again endorsed the bill in 1930, "no matter what some lawyer may tell you, when the equity court has jurisdiction it is responsible to nothing and nobody" (1930 *AFL Proceedings* 359).

AFL Vice President Matthew Woll, chair of the AFL committee that had recommended that the bill be endorsed, was given the unpleasant task of responding to Furuseth. During the 1930 convention, Woll responded to Furuseth's revived attack with an explanation of why the Norris bill would succeed. Woll's explanation reveals quite clearly that the AFL leadership had come to understand the failure of the Clayton Act as the result of AFL-supported compromises in Congress that weakened the legislative language. Woll's defense of the Norris substitute for the Shipstead bill in December 1930 was rooted in the belief that Congress rather than the courts was responsible for the failure of the Clayton Act. Woll explained:

I agree with [Furuseth] that [the Clayton Act] extended the right of entering the equity courts to anyone feeling themselves aggrieved.... And who is it that gave the courts that power? Our Congress (362).

Woll also suggested that legislators were empowering the courts in order to "evade their responsibility" for deciding labor policy issues directly. Ironically, Woll was adopting a position closer to the one occupied by Merritt and Emery than the one occupied by AFL officials Green and Morrison during the 1928 hearings.

Furuseth never relented. He continued to attack the Norris-LaGuardia Act even after early court decisions signaled that it would be much more effective than the Clayton Act (Weintraub 1959, 189). However, the actions of both members of Congress and the AFL seem to indicate that the disagreement between Furuseth and other informed participants in the process was a sincere one. Other participants seemed to believe that the improved legislative language in Norris's bill would reverse the prior pattern and prevent hostile judges from ruling against the interests of labor organizations. The fact that legislators followed the strategy recommended by the legal experts like Frankfurter rather than the strategy developed independently of such experts by labor leaders reflects the conviction that the courts would respond more favorably to clear statutory language than they had to the muddled compromises in the Clayton Act.[42]

Immunizing Collective Activities: What Activities Are Exempted by Section 4?

Like the second paragraph of Section 20 of the Clayton Act, Section 4 of Norris-LaGuardia contains a list of collective activities that are immunized from certain forms of injunctive relief.[43] However, the list of activities in Norris-LaGuardia is longer and more detailed. Section 4 begins by declaring that "No court of the United States shall have jurisdiction" to issue an injunction in a labor dispute to prevent persons from carrying out acts that fit the nine categories. Some items on the list are similar to items listed in Section 20 of the Clayton Act. Both laws contained descriptions

---

[42] Since the Shipstead version of the bill died in committee, it is not possible to know for sure what support the bill would have had on the floor of the Senate and House. However, there was one Senate vote on an amendment that did provide members of that chamber with a chance to register support or disapproval of Furuseth's vision of confining courts of equity to protecting "tangible and transferable" property. Shortly before passage of the Norris bill, Senator Shipstead introduced an amendment to add the word "tangible" to the provision requiring that injunctions only be issued when there was a threat of substantial and irreparable damage to "property." After offering praise for Andrew Furuseth and calling his task "unpleasant" Norris announced that he had to oppose the amendment on the advice of the legal experts who had helped draft the bill. Shipstead did not convince many colleagues. The amendment received only six votes. The amendment is introduced, debated, and rejected at 75 *Congressional Record* 5004–8.

[43] Like Section 7, sections 4 and 5 take direct aim at the jurisdiction of the federal courts: All three begin with the phrase: "No court of the United Sates shall have jurisdiction...". However, I associate sections 4 and 5 with the substantive changes in the *second* paragraph of Section 20 of the Clayton Act because they limit court interference by providing a list of immunized collective activities. There are other Norris-LaGuardia provisions that place procedural restrictions on the issuance of injunctions, but they do so without directly attacking the jurisdiction of the courts (sections 8, 9, 10, 11, and 12).

that seemed to cover quitting and striking, picketing, boycotting, paying benefits to strikers, and assembling.[44] However, the Norris-LaGuardia Act added novel descriptions targeting yellow-dog contracts (clause (b) and clause (i)), notifying others of the intention to perform any of the listed acts (clause (g)), and forming an agreement to do any of the other specified activities (clause (h)).

In sharp contrast to the narrow interpretations judges gave to the corresponding provisions of the Clayton Act, however, most judges interpreted the Section 4 provisions in a way that allowed a broad range of workers' collective activities to fall into the protected categories. Judges exempted many activities that courts had routinely enjoined in the decades before Norris-LaGuardia. Judges interpreted Section 4 as prohibiting injunctions in cases involving publicizing disputes,[45] strikes,[46] and picketing,[47] and (most closely to *Duplex Printing* and the Clayton Act) secondary boycotts.[48]

Once again, improvements in the legislative language of the Clayton Act appear to be an important reason for Norris-LaGuardia's relative success. While qualifying words like "lawful" and "peaceful" helped judges to justify injunctions in Clayton Act cases, the descriptions of the immunized activities in Norris-LaGuardia are expressed with fewer

[44] The activities listed in Section 4 of Norris-LaGuardia with counterparts in Section 20 of the Clayton Act were as follows: clause 4(a), striking; clauses 4(e) and 4(g), picketing; clause 4(e), boycotting; clauses 4(c) and 4(d), paying benefits to strikers; clauses 4(e) and 4(f), assembling. The language describing each category of activity was different in Norris-LaGuardia.

[45] *Taxi-Cab Drivers Local Union No. 889 of Oklahoma City, Okl v Yellow Cab Operating Co.* (C.C.A. Okl. 1941, 123 F. 2d 262); *Pauly Jail Bldg. Co. v International Ass'n of Bridge, Structural, & Ornamental Iron Workers* (C.C. Mo. 1939, 29 F. Supp. 15); *Miller Parlor Furniture Co., Inc. v Furniture Workers Industrial Union*, (D.C. N.J. 1934, 8 F. Supp. 209); *Cinderella Theater Co., Inc. v Sign Writers' Local Union No. 591* (D.C. Mich. 1934, 6 F. Supp. 164).

[46] *Allen Bradley Co. v Local Union No. 3, International Brotherhood of Electrical Workers* (323 U.S. 767 (1939)); *U.S. v Hutcheson* (312 U.S. 219 (1941)).

[47] *Wilson & Co. v Birl* (C.C.A. Pa. 1939, 105 F. 2d 948); *Houston and North Texas Motor Freight Lines v Local Union No. 886 of International Brotherhood of Teamsters, Chauffeurs, Stablemen, and Helpers of America* (D.C. Okl. 1938, 24 F. Supp. 619); *Diamond Full Fashioned Hosiery Co. v Leader* (D.C. Pa. 1937, 20 F. Supp. 467).

[48] Three leading boycott cases are the *International Ladies' Garment Workers' Union v Donnelly Garment Co.* (C.C.A. Mo. 1941, 119 F. 2d 892); *International Ass'n of Bridge, Structural & Ornamental Iron Workers v Pauly Jail Building Co.* (C.C.A. Mo. 1941, 118 F. 2d 615) (314 U.S. 639); *Wilson & Co. v Birl* (C.C.A. Pa. 1939, 105 F. 2d 948). Of course, Congress later made most secondary boycotts unlawful in 1947 in Section 8(b)(4)(A) of the Taft-Hartley Act.

qualifying phrases.[49] Yet even if the relative paucity of qualifying words contributed to the success of Norris-LaGuardia, it is clear that the language did not by itself prevent judges from making important policy decisions. Some judges still read Section 4 as allowing them a range of discretion in regulating workers' collective activities. Some judges continued to issue injunctions, often after calling attention to those few qualifying words that did appear in Section 4. For example, some judges claimed that the phrase "without fraud or violence" meant that the protections afforded to assembling, picketing, persuasion, quitting, and enlisting sympathy were voided any time there had been any violence involved in a case.[50] In other cases, judges who issued injunctions appear to have decided that there were implied (or perhaps "imaginary" is the better word) limitations on the exemptions. An example is provided by Judge Wham's claim, noted previously, that the language limiting the exemption for picketing to cases involving fraud or violence also limited the exemption in cases where picketing was "coercive" or "intimidating."[51]

In general, however, judges settled on interpretations of the categories in Section 4 that limited judicial discretion and prevented judges from issuing injunctions in labor disputes. Many judges read the qualifying phrases in the act quite narrowly, for example, by sticking to technical legal definitions of words like "fraud" and "violence."[52] As a result, judges often cited the provisions in Section 4 as they refused to issue injunctions in labor disputes. Employers could no longer count on judges to enjoin collective activities falling under the descriptions in the statutes.[53]

---

[49] Five of the nine specified categories of immunized activities are expressed without *any* qualifying adjectives at all. Of the four categories that do contain qualifying adjectives, two (the publicity and yellow-dog clauses) contain qualifications for cases involving "fraud or violence." That language does not seem to reach as far as more flexible words like "intimidation" and "coercion" and (especially) "lawfully." The provision in clause (d) immunizing persons who provide aid to persons involved in a dispute contains the only instance of the word "lawful," while the provision in clause (f) on assembling contains the act's lone variation of the word "peaceably."

[50] See, for example, *Carter v Herrin Motor Freight Lines,* C.C.A. Ala. 1942, 131 F. 2d 557.

[51] *Knapp-Monarch Co. v Anderson, et al.* (E.D. Ill. 1934, 7 F. Supp. 332).

[52] See, for example, *International Ass'n of Bridge, Structural, & Ornamental Iron Workers v Pauly Jail Building Company* (C.C.A. Mo. 1941, 11 F. 2d 615), *Wilson & Co. v Birl,* (C.C.A. Pa. 1939, 105 F. 2d 948).

[53] At least until passage of the Taft-Hartley Act of 1947. See note 1.

Immunizing Collective Activities: Section 4 in Congress

In contrast to the corresponding provisions in Section 20 of the Clayton Act, Section 4 of Norris-LaGuardia made it through Congress without any members successfully using amendments to qualify or otherwise weaken the original language from Norris's bill. There were, however, some unsuccessful attempts to amend the act that provoked illuminating discussions. Members of both the House and Senate offered amendments that would have softened or otherwise qualified the language in Section 4 of Norris-LaGuardia. However, in contrast to their counterparts during the Clayton Act debates, Norris-LaGuardia's floor managers in the House and Senate prevented all such amendments from passing. As a result, the descriptions of the immunized activities that Congress enacted in the Norris-LaGuardia Act in 1932 were nearly identical to the ones in the substitute bill first introduced by Norris in 1928.[54]

As legislators considered and rejected various proposals to amend the language in Section 4, the experience of the Clayton Act was repeatedly invoked to remind participants that judges would be inclined to use qualified language as an opportunity to rule against the interests of labor organizations. Interestingly, the legislators who spoke out against the amendments adding qualifying language did not appear convinced that, as a matter of policy, workers should be given unqualified freedom to engage in collective activities. They instead argued that the strong, unqualified language was necessary as an antidote to past problems of judicial interference. Ironically, the problems that led to judicial interference with the Clayton Act became the strongest argument for retaining Norris-LaGuardia's radical character.

At the same time, those legislators proposing amendments that would have weakened Norris-LaGuardia's immunities did not defend injunctions. They did admit that they preferred a system where judges had more discretion to control workers' activities and protect the "rights" of employers. For example, the 1930 report of the Senate Judiciary Committee that rejected Norris's bill provided a defense of judicial

---

[54] Only two changes were made to all of Section 4 between Norris's initial introduction of the bill in 1928 and enactment in 1932. Both changes were made to the general opening language of the section, not to the descriptions of immunized activities. Neither change appears to be an attempt to make the meaning less clear. First, the phrase "any restraining order or injunction" in Norris's proposed substitute in 1928 became "any restraining order or temporary or permanent injunction" when Norris offered the substitute in 1930. Second, the phrase "in cases" became "in any case" by amendment offered by the Senate Committee in 1932.

discretion. The report complained that Norris's bill did not leave judges the discretion "to prevent the intimidation and objectionable surveillance of nonunion employees" or to protect the "right to the peaceful enjoyment of a man's home by himself and family" (1930 Senate Report, 9). After the 1930 elections, however, the opposition to the Norris bill in Congress was more muted. Senator Felix Hebert did introduce a series of amendments on behalf of the minority members of the Senate Judiciary Committee. However, instead of defending judicial discretion as an end in itself, Hebert claimed that he favored the amendments only because they would help the bill to survive constitutional challenges by allowing judges to protect the rights of employers.[55]

After noting that he was "suspicious of the Greeks when they are bearing gifts" (4763), Senator Norris urged his colleagues to reject Hebert's proposed changes. Norris warned: "Here are amendments piled up on this desk, some of them innocent looking on their faces, that, if agreed to, would put holes in this bill through which a willing judge such as many of them are who have issued these unconscionable injunctions, would drive a camel" (4763). Senator Burton Wheeler (D-MT) who joined Norris in speaking out against the proposed changes, stated that the substitute amendment would merely preserve the status quo, and "that, I take it, is one of the things we are trying to correct by this bill" (75 *Congressional Record* 4768). Senator Norris noted a general concern with judicial hostility when he explained his desire to maintain the very particularized language in the bill describing collective activities, noting that the judiciary's track record of hostility toward labor warranted special care in this case (75 *Congressional Record* 4770). In the end, the arguments against Hebert's proposal won out. Hebert could generate little interest in his substitutes, and his amendment was eventually rejected by a vote of fifty-three to sixteen.

Similar events occurred when the bill reached the House. As the House began to take up the Norris bill in 1932, Representative LaGuardia set the tone by complaining to his colleagues about an article published a month earlier in the *Journal of Commerce*. LaGuardia read a passage from the article stating that the Norris bill was "so complicated that it might be said to be beyond the comprehension of most of the legislators" and that "[t]his

---

[55] Hebert's proposal for Section 4 was a substitute for the entire provision. The substitute version omitted the protections for yellow-dog contracts in clause (b), changed "publicity" to "fair publicity" in clause (e), added a "lawfully" to clause (f) and a "lawful" to clause (i), and added exceptions to clause (i) for cases involving "coercion" or "threats" (75 *Congressional Record* 4767).

may give rise to an opportunity for amendments that will take the sting out of the legislation" (75 *Congressional Record* 5480). Declaring defiantly, "we are not legislating today for finance," LaGuardia denounced the article's suggestion (5480). LaGuardia and other supporters of the original bill then successfully urged against adopting every proposed amendment that would have added qualifying language to Section 4. Like his Senate counterparts, LaGuardia warned that such amendments would allow too much judicial discretion and thus allow hostile judges to interfere with the goals of the act.

In the House, most of the discussion of Section 4 centered on an amendment offered by Rep. James Beck (R-PA), the most outspoken opponent of the bill in the House. Instead of adding phrases to the existing categories in Section 4, as Hebert's amendment had done, Beck's amendment appended a provision to Section 4 that added a general exception to the immunities already in the bill. Beck's amendment seemed to be designed to accommodate creatures at least as large as camels. It would have allowed judges to issue injunctions against acts "performed or threatened for an unlawful purpose or with an unlawful intent, or otherwise in violation of any statute of the United States" (75 *Congressional Record* 5507). Beck had earlier indicated that the "unlawful" activities he was after were "mass picketing, intimidation, besetting, importuning, libeling, and false statements" (75 *Congressional Record* 5471). In comparison to Hebert in the Senate, Beck was willing to openly attack the apparent goals of the bill. But like Hebert's amendment, Beck's was rejected. It lost without debate by a vote of 143 to 47.

The most revealing attempt to change Section 4 was made not by vocal opponents of Norris's bill but by two professed supporters, Rep. Earl C. Michener (R-MI) and Rep. Carroll L. Beedy (R-ME). Michener proposed an amendment that would have added words to allow judges to issue injunctions in cases of "threats and intimidation" to those provisions already allowing injunctions in cases involving "fraud and violence." Michener explained that the exemption for "fraud and violence" that was already in the bill was not broad enough.

In the debates over the Michener amendments, expectations about judicial responses appear once again to have shaped congressional decision making. Beedy and Michener acknowledged that the new language was risky because hostile judges might interpret it as an invitation to exercise discretion. Representative Beedy noted that judges had "abused" language in the labor provisions of the Clayton Act (75 *Congressional Record* 5468), but suggested that Congress could prevent such abuses with the new statute by including a clear definition of "intimidation." Such a definition was preferable to the sweeping language in Section 4 giving unqualified immunity to collective activities that could interfere with important individual rights. Michener followed up on Beedy's comment by suggesting such a statutory definition of "intimidation": "Conduct intended to arouse fear or apprehension of violence."

Representative LaGuardia, however, doubted that any such definitions could provide effective safeguards, and urged his colleagues to vote against the changes. LaGuardia acknowledged that the proposal was a good faith effort to improve the bill, but warned: "I have . . . looked up court decisions on these same words, and in the face of the experience of the past with the Clayton Act and the decisions thereunder, it would be very unsafe to permit this amendment to go into the bill" (5506). Representative Emmanuel Celler (D-NY) echoed these sentiments: "An examination of the precedents in the country and in the State and Federal Courts will show that the word 'intimidation' forms the basis of greatest abuse in labor injunctions" (5506). The arguments made by Celler and LaGuardia apparently convinced most members of the House. The House rejected all three Michener amendments adding the words "threats or intimidation" to provisions in Section 4.

It is instructive that both Celler and LaGuardia responded to the Michener amendment without opposing the substantive policy aim of the amendment. Celler and LaGuardia did not claim that they thought it good public policy to allow workers to engage in coercion and intimidation. They instead responded with arguments based on analyses of earlier judicial decisions. It is once again clear that members of Congress were attentive to judicial doctrines and consciously developing the substantive content of the act with an eye toward judicial attitudes as revealed in earlier judicial decisions. Furthermore, it appears as though claims about these legislative precedents helped the bill retain broader protections for labor than would otherwise have passed. Significantly, however, the fact that legislators did not modify the bill was not the result of labor exercising raw political power through a "pure politics." Labor leaders did not storm Washington and demand the right to intimidate their employers. It seems very unlikely that legislators would have passed any bill declaring openly that the courts should not provide remedies when workers used "intimidation" and "coercion." Nevertheless, it appears that the House was willing to pass a bill that many members felt would have the same effect because there was no safe way to include the words "intimidation" or "coercion" without indirectly inviting judicial intervention. Such legislative decisions only make sense when looked at in the context of earlier legislative "failures" in the courts. If the Clayton Act experience had not left legislators so worried about the courts, they would undoubtedly have passed a different, probably less radically worded, statute.

The debates in both the House and Senate on proposed amendments to Section 4 make it clear that members of Congress were conscious of, and perhaps obsessed with, the potential for judicial interference, and that concerns about judges had an important effect on the language in the statute. However, two other incidents during floor debates demonstrate that some participants felt that careful legislative drafting was not the only way to influence judges. Both of these incidents involved leading supporters of the bill consciously shaping those parts of the legislative record that they expected judges to examine when interpreting the statute.

One incident involves a speech by Senator Wagner addressing "broad questions of policy which underlie the pending... bill" (75 *Congressional Record* 4915) by providing a detailed history of earlier efforts to curtail labor injunctions though legislation. With passage of the bill assured, Wagner's fascinating speech addresses not his colleagues in the Senate, but the judges on the federal bench. Wagner explained: "The record should be complete so that when the courts come to pass upon what we are doing here today they may be fully informed of the purposes which moved us and of the ends we desired to accomplish" (4915). Wagner worked to make it very clear to judges that Congress in 1932 was opposed to the positions the courts had pursued in the aftermath of the Clayton Act, and suggested to the judges that they had hurt their prestige by weakening earlier congressional enactments: "That the need for this legislation still exists reflects no glory upon American jurisprudence" (4915).

The second incident occurred as Senator Norris made comments in response to an amendment offered by Sen. John J. Blaine (R-WI). Blaine was a member of the original subcommittee that introduced the Norris bill in 1928, and a supporter of injunction reform. But just before passage of the bill, Blaine angered Norris by suggesting publicly that the courts might rule the bill unconstitutional. Blaine made the comment in a speech supporting his pet amendment, which would have added a provision allowing workers to collect treble damages when employers caused an injury through the use of strikebreakers or *agents provocateur*. The treble damages provision was designed to counter the Sherman Act provision allowing for treble damages in antitrust cases. Blaine allowed his doubts about the rest of Norris-LaGuardia to come to the surface as he defended his amendment: "I do not know what the courts are going to do when this bill shall become a law, and none of us can predict what they will do." However, even if the courts did weaken or strike down the new law, "then the important thing that we will have accomplished, in addition to the present law, is this very wholesome measure giving threefold damages to the workingmen when the employer has employed spies and other agents to bring about a strike and to commit unlawful acts" (5014).

Blaine's rhetorical strategy in support of his amendment clearly upset his colleague Senator Norris. Norris exploded:

When the court passes on the act, as it ultimately will, if it holds that the act is unconstitutional the Senator from Wisconsin [Blaine] will probably have the honor of reading in an opinion from the Supreme Court that the great lawyer, ... the member of the subcommittee that framed the bill, ... had almost himself confessed that the whole thing was a hoax. Anyway, and that all he expected to have out of it was that little amendment that he thought of just a few minutes before the vote was taken (75 *Congressional Record* 5016).

Norris reminded Blaine of the Court's opinion in *Duplex*:

when they were taking the life blood out of the Clayton Act, ... [t]hey quoted reports from the Committee on the Judiciary in the Senate, they quoted speeches and controversies taking place on the floor of the House of Representatives, and I had hoped that we would get through this bill and enact it into law and that no court with a fine-tooth comb in going over the debates, could ever find any doubt cast upon the constitutionality of the bill by any of its friends. But I am afraid I will have to give that hope up now (5016).

Norris's angry response to Blaine was aimed at two audiences and served two purposes. First, it apparently convinced his colleagues to oppose the amendment. Only three senators voted for Blaine's amendment.[56] But second, Norris tried to cleanse the record that would be encountered by the judges who would inevitably be called on to interpret the act.

Norris's response to Blaine shows that like Wagner, he expected the judges who eventually interpreted the act to be influenced by things said by legislators in Congress. A clean record of careful deliberations would demonstrate a much stronger consensus in favor of reform. It also meant that judges could continue to issue injunctions only by doing something that they never had to do in Clayton Act cases: Directly reject a policy position that had been clearly established in Congress. The possibility of a hostile judicial response could not be eliminated entirely, but

---

[56] Along with Blaine, Senators Shipstead and LaFollette voted for the amendment. Sixty-nine senators voted no, twenty-four did not vote (75 *Congressional Record* 5017).

Norris's efforts insured that rulings against labor organizations would come at much higher cost to judicial legitimacy than the decisions on the Clayton Act.

Members of Congress tried to pressure judges in other ways. Several times during floor debates, members mentioned the recent judicial nominations that had been rejected by the Senate because the nominees had supported labor injunctions. Several members referred to the failed nomination of Circuit Court Judge John Parker to the Supreme Court.[57] Both Norris and LaGuardia mentioned the pending nomination of Judge James Wilkerson during floor debates.[58] Parker's and Wilkerson's nominations to federal judgeships had been challenged in part because of their records in labor injunction cases.

Taken together, the Senate and House amending activity on Section 4, along with the efforts to manage the content of floor debates show how the possibility of judicial interference shaped the behavior of supporters and opponents of the bill. The arguments that Norris-LaGuardia supporters used when they urged colleagues to vote against qualifying amendments reflect the belief that strong legislative language could have an important effect on the way even hostile judges would interpret the act. However, the discussions that occurred in connection with Section 4 also reveal that participants in the legislative process did not see improvements in legislative language as a foolproof strategy. Participants remained very concerned about the possibility that the courts would continue to issue hostile rulings. However, they also did not feel that legislative language was their only available weapon for controlling the courts. Supporters of injunction reform felt that judges would be responsive to a broad range of signals that they created in the legislative record, signals that would supplement the improvements made in legislative language. Significantly, legislators did not behave as though they were helpless in the face of a

[57] Parker was rejected in part because of his controversial decision to allow an injunction to protect a yellow-dog contract in the notorious *Red Jacket* case. Parker was also opposed by the NAACP for racist statements he had made earlier in his political career. Two sympathetic scholars of labor law have called the rejection of the mellowing Parker "one of the saddest pieces of injustice in senatorial annals" (Gregory and Katz 1979, 180–1). But at the time it was a very important symbolic victory for progressive critics of the courts. For discussion of the intrusion of the judicial nominating process on the development of Norris-LaGuardia, see Bernstein 1960, 403–10.

[58] Norris at 75 *Congressional Record* 4509, LaGuardia at 5479. For a discussion of the Wilkerson nomination in the context of the Norris-LaGuardia debates, see Bernstein 1960, 411–12.

hostile judiciary, or as though the only thing that would affect judicial responses were the policy preferences of judges. The legislators' arguments
about legislative language and political context reflect their well-informed
expectations about how the signals they sent about the immunities expressed in Section 4 would shape judicial reactions to those provisions.

Immunizing Collective Activities, Part 2: Who Is Protected by Section 4?

The broad readings that most judges gave to the immunities listed in
Section 4 of Norris-LaGuardia did not guarantee that the new act would
be much more successful than the Clayton Act. After all, the most damaging part of the Supreme Court's key ruling on the Clayton Act was not
the Court's reading of the highly qualified language in Section 20, but the
Court's claim that the immunities in Section 20 typically applied only to
a small percentage of the workers who might engage in collective activity
during a labor dispute. The Court ruled that the immunities in Section 20
applied only to persons who were immunized "participants" in labor
disputes, that is, persons who were very closely linked by a legitimating
"self-interest" to the employment practices of a targeted firm.

Thus, for Section 4 of Norris-LaGuardia to succeed where the Clayton
Act had failed, the courts had to do more than adopt a broader interpretation of *what* activities were immunized by the language in Section 4. The
courts also had to find that the immunities covered a much broader range
of persons. The Norris-LaGuardia provisions were more successful than
the corresponding provisions in the Clayton Act in part because judges
often ruled that Norris-LaGuardia's immunities applied to a broader
range of persons. An example illustrating the difference in judicial responses appears in the first Supreme Court case on Norris-LaGuardia,
Senn v Tile Layers Protective Union.[59]

The case grew out of tiling contractor Paul Senn's request for an injunction to prevent the tile layers union from picketing his business. Senn ran

---

[59] 301 U.S. 465 (1937). This case does not provide a clean test of Norris-LaGuardia
because it also involved Wisconsin's state "little Norris-LaGuardia Act." The Court
reviewed a decision by the Supreme Court of Wisconsin on the constitutionality of
provisions of Wisconsin's state labor code that were nearly identical to the Norris-
LaGuardia provisions. Because of the overlapping state statute, the Court's ruling
also involved a Fourteenth Amendment challenge to the state statute that is not
directly relevant to the meaning of the Norris-LaGuardia Act. The Wisconsin provision is Wisconsin Statutes, 1937, c. 103, §103.62.

his small business out of his home and performed much of the tiling work himself, along with four employees. The tile layers picketed his business as part of a broad effort to enforce a union rule prohibiting contractors from performing work on tiling jobs themselves rather than hiring unionized workers. The union members who picketed Senn were not employed or seeking employment at Senn's company.

The *Senn* case is similar to the *Duplex* case because workers were collectively targeting a company at which they were not seeking employment. If anything, Senn had a stronger case than the Duplex Company because the pickets interfered not only with his right to conduct his business but also his right to work in his chosen profession. The Supreme Court nevertheless ruled that the lower court could not issue an injunction in the case. The Supreme Court's opinion shows that the justices on the Court at that time were much more willing to recognize shared interests among workers of different firms in the same industry. The Court accepted that the union rule against contractors performing work was "adopted by the defendants out of the necessities of employment within the industry and for the protection of themselves as workers and craftsmen in the industry" (301 U.S. 468, 480). Thus, there was "no basis to the suggestion that the union's request that Senn refrain from working with his own hands, or their employment or picketing and publicity, was malicious" (480).[60]

Once again, the most obvious explanation for the different outcomes in the Clayton Act and Norris-LaGuardia cases are differences in the language in the two laws. In contrast to Section 20 of the Clayton Act, which did not clearly lay out who was covered by the expressed immunities, the Norris-LaGuardia Act contained a separate Section 13 that provided definitions of the key terms contained elsewhere in the act. Section 13 of Norris-LaGuardia defined cases that "grow out of a labor dispute" as those cases involving:

persons who are engaged in the same industry, trade, craft, or occupation; or have direct or indirect interests therein; or who are employees of the same employer; or who are members of the same or an affiliated organization of employers or employees (clause a).

---

[60] The following year, the Court went even further to divorce the immunities in Norris-LaGuardia from the employer/employee relationship. In *New Negro Alliance v Sanitary Grocery*, (303 U.S. 552) the Court ruled that a citizen's group protesting racially discriminatory hiring practices at a Washington, D.C. grocery store were engaged in a "labor dispute," and thus protected by the Norris-LaGuardia Act. This time, the ruling came even though none of the protesters were employed or interested in being employed at the store or at any other grocery store.

Section 13 further stated that a person or association should be held to be a "person participating in a labor dispute" if

relief is sought against him or it, and if he or it is engaged in the same industry, trade, craft, or occupation in which such dispute occurs, or has a direct or indirect interest therein, or is a member, officer, or agent of any association composed in whole or in part of employers or employees engaged in such industry, trade, craft, or occupation (clause b).

Section 13 also defined the term "labor dispute" to include

any controversy concerning terms or conditions of employment, or concerning the association or representation of persons in negotiating, fixing, maintaining, changing, or seeking to arrange terms or conditions of employment, *regardless of whether or not the disputants stand in the proximate relation of employer and employee* (clause c, emphasis added).

The detailed definitions in Section 13 appear to aim directly to overturn the narrow conception of workers' self-interest that supported decisions like *Duplex*. While the considerable detail of Section 13 did not make it *impossible* for judges to offer twisted rulings that favored employers, the Supreme Court eventually established interpretations of the definitions in Section 13 that would have prevented the injunction in Duplex.[61]

Defining "Labor Dispute": Sections 4 and 13 in Congress

In contrast to the other provisions that have been discussed in this chapter, the definitions of labor dispute in Section 13 of Norris-LaGuardia did

---

[61] In some of the very first Norris-LaGuardia cases, a few lower court judges did limit the immunities conferred in Section 4. In the case *United Electric Coal Companies v Rice* (7th C.C.A., 1935, 80 F. 2d. 1), the Seventh Circuit Court ruled that the immunities given to strikes and pickets in Section 4 did not apply because the dispute was between two unions and not between workers and their employer. This ruling came despite seemingly straightforward language in Section 13 (a)(3) stating that the term included disputes "between one or more employees or associations of employees." The same circuit court indirectly reaffirmed this decision in another case involving a jurisdictional dispute, *Lauf, et al. v E.G. Shinner & Co., Inc.* (C.C.A. 7th, 82 F. 2d. 68, 1937, 90 F. 2d. 250). *Lauf v Shinner* became the first Supreme Court test of who was covered by the exemptions expressed in Section 4 (303 U.S. 315 (1938)). The Supreme Court dissolved the lower court's injunction and chastised the judges below for ruling that jurisdictional disputes were not "labor disputes" within the meaning of the act. To support its ruling, the Court simply quoted the language defining "labor dispute" in Section 13 of Norris-LaGuardia. Like *Senn,* this case did not provide a clean test of Norris-LaGuardia because it was complicated by state law issues that arose under Wisconsin's antiinjunction law.

not receive much discussion as members of Congress developed and debated the statute. Nevertheless, there is evidence that observers and participants understood the significance of those definitions before the act reached the courts. Shortly after the original Norris bill was first introduced in Congress, Felix Frankfurter, one of the principle drafters of Norris-LaGuardia, explained why it was crucial to define who counted as participants in labor disputes. Frankfurter and his coauthor Nathan Green noted in *The Labor Injunction* that:

the central problem of the law of industrial relations is to determine the purposes that justify the combination of laborers by marking the outposts of the concept of "self-interest." How far laborers may combine to strive for concessions that are not of immediate benefit to them but which strengthen the union organization; how far a union in one craft may use its power to achieve the unionization of non-union plants within the same craft; how far a union of one craft may exert its power in aid of unions in another craft, and how dependent one craft must be upon the other to justify co-operative tactics, these and like issues are all the crucial ones (1930, 215–16).

Frankfurter and Green then claimed that the language in what later became Section 13 "settles all of these questions so far as application for equitable relief is concerned" (216). In particular, they noted that the decision in *Duplex* would be "rendered innocuous" by the definitions in Norris's proposed statute (216).

Some outside observers were less convinced that Section 13 would be adequate. The most comprehensive criticism of the language in Section 13 was made shortly after the bill passed by Chicago Business School professor Jay Finley Christ (1933, 250–4). Christ's article in the *Journal of Business* subjected the definitions in Section 13 to a detailed textual analysis and reached much different conclusions. Calling the language in Section 13 "extremely clumsy" (252) Christ used a list of rhetorical questions to draw attention to crucial ambiguities and uncertainties in the act.[62] Christ also examined several important cases where judges had been accused of issuing improper injunctions and asked whether the new act would have changed the outcome in any of the cases. Christ acknowledged that Norris-LaGuardia would probably prevent injunctions in secondary boycott cases like *Duplex Printing v Deering* (254). But he predicted that other judicial rulings that had been criticized by

---

[62] The questions are in twelve footnotes, numbered 233–44, on pages 251–4.

supporters of the law would be unaffected by the new statute.[63] Christ concluded:

The plain fact of the matter seems to be that the whole of the effectiveness of Section 4 rests upon the definitions in Section 13, and that for all the elaborateness of those definitions, the Act is vague and unsatisfactory precisely at its principal crucial point. For all the words used, there is no specific definition of the types of cases to which the provisions of Section 4 are to be applied.... It seems fair to say that the Norris Act, so far as it may be related to injunctive relief against boycotts, picketing, and sympathetic strikes, consists largely of illusions and futilities (footnotes omitted) (258–9).

Christ's analysis makes it clear that at least some observers doubted that legislators could successfully overcome earlier judicial interference with the legislative language in Section 13. Christ's pessimistic predictions were ultimately proven wrong. Nevertheless, his comments, along with those of Frankfurter and Green, make it clear that influential observers recognized that Section 13 was crucial to reversing earlier court rulings that had hurt the interests of labor organizations.

While academic commentators recognized the significance of Section 13, that provision was never at the center of attention in Congress. There was little discussion of the definitions during floor debates, and Section 13 remained unchallenged and virtually unchanged from its initial appearance in Norris's substitute bill of 1928 to final enactment.[64]

---

[63] Christ cited *Bedford Cut Stone Co. v Journeymen Stone Cutters* (274 U.S. 37 (1927)), (255), and *Loewe v Lawlor* (208 U.S. 274 (1908)), (258).

[64] There are a total of nine differences between the definition in the original Norris bill and the final version in Norris-LaGuardia. Only one of the changes appeared to narrow the definitions so that fewer persons would be protected by the act. In clauses (a) and (b), definitions were broadened by adding language to include persons who had "a direct or indirect interest" in the dispute. The Senate Committee that reported the bill in 1930 made these insertions.

Three other changes were made to the definition of a case "involving or growing out of" a labor dispute in clause (a). One improved the grammar by changing a "when" to an "if." One changed the phrase "same organization" to "same or affiliated organization," and one added the final disjunctive clause in the definition extending the term to persons referred to by the definitions in clauses (b) and (c).

One other change was made to the definition of a person participating in a labor dispute in clause (b). The clause including members of "any association of employers or employees" became "any association composed in whole or in part of employers or employees." The new language appeared for the first time in the bill introduced by Norris in 1932, S. 935.

Two changes were made in the definition of a "labor dispute" in clause (c). As originally introduced in 1928, the definition referred to controversies over the "terms and conditions" of employment. That phrase was changed to "terms or conditions"

The 1932 House Report on the Norris bill says that: "Section 13 contains definitions which speak for themselves."[65] The authors of the report added that it was "hardly necessary to discuss them"[66] other than to point out that the definition of persons participating in a labor dispute was designed to reverse the outcome in *Duplex*. In the Senate, the committee report stated: "It is not believed that any criticism has been or will be made to these definitions" and explained that the "main purpose" of the definitions was to provide for "limiting the injunctive powers of the Federal courts only in the special type of cases, commonly called labor disputes, in which these powers have been notoriously extended."[67]

The records do, however, contain one revealing floor speech made in connection with Section 13. That speech came after minority members of the Senate Judiciary Committee suggested an amendment to Section 13 that would have deleted the words "regardless of whether or not the disputants stand in the proximate relation of employer and employee" from the definition of a "labor dispute." The targeted clause is, of course, the one that aims most directly at the ruling in *Duplex*. The Supreme Court later quoted that clause in a crucial early ruling on Norris-LaGuardia that dissolved a lower court's injunction, *Lauf v Shinner* (301 U.S. 315 (1938)). Even before the proposal to remove the clause was formally offered as an amendment, Senator Wagner made a preemptive strike. Wagner denounced the proposal in a floor speech that specifically associated the targeted clause with the Supreme Court ruling in *Duplex Printing v Deering*. Wagner explained: "What the minority has done has been to adopt the definition almost verbatim from Section 20 of the Clayton Act, which has been held by the Supreme Court in the Duplex case . . . to apply only

of employment when the substitute Norris bill was reintroduced in 1930. The Senate committee recommended that it be changed back to the original in its report in 1930. But in 1932, the committee recommended that it be changed back again to "terms or conditions." That change was made without debate or discussion on the Senate floor (75 *Congressional Record* 4761). A final change from the original bill was made by amendment in both the Senate and the House. Both amendments deleted a clause to include "any other controversy arising out of the respective interest of the employer and employee." The only explanation made for the change came in the Senate, where Senator Walsh said he was offering the amendment on behalf of unnamed "friends of the bill" who feared the definition might otherwise cause "embarrassment in the prosecution of actions for personal injury and death" (5008). The House made the same change without any floor discussion (75 *Congressional Record* 5510).

[65] House Report 669, 72nd Congress, 10.
[66] House Report 669, 72nd Congress, 10.
[67] Senate Report 163, 72nd Congress, 25.

to an employer and his employees. Should this amendment carry, we shall find the legitimate effort of unions to extend their organizations again frustrated" (75 *Congressional Record* 4916). Although Wagner did not capture what the court had said in *Duplex* with complete precision, his denunciation of the amendment was effective. The amendment was withdrawn without ever being voted on. Wagner's comment suggests that even though the definitions in Section 13 were not the focus of attention as Norris-LaGuardia made its way through Congress, the bill's key supporters understood why the language in Section 13 was important. The definitions there would determine whether the courts could continue to issue antilabor rulings like *Duplex*.

In conclusion, it is clear that drafters of the Norris bill and other observers recognized the importance of Section 13 before passage, and that the act's key supporters tried to explain to colleagues how the language in Section 13 aimed at earlier adverse court decisions. Of course, the Supreme Court decision to adopt an interpretation more favorable to labor's expressed interest can once again be plausibly attributed to changes in judicial attitudes that had begun to occur before passage of Norris-LaGuardia. However, those changes in judicial attitudes cannot be understood as something that was occurring separately from the legislative process. One of the bill's drafters, Felix Frankfurter, was the coauthor of the academic study that identified many of the judicial trends that were later recited by defenders of the bill. The language in the bill was deliberately designed to take advantage of those trends. Changes in judicial attitudes were also a factor affecting the support the bill received in Congress and from the AFL. For example, supporters of the bill several times tried to reassure skeptical colleagues by noting that even conservative judges like William Howard Taft had started to articulate broader conceptions of workers' self interests.[68]

LESSONS FROM A LEGISLATIVE VICTORY: CONGRESS, LABOR ORGANIZATIONS, AND THE NORRIS-LAGUARDIA ACT

The Norris-LaGuardia case study yields a number of interesting lessons about the courts as barriers to change through democratic legislative processes and the ability of legislators to triumph over the courts. Before turning to a consideration of these lessons it is worth making a few concluding

---

[68] References to Taft during floor debates can be found in 75 *Congressional Record* 4619, 4690, 4694, 5489.

observations about the attitudes of participants in the legislative process as revealed through the judicial and congressional decisions that gave meaning to the Norris-LaGuardia Act.

First, it is clear that members of Congress and other participants in the legislative process were very conscious of the potential for court interference. Participants frequently associated the goals of the statute with previous attempts at legislative reform that had run into difficulties in the courts and frequently discussed how to prevent a repeat of those failures.

Second, most of the participants in the legislative process, including both labor leaders and the principal framers of the Norris bill, associated the failure of the Clayton Act with weaknesses and ambiguities in the legislative language. Although many of these same participants were also critical of judges, the lesson they learned from the failure of the Clayton Act was that the key to avoiding a repeat of that disappointing failure was to ensure that legislators did not water down the language in the new bill as it made its way through Congress.

Third, the active participants in the legislative process, with the lone exception of Andrew Furuseth, thought Norris-LaGuardia's improvements over the language in the Clayton Act made it more likely that the courts would respond favorably to the new law. A few critics of the bill, most notably Felix Hebert in the Senate, suggested the clarity of Norris-LaGuardia's legislative language would result in the bill being invalidated by the courts. However, none of the critics in Congress proposed an alternative language that participants widely understood as being less ambiguous than the language in Norris's bill.

A fourth observation is that despite the near consensus that the language in Norris-LaGuardia was an improvement over the language in the Clayton Act, participants still remained uncertain about precisely how the courts would respond. While many participants seemed to feel that the language in the bill improved on the Clayton Act, they did not see the bill as foolproof. No one claimed that the language in Norris-LaGuardia was so clear that judicial interpretations would play no role in the statute's development.

Thus, a fifth and final observation is that optimism about the likely court reactions was based not only on participants' assessments of the legislative language, but also on their understanding that judicial attitudes toward labor's collective activities had changed since the rulings on the Erdman and Clayton acts. Key supporters of the bill showed a sophisticated understanding of recent trends in the case law as they guided the bill toward passage and responded to charges that the courts would weaken the bill. Those supporters also tried to encourage those trends by making sure that a congressional purpose was communicated unambiguously in the statutory text and legislative records.

Taken together, these observations suggest that the courts had an important influence on the legislative process, but also suggest that determined, sincere, and unified legislators can take steps to minimize judicial interference. Neither the *legislative language* nor the *judicial attitudes* hypothesis by itself fully captures the reasons for the success of the Norris-LaGuardia because, from the perspective of the participants, improvements in legislative language and softening of judicial attitudes were deeply interconnected elements of legislative and political strategies.

The stark confrontations between Congress and the courts that many participants expected never materialized. However, the absence of highly visible conflicts among the branches does not mean that the courts had no impact on the development of Norris-LaGuardia. It seems clear that legislators never would have passed such broad and unqualified protections for workers' collective activities if not for fears about judicial reactions to more qualified statutory language. Accounts that try to measure the impact of separate branches by identifying the attitudes of judges and focusing on cases where those attitudes conflict openly with the expressed will of "Congress" will miss such important avenues of judicial influence.

Given these observations, the Norris-LaGuardia case seems to support a rather optimistic assessment of American democracy. Perhaps worries about the influence of unelected judges on labor policy can now be dismissed with the simple observation that labor organizations were able to get the changes they wanted just as soon as they had the power to force elected legislators to act decisively and sincerely. However, before rushing to such a happy conclusion, it is worth pausing for a moment to reconsider the role of labor organizations in the design and passage of Norris-LaGuardia. While scholars often presume that passage of statutes like the Clayton Act and Norris-LaGuardia signal that labor organizations were able to exercise power effectively in the "pure politics" of the legislative branch, the full record on Norris-LaGuardia produces a very different picture.

On the positive side, support in Congress for placing limits on injunctions was clearly much higher in 1932 than it had been in 1914. Support for injunction reform was broad enough that both major parties had included planks acknowledging judicial abuse of injunctions and supporting antiinjunction legislation in their platforms for the 1928 election.[69] More-over, that increase in support is obviously connected to democratic pro-cesses. For example, changes resulting from the election of 1930 were the difference between Norris's bill dying in committee and being enacted into law. On the other hand, the increase in support for reform does not appear to be the result of some active or replicable electoral strategy pursued by labor organizations. The consensus in Congress in favor of injunction reform in 1932 cannot plausibly be attributed solely to efforts by labor organizations to use conventional democratic processes to pressure mem-bers of Congress to support their position, for example, by threatening to use their electoral might to replace legislators who refused to support labor's goals. Neither the AFL nor any other labor organization effec-tively employed such conventional political tactics in the years leading up to passage of Norris-LaGuardia. The bill was passed when labor was in a very vulnerable political position, and labor organizations played a very small role in shaping the content of Norris-LaGuardia or pressuring Congress to pass it.

These claims may at first seem implausible. Norris-LaGuardia was passed after the Democrats' gains in the 1930 elections and just before FDR's electoral triumph in 1932. As a result, it is easy to associate its passage with political strength labor gained in the New Deal coalition that emerged through those realigning elections. It must be remembered, however, that labor was not yet an important part of that coalition at the time Norris-LaGuardia was enacted.[70] In 1932, labor organizations were still reeling from the decade of conservative Republican dominance and the crisis of the Great Depression. Dramatic depression-era strikes like the sit-down strikes against General Motors would soon alter labor's place in the underlying political structure. But those transformative strikes had not yet occurred when Norris-LaGuardia passed.

The political weakness of the AFL during the years Congress debated Norris-LaGuardia was made worse by the shattering ideological struggles that were occurring within the labor movement. AFL leaders had to strug-gle to adjust what remained of Samuel Gompers's vision of trade unionism and voluntarism to the new political realities and the Great Depression. The resulting ideological shifts allowed the AFL to support the state-administered collective bargaining plan in the Wagner Act just three years

---

[69] Johnson 1978, vol. 1, 275, 286.
[70] For an illuminating discussion of labor's political influence across this period, see Plotke 1996, ch. 4.

after Congress enacted Norris-LaGuardia, but later contributed to the AFL/CIO split and to the AFL's destructive efforts to sabotage the National Labor Relations Board (NLRB) in the late 1930s.[71] The bitter opposition of old-guard figures like Furuseth is but one manifestation of these deeper internal struggles.

Such ideological struggles are important here because they help to explain why labor never spoke with a unified voice in favor of Norris-LaGuardia as a top legislative priority. The goal of ending injunctions and yellow-dog contracts was a top priority under the old-guard AFL's voluntarist ideology, which emphasized workers' rights in a *laissez faire* economic system. That same voluntarist ideology meant that AFL leaders opposed most labor legislation (other than antiinjunction legislation) until the Depression.[72] By 1932, however, the antistatist pillars of the voluntarist vision were crumbling. As a result, antiinjunction legislation was no longer the top legislative priority of even the largely voluntarist AFL. Such legislation was certainly not "labor's" top legislative priority in 1932.

Evidence of these ideological changes can be found in the legislative demands made by the AFL in the early 1930s. After the Democrats' gains in the 1930 elections, AFL President William Green presented the new Congress with a list of legislative demands. Green informed Congress of the dire condition of workers: "Confidence has been destroyed, and a state of mind bordering on hysteria prevails throughout the land."[73] Green's list reveals that Gompers's vision of a trade union movement that could succeed without protection from the state was dead. The list included a massive public works bill, a five-day workweek, programs for keeping youth in school, and a demand for some kind of administrative machinery for structuring worker/management agreements. Green's petition did declare that "Labor regards the injunction relief measure as of transcendent legislative importance" (75 *Congressional Record* 3636). But the request for injunction legislation came only at the end of the long list of other, less voluntarist, legislative demands.[74]

That injunction legislation had been moved to a back burner is also clear from the way the AFL presented the fight for Norris-LaGuardia to its membership. In 1914, the AFL president hailed passage of the Clayton Act

---

[71] Horowitz 1978. Gross 1981, chs. 4–10, documents the AFL's costly efforts to undermine the NLRB.

[72] On this point, see Hattam 1993, 165.

[73] The petition was reprinted in 75 *Congressional Record* 3636.

[74] On the AFL's proposals, see Bernstein 1960, 403, 411.

with a prominent editorial in the *American Federationist* that contained exaggerated praise for the bill. In contrast, passage of Norris-LaGuardia in 1932 warranted only a small note in the *American Federationist* that blandly summarized the content of the bill.[75]

Despite the fact that the AFL did not make antiinjunction legislation a top priority, many members of Congress claimed that their support for Norris-LaGuardia was a way of rewarding the AFL. On the surface, such declarations suggest that political pressure applied by the independent power of the AFL was a decisive factor. However, that appearance of AFL power has to be tempered by the fact that legislators completely ignored the rest of the AFL's more pressing legislative demands.

Furthermore, the details of Norris-LaGuardia were shaped not by labor leaders or their close allies in Congress, but by elite academic and legal experts whose *independence* from labor organizations became one of the main selling points of the bill. The bill drafted by labor leader Andrew Furuseth was rejected in favor of a bill drafted by outside experts who ridiculed Furuseth's vision of reform. Floor leaders for the Norris-LaGuardia Act urged colleagues to vote for the bill not because labor organizations were endorsing it, but because the experts who drafted the bill were independent of the labor movement.

Why Did Norris-LaGuardia Pass?

If the strong congressional consensus that contributed to the success of Norris-LaGuardia in the courts cannot be attributed solely to the direct political action of labor organizations or the ability of the AFL to extract concessions from a broadly sympathetic Congress, what other factors explain support for Norris-LaGuardia in Congress? I submit that support for the act grew out of an odd convergence of interests, many of them held by political and economic elites who were otherwise unsympathetic to the goals of labor and labor organizations.

---

[75] Bernstein 1960, 415. Although the AFL was weak and injunction reform no longer a primary obsession, AFL leaders did recognize the significance of the growing consensus in favor of injunction reform outside the labor movement. In his 1932 petition to Congress, Green noted: "Public opinion slowly responded to the constant appeals of organized labor for the enactment of injunction relief legislation. It began to understand that labor was fully justified in the protests it made against the abuse of the writ of injunction in labor controversies. As a result the two great political parties included in their platforms a pledge both specific and implied to support injunction-relief legislation" (75 *Congressional Record* 3636).

One important part of the coalition favoring injunction reform in the early 1930s were persons who were closer to business than to labor, and largely sympathetic to the judiciary. Such persons were able to support the Norris-LaGuardia reforms because they had learned that the existing system of judicially administered labor relations no longer protected the interests of employers or workers. By the late 1920s, opposition to injunctions and the yellow-dog contract was being voiced not just by labor groups but also by elite legal academics, academic experts in industrial relations, and other progressive and conservative voices. In contrast, most employers' representatives had defended the use of injunctions during the debates on the Clayton Act.

Comments made by Andrew Furuseth during the 1928 Senate Hearings on his Shipstead bill demonstrate the AFL's willingness to take advantage of these trends. His comments also provide some clues about why employers had grown less fond of using repressive means like injunctions to control worker unrest. Furuseth pointedly noted that notorious anti-labor judicial rulings like *Loewe v Lawlor* (208 U.S. 274, 1908) had hurt not just the interests of workers (the "war veterans" who were forced to pay treble damages under the Sherman Act) but ultimately employers as well. Furuseth noted:

Loewe hats are finished. Loewe is now a poverty stricken man and lives upon charity. So this system ultimately does not protect men or business. It can not. What it does is this. It gradually teaches the men and women to look upon courts as their enemies, as an instrument in the hands of other people for the purpose of robbing them of either citizen's rights in the United States. More and more and more that situation, that feeling, is coming to the front, ... it is the most disheartening thing of all, the destruction, ultimately, of the respect in which the judiciary is held" (1928 Senate Hearings, 28–9).

Furuseth told a similar story about the bankrupted owners of the Buck's Stove and Range Company. Furuseth repeatedly referred to judicial intervention in labor disputes as a "cancer" destroying respect for American institutions.[76]

Furuseth's comments also hint at another general concern that contributed to congressional support for Norris-LaGuardia: A concern about maintaining respect for the courts. Beginning with the speech by Norris that opened congressional floor debate on his bill (75 *Congressional*

---

[76] The discussion of *Buck's Stove* is at 1928 Senate Hearings, 28. References to "cancer" are at 887, 889, 897.

Record 4502), members of Congress repeatedly emphasized that injunctions were weakening the courts by hurting judicial prestige. Thus, when opponents of Norris's bill defended the independence of the judicial branch as the "keystone of the arch" created by Madison and the other constitutional framers, supporters of the bill could fire back with the claim that the legislation was necessary to save the courts from the consequences of their own outrageous conduct.[77] The responsiveness of members of Congress to arguments about judicial reform also reflects the fact that the goals of labor organizations converged with the goals of the broader coalition in Congress that had been fighting for judicial reforms for much of the century.[78]

The efforts of labor leaders to point out problems created by injunctions may have had some effect on public opinion regarding labor's grievances. Some legislators recognized and called attention to shifts in public opinion. Representative Philip Swing (R-CA) noted on the floor of the House in 1932 that the AFL deserved praise for efforts to produce a "change in public sentiment" toward the labor injunction (5491). Ironically, one important factor attributable to the AFL that helped strengthen support for the Norris bill was the failed labor provisions of the Clayton Act. Several times during floor debates, members of Congress defended the new bill against charges of radicalism by claiming that Congress had, in effect, already passed the Norris-LaGuardia Act when they passed the Clayton Act in 1914. In his opening remarks on the House bill, Representative LaGuardia claimed: "There is not an underlying principle written into this bill which Congress did not enact into law back in 1914, when the Clayton Act was passed" (75 *Congressional Record* 5478). Rep. Thomas McKeown (D-OK) responded to charges of radicalism by claiming: "The bill does nothing more or less than put into actual effect what the congress did years ago when they passed the Clayton Act" (5486). Some members claimed that the only reason it was even necessary to pass the new bill was that the courts had ignored the earlier enactment. As Representative Beedy explained, "if the provisions of the Clayton Act, as originally written, had not been abused, we should never have been

---

[77] Representative Beck made the "keystone" comment at 75 *Congressional Record* 5476. Responses were made by LaGuardia (5478–9), Oliver (5481), McKeown (5486).

[78] Ross (1994) provides the best account of various anticourt proposals in Congress. The leaders of this broad coalition orchestrated the opposition to Judge Parker and Judge Wilkerson in the Senate. Labor interests were sometimes a spirited component of the political opposition to judges, but were never the whole story.

called upon to consider this so-called anti-injunction bill of the present day" (5468).[79]

At times, members of Congress used selective reconstructions of the history of earlier legislative enactments to generate claims that were bizarre. During the House debates, Representative Celler suggested that antitrust relief for labor organizations was "an integral part of Wilson's gospel of 'the new freedom'" (75 *Congressional Record* 5488) and credited Wilson with the 1913 appropriations rider that prohibited the Justice Department from prosecuting labor organizations under the Sherman Act. In reality, Wilson had opposed the appropriations rider and greeted its passage with a sinister message indicating that his administration intended to ignore it. Wilson also later forced legislators to accept compromises that weakened the Clayton Act's antitrust exemption for labor.[80]

The efforts to reconstruct judicial interference with the Clayton Act as a reason for supporting the new Norris-LaGuardia Act are quite illuminating. They show how apparent legislative failures growing out of judicial intervention can influence subsequent democratic processes. The Clayton Act was useless as a statute defining new legal protections for workers, but it later became a very powerful political weapon.

The AFL's willingness to compromise in 1914 precipitated judicial rulings that fed congressional frustration with the courts. Looked at in this respect, the allegedly "pure" politics of the legislative branch begin to take on many of the features of the legal process that are denigrated by critical scholars. The legislative process tangles outside groups in the same sorts of complications that occur when they attempt to pursue or defend their interests in the courts. Just as small legal victories growing out of long-term litigation strategies provide legal precedents supporting escalating demands, the *statutory* precedent created by the very limited Clayton Act later provided a powerful political weapon for labor sympathizers in the early 1930s. The AFL's compromises on the Clayton Act did not end the

[79] Similar claims were made by Browning (5470) and Celler (5488). Of course, the irony of such claims is that they ultimately undermine the argument, often made by the same supporters, that Norris-LaGuardia would not run into difficulty in the courts. However, it is clear that legislators expected judges to be more sympathetic to labor organizations than they had been in the past. Such expectations explain why legislators never had to fully resolve the tension between blaming the courts for the Clayton Act and remaining optimistic about Norris-LaGuardia's prospects.

[80] Even very careful scholars continue to make the same mistake about Wilson's role. For example, Seymour Martin Lipset and Gary Marks identify Wilson as the "engineer of the Clayton Act" and suggest that his opposition to injunctions helped the Democrats win support from potential members of the Socialist party (2000, 52).

use of injunctions against labor organizations any more than Supreme Court rulings in National Association for the Advancement of Colored People (NAACP)-sponsored cases like *Missouri ex rel Gaines v Canada* (305 U.S. 337 (1938)) and *Sweatt v Painter* (339 U.S. 629 (1950)) ended segregation.[81] However, the *legislative* precedent set with the Clayton Act, and the predictable judicial reaction that it set off, did become a powerful rhetorical weapon in subsequent legislative fights against the injunction. The AFL leaders who supported the Clayton Act of 1914 probably hoped that change would come sooner than 1932. Nevertheless, there can be little doubt that the appearance of unjust judicial usurpation created by the judicial decisions on the Clayton Act contributed mightily to the "change in public sentiment" that made Norris-LaGuardia possible. The problem for labor was not that the judges were fully independent and unreachable by reform legislation. The problem was that it took nearly two decades before legislators were moved to "correct" the court's earlier rulings.

A final observation is that one element that helps to explain congressional support for the Norris-LaGuardia Act was that legislators expected passage of the new law to affect the way workers organized. During the floor debates over Norris-LaGuardia, numerous legislators expressed the view that responding favorably to demands for antiinjunction legislation would help defeat labor radicalism. These claims did not come from the periphery of debates. Senator Norris mentioned the importance of preempting radicalism in his opening floor speech introducing the bill (75 *Congressional Record* 4502). Claims about the need for the bill to prevent communism and "bolshevism" dominated House debates. Representative John Nelson (R-ME) claimed that the yellow-dog contract was "the one thing that breeds more communistic thought in America than anything else in our national life" (5468). Representative Hattom Sumners (D-TX) claimed that judges issuing unjust injunctions "can do more to establish bolshevism in this country than all the soap box orators you can put on the streets" (5500).

During House debates, members elaborated the strategy in greater detail. Representative Michener claimed:

The American Federation of Labor has done more than any other group or class of our people in maintaining peace and order during this depression. It has fought communism at every turn of the road, when, as a matter of fact, organized labor would have been the ideal vehicle to carry communism to our people, and without

---

[81] On the NAACP's campaign, see Kluger 1975, Tushnet 1987.

this restraining influence no one knows what our political and social situation might be today (5465).

Representative McKeown later warned:

if it were not for the American Federation of Labor, we would be running all over this country right now trying to run down all the Bolsheviks we would have in this country, we would have so many we would not know how to catch them all (5486).

Several other members followed up on these comments by suggesting that the bill was an appropriate reward for the AFL's "spirit of toler- ance" during the economic crisis.[82] These claims suggest once again that as members of Congress consider reform legislation they consider not just the immediate policy effects of that legislation but also the effect that passage of legislation has on the way interests are organized in future political battles over new policies. While historian Irving Bernstein dis- misses the comments about communism as an "irrelevancy" (1960, 413), concerns about radicalism were expressed so frequently that it appears safe to conclude that they played some role in animating at least some of those members who crafted and voted for the bill.

In conclusion then, it is clear that the support among legislators that made Norris-LaGuardia's success possible grew out of an unusual conflu- ence of interests. The unusual nature of the coalition supporting the act should give pause to any claim that Norris-LaGuardia's success demon- strates the permeability of the institutional processes of the American state. The AFL could only win its decisive legislative triumph because the usual enemies of labor were allied in support of the reform. This is not, however, a very happy lesson for labor or other insurgent organizations. It is little comfort to social groups to be told that their efforts to use democratic processes will produce desired changes in policy each time their goals are the same as those of their most powerful enemies!

Thus, while Norris-LaGuardia shows that political processes in the legislature can triumph over the courts, it also suggests that the thresh- old that has to be crossed to produce such resounding successes is quite high. The greatest irony of Norris-LaGuardia, labor's greatest legislative triumph, is that labor played only a small role in securing its enactment.

---

[82] Beady (75 *Congressional Record* 5468). See also Representative Swing (5491).

6

Legislative Deferrals and Judicial Policy Making in the Administrative State

A Brief Look at the Wagner Act

Even before court rulings on the Norris-LaGuardia Act signaled the end of the long-standing system of judicial regulation of labor in the United States, members of Congress were at work creating a new administrative system for regulating labor relations. That process culminated in 1935 when Congress enacted what is still the most important piece of labor legislation in American history, the National Labor Relations Act, more commonly known as the Wagner Act. The Wagner Act established a permanent administrative agency, the National Labor Relations Board (NLRB) and gave it the power to certify labor organizations as bargaining agents for groups of employees, to hear complaints and, with the supervision of the federal courts, to develop remedies against employers' "unfair labor practices."

The Wagner Act also presents one of the most persistent and important puzzles in American politics and political development. On the surface, the act held out tremendous promise for labor organizations. The Wagner Act encouraged, facilitated, and protected certain kinds of organizing activities, and thus had the potential to transform American society and politics by nurturing an independent and politically powerful labor movement. Yet things did not turn out that way. All three branches of government have since retreated from Senator Wagner's original vision of using the administrative powers of the state to help workers improve their bargaining position in conflicts with employers. Policy developments since 1935 have compounded employers' economic advantages by keeping a large sphere of management prerogatives outside collective bargaining, restricting and sometimes banning the use of certain collective activities like boycotts, and encouraging workers to settle disputes through administrative processes that tame conflict between employers and employees.[1] The result has been a labor movement that never reached its potential for independent political action, and that has now declined almost to the point of political and social irrelevance.

Because of the distance between the Wagner Act's potential and what actually occurred, both the reasons why the Wagner Act passed and the act's subsequent difficulties have been the subject of intense interest and debate among historians, legal academics, and political scientists. The Wagner Act developed out of an unusual combination of political, economic, and social forces that made many legislators eager to pass new labor legislation. Those same forces, along with some personal initiative, gave Sen. Robert Wagner (D-NY) and his visionary assistant Leon Keyserling an unusual level of control over the final product. Faced with a catastrophic depression and the collapse of President Roosevelt's recovery program, Wagner and Keyserling pursued a vision of using administrative protection for labor organizations to stabilize the economy and facilitate recovery. Wagner and Keyserling felt that by providing statutory protection for workers' collective activities, the new legislation would help the recovery by improving the bargaining position and purchasing power of workers.[2] In order to fulfill this vision, the new law needed to encourage workers to organize and thus to increase their economic power.

Although it is indisputable that the Wagner Act's principal framers expected it to create sweeping changes, the precise policy intentions of Congress as a whole on specific issues are sometimes quite difficult to identify with precision. To get the law enacted, the act's sponsors had to strike a difficult balance between competing policy goals and conflicting political interests. The statute would create a new administrative system that would make it easier for workers to engage in collective activities. But

---

[1] Criticisms of the Wagner Act along these lines can be found in Stone 1981. See also Atleson 1983, Tomlins 1984.

[2] On the role of Robert Wagner and Leon Keyserling in the drafting process, see Casebeer 1989. I am not convinced that one can move easily between talking about Keyserling's or Wagner's intent to talking about "Congress's" intent. Casebeer provides some fascinating documentation regarding Wagner's and Keyserling's broad goals and ideas before passage, but the materials uncovered much later by Casebeer do not always present those ideas and goals in the same way that Wagner publicly presented them to his Senate colleagues around the time of passage. There were also many compromises made to ensure passage of the bill. For general accounts on the development of the final version of the Wagner Act, see Bernstein 1950, chs. II, V, and VI; Gross 1974, chs. 1–4; Irons 1982, chs. 1 and 10–11; Tomlins 1985, ch. 4; Gordon 1994, chs. 5–6, and Brand 1988, ch. 9.

the statute also had to have some means of limiting workers' collective aspirations in order to prevent renewed labor militancy from disrupting the fragile economy.[3]

The Wagner Act's architects never struck the final balance between these two concerns with precision. It was simply impossible to do so. The Wagner Act was passed at a volatile moment in U.S. history, and was designed to set in motion a variety of largely unpredictable organizational activities. Most perceptive commentators have already noticed that the act's drafters did not try to fix the meaning of the new law at the time of passage. They instead specified a set of administrative and judicial policy-making mechanisms that would shape the meaning of the statute in the years that followed. Ultimately, the meaning of the act would be determined by subsequent struggles among mobilized workers, intransigent employers, and the judges and NLRB lawyers who shaped the early court cases on the act.[4]

From the perspective of labor organizations, the problem with the Wagner Act has been that the policy developments that resulted from those struggles and institutional processes have gone mostly against the interests of labor organizations. Before evaluating any post-enactment developments, however, it is important to note that the Wagner Act was never an unqualified victory for labor organizations. By establishing a permanent administrative board with the power to determine employee bargaining units and to settle jurisdictional disputes among labor organizations, the

[3] By emphasizing that the Wagner Act was designed in part to encourage organizing activity, I do not mean to deny that there was already a good deal of new labor organizing and labor militancy occurring before passage of the act, nor to deny that such organizing had an effect on the decision to pass the Wagner Act. Goldfield (1989b, 1990) emphasizes such activity and suggests that it *caused* passage of the Wagner Act. Goldfield is right that the context created by labor militancy made legislators more likely to pass labor legislation. However, it cannot plausibly be claimed that the activity *caused* members of Congress to pass the precise statute that passed. Moreover, it may be more useful to think of the Wagner Act as an effort to guide and shape future organizing activity than it is to think of the Wagner Act as a reflection of past organizing activity. Since I am concerned with specific features of the Wagner Act and specific consequences of those features, I follow Skocpol and Finegold (1990) and Plotke (1989; 1996, ch. 4) by looking at the variety of concurrent causes that gave shape to specific provisions of the Wagner Act; provisions that helped to determine the subsequent development of the labor movement.

[4] Klare (1978) and Plotke (1989) both emphasize that events after passage shaped the meaning of the act. Another important group of participants who shaped both the content of the act and its subsequent development were a group of lawyers from the original labor boards established under the National Recovery Administration between 1933 and 1935. See Irons 1982, chs. 12 and 13; Gross 1974, chs. 5 and 6.

Act ensured that a government agency would be making fundamental decisions about how workers could organize and what types of activities were protected. Samuel Gompers's worst nightmare of a labor movement dependent upon state recognition and state management had come true. However, in 1935, many labor organizations were willing to accept such state regulation in return for the Wagner Act's promises of protection for workers and labor organizations. The statute required employers to bargain in good faith with the labor organizations certified by the NLRB, and gave the NLRB the power to provide remedies for employer practices that discriminated against union members or otherwise discouraged workers from organizing and exercising collective economic power.

The trade-off between supervision and protection did not ultimately evolve into a set of policies that were as favorable as many labor organizations hoped. Decisions made by the NLRB and the courts have withdrawn many of the original protections that workers hoped the Wagner Act would provide. More significantly, Congress later added a variety of new restraints on the activities of workers and labor organizations to the statutory framework, most notoriously with the Taft-Hartley Act of 1947. Labor organizations may have hoped that new union organizing facilitated immediately after passage of the Wagner Act would have placed labor organizations in a strong enough political position to protect themselves against such developments. In the long run, however, passage of legislation that appeared to change profoundly the organizational capacities of a very large social group did not leave labor in a position to fight off future legislative attacks.[5]

Scholars have offered a variety of explanations for both the unfulfilled promise of the Wagner Act and the act's role in the unfulfilled promise of American labor. Different explanations have placed blame on the different branches of government. Congress is an obvious culprit for passing the subsequent legislation that weakened the statutory protections given to workers or placed new controls on the activities of labor organizations.[6] Nevertheless, many analysts also recognize that legislators did not

---

[5] Of course, economic transformations also played a role in that decline. For accounts of labor's decline that look more broadly at both economic and political factors, see Goldfield 1989 and Gordon, Edwards, and Reich 1982. My point here is only that the Wagner Act did not produce a labor movement strong enough to respond more effectively to these economic changes.

[6] The provisions of the Taft-Hartley Act of 1947 and Landrum Griffin Act of 1959 are summarized in Cox, et al. 1991, 92–8. Critiques of these developments can be found in Tomlins 1985, ch. 8 and Dubofsky 1994, 220–2.

act in a vacuum and thus that the statutory changes did not result from some pure form of democratic political competition. Legislators made the first statutory changes only after rulings by the courts and the NLRB had already established policies that affected the capacity of workers to organize. These earlier decisions by actors in other branches helped to create a political climate in which legislators would make subsequent statutory changes. For example, both Christopher Tomlins and James A. Gross track early administrative decisions made by the NLRB and show how they set the stage for the congressional retreat in the Taft-Hartley Act of 1947.[7] Others have placed blame on decisions made in the federal courts. For example, in an influential set of law review articles, Karl Klare examines a set of early Supreme Court decisions on the Wagner Act and blames subsequent policy developments on a judicial "deradicalization" of the statute that limited workers' capacity for effective collective action.[8]

While some scholars have disagreed with the way Klare characterizes judicial decisions, no one denies that judges have decided important policy issues regarding the Wagner Act. The judicial policy making began very soon after the act passed, with the Supreme Court resolving a number of important policy questions before World War II. This reemergence of judicial policy making is puzzling because it coincided with the expansion of an administrative system for regulating labor relations and because it came so soon after the Norris-LaGuardia Act's successful destruction of the older system of judicial control of labor relations.[9]

Explanations for the continuing ability of the courts to make labor policy typically focus on very general claims about the institutional power and independence in the post-New Deal administrative state. Such explanations can be improved, however, by looking more carefully at how the ability of judges to exercise institutional power to decide labor policy has remained dependent on decisions made by legislators. For example, the text of the Wagner Act carefully spelled out a place for judges in the

---

[7] Tomlins 1985, Gross 1981. Both Tomlins and Gross make it clear that the administrative decisions were themselves influenced by political pressures on the board.

[8] Klare's position on the Wagner Act is set out in Klare 1978. He makes some important amplifications and clarifications in Klare 1985, an article that also contains a lengthy reply to the attack on Klare in Finkin 1984. For a conventional attack other than Finkin, see University of Pennsylvania Law Review 1981. For more sympathetic and illuminating readings of Klare, see Gordon 1984 and Trubeck 1984.

[9] Orren (1991, 222) makes a related point about the irony of a return of judicial control so soon after passage of the Norris-LaGuardia Act.

administrative processes that would determine the meaning of the Wagner Act after enactment. Sections 10(e)-(h) of the statute assign specific oversight and enforcement responsibilities to specific courts, and specify procedures for parties affected by administrative processes to invoke judicial review. Such provisions are part of a broader pattern in which legislators would again and again give judges important and sometimes carefully specified oversight powers in the growing administrative state.[10]

Scholars differ on precisely how to characterize and measure the effect of this judicial oversight power and precisely how much judicial oversight power is required by the Constitution. In trying to measure the impact of the decisions judges make as they oversee administrative processes, most conventional scholars have focused on the often-unanswerable question of whether the positions established by judges match the baseline positions favored by elected legislators. For most scholars, this approach has led to a focus on the immediate policy consequences of particular interpretive decisions. More recently, critical scholars like Klare have attempted to draw attention to longer term, indirect effects that come about because of the ideologies encoded in the written opinions judges use to justify their decisions across series of cases.

In contrast, this chapter approaches questions about judicial power by focusing on the question of why the courts were able to play any significant role in the development of labor policy. I do this by focusing on decisions made in Congress that empowered judges rather than subsequent decisions by judges exercising those discretionary powers. This chapter is only able to make a very preliminary inquiry into the institutional sources of judicial influence on the development of the Wagner Act. The Wagner Act is so complicated that it is impossible to provide a complete account of judicial decision making in a single chapter, or even a whole book. Because the Wagner Act has remained central to collective bargaining law for several decades, almost every provision of the act has generated voluminous case law. Short summaries of all the cases where judges have made significant interpretive decisions on the Wagner Act cover hundreds of pages in the *United States Code Annotated*. Furthermore, judicial involvement has taken a variety of forms and become more complicated as legislators have continued to pass new statutes modifying or amending the Wagner Act. There is undoubtedly no single explanation that can account for the full variety of judicial intervention in all the Wagner Act cases.

---

[10] See Strauss 1989, esp. chs. 2, 7, and 8; Shapiro (1988) for more general overviews of judicial oversight of administrative processes.

My more limited goal in this chapter is to establish only that conscious legislative choices have continued to be a source of judicial power in the post New Deal administrative state. My strategy, as with Norris-LaGuardia, is to focus on a small set of early interpretive questions that the courts addressed before Congress complicated the interpretive task by passing new statutes. For the sake of brevity, I have chosen two closely related policy issues that raised important questions about the Wagner Act provision that was perhaps the most important for labor organizations, the guarantee of the right to strike in Section 13 of the act. The right to strike was, of course, the most sacred tenet of the voluntarist ideology that had shaped the American Federation of Labor's (AFL's) drive for anti-injunction legislation before the Depression. Of all the collective activities that might have been given protection by the government, none was more important to workers than the right to strike. It seems safe to assume that any judicially imposed limitations on the right to strike would go to the heart of whatever it was that labor organizations had hoped to gain from the Wagner Act. Threats to the right to strike under the Wagner Act were, in effect, threats that the old system of regulation by injunction would be replaced by an equally restrictive system of regulation through administrative processes.

I will focus here on the two policy questions related to the right to strike that arose in two early Wagner Act cases before the Supreme Court. The first is the question of whether employers can hire permanent replacements for striking workers and deny reinstatement at the conclusion of a strike. The second is the question of whether employees give up the protections of the Wagner Act if they strike during the term of a collective-bargaining agreement. The Court decisions resolving these two issues are among the several decisions that Karl Klare criticizes in his innovative account of the impact of the Supreme Court on the development of labor law and the labor movement in the United States (1978). By choosing cases that Klare uses to illustrate the independent power and influence of the court, I am once again deliberately biasing my case selection *against* my hypothesis that the power of the courts grew out of deliberate legislative deferrals. My goal is to see whether Congress bears some responsibility for two of the judicial rulings that are used to build the strongest argument that the courts had an independent impact on the development of labor policies and the labor movement.

My findings with respect to the right to strike cases are revealing. I find that judges had to make important policy choices largely because of legislative deferrals. Members of Congress chose to leave the reinstatement and midterm strike issues unresolved with the expectation that judges would take responsibility for making policy choices. This finding for the small number of policy issues considered here does not provide a full account of judicial decision making on the Wagner Act. However, it does demonstrate the continuing relevance of deferrals and legislative deference in the modern administrative state. Even as members of Congress were perfecting the art of delegating policy decisions to new regulatory agencies, they still were deliberately leaving some policy issues for judicial resolution.

I also find, however, that the more complex administrative system created by the Wagner Act gave legislators more complicated options as they shifted policy choices outside the legislative branch. Creating the NLRB as an additional source of power and responsibility is a significant innovation. Legislators could now use specificity in legislative language to limit the role of the courts without being specific about policy outcomes.

Legislators carved out a general role for the courts by assigning the circuit courts broad powers to review and reverse NLRB decisions and to enforce NLRB rulings in sections 10(e)-(h). However, legislators also effectively used statutory language to limit judicial oversight with respect to some specific policy issues. They did this by including provisions in the act that specifically assigned the NLRB the power to rule on particular policy questions while omitting provisions inviting judges to review those decisions. For example, provisions in sections 9(b)-(c) state that the NLRB has the power to determine employee-bargaining units and certify collective-bargaining representatives for groups of workers. Unlike board orders related to unfair labor practices, there were no provisions providing for judicial review of board bargaining unit and certification decisions.[11] The legislative strategy worked. When members of Congress protected the discretion of the NLRB by stating that the board had final say on certain types of decisions, judges were usually willing to respect the NLRB's judgments about fact and policy and decline review. Thus, when aggrieved labor organizations asked the Supreme Court for help in connection with a certification decision, they were told that "these are

---

[11] Section 9(b) states: "The Board shall decide in each case whether, in order to insure to employees the full benefit of their right to self-organization and to collective bargaining ... the unit appropriate for the purposes of collective bargaining shall be the employer unit, craft unit, plant unit, or subdivision thereof." The provisions in Section 10 allowed for judicial review of board enforcement orders. The Supreme Court ruled in 1940 that those provisions were not applicable to Section 9(b) and (c). *AFL v NLRB* (308 U.S. 410 (1940)).

arguments to be addressed to Congress and not to the Courts."[12] In contrast, judges were more influential on issues like replacement workers and midterm strikes because legislators chose to be much less specific about whether the board or the Courts should have the final say on those issues. When Congress was less clear, judges could treat general language inviting judicial oversight of board decisions as an invitation to second-guess the board's policy judgments. Judges needed only to claim that the board had misinterpreted the Wagner Act when the board made its decision.

The legislative baseline framework conditions scholars to think of ambiguities and uncertainties in statutes as accidents that legislators would just as soon avoid. However, when legislators deliberately treat some policy issues with more specificity than others, or establish judicial review for some decisions but not for others, the choices they make presumably reflect strategic decisions about how large a role members of Congress want interpreting judges to play. My goal here is primarily to show that the failure of legislators to resolve the meaning of the right to strike provision was not simply an accident. Legislators clearly foresaw the specific issues that later had to be decided by judges, but members empowered judges by making choices that left the congressional position unclear.

THE SUPREME COURT AND THE RIGHT TO STRIKE

Before turning to the cases, it is worth considering Karl Klare's innovative and influential argument in more detail. Klare focuses on a set of Supreme Court decisions on the Wagner Act decided before World War II. Each of the cases addressed interpretive questions that arose over statutory language. In each of the cases, the justices claimed that Congress had not specifically addressed the particular policy issue under dispute, and then established a new binding policy as they resolved the interpretive controversy. Since Congress had not resolved the specific policy issues at stake, the justices in each case justified their interpretation of the statute by claiming that the policy they chose matched the broader goals expressed by "Congress" when the statute passed. Following standard interpretive conventions, the Court identified those goals by searching selectively through legislative records.

So long as the congressional failure to resolve the issue was the result of some accident or oversight, the strategy of looking to broader congressional goals to resolve specific policy issues that were not addressed clearly

---

[12] *AFL v NLRB* (308 U.S. 401, 411–12 (1940)).

in the statute makes sense. It is certainly likely that legislators might not have foreseen some unresolved policy issues arising under the Wagner Act. The Wagner Act was a very complicated and somewhat revolutionary statute, was passed at an economically volatile time, and set in motion a wide range of unpredictable social and political forces. Given the complexity of the issues addressed, it is very easy to believe that many policy questions arose that legislators had never considered before passage.

For example, one policy question that the Supreme Court had to decide under the Wagner Act was whether the act covered unions of supervisory employees. After the organizing activity that followed passage of the Wagner Act stimulated a wave of supervisor organizing drives in the 1940s, the question of whether supervisors' unions were covered by the act ended up before the Supreme Court in 1947.[13] Before ruling in favor of the supervisors, the justices noted that Congress had not in any way addressed the supervisor issue when it passed the Wagner Act, and suggested that it had never occurred to Congress that supervisors would form unions. Justice Douglas explained that the issue of supervisor organizations was not "in the consciousness of Congress" at the time the Wagner Act was passed.[14]

With respect to supervisor organizing, the Supreme Court may have been right that the issue in question never occurred to Congress.[15] Confronted with such an unforeseen policy controversy, there is nothing particularly suspect about looking to the general goals that legislators expressed at the time of passage. Klare's criticism is not that the justices on the Supreme Court looked for general goals expressed by Congress, but that the justices made very selective claims about congressional goals as they attempted to justify their decisions. After making his own inquiry into the legislative records, Klare finds that legislators expressed not just the few goals emphasized by the Court in its line of decisions but also a variety of other goals that seemed to contradict the outcomes chosen by the court. Instead of trying to reconcile the competing goals, the Court

---

[13] *Packard Motor Car Company v NLRB* (330 U.S. 485 (1947)). Klare's discussion of this case is in Klare 1985, 789. See also, Seitz 1984.

[14] *Packard Motor Car Company v NLRB* (330 U.S. 485 (1947), 500). Douglas's opinion is a dissent, but the view expressed seems to have been shared by the majority as well. Congress quickly reversed the Supreme Court and banned supervisor unions in the Taft-Hartley Act.

[15] I was unable to find any evidence in the legislative records on the Wagner Act showing that any members of Congress anticipated that supervisors would form unions and seek protection under the Wagner Act. See discussion of *Packard* in Klare 1985, 789.

simply ignored or downplayed those goals that suggested a more prolabor reading of the act. By showing that legislators had also expressed goals that undercut the interpretations chosen by the Court, Klare refutes the justices' claims that they were simply following the will of Congress. The justices did cite some congressional goals that matched their chosen outcome. However, that does not mean that the Court was following the will of Congress. Klare's argument is that the judges were in reality picking and choosing from among the goals expressed in Congress to find those that matched their preferred position.

Most importantly for Klare, the Supreme Court established a clear pattern in the early cases that settled the first interpretive controversies. The Court systematically favored the proemployer goals of the act. These included the need for industrial stability and the need to make collective-bargaining contracts binding on workers. Meanwhile, the same Court ignored the act's more prolabor goals of redistributing income and equalizing bargaining power among workers and employers. Klare concludes that the accumulated effect of decisions emphasizing employer-friendly goals was a judicial "de-radicalization" of the Wagner Act.

I focus here on two of the early Supreme Court cases that Klare identifies as showing the power of the courts to shape policy and influence subsequent events: *NLRB v Mackay* and *NLRB v Sands*.[16] *Mackay* produced an influential Supreme Court ruling on permanent replacements for striking workers while *Sands* addressed the issue of midterm strikes. Both cases raised questions related to the guarantee of a "right to strike" that legislators included in Section 13 of the act. Section 13 stated:

Nothing in this Act shall be construed so as to interfere with or impede or diminish in any way the right to strike.

The precise meaning of this provision was the subject of considerable controversy both before and after enactment. In both Congress and the courts, participants agreed that, at a minimum, the right-to-strike provision protected workers by prohibiting government officials, including judges, from directly interfering to prevent workers from striking. Participants disagreed, however, on whether or how far this guarantee of the right to strike extended beyond this minimal level of protection against official interference. Some observers read the guarantee as providing additional

---

[16] *NLRB v Mackay Radio and Telegraph Company* (304 U.S. 333 (1938)) is discussed in Klare 1978, 301–3 and Klare 1985, 804–8. *NLRB v Sands Mfg. Co.* (306 U.S. 332 (1939)) is discussed in Klare 1978, 303–5, 319–20, and Klare 1985, 798–804.

positive protection against employer interference with the right to strike. For example, Section 13 might be read as giving the NLRB the power to assist striking workers by giving broad readings to the statute's protections against unfair labor practices. Such protection might include limits on the hiring of permanent replacements for strikers or a requirement that employers reinstate striking workers once a strike was settled. NLRB practices regarding such issues would do much to determine whether strikes remained effective economic weapons.

In both *Sands* and *Mackay*, the Supreme Court's answer to the question of whether the right to strike provisions in Section 13 went beyond negative protection from government interference hinged on subsidiary questions about other provisions in the act. In particular, both cases hinged in part on the question of whether workers who went on strike qualified as "employees" under the Wagner Act. The Court's answer to that question depended on the Court's interpretation of yet another statutory provision, the definition of "employee" in Section 3(3). Only employees were entitled to the positive protections that the Wagner Act gave to workers, such as protection from discrimination for union activities and the right to vote in certification elections.

The question of who counted as an employee was relevant in *Mackay*, a case where the immediate question before the Court was whether workers who went on strike had the right to reinstatement when the strike ended. If the strikers remained "employees," the Board could treat the employer's refusal to reinstate strikers as a form of prohibited discrimination against employees. In *Sands*, the "employees" question was important because the Supreme Court had to decide whether strikebreakers should have status as protected "employees" able to authorize a new union for the company's workers.

In both cases, the Court ended up adopting a narrow reading of "employee" that favored the interests of employers over the interests of workers. The result was that the "right to strike" provision in Section 13 protected only against direct government interference with strikes without providing any additional protection from the predatory activity of employers.

Mackay and Permanent Replacements

The Supreme Court's ruling on permanent replacements grew out of an attempted strike against the Mackay Radio and Telegraph Company of California. The strike failed after only a few days because the company was able to find and hire replacements for the striking workers. After realizing that the strike was failing, the workers announced a willingness to return to their jobs. The company agreed to reinstate all the workers except six who had been particularly active in union activities before the strike. Those six workers were told that their places had been permanently filled. After receiving a complaint from those workers, the NLRB ruled that the company had discriminated against the six employees because of their union activity. The Board found the discrimination to be in violation of Section 8(3) of the Wagner Act, which makes it an unfair labor practice for an employer to "discourage membership in any labor organization" by "discrimination in regard to hire or tenure of employment." Following procedures described in Section 10 of the act, the NLRB held hearings to establish facts about the dispute. The NLRB then ruled that the company had engaged in an unfair labor practice and issued a cease and desist order requiring the company to reinstate the six workers.

After a lower court disagreed and refused to enforce the order, the Board's appeal ended up before the Supreme Court. The Supreme Court unanimously overruled the lower court and ordered enforcement of the original NLRB order. Thus, the immediate outcome was a victory for the six workers, who regained their jobs. However, the Supreme Court also stated in a dictum that it was not, in general, an unfair labor practice for employers to hire permanent replacements for striking workers or to refuse to reinstate striking workers after a strike. So long as the reason for hiring the permanent replacements was to "carry on the business" and not to break the union or discriminate against its most active members, employers had the right both to hire replacements and to offer *permanent* employment as an inducement to strikebreakers. In making this statement, the Court was rejecting an alternative interpretation of the "right to strike" provision in Section 13. On the alternative interpretation, the guarantee of a "right to strike" meant that workers were entitled to reinstatement when a strike was concluded. By allowing employers to use permanent employment as an inducement to strikebreakers, the Court made it more difficult for unions to use strikes as economic weapons.

The Court based its conclusion on the assertion that the employer had a "right to protect and continue his business by supplying places left vacant by the strikers" (304 U.S. 333, 345). The Court ruled that this right to conduct business included the right to use *permanent* replacements to break strikes and a right to refuse to reinstate workers who went out on strike. The Court failed to explain the sources of these employer rights, which were not mentioned anywhere in the text of the Wagner Act. The court did not cite any legislative text or legislative history that supported its decision to give protection to these very specific rights. The Court simply asserted that these apparently inherent rights of employers outweighed the right to strike that Congress had explicitly guaranteed in the text of the Wagner Act.

Sands and Midterm Strikes

A little over a year after *Mackay*, the Supreme Court made a controversial ruling on midterm strikes, that is, strikes that take place during the term of a collective-bargaining contract, in the case of *NLRB v Sands* (306 U.S. 332 (1939)). *Sands* grew out of a dispute between the Sands Manufacturing Company and the independent union representing Sands' employees. The dispute was over the meaning of provisions regarding seniority in a collective-bargaining agreement between the company and the union. After negotiations over the issue broke down, the workers announced that they would not work under the company's asserted interpretation of the contract. The company responded by closing down the plant and locking out the workers.

The lockout lasted several days before the plant reopened with a new group of employees. The new workers were members of a different union, one affiliated with the AFL. The company quickly executed a new collective-bargaining agreement with the new union. The NLRB later held hearings and heard evidence suggesting that the company had rigged the entire confrontation with the original workers in order to justify the lockout and replace the independent union with the more cooperative AFL-affiliated union. The NLRB concluded that the company had engaged in an unfair labor practice by prematurely locking out the original workers rather than continuing with negotiations.

The Supreme Court, however, reversed the NLRB's decision. In its ruling, the Court rejected the board's findings that the company had not bargained fairly. The Court simply claimed that the company's prior history of dealing fairly with the union "definitely refutes" (341) the NLRB finding that the company had acted unfairly in the seniority dispute. The Court's aggressive decision to second guess the board on this point came even though Section 10 of the Wagner Act explicitly discourages judicial review of NLRB findings of facts. That section, which specifies the procedures for judicial review of NLRB decisions, included a provision in clause (f) stating that: "the findings of the Board as to the facts, if supported by evidence, shall . . . be conclusive."

After rejecting the factual basis of the NLRB's ruling, the Court had to decide what the status of the original Sands employees should be. The Court found that by merely threatening to go on strike during the term of an agreement, the original Sands employees forfeited their status as "employees" of the Sands Company. Thus, the original workers who were locked out were not entitled to vote in the certification elections for the new union. The Court's ruling guaranteed that the AFL-affiliated union favored by the company would be allowed to represent the remaining workers at the plant. The immediate result of the ruling was that the original Sands employees paid for the midterm strike with their jobs.

The Court's ruling in *Sands* seems especially harsh given that the collective-bargaining agreement between the company and the original union did not contain any clause forbidding strikes during the term of the agreement. The agreement also did not have any provisions offering arbitration or any other procedure short of a strike to settle disputes that occurred during the term of the contract. The agreement however, did contain a clause stating that if disputes arose during the term of the contract, the union was free to "act as they saw fit," provided only that they waited forty-eight hours. That contractual provision seemed to invite workers to strike during the term of the contract.

The Supreme Court, however, was not swayed by absence of a "no strike" clause or even by the provision authorizing action after forty-eight hours. The Court declared that the forty-eight hour provision did not apply because the dispute was not a genuine dispute over the terms of the contract. The Court ruled that the "interpretation" of the seniority rules that the union offered was not really an interpretation, but a unilateral demand for the company to abandon the contract. That demand, the Court claimed, itself amounted to a breach of contract. Thus, the Court concluded that the shutdown of the plant and hiring of new workers was the result of the union's breach, and thus not an unfair practice by the employer (Klare 1985, 798–804).

The Court's next leap was to find that because the union broke the contract, none of the original workers qualified as "employees" under the Wagner Act. This conclusion required the Court once again to go beyond the text of the statute. The Wagner Act did not contain a provision stating that a breach of contract should deny a worker status as an "employee" under the act. In fact, the Wagner Act said nothing at all about how breaches of contract should be treated.

On its face, the Court's ruling is rather incredible. Despite an explicit guarantee of the right to strike in Section 13, the court decided that a threat to strike was enough to void all the protections afforded the workers in both the Wagner Act and in the actual collective-bargaining agreement. Nevertheless, the Court tried to justify its ruling by making a claim about congressional intent in passing the act. The Court declared that the "legislative history of the statute goes far to indicate that the purpose of the statute was to compel employers to bargain collectively with their employees to the end that employment contracts binding on both parties should be made" (342). The Court seemed to think that the only way to secure that goal was to create a policy whereby workers who threatened to strike during the term of a contract lost all the protection afforded by the Wagner Act. The Court also felt that it was necessary to deny workers status as "employees" in order to discourage workers from violating their collective-bargaining agreements. By all measures, the Court seemed to be reaching. The Wagner Act did not contain a single provision establishing mechanisms for ensuring compliance with the terms of a contract. Nevertheless, the justices treated the goal of securing compliance as though it was the overriding goal of Congress.

To support its finding that the overriding "purpose" of the statute was to establish enforceable collective-bargaining agreements, the Court could cite only a page number from a single committee report.[17] The page cited contains a passage explaining the "duty to bargain" under the statute, but contains not the slightest hint that the main purpose of the act was to make collective-bargaining agreements binding on workers. Looking for the "purpose of the statute" in a passage that addressed the duty to try to reach collective-bargaining agreements was a good way for the justices to ensure that they would find a "purpose" that supported their decision to emphasize the binding nature of agreements. The justices had to ignore the seemingly more relevant opening section of the same committee report, which was entitled "General Objectives of the Bill."[18] That opening section counts "economic adjustment" and "industrial peace" as goals of the act and makes a variety of claims about the advantages of collective bargaining. It says nothing at all about the need to enforce worker obligations under collective-bargaining agreements by punishing workers who threatened to strike.

---

[17] The Court cited Senate Report 573, 12, Senate Committee on Education and Labor, 74th Congress, 1st Session. The report is reprinted at the *Legislative History of the National Labor Relations Act, 1935*, National Labor Relations Board (hereafter referred to as *LH*), 2300–19.

[18] Senate Report 573, 1–4; reprinted at *LH*, 2300–3.

The Court's ruling in *Sands* provides a very useful illustration of the problem that Klare finds across a larger number of early Wagner Act rulings. The Court clearly seems to be selectively identifying the goals and purpose of the Wagner Act, and using selective claims about some goals to justify policy choices that seem inconsistent with other important goals expressed by legislators. The Court may have been right that many legislators wanted workers and employers to form binding collective-bargaining agreements. However, legislators expressed other goals when the Wagner Act passed, some of which do not seem compatible with the harsh ruling that the Court made in *Sands*.

As with the ruling in *Mackay*, the ruling in *Sands* rejected a broad interpretation of Section 13 as providing positive state protection of the right to strike. The Court's ruling did not prohibit workers from striking during the term of a contract, but it went a long way toward rendering such strikes useless by ensuring that workers would lose if they tried to strike during the term of a contract. More generally, the interpretive controversies surrounding replacement workers and midterm strikes provide a useful picture of the difficulties that occurred as the board and the courts worked to implement the Wagner Act. Legislators did not attempt to settle in the text every policy issue that could arise under the statute. They recognized that unforeseeable issues would arise, and wanted the board to be able to respond flexibly to particular situations as they arose. Thus, the text of the statute established procedures for the labor board and judges to follow as they resolved policy controversies while leaving many specific policy issues unresolved. While legislators included text that provided very specific guidance on a few core policy issues, legislators were mostly content to state general policy goals for administrators and judges to follow as they exercised discretion. Such legislative strategies are now standard in the modern administrative state.

Klare's criticism of the justification offered by the Supreme Court in cases like *Mackay* and *Sands* is compelling. The justices do seem to have been making substantive choices about policy as they prioritized the many goals expressed by legislators, and not simply following the will of Congress. However, Klare's criticism of the Supreme Court's justification does not go very far toward explaining the relationship between Congress and the Courts in these cases. One striking feature of the Wagner Act, which Klare reveals but does not explain, is that legislators made it particularly easy for judges to exercise discretion by expressing multiple and sometimes incompatible goals in the text of the statute. Because the legislators did not provide sufficient guidance about which goals were most important, they made even their general motives for passing the act ambiguous. It was the congressional failure to prioritize relevant goals that made it easy for judges to exercise discretion as they chose from among competing goals.

To analyze the impact of the judges who make particular policy choices as they oversee administrators' decisions, scholars need to understand more fully the choices made by legislators that determined the level of judicial discretion. Thus, my analysis of *Mackay* and *Sands* in the remainder of this chapter is based on a more detailed look at how well legislators anticipated the issues decided by judges and at what legislators did to limit or expand the power of judges to determine how those issues would be resolved. The resulting account provides a more complete picture of the relationship between the processes in Congress that add new words to the statute books and the judicial decisions that determined the meaning of the Wagner Act.

THE WAGNER ACT IN CONGRESS: REPLACEMENT WORKERS AND MIDTERM STRIKES

In both *Mackay* and *Sands*, the Supreme Court had to look beyond the text of the statute to broader congressional goals because the statute failed to resolve important policy issues that arose during implementation. The text of the Wagner Act contains no mention of replacement workers, reinstatement of strikers, or midterm strikes. However, a full inquiry into the legislative history reveals that the failure of legislators to address the replacement and midterm strike issues in the text of the act was not due to accidents during drafting, an inability of legislators to foresee that the issues would arise, or an inability to develop statutory language that would signal clear congressional intent to the courts. Both the permanent replacement and midterm strike issues were repeatedly brought before the "consciousness of Congress" before the Wagner Act was enacted, but legislators rejected proposals to address these issues more decisively in the statutory language.

The justices who decided the cases looked at the legislative record, but failed to find any evidence that legislators had made decisions about replacement workers and midterm strikes. The Court's failure to find such evidence does not show, however, that legislators never considered those issues or made decisions about them. The real problem was that the Court never considered the most revealing parts of the legislative history because the justices followed interpretive conventions that tell judges to ignore most legislative records. The justices looked at committee reports and selected parts of the floor debates from 1935, but ignored most of the record of two congresses' lengthy deliberations on the bill that eventually became the Wagner Act. For this chapter, I will consider that broader record.[19] While I find that legislators did not make a clear policy choice on the replacement and midterm strike issues, they did make some important decisions directly related to those issues. Those decisions helped to determine which actors would later resolve those policy issues. The broader record shows that the textual ambiguity that the court had to resolve was the result of deliberate legislative deferrals to the courts.

Proposed Labor Relations Bills in Congress: 1934–1935

The Wagner Act did not suddenly spring full grown from Congress. It reflected a variety of prior experiences with administrative labor boards and two years of deliberation on various proposals for a new system of state administration of labor disputes.[20] The immediate roots of the Wagner Act go back to the labor boards set up as part of Roosevelt's National Recovery Administration (NRA).[21] Between 1933 and 1935, the NRA set up boards to deal with labor problems and to supervise processes for recognizing collective-bargaining agents. The NRA boards failed to end labor unrest, in part because they lacked the power to enforce their own rulings. Nevertheless, the experiences of the NRA boards and the case law they developed gave the Wagner Act's architects a wealth of experience to draw upon as they tried to anticipate issues that might arise once a more powerful and permanent board went into operation.[22]

Efforts to pass an independent statute establishing a national labor board with effective powers of enforcement began in 1934 when Wagner introduced a bill (the "1934 Wagner bill") that later became the model for the Wagner Act in the next congress.[23] In 1934, the Senate Committee on Education and Labor held lengthy hearings on Wagner's bill

---

[19] Klare also criticizes the interpretive conventions followed by the judges, and offers an explanation of his own, somewhat different reasons for looking beyond standard sources of legislative history, see Klare 1985, 779–86.

[20] This subsection relies on Bernstein 1950, still the best historical source on the *legislative* processes leading to passage of the Wagner Act.

[21] Deeper roots go back to the Railway Labor Act of 1924. See Bernstein 1950, ch. IV.

[22] For accounts of the NRA labor boards and their effect on the development and implementation of the Wagner Act, see Gross 1974, chs. 1–4; Irons 1982, ch. 10; and Bernstein 1950, ch. III.

[23] S. 2926, 73rd Congress, 2nd Session.

before reporting a substitute bill devised by Committee Chair David Walsh (D-MA).[24] The Walsh bill was criticized by the American Civil Liberties Union (ACLU) as a "sham and a fraud,"[25] opposed by the National Association of Manufacturers, and ignored by the AFL (Bernstein 1950, 75). Before Walsh's bill had a chance to die, however, a new round of labor disputes in the steel industry disrupted temporary quiet on the labor front. After the NRA labor boards proved unable to resolve the crisis, President Roosevelt sought an emergency legislative response. The result was a hastily assembled stopgap measure known as Public Resolution 44. The new resolution allowed Roosevelt to establish a new labor board. That board was the first "National Labor Relations Board." The new board had more extensive powers than the old National Labor Board under the NRA, but it remained under the rubric of the temporary NRA and still lacked strong enforcement powers (Bernstein 1950, ch. VI).

Political conditions changed again when the 1934 elections gave the Democrats huge gains in both the House and Senate. When the new congress arrived in 1935, Wagner had another chance to push his more comprehensive labor relations statute. The 1934 elections were also followed by a new wave of labor unrest that made the need for a permanent board with enforcement powers seem more urgent than ever. Wagner in 1935 introduced a new bill that restored many of the principles and much of the language of his original 1934 bill.[26] Members of Congress eventually enacted an amended version of Wagner's 1935 bill as the Wagner Act.

The new bill gathered momentum in Congress and moved toward passage despite the absence of any interest or support from President Roosevelt. The Senate easily passed the new Wagner bill on May 16 and sent it to the House for consideration. But as the House considered the bill, its momentum was suddenly disrupted when the Supreme Court struck down the law establishing the NRA on May 27, 1935 (*Schecter Poultry v United States* (295 U.S. 495)). The Court's decision made it seem both more urgent and more difficult to establish an effective labor policy. Passage was more urgent because the Court had struck down the law establishing the existing labor boards and left the Roosevelt administration without any viable recovery program. The decision made the problems confronting legislators more difficult because it created uncertainty about whether any

---

[24] The substitute bill was titled the "National Industrial Adjustment Act." It was reported under the same number: S. 2926, 73rd Congress, 2nd Session.

[25] Letter from A. F. Ward to Wagner, June 5, 1934, quoted in Bernstein 1950, 75.

[26] S. 1958, 74th Congress, 1st Session.

new labor relations law could survive the Court's constitutional scrutiny. *Schecter* also seemed to limit the ability of legislators to delegate decision-making authority to regulatory agencies and Congress's power to regulate interstate commerce.

The legislative drafters working under Wagner immediately went to work rewriting the bill's statement of public policy to try to accommodate the Court's objections to the NRA. Keyserling and Wagner drafted a set of amendments to the bill and, with the backing of Roosevelt, had the changes added to the bill in the House. Many outside observers and members of Congress remained concerned (or in some cases hopeful) that the Supreme Court would strike down the new law (Bernstein 1950, 119–21). Nevertheless, the House passed the bill on June 19th. After a conference committee successfully worked out House/Senate differences, Roosevelt signed the Wagner Act into law on July 5, 1935.

The full record of congressional deliberations on the 1934 and 1935 Wagner bills, the substitute Walsh bill, and Public Resolution 44 provides a much fuller picture of legislators' understandings, expectations, and preferences than the more limited picture that the Court considered in *Mackay* and *Sands*. The full record reveals that legislators had considered the policy issues decided by the Supreme Court long before the Wagner Act passed. At least some participants in legislative deliberations anticipated that controversies involving permanent replacements and midterm strikes were likely to arise under the new law. Several participants in Congress introduced amendments or alternative proposals intended to provide a clearer indication of how Congress wanted the permanent replacement and midterm strike issues resolved. Legislators decided to reject these suggestions and alternative provisions. As a result, policy questions that had been actively debated were left unresolved in the final version of the Wagner Act. It was no accident that courts later had to resolve the interpretive questions left unanswered by members of Congress when the Wagner Act passed.

The Evolution of the Right to Strike Provision in the Wagner Act

The first clues about congressional attitudes toward the issues raised in *Sands* and *Mackay* can be found in the evolution of the provision that was relevant to issues decided in both cases: The "right to strike" provision in Section 13. The evolution of Section 13 in Congress appears at first to be straightforward and uneventful. The final wording of Section 13 of the Wagner Act is identical to the corresponding provision in the original bill introduced by Wagner in 1934. However, legislators adopted the original right to strike provision only after the provision had stimulated a great deal of discussion and debate. At one point, the Senate replaced the provision with an alternative that more clearly addressed the policy questions that would later arise regarding Section 13. However, the Senate eventually switched back to the original language from Wagner's first bill. Much of the more general debate over the right to strike provision focused on specific policy issues that some participants felt should be resolved before passage of the new law. Those participants complained that the vaguely worded promise of the right to strike in Section 13 left the courts free to decide a variety of important policy issues. Many of the participants urged Congress to adopt clearer legislative language to resolve those issues before enactment. Taken together, the discussions, debates, and alternative proposals indicate that members of Congress were aware that the vaguely worded guarantee in Section 13 did not, by itself, determine the relationship between the statutory right to strike and other rights and duties addressed in the statute. Members of Congress thus made a conscious decision to leave those crucial policy questions to be resolved elsewhere.

A first clue about how participants understood Section 13 before passage is found in the explanation Senator Wagner gave for including the provision at all. When he appeared as the first witness before the Senate hearing on his 1934 bill, Wagner explained that he included an explicit acknowledgment of an unbounded right to strike in order to gain the confidence and support of labor organizations.[27] The importance of that provision to labor organizations was later confirmed by Sidney Hillman of the Amalgamated Clothing Workers, who informed the committee that the right to strike was "a right that labor cannot possibly give up under any circumstances."[28]

Representatives of employers who appeared before the same Senate committee were unhappy with the provision and complained vigorously that it was unfair to give workers an unbounded right to strike. Such an unqualified declaration of the right to strike was inappropriate, the employers claimed, in a legislative proposal that placed so many limits on the rights of employers. None of the employers denied that workers should have the right to strike. None denied that the right to strike was already protected by law. The employers were concerned, however, that a statutory declaration of the right to strike might have a dangerous symbolic

[27] *LH*, 40–1.
[28] *LH*, 153.

power. The provision would signal legislators' strong approval of strikes as economic weapons and lead the courts to provide additional, positive state protection for striking workers.[29]

Some of the witnesses before the committee raised questions about what the right to strike provision would mean in connection with specific policy issues. Although it was not easy to anticipate all the issues that would arise after the Wagner Act went into effect in the volatile atmosphere of the 1930s, participants did anticipate many of them. Attentive participants could draw on the experiences of the labor boards under the NRA. And during congressional hearings, numerous witnesses tried to draw the attention of the committee to some of the important issues that had arisen under the NRA but that had been left unresolved in Wagner's bill.[30]

The most interesting summation of the experiences under earlier labor boards was presented to Congress by Isadore Polier of the International Juridical Association. In a brief submitted to the Senate committee in 1934, Polier documented several examples of restrictions that judges had placed on the right of workers to strike under the NRA.[31] Based on this evidence, Polier made some specific suggestions regarding legislative language that would have clarified the meaning of the right to strike granted in Section 13. Two of Polier's suggestions were directly relevant to issues later raised in *Sands* and *Mackay*. First, Polier suggested adding a provision stating that the right to strike "shall not be held to be interfered with, impeded, diminished or affected in any way" by "compliance of an employer with the provisions of this act" (*Legislative History of the National Labor Relations Act, 1935*, National Labor Relations Board, 1052–3, hereafter referred to as "*LH*"). If such a provision had been included, it would not

---

[29] For an example of an employer representative's complaints about the potential symbolic value of the right-to-strike provision, see testimony of Guy L. Harriman, *LH*, 494. Other employers' complaints can be found in the testimony of Leslie Vickers, *LH*, 717, and L. L. Balleisen, *LH*, 692. For the more skeptical fears of the representative of a radical labor organization, see the complaints of William Dunne of the Trade Union Unity League, *LH*, 1028. Dunne warned the committee that the guarantee of the right to strike was worthless because the courts were likely to be hostile toward labor organizations.

[30] The battleground labor provision of the National Industrial Recovery Act of 1933, which established the NRA, was Section 7(a). Section 7(a) stated that the codes of fair competition established by the NRA had to guarantee that employees had the right to organize and bargain collectively through chosen representatives, that no employee could be required to join a company union, and the employers would comply by hours and wage limits established under the act.

[31] The brief is reprinted in *LH*, 1050–6.

have guaranteed a different outcome in *Mackay* or *Sands*, but it would at least have forced the justices to alter their reasoning. In both cases, the Supreme Court declined to extend protection to striking workers after giving great weight to the employer's prior history of compliance with the Wagner Act. In *Sands*, for example, the Court found that the company's prior compliance with the act was sufficient grounds to reject the NLRB's evidence that the company had dealt unfairly with the union.

A second Polier suggestion is directly relevant to the issues raised in *Sands*. Polier recommended that Congress add a provision stating that the right to strike guaranteed in Section 13 could not be diminished by "the existence of any contract between an employer and an employee and/or labor organization" (*LH*, 1053). If legislators had followed this second suggestion and included such a provision, Congress would have directly addressed the issues raised in *Sands* in the text of the statute. Again, it seems likely that such a provision would have been relevant to the Court's thinking in *Sands*. Affirming in the text that workers had the right to strike during the contract term would have made it difficult for the Court to rely on the "contract" between the Sands Company and its employees to justify its ruling.

Polier's brief demonstrates that it was possible for an attentive observer of the labor boards of the NRA to anticipate the interpretive questions that would later arise in *Mackay* and *Sands*. Polier also clearly associated his suggestions for statutory wording with concerns about the courts: "The specific enumerations suggested should serve not only to avoid the judicial use of the bill to outlaw strikes, but also to make clear to the public that the use of the strike is entirely proper and 'respectable' " (*LH*, 1053).

Of course, the inclusion of Polier's brief in the published version of the committee hearing does not guarantee that even a single member of Congress read the brief or that members of Congress were aware of the issues the brief raised. Perhaps Polier's powers of foresight were somehow better than the average legislator's. However, additional evidence shows that Polier was not the only person to recognize that the unadorned Section 13 would ultimately allow judges to resolve the important policy issues raised in *Sands* and *Mackay*.

One important source of additional evidence showing that legislators were aware of the interpretive questions later decided by judges is found in the activities surrounding changes made to the right to strike provision by the Senate Committee in 1934. Senator Walsh's substitute bill had an entirely new provision regarding the right to strike. Both the text of the substitute provision, and the comments that Walsh's version elicited, make it clear that members of Congress were well aware of the crucial distinction between adopting a minimal guarantee against state interference with strikes and adopting a broader positive affirmation of the right to use strikes as economic weapons.

Walsh's replacement for the Wagner bill's right to strike provision stated:

Nothing in this resolution shall be construed to require any employee to render labor or service without his consent, or to authorize the issuance of any order or injunction requiring such service, or to make illegal the failure or refusal of any employee individually, or any number of employees collectively, to render labor or service.

The language in the Walsh version suggests a minimal right against government interference, and is clearly consistent with the interpretation eventually adopted by the Supreme Court in cases like *Mackay* and *Sands*. Significantly, however, legislators rejected the clearer and more minimalist Walsh version and returned to the original, more open-ended Wagner version by the time the Wagner Act passed.

A year after Walsh first proposed his version, the members of the Senate Committee on Education and Labor explained the reasons for returning to the original version. In a memo explaining each of the differences between the new 1935 Wagner bill and the Walsh bill of a year earlier, the committee explained that the problem with the right to strike language in the Walsh bill was that it "merely provide[d] that nothing therein shall 'make illegal' the failure or refusal of any employee ... to render labor or service." The Wagner version, the memo explained, was better because it contained an "affirmative declaration of the right to strike" (*LH*, 1371). Clearly, the committee wanted the provision to reach further than the Walsh bill's declaration of a minimal right against government interference. However, even though legislators recognized the importance of restoring the affirmative declaration of the right to strike, neither the committee nor the rest of Congress was willing to include language specifying exactly how much further the act was supposed to go. Legislators were also unwilling to add text explaining how the NLRB and the courts should balance the right to strike against employers' rights and responsibilities under the complicated administrative system of the Wagner Act. The result was that the precise meaning of whatever "affirmative declaration" the committee hoped to make was not established before the Wagner Act passed Congress. Its meaning would only be determined as disputes arising under the Wagner Act reached the NLRB and the courts.

Permanent Replacements and Reinstatement in Congress

It is now appropriate to move from these general questions about the right to strike provision to the more specific policy issues addressed by the Supreme Court in *Mackay* and *Sands*. The final version of the Wagner Act, as already noted, did not contain any language indicating a position on replacement workers or the reinstatement of workers after strikes. The failure to include such language was not, however, the result of an accident or legislators' inability to foresee that such issues would be important. The issue of replacement workers was broached several times during deliberations on early versions of the Wagner Act. Proposals considered by legislators contained language that directly addressed replacement and reinstatement issues. For example, the 1934 Wagner bill contained two provisions that referred to "replaced" workers and "reinstatement" of workers after strikes. However, language addressing the replacement worker issue in the original Wagner bill was removed after it generated considerable controversy. The provisions were not included in the substitute Walsh bill and did not reappear in either Public Resolution 44 or the Wagner Act. The fact that such proposals appeared early on, created controversy, and then disappeared suggests that important members of Congress were aware of the issues but decided to avoid controversy by leaving the issues unresolved.

The first relevant provision in the 1934 bill was in Section 5, the section of the bill defining unfair labor practices.[32] Clause (6) of Section 5 stated that it was an unfair labor practice:

To engage in any discriminatory practice as to wage or hour differentials, advancement, demotion, hire, tenure of employment, *reinstatement*, or any other condition of employment, which encourages membership or non-membership in any labor organization (emphasis added).

The corresponding provision in the Wagner Act as enacted was Section 8(3). That provision specified only "hire or tenure or any term or condition" of employment, omitting all reference to reinstatement.

A second relevant provision from the 1934 Wagner bill was part of the definition of "employee" in Section 3(3).[33] The 1934 version of the definition included a provision stating, "the term 'employee' shall not include

---

[32] Section 5(6) of S. 2926.
[33] The corresponding provision is in Section 2(3) of the Wagner Act.

an individual who has replaced a striking employee."[34] The provision was omitted from the 1935 Wagner bill and the Wagner Act.

Of the two provisions, the second, which denied strikebreakers status as employees, attracted the most attention during Senate hearings on the 1934 bill. Numerous witnesses representing employers and employers' organizations vigorously opposed the reference to replacement workers in Section 3(3) of the 1934 bill. Although some employers appeared confused about the legal ramifications of the provision,[35] most saw immediately that it would make it more difficult for employers to defeat strikes by hiring replacement workers. For example, S. G. Brooks, representing several groups of Ohio businesses, noted that if replacement workers did not count as "employees" under the bill, they could not vote in new elections to choose new representatives. Brooks was concerned that the provision would make it impossible to do precisely what the Sands company had done: Use replacement workers to vote out an existing union. Brooks also noted that excluding replacement workers as "employees" would make it an "unfair labor practice" for an employer to do precisely what the management of the Sands Company did: Form a new collective agreement with replacement workers (*LH*, 726).

If legislators had adopted the Wagner bill with these original provisions intact, Congress would have collectively spoken more directly to issues the Supreme Court later had to decide in *Sands* and *Mackay*. Members of Congress would have signaled its intention on two points that the Supreme Court seemed to deny in *Sands* and *Mackay*: 1) The right to strike included at least some protection against permanent replacements, and 2) any relevant right employers had to "carry on the business" by hiring replacement workers was not unlimited within the new administrative system of labor relations law. However, legislators did not vote to adopt the original Wagner bill language in 1935. Members of Congress were unable or unwilling to pass a bill indicating any position on, or even awareness of, the replacement and reinstatement issues.

Furthermore, it is clear that members of Congress did not adopt the statute in its final form because they somehow thought that the adopted version established a clearer policy on strikebreakers than the original version. The congressional committees that reported the second Wagner bill were unable to say which policy position the new bill took on permanent

---

[34] S. 2926 (*LH*, 2).
[35] For example, William Whitehead of Institute of American Meatpackers, *LH*, 1042.

replacements. The Senate report on the 1934 Walsh bill said that it would be up to the board to decide on a case-by-case basis whether replaced workers continued to be "employees."[36] The Senate report on the 1935 Wagner bill is even less helpful. The committee's explanation of the entire antidiscrimination section was the rather disingenuous statement that the provision was "self-explanatory."[37] The meaning of that "self-explanatory" provision has since been disputed in hundreds of court cases.

The most obvious explanation for the decision to avoid a clear resolution of the replacement and reinstatement issue is that the bill's supporters wanted to avoid a fight. They may have calculated that the provision was not important enough to sacrifice support for the bill or to create delays in passage. While the official records do not establish this conclusion with any certainty, it is clear that the provision denying strikebreakers status as "employees" was a political lightning rod in the 1934 hearings. The reaction to the strikebreaker provision contrasts sharply with the very general complaints employers made about the affirmation of the "right to strike" in Section 13. None of the employers who testified asked the committee to remove the right to strike provision, perhaps because they guessed that the courts would render it harmless. However, the same witnesses repeatedly singled out the strikebreaker provision in Section 3(3) for removal. The objections made by employers square perfectly with the decision by legislators to retain the ambiguous right to strike provision while removing the offending part of the definition in 3(3).

An alternative explanation for the removal of the strikebreaker provision is the one actually stated in the 1934 Senate report on the Walsh bill: The bill's supporters made a conscious decision to leave the permanent replacement issue for the labor board to decide. Perhaps legislators preferred to take advantage of the expertise and flexibility of the board. The supporters of the bill may have worried that the complicated issues likely to arise in permanent replacement cases were too delicate to be bluntly resolved with a rule that went the same way for every situation. Although this explanation concedes that Congress delegated the decision to the regulatory agency, it does not concede that Congress anticipated that the courts would step in, reverse the NLRB's findings of fact, and establish the blunt policy resolution of their own choosing.

The problem with this second explanation, however, is that legislators failed to add any statutory language on replacement workers that

---

[36] Senate Report 1184, S. 2926, 73rd Congress, 2nd Session, *LH*, 1102.
[37] Senate Report 573, S. 1958, 74th Congress, 1st Session, *LH*, 2311.

would have protected the NLRB's discretionary judgments from judicial interference. As noted previously, legislators sometimes included language indicating that the courts should leave specific policy questions to the discretion of the board. Legislators included provisions mentioning some issues and committing them to the board's discretion, and other provisions that seem to limit judicial review of some board decisions. The provision (9(b)) regarding certification of bargaining units is an example. In the case of permanent replacements, however, legislators removed all references to the issue in the text without indicating a congressional position regarding who should make decisions. The failure to commit decisions on replacements to the discretion of the NLRB created ambiguity: Did legislators want questions regarding replacement to be resolved by the experts on the board on a case-by-case basis? Or, did legislators neglect to resolve the issue despite a preference that the replacement issue be settled with a firm rule that matched their broader goals in enacting the statute? The failure of legislators to give any indication of their position meant that judges were left free to roam in the legislative records in a selective quest for some broader congressional "purpose" that might justify a judge-made rule for resolving conflicts over replacement and reinstatement. Members of Congress specifically empowered the courts to review the board's enforcement orders, presumably to ensure that the board exercised discretion in a way that comported with broader congressional goals. It seems unfair to characterize the resulting judicial rulings as unwarranted or even unwanted interference.[38]

Moreover, even if the second explanation is correct, the more basic fact remains. The failure of legislators to decide the permanent replacement issue or to assign the issue to the NLRB was not the result of it being impossible for legislators to foresee that the issue would arise or to anticipate that the absence of clear instructions in the statutory text would ultimately empower the courts to decide. Legislators addressed the replacement issue in two provisions in an earlier version of the bill. The issue was obviously brought before the "consciousness of Congress" during the debates leading to passage of the Act. Congress, however, decided not to decide.

---

[38] It is worth noting that Congress provided an avenue of judicial redress for the type of board decision that was most likely to upset employers (cease and desist orders related to employers' unfair labor practices) but did not provide a similar avenue for the types of decisions that were most likely to upset workers (bargaining unit and certification decisions).

Of course, it is possible that judges would have taken the same position on replacement workers even if legislators had retained the two relevant provisions from the first Wagner bill in the Wagner Act. Neither provision from the 1934 Wagner bill suggested an absolute right to reinstatement. The reference to "reinstatement" in the original bill may well have been consistent with the position the Supreme Court took in *Mackay*. However, if legislators had provided more indication of how the NLRB and the courts should balance the right to strike against the interests of employers, or if legislators had included a provision indicating that they expected the NLRB to decide issues of reinstatement, judges almost certainly would have had to modify the rationale they used to find that the Wagner Act allowed permanent replacements. Only the complete absence of any indication in the text that members of Congress were conscious of the replacement issue allowed the *Mackay* Court to assert that legislators wanted to leave employers with an unlimited "right to protect and continue... business by supplying places left vacant by strikers."[39]

Ensuring Worker Compliance with Collective Bargaining "Contracts"

When *Sands* confronted the Supreme Court with the midterm strike controversy in 1939, the justices could not find any statutory provision indicating directly how legislators wanted the courts to treat midterm strikes. Legislators had neglected to provide any statutory mechanism for enforcing contracts. As a result, the Court assumed responsibility for deciding which policy choices regarding midterm strikes would best achieve the broader goal of facilitating smooth enforcement of collective-bargaining agreements.

On the midterm strike issue, the evidence indicates that the silence of Congress in the statute was not due to an accident or to an inability to foresee that cases raising the issue would be decided in the courts. Numerous witnesses who appeared before committees on the 1934 and 1935 Wagner bills expressed concern that the bill did not contain any provisions to ensure that workers would follow collective-bargaining agreements once they were formed. Legislators also considered and rejected a number of proposals that would have provided mechanisms for enforcing collective-bargaining agreements, including a proposal for doing precisely what the Supreme Court later decided to do: Giving midterm strikers unfavorable treatment. Members of Congress decided, however, not to include any

[39] 304 U.S. 333 (1938), 345.

of these clarifying provisions in the final version of the bill, and instead allowed the courts to decide how midterm strikes should be treated.

When the midterm strike issue reached the Supreme Court, the justices claimed that they were matching the purpose of Congress because they selected an outcome that advanced the purported congressional goal of making collective-bargaining contracts binding and enforceable. The Court did not consider the alternative statutory provisions for ensuring smooth enforcement of collective-bargaining agreements that members of Congress voted to reject before adopting the final version of the Wagner Act.

For example, one proposal considered in Congress was to ensure enforcement of contracts by giving enforcement powers to the NLRB. The key advocate for board enforcement of contracts was William H. Davis of the Twentieth Century Fund, a prototype of the corporate-sponsored think tank. Before Senate committees in both 1934 and 1935, Davis recommended that the committee add a provision requiring that collective-bargaining contracts be registered with the NLRB and that worker violations of registered contracts be treated as unfair labor practices.[40]

Davis's suggestion never went very far. When Davis made the recommendation before a Senate committee in 1935, Senator Wagner responded by claiming that a provision giving the NLRB powers to enforce contracts was not necessary. Wagner told Davis that the real hurdle had always been getting employers to come to the bargaining table to make agreements, not getting workers to follow agreements once made.[41]

However, not all the participants in the legislative process agreed with Wagner's position that there was no need to add a provision for enforcement of collective-bargaining contracts. Several participants suggested additional provisions that would have established various incentives for adhering to contracts. For example, Donald Richberg, General Counsel of the NRA and an important administration figure with influence in Congress, made a speech in January 1935 that was later reprinted in the *Congressional Record*. Richberg suggested that the new labor bill include a provision that set an explicit limit on the right to strike during the term of a contract.[42] Richberg suggested that strikes be forbidden during a cooling-off period when disputes could be submitted to an impartial arbitrator (*LH*, 1292).

---

[40] See 1934 Senate Hearings, *LH*, 1317; 1935 Senate Hearings, *LH*, 2092, 2101–3.
[41] The exchange with Wagner is in *LH*, 2101–3.
[42] 79 *Congressional Record* 265, *LH*, 1284–94.

In some respects, Richberg's suggestion would have gone even further than the Court did in *Sands*. The Supreme Court limited the effective use of strikes as economic weapons by denying the Sands workers status as employees. But the Court did not *prohibit* the workers from going on strike. In other ways, however, Richberg's suggestion was much milder than the policy the Supreme Court established in *Sands*. Richberg's limit on the right to strike applied only during a cooling-off period and only when there was a prior agreement to submit disputes to arbitration. In *Sands*, the Court ruled against the workers even though the contract stated that the workers could "act as they saw fit" after a cooling-off period and did not have any procedure for submitting disputes to arbitration.

For the most part, suggestions for adding provisions regarding contract enforcement were rejected in congressional committees. As a result, there were few opportunities for the full membership of either the House or Senate to vote on such proposals. In one instance, however, an amendment that would have clarified the meaning of Section 13 for cases like *Sands* was considered by the entire membership of the House. A floor amendment offered by Rep. Frederick Biermann (D–1A) on the final day of debate on the Wagner Act made a direct reference to midterm strikes. The amendment would have replaced the right to strike declaration in Section 13 with a new provision that guaranteed the right to strike only before an agreement was reached. The version in the amendment then provided that "After that agreement has been made, and so long as it shall be observed by the employer, a strike shall be considered as a violation of the spirit of the Act" (79 *Congressional Record* 9731).

If adopted, the Biermann amendment would have established strong congressional support for the position later taken by the Supreme Court in *Sands*. However, the Court never had the opportunity to interpret the language in the Biermann amendment because it never became part of the Wagner Act. The full House voted narrowly to reject the amendment after the chair of the committee with jurisdiction, Rep. William Connery, denounced it. Connery claimed that the amendment would "take the heart out of it and kill the bill." He said it was "another way of interfering with labor's right to strike, which is not a right that comes from Congress but is a divine right which comes from the Almighty God" (*LH*, 3227). Even after this quick condemnation by the bill's floor manager, the amendment initially passed 115-109 on a standing vote. It was only after Connery demanded a teller vote and rounded up additional legislators that the amendment was defeated by 140 to 107.

The strong statement by the committee chair that a provision like the one offered by Biermann would defeat the purpose of the bill, and the eventual decision by the full House to reject the amendment suggests that the Court made a mistake about the "purpose" of Congress when it decided *Sands*. The rejection of the Biermann amendment seems to support the claim that Congress, or at least the House, rejected the precise policy that the Court ended up choosing in *Sands*. At the very least, the decision to reject the Biermann amendment seems much more relevant to the decisions in *Sands* than the single page number from the Senate Committee report that the Court actually cited in its opinion.[43]

In his analysis of *Sands*, Klare criticizes the justices on the Court for failing to take note of the failed Biermann amendment as they engaged in their selective perusal of the legislative history (1985, 802–4). Rather than repeat Klare's criticism here, I want simply to note that regardless of whether the fight over the Biermann amendment says anything about the collective intent of Congress, the fight clearly demonstrates that representatives were aware of the right to strike issue and concerned about the relationship between the right to strike provision and midterm strikes right up to the day of passage. The amendment drew the attention of the House membership to the same policy question that later had to be settled by the Court in *Sands*. Legislators chose to retain the ambiguous right to strike provision without taking a clear position on whether midterm strikes were consistent with the "spirit of the Act." While it is impossible to know for sure that such an alternative provision would have changed the outcome in a case like *Sands*, it is clear from the controversy over the Biermann amendment that the failure to settle the midterm strike issue was not the result of legislators failing to anticipate that the issue would become important. The close vote on the Biermann amendment on the final day of floor discussion of the Wagner Act suggests that legislators ultimately failed to act decisively because the issue remained quite controversial in 1935. Members of Congress decided to leave the issue for the NLRB and courts to resolve, at least until 1947 and the Taft-Hartley Act.

CONCLUSION

While the legislators who created the Norris-LaGuardia Act seemed to have learned some important lessons about using clear legislative language to limit the involvement of the courts, those lessons seem to have

[43] See note 17.

been abandoned just three years later when Congress passed the Wagner Act. The decision in Congress to remain silent on both the permanent replacement and midterm strike issues was in effect a decision to leave these important and controversial issues to be decided by the NLRB and, ultimately, by the courts. Although the act created a permanent labor board authorized to make decisions on some of the issues left unresolved, the act also assigned broadly defined powers to review NLRB rulings to the courts. The fact that legislators decided to delegate authority to an administrative board complicates the task of figuring out exactly which issues legislators expected the Courts to decide. However, the evidence presented here suggests the ability of judges to determine particular policy outcomes is not simply a fixed feature of institutional design. Legislators can limit judicial discretion by establishing clear standards in the text or by including language that protects the discretion of the administrative agency. Alternatively, legislators can expand judicial power by failing to indicate a position and leaving judges free to find a position in ambiguously expressed legislative goals.

On the issues of permanent replacements and midterm strikes, the evidence indicates that the reason the Court was able to issue influential rulings on important policy issues was not that legislators were unable to foresee issues or take steps to limit judicial discretion. Judges made policy decisions only after members of Congress discussed the controversial issues during deliberations without providing a clear resolution. As with the Clayton Act, my three conditions for declaring a statutory provision to be a legislative deferral have been met. Members of Congress identified the issues as important, called the attention of their colleagues to ambiguities in the statute that would have to be resolved by judges, and proposed alternative legislative language that many participants felt would better resolve the issues. The issues were clearly before "the consciousness of Congress" at the time the statute passed. In the end, however, legislators passed the new statute before reaching any agreement on how these issues should be resolved.

Because legislators deferred to the courts, the extent to which decisions made by unelected judges were barriers to workers' efforts to use the democratic process cannot be measured by asking whether the judges successfully matched a baseline produced through some pure democratic process in Congress. The same legislative process that led to the decision to pass the Wagner Act also led to the decision to create the ambiguity that allowed the courts to settle important policy issues. Thus, the impact of the courts as barriers to democratic process must be looked at not in terms of the independence of judges, but also in terms of the democratic forces that made empowering judges through legislative ambiguity an attractive political strategy.

This short inquiry into the Wagner Act has not provided a complete account of those processes, but it has established that even in the more complicated administrative system for regulating labor organizations, opportunities for legislators to defer to the courts remain. The success of Norris-LaGuardia in limiting judicial policy making was not repeated in the case of the Wagner Act. However, the return of judicial policy making came about not because the courts developed mysterious powers that allowed judges to rise Phoenix-like from the ashes. Judges had power because it remained in the interests of legislators to preserve the courts as a check on the power delegated to the administrative board.

By demonstrating that deferrals persisted even as legislators were perfecting the practice of delegating to executive branch agencies, this chapter suggests that deferrals are more than historic curiosities, relics of an older system of judicial regulation of labor. Deferrals still need to be accounted for if scholars are to understand how the development of the post–New Deal administrative state has affected democratic accountability. The most accomplished critics of delegation to executive branch agencies assert that American democracy was much healthier in the nineteenth century and early twentieth centuries, before legislators developed the habit of delegating (Lowi 1979, Schoenbrod 1993). My case studies of the Erdman and Clayton acts have already shown that such scholars overestimate the integrity of legislation passed before the New Deal. This chapter establishes an additional important point: Scholars concerned about the lack of direct accountability in the expanded administrative state need to pay attention to the full range of strategies legislators use to shift responsibility to actors outside the legislative branch.

7

Conclusion

The preceding chapters have examined the circumstances that allowed judges to make influential decisions about the meaning of four federal labor statutes, decisions that shaped both labor law and the labor movement in the United States. In one of the three cases, the Supreme Court struck down an important prolabor provision of the statute on constitutional grounds. In the other three cases, judges stopped short of striking down provisions, but nevertheless made important policy decisions as they settled interpretive controversies about the meaning of legislative language. Each time judges settled interpretive controversies about a statutory provision, they justified their choices by claiming that they were following the will of Congress rather than their own personal policy preferences.

Up to now, scholars who have criticized those judicial decisions have focused on questions about whether or not the judges' decisions correctly matched the policy outcomes preferred by the elected legislators who created the statutes. Critics of the courts have drawn attention to the fact that the judicial rulings went against policy goals that many members of Congress and labor leaders articulated when the statutes passed. Because judicial rulings thwarted those expressed goals, critics have concluded that unelected judges were able to obstruct legislative reforms and thus were significant barriers to labor's efforts to produce change through the democratic processes of the legislative branch.

The conclusions growing out of this study are different. Using a set of research procedures that uncover evidence that other scholars have ignored, I have found that it is not possible to understand the impact and legitimacy of the judicial decisions by asking whether policies established by judges match some policy outcome preselected in Congress.

Judges had to settle interpretive controversies in these cases largely because legislators were unable and unwilling to establish a consensus on a particular policy outcome.

My findings in the case studies also draw attention to more general problems with the strategy of using legislative branch outcomes as a democratic baseline against which to measure the legitimacy of policy outcomes in a separation of powers system. In all four case studies, participants in the legislative process tried to anticipate and shape the role that judges would later play when the statute was implemented. The ability of participants to anticipate the important role that judges would play allowed them to engage in a variety of strategic behaviors that made the outcomes of legislative processes ambiguous and sometimes deceptive. The complications created when participants adjust their behavior to anticipated judicial reactions are important even in cases where legislators do not ultimately decide to defer to the courts. In all four of my case studies, participants' expectations about judicial reactions shaped the content of the statute before it was enacted. As a result, decisions made in Congress do not establish an independent democratic baseline against which to measure the influence of the judicial branch. Given that anticipated judicial reactions influence the content of statutes, the outcomes of legislative processes do not provide some pure reflection of underlying political competition, uncontaminated by the influence of unelected judges. In all four cases, elected legislators would have produced different legislation, and thus a different baseline, if they had not expected judges to play any role in the implementation of the statutes.

Such findings mean that scholars cannot develop a complete understanding of the impact and legitimacy of judicial decisions by making comparisons between the outcomes produced by the courts and the allegedly more democratic or pure outcomes produced earlier by elected legislators. The "baseline" that legislators establish in a separation of powers system will be different from the baseline that the same legislators would establish in a system where judges were effectively confined to some less important role. Moreover, the cases also show that legislators are in some cases willing to empower judges as a means of limiting accountability for difficult decisions. Thus, not only does judicial power affect legislative decision making before statutes pass, but decisions in Congress affect the capacity of judges to influence policies after legislation passes. As a result, it is not possible to isolate and compare legislative and judicial branch outcomes in the way the legislative baseline framework demands. Efforts to artificially isolate and construct isolated positions cannot provide a complete or accurate understanding of the impact and legitimacy of the courts.

FACTORS AFFECTING DECISIONS TO EXPAND THE ROLE OF THE COURTS

The question to turn to now is whether my four case studies provide any insight that could lead toward development of a coherent alternative framework for understanding the impact and legitimacy of judicial decisions.

One possibility would be to claim that judicial policy choices simply cannot be undemocratic in cases where the power of judges to make policy choices is the result of deliberate deference by elected legislators. Such a claim recognizes that regardless of which policy choice judges make, it is unfair to criticize judges for thwarting democratic processes since choices made by elected legislators empowered the courts. Making the analytic claim that all resulting judicial decisions were "democratic" would preserve some of the simplicity and elegance of the legislative baseline framework. However, such an approach does not seem particularly satisfying or helpful in light of the four case studies presented here. Although elected officials made the decisions that created a role for the courts, the evidence here suggests that the availability of certain types of compromises had an important and perhaps destructive impact on democratic accountability. In particular, the availability of the courts as another location of power and responsibility seems to have complicated the efforts of workers and labor organizations to use electoral processes to produce desired changes in policy. Moreover, the gains legislators and labor leaders made by deferring to the courts were realized in part because legislators and labor leaders deliberately created the impression that new statutes accomplished more than they did. This in turn suggests that the participants made deliberate efforts to deceive the workers whose interests were allegedly being served by the statutes. If legislators and labor leaders expected workers to understand fully that the legislative compromises deliberately shifted responsibility to less accountable and likely hostile judges, the compromises would presumably not have been made.

Thus, the categorical claim that judicial decisions are democratic so long as elected officials made the decisions that expanded the role of the courts does not seem very helpful. It seems important to engage in the difficult task of developing a general framework for characterizing the threat that legislative deference to the courts poses to democratic accountability.

The first step toward building such an account is to develop some general claims about circumstances that might lead legislators to defer to the courts. Some initial hypotheses can be developed by uncovering the common features of the three case studies where legislators expanded the role of the courts, features that distinguish those cases from Norris-LaGuardia, the one case where legislators curtailed the power of the courts.

Compromises and Accountability in Congress

A first relevant factor unique to the three cases where legislators deliberately allowed judges to decide important policy issues was that legislators were deeply divided about how to resolve the policy controversies addressed by the statute. In all three cases, there was a lack of consensus over the direction of policy. Efforts to accommodate the conflicting interests of different groups led to compromises that weakened legislative language or obscured its meaning as the legislation moved toward passage. In contrast, the one case where legislators limited the role of the courts, the Norris-LaGuardia Act, was also the one case where there was a broad consensus in Congress in favor of limiting the role of the courts and making some specific policy changes.

This first observation draws attention to some important concerns about the impact of the courts on democratic accountability. The availability of judges as policy makers meant that members of Congress could deflect conflicting political pressures without having to take full responsibility for making divisive choices. Thus, wittingly or not, judges helped to shield legislators from the electoral consequences of difficult choices. Furthermore, the issues selected for judicial resolution were not innocuous or technical issues that were particularly suited for resolution through the principled legal reasoning employed by judges. The issues left for judicial resolution had already generated long-lasting conflicts among well-organized and well-mobilized constituencies. Had legislators been forced to take responsibility for resolving those conflicts, it would have been much easier for the relevant constituencies to shape appropriate and effective political responses through democratic processes like congressional elections.

Organizational Imperatives and Organizational Side Effects

The second factor distinguishing the cases where the courts later played an important role is that both legislators and labor leaders felt a particular type of pressure to ensure that Congress enact a new piece of legislation. In all three of the cases where legislators compromised by expanding the role of the Courts, the pressure to pass legislation was not simply pressure to achieve particular policy results. Participants did feel pressure to do something quickly, but they also felt that they could satisfy that short-term imperative even if they enacted compromise legislation that included provisions that hindered the law's chances of accomplishing all of its advertised policy goals. In all three cases, legislators and labor leaders were willing to sacrifice some certainty on policy goals because they also valued some side effects that passage of legislation could create regardless of whether the statute achieved all of its advertised policy goals. In particular, participants hoped that the excitement and interest created by the decision to pass legislation could serve important short-term organizational imperatives even if judges later made rulings that prevented the law from creating lasting or important changes in labor policy. Although the participants did not always publicly explain that such extra-policy side effects were an important reason for creating or supporting the statutes, the supposition that such side effects were important to participants helps to explain the otherwise inexplicable choices that many participants made during the legislative process.

Because this second factor is crucial to assessing the impact of the courts as barriers to democratic accountability, it is worth recounting some specific circumstances for each of the three cases where legislators expanded the role of the courts. In the case of the Erdman Act, legislators wanted to make some response to the crisis of the Pullman Strike and to assert that Congress had some role to play in creating labor policies that could prevent future crises. Unfortunately, the labor organizations most affected by the Erdman Act were not strong enough to force legislators to make anything more than a symbolic enactment that was incapable of achieving its advertised goal of ending labor unrest on the railroads. Although the Erdman Act was ostensibly concerned with setting up a system for arbitrating railroad labor disputes, many members of Congress realized that the bill would not achieve that goal. Legislators were instead using the statute to signal its responsiveness and to discourage labor radicalism by rewarding one group of conservative railroad labor organizations.

In the case of the Clayton Act, Democrats facing midterm elections wanted to avoid the embarrassment of breaking an important campaign promise to labor organizations. In normal circumstances, the campaign promise might have put the American Federation of Labor (AFL) in a strong position to insist that the Democrats support a stronger proposal like the Pearre bill, which the AFL had been backing for the preceding decade. But in 1914, the ability of AFL leaders to secure passage of their favored bill was limited by internal pressures that made it very difficult for AFL leaders to hold out for stronger legislation. The AFL leaders who made the controversial decision to endorse Wilson could not risk coming away from their negotiation with Wilson and the Democrats empty handed. Such factors help to explain why AFL leaders abandoned a bill that they felt was much more likely to achieve their goals, and even helped to block some amendments that would have clarified and strengthened the immunities given to workers in the Clayton Act.

In the case of the Wagner Act, both members of Congress and the Roosevelt Administration faced the ongoing economic emergency of the Great Depression, an increasingly energetic labor movement, and the collapse of the administration's recovery program. Members of Congress felt an urgent need to use new legislation to improve the administrative capacities of the labor boards set up by emergency recovery legislation. Legislative leaders like Robert Wagner recognized the need for a statute that would help the recovery by strengthening the bargaining position of workers and rewarding labor organizations willing to submit to a stabilizing administrative system. However, labor organizations were neither strong nor unified enough to give permanent shape to important details of the Wagner Act, details that later turned out to be crucial to the development of the labor movement. Legislators responded with a law that gave the National Labor Relations Board (NLRB) and the courts responsibility for making a wide variety of important decisions about the meaning of the new law.

The more successful Norris-LaGuardia Act provides a useful contrast to the other three cases. While Norris-LaGuardia was also enacted during a period of economic emergency, it was also the only one of my cases where there was a consensus on a particular change in policy at the time the statute passed. Few members of Congress spoke in opposition to the policy changes that the statute aimed to achieve. Even business groups limited their criticisms of the proposal. Most employers had stopped using yellow-dog contracts and were no longer willing to defend labor injunctions at the hearings leading to passage of the statute.

The observation that participants in legislative processes were motivated in part by concerns about the organizational effects of statutes reveals an important problem with the legislative baseline framework that occurs in all cases, not just cases where legislators defer to the courts.

The problem is that legislative outcomes cannot be taken as a baseline measure of the relative strengths of competing groups who take part in electoral processes. Legislation is itself a tool for manipulating those relative strengths. This problem emerges in all four of my cases. Participants in every case were very concerned with the question of how the decision to enact legislation (or, alternatively, a refusal to enact legislation) would affect the relative strengths of rival labor organizations. Members of Congress spent a great deal of time discussing the effects legislation would have on the way labor interests were organized and on the ideologies of labor organizations, and sometimes explained their choices by noting how the legislation would change the way workers were organized. Legislators were particularly interested in using legislation to placate moderate labor organizations and strengthen their leaders, and thus to prevent more radical labor organizations and leaders from becoming more powerful.

The interests of legislators and the interests of the participating labor leaders were much more likely to converge around these organizational issues than around the policy goals of labor leaders. From 1898 until passage of the Wagner Act, there was never majority support in Congress for establishing an effective regulatory system that protected workers' right to organize spontaneously, as they saw fit, and without judicial intervention. But throughout the same time period, there was a consensus among legislators that it was better to have a labor movement dominated by conservative trade union organizations like the AFL and the railroad brotherhoods than a movement dominated by radical industrial unions like the one headed by Eugene Debs. Thus, it is not surprising that legislators and labor leaders used legislation to help influence organizing strategies and ideologies. The result is that outcomes of apparently permeable legislative processes cannot be understood as pure reflections of underlying political conditions that exist independently of what legislators or judges do. In some cases, legislation is less a mirror of the intensity of the preferences of the affected groups than a tool used to manipulate the relative strengths and weaknesses of those groups.

Shaping Institutions and Shaping Movements

Taken together, these observations about the circumstances that give rise to legislative decisions that expand the role of the courts help to solidify concerns that such decisions threaten democratic accountability. A system where policies are created through the interactions of three interdependent branches can make it much easier for those in power to resist the changes sought by potentially radical social movements. For workers hoping to change policies, choosing leaders who could accomplish the very difficult task of winning legislation in Congress was not enough to produce desired changes in policies. Workers also needed to overcome efforts to distort the meaning of legislative outcomes and efforts to manipulate which worker organizations would survive. In the cases examined here, legislators were able to establish their responsiveness by passing nonresponsive statutes, and labor leaders were able to demonstrate their effectiveness by endorsing ineffective statutes. The result was a set of failed attempts at reform, and a population of labor organizations that must be understood as being at least partly the result of decisions made by elite actors without the full knowledge and participation of the workers themselves.

Such findings suggest that judicial rulings associated with legislative deference can be understood as barriers to democratic accountability. Definitive judicial rulings often come years after legislation passes, and are accompanied by opinions that attempt to legitimate judicial choices by referring to complicated and ever-shifting sets of technical legal rules. These essential features of the judicial process make it difficult for nonspecialists to evaluate the outcomes of the legislative process and to assign responsibility when the proximate cause of legislative failure is a decision made by a judge. The compromises worked out in Congress were made only because the active participants in those processes recognized that nonspecialist workers depended on their leaders when evaluating and interpreting the actions of both Congress and the courts.

These observations provide some support for claims made by critical scholars like Karl Klare (1978), James Gray Pope (1997), and Girardeau Spann (1994). Such scholars have focused on the peculiar nature of legal reasoning, and have blamed that style of reasoning for dampening the enthusiasm for political action among various social classes and groups. On these accounts, judicial reasoning helps to preserve the status quo by establishing ideologies that make contingent and unfair outcomes seem necessary and legitimate.[1] However, my cases suggest somewhat different conclusions about the importance of judicial reasoning. These cases suggest that the problem goes beyond any particular set of biases judges happen to possess at a given time, and beyond the specific content of

[1] Others argue, however, that legal action can in some circumstances be radicalizing. See McCann (1994).

judicial ideologies. The reliance of judges on obfuscating forms of reasoning may create barriers for workers even when judges fail to convince
workers that their antilabor ideologies are neutral or legitimate. Labor
leaders and legislators had specialized knowledge that helped them to anticipate how judges would resolve complicated doctrinal questions, and
used that specialized knowledge to structure compromises. Thus, the feature of judicial reasoning that made it difficult for workers to win policy
victories was not just that judges pushed policies in an antilabor direction, or that judges had magical powers to legitimate their choices. The
problem was that the complicated nature of judicial reasoning increased
workers' dependency on elite actors and gave those actors the power to influence the way workers organized and worker organizations developed.
That dependency also made it more likely that the way workers organized for political action could be shaped by the strategic, self-interested
actions of legislators and labor leaders rather than the informed, spontaneous decisions of the workers themselves. The cases also suggest that
it is not simply judges who make use of legal rhetoric to legitimate outcomes. Legislators also used the opacity of legislative compromises to
increase their own legitimacy. Legislators were never forced to say "no"
to the demands of labor organizations. They could instead create deceptive responses that were attractive to legislators precisely because they
made legislators and the legislative process appear responsive and thus
legitimate.

The case studies also draw attention to the flexibility of the institutional
powers possessed by courts. Earlier studies of these same cases have noted
that labor organizations adopted ideologies as a response to those structural features of the American state that protect the independence of the
courts and give the courts very important policy-making powers. The
findings here suggest that the changes in labor ideologies were not simply responses to the fixed institutional capacities of different branches
of government but the result of a more dynamic process that itself produced important changes in institutional capacities. Significantly, the case
studies suggest that elected legislators played a guiding role in the often
painfully slow process of wresting control over labor relations from the
courts. The findings also show that the forces that shaped the way workers
responded to institutional arrangements were not situated entirely *within*
the labor movement. The emergence of certain labor ideologies does seem
to have been affected by institutional features of the evolving separation
of powers system. But the processes of ideological development were not
determined solely by the spontaneous and independent responses crafted

by labor leaders. Those processes were also affected by the conscious manipulation of state actors.

BEYOND THE VALLEY OF THE LEGISLATIVE BASELINE FRAMEWORK

The fact that the basic assumptions of the framework do not hold up in some cases, even the important and pivotal cases considered here, is not reason by itself to abandon a theoretical framework that has been useful and productive in structuring judicial decisions and scholarly inquiry into the courts. The test of a theoretical framework is not whether all its assumptions stand up in every case. A better test is whether it 1) leads scholars to focus on important questions and problems, 2) generates successful constructs for addressing those questions empirically, and 3) leads scholars to useful and convincing answers to questions that the framework identifies as important. Judged by this standard, the legislative baseline framework remains powerful and useful. Because neither I nor anyone else has yet come up with an equally powerful alternative, I will not conclude this book by stating that the framework should be completely abandoned.

Nevertheless, there is good reason to believe that scholars interested in questions about the impact and legitimacy of judicial policy making would gain by adopting what I will now call a *deferral perspective*. Adopting a deferral perspective would mean that scholars and judges interested in the impact or legitimacy of judicial decisions would ask of every judicial policy decision whether and to what extent the capacity of judges to influence policy outcomes was shaped by earlier choices made by elected legislators. Scholars adopting this perspective would have to investigate the possibility that legislators invited or allowed judges to make policy instead of simply assuming that legislators wish to minimize the role of the courts. Scholars could continue to apply the analytic strategies of the legislative baseline framework, but only in cases where they can first rule out the possibility that legislators deliberately deferred to the courts.

There are a number of reasons to believe that judges and scholars would benefit from adopting this deferral perspective. The first is one that I discussed in some detail in Chapter 1: Scholars who follow the legislative baseline framework while ignoring the possibility of deliberate legislative deference to the courts are likely to miss some important connections between judicial policy making and democratic processes. The framework makes it likely that scholars will misinterpret judicial rulings that occur after legislative deferrals as cases where judges thwarted democratic processes. Each of the three statutes that I identify here as one where legislators deliberately expanded the power of the courts has been previously identified as a case where judges reversed potential victories won by labor organizations in legislatures (e.g., Hattam 1993, Forbath 1991, Jones 1957, Kutler 1962, Klare 1978). The judicial decisions on all three statutes seemed significant because the unelected judges appeared to reverse the will of elected legislatures. The findings presented in this book suggest that the gap between the outcome advertised by elected officials in Congress and the outcome later produced by unelected judges is not simply the result of differences in the way legislators and judges can be held accountable by voters. The connections (or lack of connections) between decision makers in each branch and electoral processes are more complicated and variable than the legislative baseline framework comprehends.

A second reason for paying more attention to deferrals is that doing so can lead scholars to better understandings of historical events and processes. A deferral perspective will lead scholars to examine important sources of evidence that scholars who follow the legislative baseline framework ignore. The small number of empirical studies of legislative deference to the courts demonstrate how much scholars can learn from looking for and uncovering legislative deference to the courts. Mark Graber's study of legislative deference uncovered evidence that supported his dramatic reinterpretations of several important instances of judicial review.[2] This book produces a dramatic challenge to the dominant interpretation of four crucial labor statutes that, by all accounts, together had a profound effect on the development of the American labor movement and American social policies. Taken together, Graber's study and my own make a powerful case for conducting additional historical inquiries into legislative deference as a source of judicial power. Both studies provide fresh insights on important issues (slavery, abortion, antitrust, labor relations) that have been widely studied. Of course, giving up the assumptions of the legislative baseline framework is not without costs. A deferral perspective forces scholars to look more carefully at a much larger historic record, a time-consuming process that more conventional methods allow

---

[2] Graber (1993) finds evidence of strategic ambiguity without doing as much violence as I do to the accepted conventions for reading legislative records. His evidence regarding the Sherman Act, for example comes from speeches given by the bill's floor managers (50–3).

scholars to skip. However, the simplicity provided by a theoretical framework has to be balanced against the ultimate goal of getting the facts right. Graber's study and my own together suggest that the balance can be profitably restruck if scholars change their presumptions about congressional decision making and interbranch interaction.

A third reason for adopting a deferral perspective is that doing so opens up a wide range of important and interesting questions for scholarly inquiry. Some of the scholarly debates that grow out of the legislative baseline framework seem to have reached dead ends (e.g., debates over theories of constitutional interpretation as constraints on judges). Others seem to have divided into competing camps that mostly talk past one another (e.g., behavioral versus institutional accounts of judicial decision making). (On this last point, see Gillman 2001.) While the deferral perspective is not likely to resolve such impasses, any strategy that opens up fresh questions might be worth following.

A deferral perspective makes fresh inquiries possible because it makes questions about how judges decide particular cases recede in importance, while making questions about how judges end up in a position to decide policy issues seem much more important. A deferral perspective also shifts attention away from decisions made by judges to decisions made in the other branches. Understanding legislative deference might help to explain why actors in the other branches can be receptive to judicial efforts to expand their power, and why such actors are so reluctant to attack the institutional bases of judicial power.

A deferral perspective can also allow scholars to explain how variations in judicial power within time periods contribute to changes across time periods. Legislators sometimes use deferrals to empower judges to decide particular policy controversies. However, in order for deferrals to serve the interests of legislators, judges need to have institutional power and independence. If voters believed that legislators could simply turn the courts on and off like a spigot, or control judges like marionettes, legislators would eventually seem responsible for the decisions that they shift to the courts. This observation helps to explain why deferrals that empower judges to resolve isolated policy issues might gradually contribute to a general expansion of judicial power. It may be that the only way legislators can create the beneficial appearance of judicial independence is to actually allow the courts real independence. (This observation helps to explain why legislators almost never use their considerable institutional powers for reversing the courts.) Judges may themselves play a more central role in this process by using the influence growing out of deferrals to create expectations that make it easier to exercise power in other cases.[3]

The extent to which inquiries into such issues will yield a better understanding of the policy-making role of the courts remains to be seen. Nevertheless, it seems clear from the case studies presented here that scholars need to be more careful about the assumptions they make, and that scholars need to trace the roots of judicial discretion in legislative decisions before drawing conclusions about the judicial policy making as a barrier to electoral accountability. While the simplifying assumptions and interpretive conventions of the legislative baseline framework make the researcher's and judge's tasks much easier, they also make it much more likely that the nature of the courts as barriers will be misunderstood.

---

[3] Some scholars associated with both the historical and rational choice varients of the new institutionalism have recently made very productive inquiries into judicial power that draw attention to the way the expansion of judicial power serves the interest of political actors, for example, Graber 1999, 1998; Gillman 2002; Rogers 2001.

Reference List

PRIMARY SOURCES ON FEDERAL LEGISLATION

<u>Erdman Act: 30 Statutes at Large 424. 1898.</u>

Olney's Bill
    H.R. 8556, 53rd Congress
    H.R. 269, 54th Congress
    H.R. 4332, 55th Congress
    S. 3662, 55th Congress

Railroad Labor Bills in the 53rd Congress
    S. 1563, Allen bill
    S. 2177, George bill
    H.R. 7697, Hudson bill
    H.R. 7382, 8214, Tawney bill
    H.R. 7632, Boatner bill

Reports

53rd Congress:
    House Report 1754, on H.R. 8556

54th Congress:
    House Report 1058, on H.R. 268

55th Congress:
    House Report 4334, on H.R. 4332
    Senate Report 591, S. 3662

<u>Clayton Act: 38 Statutes at Large 730. 1914.</u>

Published Legislative History: *The Legislative History of the Federal Antitrust Laws and Related Statutes. Part 1: The Antitrust Laws,* vols. 2 and 3. Earl W. Kintner, ed., New York: Chelsea House Publishers.

The Hoar/Grosvenor Bills
H.R. 8917, 56th Congress
H.R. 11060, S1118, 57th Congress
H.R. 89, 58th Congress
H.R. 4445, 59th Congress

The Pearre Bill
H.R. 18171, 18446, 18752, 59th Congress
H.R. 94, 60th Congress

The Wilson Bill
H.R. 11032, 62nd Congress

The Bartlett Bacon Bill
H.R. 23189, 62nd Congress

Antiinjunction and Procedural Bills of 1912
H.R. 23635, 62nd Congress
H.R. 22591, 62nd Congress

The Clayton Antitrust Bill: 1914
H.R. 15657

Hearings

1900 House Hearings. *Report of a Hearing before the Committee on the Judiciary of the House of Representatives, March 23, 1900,* House Judiciary Committee, 56th Congress, Senate Document 58.

1904 House Hearings. *Hearing before the House Judiciary Committee: Anti-Injunction Bill,* 58th Congress. H.R. 89.

1906 House Hearings. *Hearing before the Committee on the Judiciary of the House of Representatives in Relation to Anti-Injunction and Restraining Orders,* 59th Congress. H.R. 94.

1908 House Hearings. *Hearings on the So-Called Anti-Injunction Bills and All Other Labor Bills,* House Committee on the Judiciary, 60th Congress.

1908 Senate Antitrust Hearings. *Amendment of the Sherman Antitrust Law: Hearings before the Senate Committee on the Judiciary,* 60th Congress.

1912 Senate Hearings. *Limiting Federal Injunctions: Hearing before a Subcommittee of the Committee on the Judiciary, United States Senate*, 62nd Congress. H.R. 23635.

1912 Senate Hearings: Spelling Testimony. *Limiting Federal Injunctions: Argument of Thomas Carl Spelling, Esq. before a Subcommittee of the Committee on the Judiciary*, Senate Document 944, 62nd Congress. H.R. 23635.

Reports and Documents

56th Congress:
>House Report 1987, on H.R. 8917
>House Report No. 2007, on H.R. 8917
>*Petitions and Remonstrances for and Against the Passage of the Bills "To Limit the meaning of the word 'conspiracy' and use of 'restraining orders and injunctions' in certain cases*, (S. 1118, S. 4553, and H.R. 11060), Uncollected House Document, Library of Congress.

57th Congress:
>House Report 1522, on H.R. 11060
>House Report 1650, on H.R. 11060
>House Document 190, "A Compilation of Documents Relating to Injunctions in Conspiracy Cases"

60th Congress
>Senate Document 504, *Certain Injunction and Labor Cases*
>Senate Document 406, *Special Message of the President of the United States*, March 25, 1908

62nd Congress
>House Report 588, on H.R. 23189
>House Report 612, on H.R. 23635
>House Report 613, on H.R. 22591
>Senate Document 440, "Wilson Anti-Injunction Bill: Labor's Reasons for its Enactment" (Gompers report to the 1911 AFL convention)

63rd Congress
>House Report 1168, on H.R. 15657
>Senate Report 698, on H.R. 15657
>Senate Document 614, "Recent Antitrust and Labor Injunction Legislation," Annual Address Before the American Bar Association by William Howard Taft

Norris-LaGuardia Act: 47 Statutes at Large 70. 1932.

The Shipstead Bills
> S. 1482, 70th Congress
> S. 2497, 71st Congress

The Norris Bill
> S. 935, 72nd Congress

The LaGuardia Bills
> H.R. 10082, 70th Congress
> H.R. 122, 71st Congress

Reports

71st Congress
> Senate Report 1060, on S. 2497

72nd Congress
> Senate Report 163, on S. 935
> House Report 669, on H.R. 5315

Hearings

1928 Senate Hearings. *Limiting Scope of Injunctions in Labor Disputes: Hearing before a Subcommittee of the Judiciary, United State Senate,* 70th Congress, 1st Session. S. 1482

1930 Senate Hearings. *Defining and Limiting the Jurisdiction of Courts Sitting in Equity: Hearing before Subcommittee of the Committee on the Judiciary,* 71st Congress, 2nd Session. S. 2497.

The Wagner Act: 49 Statutes at Large 449. 1935.

Published Legislative History.

Legislative History of the National Labor Relations Act, 1935. National Labor Relations Board. Washington, DC: Government Printing Office.

Bills
> S. 2926, 73rd Congress
> S. 1958, 74th Congress
> H.R. 6288, 74th Congress

Hearings

1934 Senate Hearings. *Hearing before the Senate Committee on Education and Labor,* 73rd Congress. S. 2926.

1935 Senate Hearings. *Hearings before the Senate Committee on Education and Labor,* 74th Congress. S. 1958.

1935 House Hearings. *Hearings before the House Committee on Labor,* 74th Congress. H.R. 6288.

Reports

73rd Congress
    Senate Report 1184, on S. 2926

74th Congress
    Senate Report 573, on S. 1958
    House Report 1147, on S. 1958

PERIODICALS

American Labor Legislation Review, American Association for Labor Legislation
American Federationist, American Federation of Labor
Life and Labor, National Women's Trade Union League
The Industrial Worker, Industrial Workers of the World

AFL-RELATED PRIMARY MATERIALS

Samuel Gompers Letterbooks. Library of Congress.

AFL Records: American Federation of Labor Records: The Gompers Era, Sanford, NC: Microfilming Corporation of America.

Proceedings of the American Federation of Labor.

American Federation of Labor, History, Encyclopedia and Reference Book. Vols. I (1919), II (1924), III (1960). Washington, DC: American Federation of Labor.

References

Ackerman, Bruce. 1991. *We the People: Foundations.* Cambridge, MA: Harvard University Press.

Atleson, James B. 1983. *Values and Assumptions in American Labor Law.* Amherst, MA: University of Massachusetts Press.

Balbus, Isaac. 1977. "Commodity Form and Legal Form: An Essay on the 'Relative Autonomy' of the Law." *Law and Society Review* 11:571–88.

Bennett, Robert W. 2001. "Counter-Conversationalism and the Sense of Difficulty." *Northwestern University Law Review* 95:845–906.

Bernstein, Irving. 1950. *The New Deal Collective Bargaining Policy.* Berkeley: University of California Press.

Bernstein, Irving. 1960. *The Lean Years.* Boston: Houghton Mifflin.

Bickel, Alexander. 1962. *The Least Dangerous Branch.* New Haven: Yale University Press.

Bobbitt, Philip. 1982. *Constitutional Fate.* New York: Oxford University Press.

Brand, Donald R. 1988. *Corporatism and the Rule of Law: A Study of the National Recovery Administration.* Ithaca, NY: Cornell University Press.

Carter, Lief H. 1998. *Reason in Law,* 5th ed. New York: Longman.

Casebeer, Kenneth. 1989. "Drafting Wagner's Act: Leon Keyserling and the Pre-committee Drafts of the Labor Disputes Act and the National Labor Relations Act." *Industrial Relations Law Journal* 11:73–131.

Casper, Jonathan D. 1976. "The Supreme Court and National Policy Making." *American Political Science Review* 70:550–63.

Chong, Dennis. 1991. *Collective Action and the Civil Rights Movement.* Chicago: University of Chicago Press.

Christ, Jay Finley. 1930. "The Federal Courts and Organized Labor. I." *Journal of Business* 3:205–49.

Christ, Jay Finley. 1932. "The Federal Courts and Organized Labor. III. Since the Clayton Act." *Journal of Business* 5: 47–75, 103–29, 283–300, 380–99.

Christ, Jay Finley. 1933. "The Federal Courts and Organized Labor. III. Since the Clayton Act, continued." *Journal of Business* 6:157–261.

Clayton, Cornell W. and Howard Gillman, eds. 1999. *Supreme Court Decision-Making: New Institutionalist Approaches.* Chicago: University of Chicago Press.

Cochrane, Cornelius. 1927. "Why Organized Labor is Fighting 'Yellow Dog' Contracts." *American Labor Legislation Review* 15:227–32.

Cover, Robert. 1983. "The Supreme Court, 1982 Term–Foreword: Nomos and Narrative." *Harvard Law Review* 97:4–68.

Cox, Archibald, Derek Bok, Robert Gorman, and Matthew W. Finkin. 1991. *Labor Law: Cases and Materials,* 11th ed. Westbury, NY: Foundation Press.

Cushman, Barry. 1992. "Doctrinal Synergies and Liberal Dilemmas: The Case of the Yellow-Dog Contract." *Supreme Court Review* 7:235–93.

Cushman, Barry. 1998. *Rethinking the New Deal Court: The Structure of a Constitutional Revolution.* New York: Oxford University Press.

Dahl, Robert A. 1956. "Decision Making in a Democracy: The Supreme Court as a National Policy-Maker." *Journal of Public Law* 6:279–95.

Dahl, Robert A. 1961. *Who Governs.* New Haven: Yale University Press.

Dubofsky, Melvyn. 1969. *We Shall Be All: A History of the Industrial Workers of the World.* Chicago: Quadrangle Books.

Dubofsky, Melvyn. 1994. *The State and Labor in Modern America.* Chapel Hill: University of North Carolina Press.

Ducat, Craig R. 1999 *Constitutional Interpretation,* 7th ed. Belmont, CA: Wadsworth.

Edelman, Murray. 1957 "New Deal Sensitivity to Labor Interests." In Milton Derber and Edwin Young, eds., *Labor and the New Deal.* Madison: University of Wisconsin Press, 159–91.

Edelman, Murray. 1977. *Political Language.* New York: Academic Press.

Eggert, Gerald G. 1967. *Railroad Labor Disputes: The Beginnings of Federal Strike Policy.* Ann Arbor: University of Michigan Press.

Eggert, Gerald G. 1974. *Richard Olney: Evolution of a Statesman.* University Park: Pennsylvania State University Press.

Ely, John Hart. 1980. *Democracy and Distrust.* Cambridge, MA: Harvard University Press.

Epstein, Lee and Thomas G. Walker. 2001. *Constitutional Law for a Changing America: Institutional Powers and Constraints,* 4th ed. Washington, DC: Congressional Quarterly Press.

Ernst, Daniel. 1989a. "The Yellow-Dog Contract and Liberal Reform, 1917–1932." *Labor History* 30:251–74.

Ernst, Daniel. 1989b. "The Labor Exemption: 1908–1914." *Iowa Law Review* 74:1151–73.

Ernst, Daniel. 1995. *Lawyers Against Labor.* Urbana: University of Illinois Press.

Eskridge, William N., Jr. 1991. "Overriding Supreme Court Statutory Decisions." *Yale Law Review* 101:331–455.

Eskridge, William N., Jr. 1994. *Dynamic Statutory Interpretation.* Cambridge, MA: Harvard University Press.

Eskridge, William N., Jr. and Philip P. Frickey. 1987. *Cases and Materials on Legislation.* St. Paul, MN: West Publishing Company.

Eskridge, William N., Jr., Philip P. Frickey, and Elizabeth Garrett. 2000. *Legislation and Statutory Interpretation.* New York: Foundation Press.

Farber, Daniel A. 1989. "Statutory Interpretation and Legislative Supremacy." *Georgetown Law Journal* 78:281–318.

Finkin, Matthew W. 1984. "Revisionism in Labor Law." *Maryland Law Review* 43:23–92.

Foner, Philip S. 1955. *The History of the Labor Movement in the United States Volume 2: From the Founding of the American Federation of Labor to the Emergence of American Imperialism*. New York: International Publishers.

Foner, Philip S. 1980. *The History of the Labor Movement in the United States Volume 5: The AFL in the Progressive Era 1910–1915*. New York: International Publishers.

Forbath, William. 1991. *Law and the Shaping of the American Labor Movement*. Cambridge, MA: Harvard University Press.

Frankfurter, Felix and Nathan Green. 1930. *The Labor Injunction*. New York: MacMillan.

Fraser, Steven. 1991. *Labor Will Rule: Sidney Hillman the Rise of American Labor*. Ithaca, NY: Cornell University Press.

Frickey, Philip P. and Daniel A. Farber. 1988: "Legislative Intent and Public Choice." *Virginia Law Review* 74:423–69.

Friedman, Barry. 2000. "The History Of The Countermajoritarian Difficulty, Part Four: Law's Politics." *University of Pennsylvania Law Review* 148:971–1064.

Geoghegan, Thomas. 1991. *Which Side are You On?:Trying to be for Labor When It's Flat on Its Back*. New York: Plume.

Gillman, Howard. 1993. *The Constitution Beseiged: The Rise and Demise of Lochner Era Police Powers Jurisprudence*. Durham, NC: Duke University Press.

Gillman, Howard. 1999. "The Court as an Idea, Not a Building (or a Game): Interpretive Institutionalism and the Analysis of Supreme Court Decision-Making." In Cornell W. Clayton and Howard Gillman, eds., *Supreme Court Decision-Making: New Institutionalist Approaches*. Chicago: University of Chicago Press, 65–87.

Gillman, Howard. 2001. "What's Law Got to Do with It? Judicial Behavioralists Test the 'Legal Model' of Judicial Decision Making," Review of Harold J. Spaeth and Jeffrey A. Segal, *Majority Rule or Minority Will: Adherence to Precedent on the U.S. Supreme Court* (Cambridge University Press, 1999). *Law and Social Inquiry* 26:465–504.

Gillman, Howard. 2002. "How Political Parties Can Use the Courts to Advance Their Agendas: Federal Courts in the United States, 1875–1891." *American Political Science Review* 96:511–24.

Gillman, Howard and Cornell Clayton, eds. 1999. *The Supreme Court in American Politics: New Institutionalist Interpretations*. Lawrence, KS: University Press of Kansas.

Gilmore, Grant. 1977. *The Ages of American Law*. New Haven: Yale University Press.

Goldfield, Michael. 1987. *The Decline of Organized Labor in the United States*. Chicago: University of Chicago Press.

Goldfield, Michael. 1989. "Worker Insurgency, Radical Organization, and New Deal Labor Legislation." *American Political Science Review* 83:1257–82.

Goldfield, Michael. 1990. "Explaining New Deal Labor Policy" (response to Skocpol and Finegold). *American Political Science Review* 84:1304–15.

Gompers, Samuel. 1925. *Seventy Years of Life and Labor: An Autobiography*, 2 vols. New York: E.P. Dutton and Company.

Goodnough, Abby. 1997. "Financial Details are Revealed in Affirmative Action Settlement." *New York Times* December 5, B5.

Gordon, Colin. 1994. *New Deals: Business, Labor, and Politics in America: 1920–1935.* New York: Cambridge University Press.

Gordon, David M., Richard Edwards, and Michael Reich. 1982. *Segmented Work, Divided Workers: The Historical Transformation of Labor in the United States.* New York: Cambridge University Press.

Gordon, Robert W. 1984. "Critical Legal Histories." *Stanford Law Review* 36: 57–125.

Gould, William B. IV. 1993. *A Primer on American Labor Law*, 3rd ed. Cambridge, MA: The MIT Press.

Graber, Mark A. 1993. "The Non-Majoritarian Difficulty: Legislative Deference to the Judiciary." *Studies in American Political Development* 7:35–72.

Graber, Mark A. 1998. "Establishing Judicial Review? *Schooner Peggy* and the Early Marshall Court." *Political Research Quarterly* 51:7–25.

Graber, Mark A. 1999. "The Problematic Establishment of Judicial Review." In Howard Gillman and Cornell Clayton, eds. *The Supreme Court in American Politics: New Institutionalist Interpretations.* Lawrence: University Press of Kansas, 28–42.

Gregory, Charles O. and Harold A. Katz. 1979. *Labor and the Law*, 3rd ed. New York: W.W. Norton.

Gross, James A. 1974. *The Making of the National Labor Relations Board: A Study in Economics, Politics, and the Law (Volume I 1933–1937).* Albany: State University of New York Press.

Gross, James A. 1981. *The Reshaping of the National Labor Relations Board: National Labor Policy in Transition, 1937–1947.* Albany: State University of New York Press.

Hattam, Victoria. 1993. *Labor Visions and State Power.* Princeton: Princeton University Press.

Hattam, Victoria. 1994. "Reply to Lovell: Politics of Commitment or Calculation?" *Studies in American Political Development* 8:103–10.

Hayes, Michael. 1978. "The Semi-Sovereign Interest Groups." *Journal of Politics* 40:134–61.

Holmes, Oliver Wendell, Jr. 1894. "Privilege, Malice, and Intent." *Harvard Law Review* 8:1–14.

Horowitz, Donald L. 1977. *The Courts and Social Policy.* Washington, DC: Brookings Institution.

Horowitz, Ruth L. 1978. *Political Ideologies of Organized Labor.* New Brunswick, NJ: Transaction Books.

Hunt, Henry T. 1928. "Make the Laws More Explicit." *American Labor Legislation Review* 16:309–11.

Irons, Peter H. 1982. *The New Deal Lawyers.* Princeton: Princeton University Press.

Ivers, Gregg. 2001. *American Constitutional Law: Power and Politics. Volume One: Constitutional Structure and Political Power.* Boston: Houghton Mifflin.

Johnson, Donald Bruce. 1978. *National Party Platforms.* Urbana: University of Illinois Press.

Jones, Charles O. 1968. "Joseph G. Cannon and Howard W. Smith: An Essay on the Limits of Leadership in the House of Representatives." *Journal of Politics* 30:617–44.

Jones, Dallas. 1957. "The Enigma of the Clayton Act." *Industrial and Labor Relations Review* 10:201–21.

Joseph, Charles M. 1928. "The Sherman Act–A Menace to Freedom." *American Labor Legislation Review* 18:297–301.

Katzmann, Robert A. 1997. *Courts and Congress.* Washington, DC: Brookings Institution Press.

Kaufman, Stuart B., Peter J. Albert, and Grace Palladino. 1991. *The Samuel Gompers Papers: Volume 4: A National Labor Movement Takes Shape, 1895–98.* Urbana: University of Illinois Press.

Kaufman, Stuart B., Peter J. Albert, and Grace Palladino. 1996. *The Samuel Gompers Papers: Volume 5: An Expanding Movement at the Turn of the Century, 1898–1902.* Urbana: University of Illinois Press.

Keller, Morton. 1990. *Regulating a New Economy.* Cambridge, MA: Harvard University Press.

Klare, Karl. 1978. "Judicial Deradicalization of the Wagner Act and the Origins of Modern Legal Consciousness, 1937–1941." *Minnesota Law Review* 62:265–339.

Klare, Karl. 1979. "Law Making as Praxis." *Telos* 123–35.

Klare, Karl. 1981. "Labor Law as Ideology: Towards a New Historiography of Collective Bargaining Law." *Industrial Relations Law Journal* 4:450–506.

Klare, Karl. 1985. "Traditional Labor Law Scholarship and the Crisis of Collective Bargaining Law: A Reply to Professor Finkin." *Maryland Law Review* 44:731–837.

Klare, Karl. 1990. "Critical Theory and Labor Relations Law." In David Kairys, ed., *The Politics of Law.* New York: Pantheon Books.

Kluger, Richard. *Simple Justice: The History of Brown v Board of Education and Black America's Struggle for Equality.* New York: Alfred A. Knopf, Inc.

Kutler, Stanley. 1962. "Labor, the Clayton Act, and the Supreme Courts." *Labor History* 3:19–38.

Landis, James M. 1938. *The Administrative Process.* New Haven: Yale University Press.

Lecht, Leonard A. 1955. *Experience Under Railway Legislation.* New York, Columbia University Press.

Lewis-Beck, Michael and John R. Alford. 1980: "Can Government Regulate Safety? The Coal Mine Example." *American Political Science Review* 74:745–56.

Lipset, Seymour Martin and Gary Marks. 2000. *It Didn't Happen Here: Why Socialism Failed in the United States.* New York: W. W. Norton and Company.

Lovell, George. 1994. "The Ambiguities of Labor's Legislative Reforms in New York State in the Late Nineteenth Century." *Studies in American Political Development* 8:81–102.

Lovell, George. 1997. *Legislative Deferrals and Judicial Policy Making in American Labor Law*. Ph.D. Thesis (Political Science), Ann Arbor: University of Michigan.

Lowi, Theodore. 1979. *The End of Liberalism*, 2nd ed. New York: Norton.

Luker, Kristin. 1984. *Abortion and the Politics of Motherhood*. Berkeley: University of California Press.

Maltzman, Forrest, James F. Spriggs II, and Paul J. Wahlbeck. 1999. "Strategy and Judicial Choice: New Institutionalist Approaches to Supreme Court Decision-Making." In Cornell W. Clayton and Howard Gillman, eds. *Supreme Court Decision-Making: New Institutionalist Approaches*. Chicago: University of Chicago Press, 43–63.

Martin, Andrew D. 2001. "Congressional Decision Making and the Separation of Powers." *American Political Science Review* 95:361–78.

Mashaw, Jerry M. 1997. *Greed, Chaos, and Governance: Using Public Choice to Improve Public Law*. New Haven: Yale University Press.

McCann, Michael W. 1994. *Rights at Work: Pay Equity Reform and the Politics of Legal Mobilization*. Chicago: University of Chicago Press.

McCann, Michael W. 1999. "How the Supreme Court Matters in American Politics: New Institutionalist Perspectives." In Howard Gillman and Cornell Clayton, eds. *The Supreme Court in American Politics: New Institutionalist Interpretations*. Lawrence: University Press of Kansas, 63–97.

McGerr, Michael E. 1986. *The Decline of Popular Politics: The American North, 1865–1928*. New York: Oxford University Press.

McNollgast. 1995. "Politics and the Courts: A Positive Theory of Judicial Doctrine and the Rule of Law." *Southern California Law Review* 68:1631–81.

Melnick, R. Shep. 1983. *Regulation and the Courts: The Case of the Clean Air Act*. Washington, DC: Brookings Institution.

Melnick, R. Shep. 1994. *Between the Lines: Interpreting Welfare Rights*. Washington, DC: Brookings Institution.

Mink, Gwendolyn. 1986. *Old Labor and New Immigrants in American Political Development: Union, Party, and State, 1875–1920*. Ithaca, NY: Cornell University Press, 1986.

Montgomery, David. 1987. *The Fall of the House of Labor*. New York: Cambridge University Press.

Murphy, Walter F. 1962. *Congress and the Court*. Chicago: University of Chicago Press.

Murphy, Walter F., James E. Fleming, and Sotirios A. Barber. 1995. *American Constitutional Interpretation*, 2nd ed. Westbury, NY: Foundation Press.

Norris, George. 1945. *Fighting Liberal: The Autobiography of George W. Norris*. New York: MacMillan.

Novkov, Julie. 2001. *Constituting Workers, Protecting Women: Gender, Law and Labor in the Progressive Era and New Deal Years*. Ann Arbor: University of Michigan Press.

O'Brien, Ruth A. 1998. *Workers' Paradox: The Republican Origins of New Deal Labor Policy, 1886–1935*. Chapel Hill: University of North Carolina Press.

Olney, Richard. 1908. "Discrimination Against Union Labor–Legal?" *American Law Review* 42:161–7.

Orren, Karen. 1991. *Belated Feudalism: Labor, the Law and Liberal Development in the United States.* Cambridge: Cambridge University Press.

Orren, Karen. 1995. "The Primacy of Labor in American Constitutional Development." *American Political Science Review* 89:377–88.

Paul, Arnold M. 1960. *The Conservative Crisis and the Rule of Law.* Ithaca, NY: Cornell University Press.

Peretti, Terri Jennings. 1999. *In Defense of a Political Court.* Princeton, NJ: Princeton University Press.

Perry, H.W., Jr. 1991. *Deciding to Decide: Agenda Setting in the United States Supreme Court.* Cambridge, MA: Harvard University Press.

Plotke, David. 1989. "The Wagner Act, Again." *Studies in American Political Development.* 3:105–56.

Plotke, David. 1996. *Building a Democratic Political Order: Reshaping American Liberalism in the 1930s and 1940s.* New York: Cambridge University Press.

Pope, James Gray. 1997. "Labor's Constitution of Freedom." *Yale Law Journal* 106:941–1031.

Posner, Richard A. 1985. *The Federal Courts: Crisis and Reform.* Cambridge, MA: Harvard University Press.

Posner, Richard A. 1986. "Legal Formalism, Legal Realism, and the Interpretation of Statues and the Constitution." *Case Western Reserve Law Review* 37:179–200.

Posner, Richard A. 1990. *The Problems of Jurisprudence.* Cambridge, MA: Harvard University Press.

Pound, Roscoe. 1909. "Liberty of Contract." *Yale Law Journal* 19:454–87.

Rabban, David M. 1994. "The IWW Free Speech Fights and Popular Conceptions of Free Expression before World War I." *Virginia Law Review* 80:1055–158.

Rae, Douglas W. 1971. *The Political Consequences of Electoral Laws.* New Haven: Yale University Press.

Rogers, James R. 2001. "Information and Judicial Review: A Signaling Game of Legislative-Judicial Interaction." *American Journal of Political Science* 45: 84–99.

Rogin, Michael. 1962. "Voluntarism: The Political Functions of an Antipolitical Doctrine." *Industrial and Labor Relations Review* 15:521–35.

Rosenberg, Gerald N. 1991. *The Hollow Hope: Can the Courts Bring About Social Change?* Chicago: University of Chicago Press.

Ross, W. G. 1994. *A Muted Fury.* Princeton: Princeton University Press.

Salvatore, Nick. 1982. *Eugene V. Debs: Citizen and Socialist.* Urbana: University of Illinois Press.

Scalia, Antonin. 1997. *A Matter of Interpretation: Federal Courts and the Law.* Princeton: Princeton University Press.

Schoenbrod, David. 1993. *Power Without Responsibility.* New Haven: Yale University Press.

Segal, Jeffrey A. 1997. "Separation of Powers Games in the Positive Theory of Law and Courts." *American Political Science Review* 91:28–44.

Segal, Jeffrey A. 1999. "Supreme Court Deference to Congress: An Examination of the Marksist Model." In Cornell W. Clayton and Howard Gillman, eds. *Supreme Court Decision-Making: New Institutionalist Approaches.* Chicago: University of Chicago Press, 237–53.

Segal, Jeffrey A. and Harold J. Spaeth. 1993. *The Supreme Court and the Attitudinal Model.* New York: Cambridge University Press.

Seidman, Joel. 1962. *The Brotherhood of Railroad Trainmen: The Internal Life of a National Union.* New York: John Wiley.

Seitz, Virginia A. 1984. "Legal, Legislative, and Managerial Responses to the Organization of Supervising Employees in the 1940s." *American Journal of Legal History* 28:193.

Shapiro, Martin M. 1983. "Fathers and Sons: The Courts, the Commentators, and the Search for Values." In Vincent Blasi, ed. *The Burger Court: The Counter Revolution that Wasn't.* New Haven: Yale University Press, 218–33.

Shapiro, Martin M. 1988. *Who Guards the Guardians: Judicial Control of Administration.* Athens, GA: University of Georgia Press.

Skocpol, Theda. 1980. "Political Response to Capitalist Crisis: Neo-Marxist Theories of the State and the Case of the New Deal." *Politics and Society* 10:155–201.

Skocpol, Theda and Kenneth Finegold. 1990. "Explaining New Deal Labor Policy" (with response by Michael Goldfield). *American Political Science Review* 84:1297–1304.

Skowronek, Stephen. 1982. *Building a New American State.* New York: Cambridge University Press.

Smith, Rogers M. 1988. "Political Jurisprudence, the 'New Institutionalism,' and the Future of Public Law." *American Political Science Review* 80:89–108.

Spann, Girardieau A. 1993. *Race Against the Court: The Supreme Court and Minorities in Contemporary America.* New York: State University of New York Press.

Stone, Katherine van Wezel. 1981. "The Post-War Paradigm in American Labor Law." *Yale Law Journal* 90:1509–80.

Strauss, Peter L. 1989. *An Introduction to Administrative Justice in the United States.* Durham NC: Carolina Academic Press.

Sunstein, Cass R. 1990. *After the Rights Revolution.* Cambridge, MA: Harvard University Press.

Tomlins, Christopher L. 1985. *The State and the Unions.* New York: Cambridge University Press.

Trubeck, David M. 1984. "Where the Action Is: Critical Legal Studies and Empiricism." *Stanford Law Review* 36:575–623.

Tushnet, Mark. 1987. *The NAACP's Legal Strategy Against Segregated Education, 1925–1950.* Chapel Hill: University of North Carolina Press.

United States Strike Commission. 1895. *Report on the Chicago Strike of June–July, 1894.* Washington, DC: Government Printing Office.

University of Pennsylvania Law Review. 1981. "Comment: The Radical Potential of the Wagner Act and the Duty to Bargain Collectively." 129:1392–1426.

Waldron, Jeremy. 1999. *Law and Disagreement.* New York: Oxford University Press.

Weintraub, Hyman. 1959. *Andrew Furuseth: Emancipator of the Seamen.* Berkeley: University of California Press.

Witte, Edwin. 1929. "New Developments in Labor Injunctions." *American Labor Legislation Review* 19:308–16.

Witte, Edwin E. 1932. *The Government in Labor Disputes.* New York: McGraw Hill.

White, G. Edward. 1980. *Tort Law in America: An Intellectual History.* New York: Oxford University Press.

Whittington, Keith A. 1999. *Constitutional Construction: Divided Powers and Constitutional Meaning.* Cambridge, MA: Harvard University Press.

Whittington, Keith A. 2001. "The Strategic Environment of Judicial Review." Paper Presented at the Annual Meeting of the American Political Science Association, San Francisco, CA.

Zinn, Howard. 1959. *LaGuardia in Congress.* Ithaca, NY: Cornell University Press.

Index